THE EVOLVING ARAB CITY

Tradition, Modernity and Urban Development

Planning, History and Environment Series

Editor:
Emeritus Professor Dennis Hardy, High Peak, UK

Editorial Board:
Professor Arturo Almandoz, Universidad Simón Bolivar, Caracas, Venezuela and Pontificia
    Universidad Católica de Chile, Santiago, Chile
Professor Gregory Andrusz, London, UK
Professor Nezar AlSayyad, University of California, Berkeley, USA
Professor Robert Bruegmann, University of Illinois at Chicago, USA
Professor Meredith Clausen, University of Washington, Seattle, USA
Professor Robert Freestone, University of New South Wales, Sydney, Australia
Professor John R. Gold, Oxford Brookes University, Oxford, UK
Professor Sir Peter Hall, University College London, UK
Emeritus Professor Anthony Sutcliffe, Nottingham, UK

Technical Editor
Ann Rudkin, Alexandrine Press, Marcham, Oxfordshire, UK

Selection of published titles

Planning Europe's Capital Cities: Aspects of nineteenth century development by Thomas Hall (**paperback 2010**)

Selling Places: The marketing and promotion of towns and cities, 1850–2000 by Stephen V. Ward

Changing Suburbs: Foundation, form and function edited by Richard Harris and Peter Larkham

The Australian Metropolis: A planning history edited by Stephen Hamnett and Robert Freestone

Utopian England: Community experiments 1900–1945 by Dennis Hardy

Urban Planning in a Changing World: The twentieth century experience edited by Robert Freestone

Twentieth-Century Suburbs: A morphological approach by J.W.R. Whitehand and C.M.H. Carr

Council Housing and Culture: The history of a social experiment by Alison Ravetz

Planning Latin America's Capital Cities, 1850–1950 edited by Arturo Almandoz (**paperback 2010**)

Exporting American Architecture, 1870–2000 by Jeffrey W. Cody

Planning by Consent: The origins and nature of British development control by Philip Booth

The Making and Selling of Post-Mao Beijing by Anne-Marie Broudehoux

Planning Middle Eastern Cities: An urban kaleidoscope in a globalizing world edited by Yasser Elsheshtawy (**paperback 2010**)

Globalizing Taipei: The political economy of spatial development edited by Reginald Yin-Wang Kwok

New Urbanism and American Planning: The conflict of cultures by Emily Talen

Remaking Chinese Urban Form: Modernity, scarcity and space. 1949–2005 by Duanfang Lu (**paperback 2011**)

Planning Twentieth Century Capital Cities edited by David L.A. Gordon (**paperback 2010**)

Planning the Megacity: Jakarta in the twentieth century by Christopher Silver (**paperback 2011**)

Designing Australia's Cities: Culture, commerce and the city beautiful, 1900–1930 by Robert Freestone

Ordinary Places, Extraordinary Events: Citizenship, democracy and urban space in Latin America edited by Clara Irazábal

The Evolving Arab City: Tradition, modernity and urban development edited by Yasser Elsheshtawy (**paperback 2011**)

Stockholm: The making of a metropolis by Thomas Hall

Dubai: Behind an urban spectacle by Yasser Elsheshtawy

Capital Cities in the Aftermath of Empires: Planning in central and southeastern Europe edited by Emily Gunzburger Makaš and Tanja Damljanović Conley

Lessons in Post-War Reconstruction: Case studies from Lebanon in the aftermath of the 2006 war edited by Howayda Al-Harithy

Orienting Istanbul: Cultural capital of Europe? edited by Deniz Göktürk, Levent Soysal and İpek Türeli

Olympic Cities: City agendas, planning and the world's games 1896–2016, 2nd edition edited by John R Gold and Margaret M Gold

The Making of Hong Kong: From vertical to volumetric by Barrie Shelton, Justyna Karakiewicz and Thomas Kvan

Urban Coding and Planning edited by Stephen Marshall

Planning Asian Cities: Risk and resilience edited by Stephen Hamnett and Dean Forbes

THE EVOLVING ARAB CITY

Tradition, Modernity and Urban Development

edited by

Yasser Elsheshtawy

Routledge
Taylor & Francis Group

LONDON AND NEW YORK

First published 2008 by Routledge

This paperback edition first published 2011
by Routledge
2 Park Square, Milton Park, Abingdon, Oxfordshire OX14 4RN

Simultaneously published in the US and Canada
by Routledge
711 Third Avenue, New York, NY 10017

Routledge is an imprint of the Taylor & Francis Group, an informa business

© 2008, 2011 Selection and editorial material Yasser Elsheshtawy; individual chapters: the contributors

Typeset in Palatino and Humanist by PNR Design, Didcot
Printed and bound in Great Britain by CPI Antony Rowe, Chippenham, Wiltshire

This book was commissioned and edited by Alexandrine Press, Marcham, Oxfordshire

British Library Cataloguing in Publication Data
A catalogue record of this book is available from the British Library

Library of Congress Cataloging in Publication Data
The evolving Arab city : tradition, modernity and urban development / edited by Yasser Elsheshtawy.
p. cm. — (Planning, history and environment series)
Includes bibliographical references and index.
1. City planning—Arab countries. 2. Cities and towns—Arab countries. I. Elsheshtawy, Yasser.
HT147.5.E86 2008
307.1'21609174927—dc22
2008001567

ISBN13: 978-0-415-66572-8 (pbk)
ISBN13: 978-0-203-69679-8 (ebk)

Contents

From our thousand year old sleep
From our crippled history
Comes a sun without ritual
To the country that's dug into our lives like graves
To the drugged and murdered country
And kills the shaikh of the sand and locusts

Time grows on its plains
Time withers on its plains
Like mushrooms

A sun that kills and destroys
Appears over the bridge
Adonis, *Prophecy*

If I had in my dreams and mirrors
a haven
If I had a ship
If I had the remains
of a city
If I had a city
In a country of children and weeping

I'd have made out of all this for the wound
A song like a spear
Piercing trees, stones and heaven
And soft as water
Amazing and overpowering like a conquest
Adonis, *The Wound*

Preface

Much has changed in the world since the publication of this book in 2008. The financial crisis has become a defining moment for urbanism in the twenty-first century – slowing the boom experienced in cities throughout the world. Within the Arab Gulf region there has been a remarkable slowdown, prompting local governments to reassess priorities and even their entire development paradigm. The focus has shifted from spectacular urbanism to one that emphasizes the everyday and the mundane – a shift from 'Big Space' to 'Little Space' – as I indicated in a recent article published in the *Brown Journal for World Affairs*. Yet significantly, my assertion in the first edition of this book that there is a 'great rift' in the Arab world has continued and in fact intensified because of the financial crisis. So even though Dubai is experiencing a slowdown other centres, such as Doha and Abu Dhabi, are emerging.

In addition, during a meeting in Beirut in December 2010 organized by the UN-ESCWA (Economic and Social Commission of Western Asia) on the notion of the inclusive city, to which I was invited to contribute under the theme of 'Urban Dualities', these divisions became even more visible. Moreover the presentations at that meeting showed the Gulf's significance as the site of an urban modernity that has escaped the region's traditional centres. This was also a common argument made at a two-day symposium held in Berlin (2010) at the ZMO (Zentrum Moderner Orient) under the theme 'Under Construction: The material and symbolic meaning of architecture and infrastructure in the Gulf region' – which validates some of the arguments made by the authors of this volume.

This book originated in the Tate Modern restaurant in London, which seems an unusual setting for contemplating the fate of Arab cities but this is where Ann Rudkin – the technical editor of the Planning, History and Environment series – suggested I work on a second volume to accompany *Planning Middle Eastern Cities* (Routledge, 2004, 2010). The idea was to include cities that were not part of the initial collection. While the first book received positive reviews, my reservations centred around finding qualified authors from the Arab world. As is the case with any endeavour in this region there are numerous difficulties and hurdles to consider. These thoughts were, however, soon forgotten while trying to decipher, and enjoy, the culinary presentations. Yet ultimately and during the IASTE (International Association for the Study of Traditional Environments) 2004 conference in Sharjah and after consulting with several colleagues, I decided to go ahead. Many of the authors in this collection are in fact colleagues whom I met during various IASTE conferences – and the theoretical orientations, themes and constructs evoked during these different meetings have shaped some of the approaches that these authors took.

While working on the introduction to the book's first edition and trying to elaborate on common themes, I was invited by the UN-ESCWA to write a report on the status of the Arab city. This proved to be particularly timely since being involved in this endeavour helped me to crystallize some thoughts, which are reflected in my introduction here. Specifically, the emergence of a 'great rift' in the Arab world, which is currently intensifying with potentially disastrous consequences, proved to be a narrative thread linking the chapters. As part of that effort I was also invited to participate in a regional meeting in Kuwait in December 2007 dealing with 'Equitable Cities'. The presence of American soldiers in full gear in the arrival hall of Kuwait Airport, as well as the discussions of the meeting itself which brought together social scientists, policy-makers and activists, highlighted the contradictions, problems and denials which exist to varying degrees in the Arab world's urban centres – which one participant characterized as a 'crisis'.

I would like to thank all the contributors for their efforts in writing these chapters, and in their timely response to my queries. I am grateful too to the social policy team from ESCWA – specifically Frederico Neto, Mona Khechen and Nadine Chalak – for giving me an opportunity to share my views with a wider Arab audience. I also would like to thank some of the commentators on an early draft of this book, particularly Janet Abu-Lughod whose poignant comments pointed me to some alternative venues with regard to global cities. In addition, special recognition should be given to the United Arab Emirates University and my colleagues at the Department of Architecture for their support and help during the writing of this book. My thanks also go the writers who reviewed the book's first edition, particularly Michelle Buckley for the *International Journal of Urban and Regional Research*, Sarah Moser for *Cities*, and Mona Fawaz for the *Urban Land Magazine*. Their comments and insights have been very illuminating. And, finally, my particular thanks and deep appreciation to Ann Rudkin for her diligent effort in editing this collection, and for keeping everyone on 'track'.

Yasser Elsheshtawy
Al-Ain, January 2011

Illustration Credits and Sources

The editor, contributors and publisher would like to thank all those who have granted permission to reproduce illustrations. We have made every effort to contact and acknowledge copyright holders, but if any errors have been made we would be very happy to correct them at a later printing.

The Contributors

Khaled Adham was raised in Egypt and Qatar, where he concluded his high school studies. After receiving his Bachelors degree from Cairo University in 1986, he practised as an architect until 1990 when he moved to the United States for postgraduate studies. In 1992 he received a Masters degree in architecture from Kent State University and in 1997 a PhD in architecture from Texas A&M University. Between 1998 and 2004, he taught architectural theory and design studios at the Suez Canal University as well as practising as an architect and urban planner from his private studio. He is now an Assistant Professor at the United Arab Emirates University in Al-Ain. His current research focuses on the impact of late capitalism on the architecture and urban developments in Cairo as well as selected cities in the Arabian Gulf.

Mashary A. Al-Naim is Associate Professor of Architectural Criticism in the Faculty of Architecture at King Faisal University, Saudi Arabia. He is the Vice Rector for the Administrative Affairs and Business Development at Prince Mohammed University (PMU) where he has been Chair of the Architecture Department. Al-Naim has served on numerous architectural and design juries (such as Arab City Award, Sultan Qaboos Award and King Abdulla Award) and has consulted on many design projects throughout the world, but especially in the Middle East and Gulf Region. He is an active researcher, a prolific journalist, and practicing architect. He is also a senior editor of *Albenaa* (the oldest and widely distributed Arabic architectural journal), and writes a weekly column in *AlRiyadh* (a major local newspaper) and a monthly column in several journals. Al-Naim has published in both English and Arabic on topics related to sustainability, environment behaviour studies, identity and symbolism in the built environment, traditional and contemporary architecture in Arab countries and architectural education and practice.

Jamila Bargach is an anthropology graduate from Rice University, Houston, Texas and is currently an Assistant Professor at the Ecole Nationale d'Architecure (ENA) in Rabat where she teaches introductory courses in anthropology and sociology, in addition to a major course on research methodology and senior-year seminars on specific topics relating to space (the Anthropology of Space; Space and the Sacred; Poverty in the City; and a forthcoming Space in Literature). Her published work includes a book entitled *Orphans of Islam: Adoption, Family, and Abandonment in*

Morocco (Rowman and Littlefield, 2002). Since joining the ENA, she started doing research on space-related issues. She was a participant researcher in the Islam and Human Rights Project, directed by Dr. Abdullahi An-Na'Im of Emory Law School, Atlanta, Georgia funded by the Ford foundation. In addition to this she has carried out extensive research on poor caravanserais in Salé as part of a joint project between ENA and the Architecture Department of Bath University. She has published articles on issues of poverty and the city and violence and the city in Arabic and French in Moroccan based journals.

Mustapha Ben Hamouche holds a Doctorate from the Institut Français d'Urbanisme, Paris VIII University; a Master of Philosophy (MPhil) from the Faculty of Arts, University of Newcastle upon Tyne and a Diplome d'Etat d'Architecte (BSC) from the Ecole Polytechnique d'Architecture et d'Urbanisme, Algiers. He joined the University of Blida, Algeria in 1986 and taught there for nearly 10 years where he was also in charge of postgraduate studies and research programmes. From 1995 to 1999 he left academia and worked as an Expert-Planner in the Town Planning Department of Al Ain, UAE. He is now Associate Professor at the University of Bahrain. He has published books and papers in Arabic, English and French on urbanization in the Gulf, urban history in the Maghreb, and the impact of Islamic law in shaping the built environment in traditional Muslim cities. At present he is working on the application of chaos and fractals theory to traditional urban fabric. He is also leading a research team at the University of Bahrain on the application of GIS to Manama's urban development.

Rami Farouk Daher is an Assistant Professor of Architecture at Jordan University of Science & Technology, Irbid and a heritage specialist interested in research related to politics and dynamics of place and heritage conservation and urban regeneration, especially the architectural heritage of recent periods (Ottoman and contemporary Bilad al Sham). He holds a PhD in architecture (1995) from Texas A&M University, a Masters in architecture (1991) from the University of Minnesota, and a Bachelor of Architecture (1988) from the University of Jordan. He also holds a Certificate in Historic Preservation (1995) from the College of Architecture at Texas A&M University. Since 1999, he has been a faculty Fellow at the Historic Resources Imaging Laboratory, College of Architecture, Texas A&M University, and since 2002 a Visiting Research Fellow at the Centre for Tourism and Cultural Change at Sheffield Hallam University. He was awarded a Fulbright Visiting Scholar Fellowship and served as a Research Associate at the Center for Middle Eastern Studies at the University of California, Berkeley (2001). In addition, he has been awarded (2002) an International Collaborative Research Grant (ICRG) from the Program on the Middle East & North Africa (MENA) of the Social Science Research Council (SSRC).

Yasser Elsheshtawy obtained a Bachelor of Architecture from Cairo University in

1986, a Masters Degree in Architecture from Pennsylvania State University in 1991 and a PhD from the University of Wisconsin-Milwaukee in 1996. His research has focused on environment-behaviour studies, architectural theory as well as the changing urban/architectural patterns of Middle Eastern cities. He has published in numerous international journals and attended conferences worldwide. He was recently awarded the JAE (*Journal of Architectural Education*) award for best article of the year for an article titled 'The Ambiguous Veil: On Transparency the Masharabiy'ya and Architecture'. His most recent publication is an edited book on Middle Eastern cities published by Routledge (2004) titled *Planning Middle Eastern Cities: An Urban Kaleidoscope in a Globalizing World*. He has lectured at Harvard Design School, Tianjin University, China, and is currently Associate Professor of Architecture at the United Arab Emirates University.

Yasser Mahgoub is Assistant Professor of Architecture in the Department of Architecture, College of Engineering and Petroleum, Kuwait University. He received a PhD in Architecture from the University of Michigan, Ann Arbor, in 1990. From 1990 to 1993 he taught at Ain Shams University, Cairo and from 1993 to 1999 at United Arab Emirates University, Al Ain. Since then he has been teaching at Kuwait University. His research interests include social and cultural aspects of architecture, sustainable architecture, architectural education and the impact of globalization on architecture. His teaching covers architectural design studios, architectural graduation projects, architectural research, and architectural professional practice courses. He practised architecture in Egypt and is currently a consultant to Kuwait University's Vice President for Planning for the New University City Campus Master Plan.

Fuad K. Malkawi is an architect and urban planner. He holds a PhD in City and Regional Planning from the University of Pennsylvania (1996), a Masters in Architecture from the University of Texas (1989). He has taught architecture and urban planning in Jordan, Oman, UAE and USA. For several years he was a regional consultant for the World Bank on city development strategies in the MENA region. He has been involved in planning several cities around the Middle East and now leads the team preparing the Sharjah Spatial Plan. He has published extensively in international journals and participated in numerous conferences worldwide. His latest publication is an historic survey of planning in Jordan published by the Institut Français du Proche-Orient (IFPO) entitled *The Condition of Physical Planning in Jordan, 1970–1990*. The city has always been the focus of his research whether in terms of its polity or its architecture. He is currently the Manager of Planning and Landscape Architecture Department at Khatib & Alami (CEC) in the UAE.

Sofia T. Shwayri is a Visiting Fellow in Lebanese Studies at St Antony's College Oxford. Previously she was an Assistant Professor/Faculty Fellow in the area of

The City at the John W. Draper Program in the Humanities and Social Thought in the Graduate School of Arts and Sciences at New York University. She gained her BA and MA in Archaeology at the American University of Beirut (1991, 1994) and an MS and PhD in Architecture at the University of California, Berkeley (1997, 2002), where she was also a Research Fellow at the Center of Middle Eastern Studies and Instructor in Peace and Conflict Studies. As part of her research interest, Sofia teaches seminars on the Contemporary City in Conflict, and Post-conflict Reconstruction of Cities. Her interest in cities springs from growing up in wartime Beirut where she witnessed more than 15 years of simultaneous destruction and reconstruction; diminishing state power against a backdrop of increasing control by private militias; the lack of any official response to the ironies of waves of displaced persons setting up informal settlements alongside refugee camps while at the same time luxury apartment buildings were being erected less than 2 kilometres away. Her PhD research expanded these themes resulting in a dissertation that focused on the relationship of intrastate wars to the making of a city, using Beirut as a case study.

Chapter 1

The Great Divide: Struggling and Emerging Cities in the Arab World

Yasser Elsheshtawy

The Minaret wept
When a stranger came – bought it
And built on top of it a chimney
                    Adonis, *The Minaret*

The Weeping Minaret

Do Arabs still exist? Not in the sense of a physical presence – but rather as a vital and contributing civilization. The great Arab poet Adonis argues the following:

> If I look at the Arabs, with all their resources and great capacities, and I compare what they have achieved over the past century with what others have achieved in that period, I would have to say that we Arabs are in a phase of extinction, in the sense that we have no creative presence in the world… We have become extinct. We have the quantity. We have the masses of people, but a people becomes extinct when it no longer has a creative capacity, and the capacity to change its world.[1]

He reflects a sense of doom and hopelessness. In his poem 'The weeping minaret' he elaborates on the role of the 'stranger' – the colonialists, multi-national corporations, occupying forces – and the degree to which they have subverted symbols of Arab identity – signified here by the minaret – and replaced them with signs of Western power, i.e. the 'chimney' (figure 1.1). In other words while much of the blame for the Arab crisis is from within, external forces are conspiring to maintain the region in a constant state of backwardness. Some Western observers went so far as calling the Middle East 'the middle of nowhere'.[2]

These are certainly popular sentiments for many in the region. There are many indicators that would indeed suggest that this is the case – that the Arabs are simply

Figure 1.1. The minaret of the Farag ibn Barquq Mosque in Cairo enveloped by informal settlements built in proximity to the City of the Dead.

not contributing in any substantive way to science, literature and the arts. Rather, they are recipients, consumers, and proponents of extremist ideologies. For instance a recent UN report estimates that the number of books published in the Arab world does not exceed 1.1 per cent of world production even though Arabs constitute 5 per cent of the world population. This number becomes even more alarming if we consider that the majority of these books are of a religious nature (Arab Human Development Report, 2003).[3] There is a growing conservatism sweeping the Arab world, even in formerly liberal and cosmopolitan cities such as Cairo, in a way responding to this perceived 'threat' by turning inward and adapting religious symbols such as the veil, which some scholars have called 'medieval modernity' (AlSayyad, 2006).

How is this related to cities? In looking at cities in the region one certainly cannot escape this sense of doom either: whether it is the dismantling of Baghdad; the bombing of Beirut; or the grinding poverty in the slums of Cairo and Rabat – all highlight the critical situation facing our urban conglomerates. They have become sites of struggle and contestation, spaces of doom rather than spaces of hope. Contrast this with the glitz and glamour of Dubai or Doha – centres that have become a model for the Arab world. By opening up to global capital they have the potential to become a 'new Arab metropolis' to use Fuad Malkawi's title in his prologue here – adapting Western forms and planning models. Unburdened by history they are free to create a new identity and in turn serve as a model for the rest of the Arab world. Perhaps they have become the new 'stranger' to paraphrase Adonis. This book provides a glimpse into a select set of Arab cities where these issues are addressed from a variety of perspectives. It should be left to the reader to decide on the accuracy of Adonis's assessment of the Arab condition.

The Arab City: Definition and the Book's Approach

The word 'Arab City' evokes a multitude of images, preconceptions and stereotypes. At its most elementary it is for many a place filled with mosques and minarets; settings characterized by chaotic, slum-like developments; a haven for terrorists; maze-like alleyways; crowded coffeehouses where people sit idling their time away smoking a *nerghile*; sensuality hidden behind veils and *mashrabiy'yas*. But it is also a place of unprecedented development, rising skyscrapers, modern shopping malls, unabashed consumerism. Most importantly it is a setting where one can observe the tensions of modernity and tradition; religiosity and secularism; exhibitionism and veiling; in short a place of contradictions and paradoxes. Each of these characterizations plays into clichés about what constitutes an Arab or Middle Eastern city. The latter term is particularly problematic – being primarily a British colonial invention – indicating the location of 'this' region in relation to both Britain and India. Furthermore, it excludes cities of North Africa. It may be

Figure 1.2a. The decay of Cairo – Manshiet Nasser informal settlement in Cairo (the garbage collectors district).

Figure 1.2b. The glamour of Dubai – the Madinat Jumeirah Complex and the Burj Al-Arab Hotel.

more accurate to describe them as Arab cities. But here again, one may object that such depictions are conducive to more stereotyping. At the same time, arguments are made that there is a divide in this region between newly emerging cities (the Gulf) and the traditional centres – a form of 'gulfication' or 'dubaization' in which these new centres are influencing and shaping the urban form of 'traditional' cities. Counter arguments are made that cities in the Middle East and North Africa are influenced by a variety of cities and regions throughout the world and that the relationship is far more complex than a one-way, linear directionality (figures 1.2*a* and *b*).

The Arab/Middle Eastern city is thus caught between a variety of worlds, ideologies, and struggles. At its very essence it is a struggle for modernity and trying to ascertain one's place in the twenty-first century. The paradoxes described above are remnants of the past: of the colonial heritage which did, and still does, play a large role in determining the region's direction. It could thus be argued that colonialism has returned – in a more subtle and disguised form – and in some instances instigated by local elements. In the movie *The Battle of Algiers* by Gillo Pontecorvo the city's traditional quarter, the *qasbah,* the site of resistance, is contrasted with the European quarter, the seat of the colonial masters. In order to deal with the insurgency, the *qasbah* is sealed and movement between the two worlds is strictly controlled (figure 1.3). While the colonials eventually left, the divide essentially remained. As a consequence the region was mired for a long time in struggles and conflicts, depriving it of the ability to develop properly. The *qasbah*'s scope simply grew to encompass the whole region. Now in the current

Figure 1.3. Film still from *The Battle of Algiers*. The entry to the *qasbah* is controlled by French soldiers.

climate of globalization and the growing influence of multi-national corporations, the 'West' has returned – yet these developments tend to be exclusive, catering to an elite segment of society – both local and foreign. The majority of locals are kept out – thus the *qasbah* phenomenon has returned but in a more refined and subtle manner. Yet, is this a phenomenon reserved for the formerly colonized only? Or, should this be understood in the wider context of globalization?

Many of these issues tie in with global city theory. For example the notion of *exclusion* is being presented as a characteristic of world cities which has been thoroughly discussed by John Friedmann and Goetz Wolff, Saskia Sassen, Peter Marcuse and others (Friedmann and Wolff, 1982; Marcuse and Van Kempen, 2000; Sassen, 2001). Furthermore, an essential component of world cities discourse is the construct of *networking*. Cities are conceived as lying on a network, and research is directed at ascertaining the level of connectivity – a *space of flows* as opposed to the *space of places* as developed by Manuel Castells (1996). More recent research by Sassen (2002) as well as Stephen Graham and Simon Marvin (2001) discussing the impact of network infrastructures on city form tends to affirm the connectivity among cities and the fragmentary nature of contemporary urban structures. Recently a number of critics have pointed out that the typical global city discourse has left out many cities; they are 'off the map' and increasingly have been calling for an examination of 'marginalized' cities. A central construct underlying these new developments is the notion of transnational urbanism in which urbanizing processes are examined from 'below', looking at the lives of migrants, for example, and the extent to which they moderate globalizing processes (Robinson, 2002; Peter-Smith, 2001). The global city discourse – whereby certain cities are offered as a model to which other cities must aspire to if they are to emerge from 'off the map' – is essentially in dispute. Underlying all these critiques is the work of urban sociologist Janet Abu-Lughod (1999) who has written extensively on Middle Eastern cities and has reminded us that globalization needs to be placed in its proper historical context (figures 1.4 and 1.5).

Cities in the Arab world are curiously left behind in this discussion. A cursory look at the literature reveals that since the publication of the earlier Middle East cities volume (Elsheshtawy, 2004a) there have been hardly any attempts to address the state of the contemporary Arab city. Exceptions exist such as Diane Singerman and Paul Ammar's collection on Cairo (Singerman and Ammar, 2006) forcefully arguing for the emergence of a 'new Middle East'. Another interesting collection dealing with the historical development of Cairo is by Nezar Al Sayyad, Irene Bierman and Nasser Rabat, all scholars residing in the US and forming what is called the *Misr Research Group*. The aim of their book is to present the case of medieval Cairo using a transnationalist perspective. While clearly geared towards historians it has value for contemporary scholarship as well (AlSayyad, Bierman and Rabbat, 2005).

Another interesting collection of chapters addressing developments in the city of Dubai from a critical perspective is by anthropologist Ahmed Kanna (2008).

Figure 1.4. Shanghai: a 'globalizing' city. City residents rest opposite an upscale shopping centre in the city's central district.

Figure 1.5. Social exclusion. The Satwa district in Dubai; the Emirates Towers on Sheikh Zayed Road appear in the background.

These chapters are unique in that they tie together a variety of perspectives – sociological, political, architectural, historical, etc. In that way the multi-dimensional nature of Arab cities is exposed and it is shown that they are plagued with many problems similar to other world cities and as such can make a positive contribution to understanding urbanizing processes in the twenty-first century. They are not a one-thousand-and-one night's fantasy relegated to studying issues of heritage, identity and *Islamic* urbanism. It is however a sad reflection on the state of Arab scholarship that no other books or substantive studies have been published in the intervening years.[4]

One of the aims of the present book is to enrich the study of urbanism and of globalizing processes, building on the previously mentioned studies, and at the same time to provide an accompaniment of sorts to the earlier book, *Planning Middle Eastern Cities* (Elsheshtawy, 2004*a*). Within this context the contributors were invited to reflect on the urban development of their respective cities from the nineteenth century to the present day. This particular time-frame was chosen to illustrate the impact of colonialism (or foreign protection) on the cities' morphology and to draw parallels (or differences) to the current discourse on globalization.

Like the first book, the eight authors here are all affiliated with their cities, either as long time residents, or having lived in the city for some time in the past. Further, the aim of both books is to introduce to a wider global audience a new generation of Arab researchers. With one exception, all the contributors teach and practise within the Middle East. Their backgrounds are primarily architectural but there are exceptions: Mustapha ben Hamouche (Manama) comes from a planning background; Sofia Shwayri from archaeology and Jamila Bargach is trained as an anthropologist. This diversity broadens the scope and perspective of the book.

I posed the following questions to the authors as a starting point for reflection on their respective cities:

◆ How did the city's encounter with modernity (whether through colonialism or globalization) shape and influence its urban form and built environment?

◆ What influences are Middle Eastern cities subjected to?

◆ How are Middle Eastern cities placed within the global city discourse?

◆ What efforts are being made to integrate with other world cities? Is national identity being subordinated in favour of 'global urbanism'?

◆ To what extent are policies of exclusion used to marginalize the lower strata of society?

◆ What images are being projected by the cities in their drive to modernize?

◆ To what extent is the 'local' utilized in projecting such images?

◆ To what extent does the post-colonial condition of some Middle Eastern cities relate to their colonial history? Is there any relationship between post-colonialism and modernity?

I also encouraged contributors to situate and complement their depictions with case studies that would exemplify the transformations which have occurred. In structuring this book I have used both a geographical and a socio-cultural marker in grouping them. Thus they are divided into two parts. The first, *Struggling Cities,* includes Rabat, Amman and Beirut. And the second, *Emerging Cities,* includes the following cities from the Arabian Peninsula: Riyadh, Manama, Kuwait, Doha and Abu Dhabi. The notion of struggle and emergence do tie in, I believe, with the general state of Arab cities and the extent to which they are coping with globalizing processes. I will briefly discuss this issue in the next section.

Emerging Themes: The Great Divide and Commonalities

The chapters in the *Emerging Cities* section reveal that the Arab city is undergoing a massive transformation which is perhaps comparable to changes which took place in the twentieth century while they were under foreign occupation or protection. However, this time the changes are fuelled by global capital – and some would argue neoliberal economic policies. These moments of change – or rupture – have resulted in a change in the cities' urban form. Also, they were instigated by both local and external elements. However, in the twenty-first century the main players are real estate conglomerates – particularly from the Gulf region, and from one specific city which stands way above the rest – Dubai. The dominance and attractiveness of the Gulf model is, of course, fuelled by an abundance of capital, creating a great divide in the region.

Various economic statistics indicate that the pace of economic growth in the GCC (Gulf Cooperation Council) is stronger than the rest of the Arab world. Several indicators of economic growth and development show a wide gap between GCC and other Arab countries. Furthermore this gap appears to have widened in recent years. Some of these numbers are quite striking. For example, the total population of GCC countries was approximately 37 million in 2006, which was roughly 12 per cent of the Arab population of the Middle East and North Africa. However, the economy of GCC countries in 2006 accounted for more than 55 per cent of the Arab world's US$1.25 trillion economy (figure 1.6).

In 1995 the GCC countries had an average per capita income of US$8,500, which was 7.3 times higher than the per capita income of the remaining Arab countries. In 2006 the GCC per capita income rose to US$19,300, which was 10.4 times larger than the average for other Arab countries. Thus, the rift widened. The per capita incomes in some GCC countries such as Qatar ($63,000) and the UAE ($38,000) were higher than many advanced industrial countries in 2006. The 2005 Human Development Index (HDI), which is reported annually by the UN, shows that Kuwait, Bahrain, Qatar, the UAE and Oman achieved the five highest

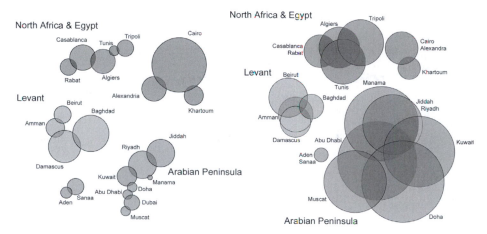

Figure 1.6. Comparison between population in major cities in the MENA region and GDP per head. Circle size is proportional to population size and GDP.

scores among Middle Eastern countries, while Saudi Arabia stood at seventh place, after Libya.

Another gap between GCC and other Arab countries is governance, which measures six parameters: voice and accountability; political stability; government effectiveness; regulatory quality; rule of law; and costs of corruption. According to the World Bank's governance indicators for 2005, on average, GCC countries achieved higher scores in all parameters. The high quality of governance in GCC countries has led to a sharp increase in foreign investment inflows. The share of GCC in total inflow of foreign investment into the Arab world has also increased.[5]

This divide in the region is of course based on oil wealth. According to the IMF the bulk of the oil windfall will be invested in the region where projects worth more than US$1,000 billion are planned. A study by McKinsey estimates that over the period 2005 to 2020 the Gulf is likely to have a US$3,000 billion oil surplus, half of which will stay in the region, with capital of another US$750 billion or so going into investments in wider Middle East and North Africa.[6] In this book some of these places of investment are discussed – particularly Rami Daher's discussion of the Abdali development in downtown Amman, and Jamila Bargach's depiction of the Sama Dubai intervention in Rabat. I have discussed these new forms of investment in Cairo in the previously mentioned collection by Singerman and Ammar (Elsheshtawy, 2006).

This 'great divide', as it were, has led to many problems. Among them an increased rate of migration from poor Arab countries to the richer ones in the GCC, as can be observed, for example, at the border between Yemen and Saudi Arabia which is crossed yearly by more than 400,000 illegal immigrants. According to one observer, expressing the interconnectedness in the region, 'GCC countries, like all other rich countries in the world, need to understand that maintaining a bizarre status of economic inequality between neighbouring countries would inevitably mean more illegal immigrants and hence more problems for all'.[7] In addition there are spatial repercussions for such economic disparity across countries which this book aims at unearthing. Cities in particular are sites where such divisions are made visible and are greatly intensified.

While the foregoing may seem to stress intra-city divisions, another way of reading the chapters would suggest some commonalities. Cities are repositories of memories. Their spaces are inscribed with meaning by their users, thus common elements/themes emerge defying artificiality and imposed binary distinctions. From this perspective Daher's Amman becomes no different from Adham's Doha, my Abu Dhabi, Shwayri's Beirut or Bargach's Rabat. One aspect that struck me in particular was the extent to which personal experiences influenced the way authors structured their chapters or how they focused on specific urban spaces. For example, Rami Daher introduces his chapter by relaying some of his childhood memories. Khaled Adham elaborates on his residence in Doha's central area and his impression of its fragmented cityscape; or my own arrival in Abu Dhabi and its association with the central market nestled among high-rise skyscrapers. Also Sofia Shwayri's depiction of the civil war in Lebanon and the extent to which it fractured Beirut's cityscape – echoing in a way her own memories of these events – responds to this notion of the subjective experience of cities.

What makes this specific reading particularly valuable is that it moves us away from only seeing divisions, to looking at what ties these cities together. Residents of cities, whether in the Gulf or in the region's traditional centres, ultimately aim at having a city that is liveable and pleasurable – an aspiration they share with residents of any city in the world. There is also an epistemological value for such an experiential approach. Many urban studies focus on statistics and numbers which hide the experience of the everyday and ordinary interactions of city residents.[8] It is here that some of the contributors to this book have begun to suggest an alternative method not found in the typical global cities literature.

The Structure of the Book

It is common in edited books to provide a capsule summary of chapters. I will not attempt to do this here. Rather, I will sketch out the main themes identified by the contributors and fill some of the gaps – issues that were not discussed, and that would aid in contextualizing the chapters. As noted above the book is divided into two main parts: *Struggling Cities* and *Emerging Cities*. This distinction is geographical but it also reflects a growing reality in the region pertaining to the extent of engagement with globalization.

Contributors in *Struggling Cities*, the traditional centres, seem to follow a political approach in that they articulate a particularly confrontational tone – setting the State and its policies versus citizens and the extent to which this impacts urban form. Prevalent ideologies were adapted with particularly negative implications on urban morphology. This is certainly the case in both Bargach's and Shwayri's chapters who describe the role of the 'State' in constructing housing environments (Rabat-Sale) and the reconstruction of Beirut following its devastating civil war. Bargach explores a connection between the experiences of residents within these constructed environments and the extent to which they 'clash' with State policies – offering a vivid portrayal of a North African city (this ties in with the work of Abu-Lughod (1980) examining housing policies in Rabat). Shwayri tries to show the role of both local and global actors in the reconstruction process of Beirut which is an addition to recent research efforts (for example, Rowe and Sarkis, 1998; Kassab, 1997). Daher approaches his city, Amman, by discussing the impact of global capital on its urban development using the case of Abdali – its new 'downtown.' All contributions suggest a struggle – a desire to move away from the restrictions of the past and of tradition and to embrace modernity. Such narratives become particularly poignant in the post 9/11 era in which the entire region is engaged in a political upheaval. In such a discourse critiques of urban development processes become common, challenging the power of the State and decision-makers and calling for a more participatory and inclusive direction (figures 1.7 and 1.8).

Authors in the second section *Emerging Cities* adopt a different tone. Here the overall articulation is more optimistic, evidenced in the choice of words: metamorphosis; rediscovering; arrival; emergence. Such terms evoke a positive response to modernizing (or globalizing) influences. At the same time there is a slightly sceptical (one might even say ironic) view in using phrases such as 'cities of sand and fog'. The overall perception (or misconception) is that Gulf cities are not authentic or that they are merely the result of capital speculation, generated by

Figure 1.7. The Solidere development in central Beirut.

Figure 1.8. Amman's new downtown: the Abdali development in a display at the Dubai Cityscape 2007 exhibition.

temporary influx of wealth. Yet a reading of these chapters indicates differences: cities which have a more developed encounter with modernity (Kuwait, Manama and Riyadh) and dormant/emergent cities (Doha, Abu Dhabi). Cities in the Gulf have been active in asserting themselves as world cities, aided by being free from historical 'burdens' as well as direct forms of colonization. Yet such a freedom has also resulted in some cities lying in a 'dormant' state, only recently beginning to emerge. Within the first category, Mahgoub in discussing the case of Kuwait, a city with a relatively long engagement with modernity, illustrates its embrace of foreign architects in the 1970s and 1980s and its current marginalization in the world city discourse. Ben Hamouche presents the case of Manama, one of the first cities in the Gulf to encounter the depletion of oil, offering a sweeping account of various modernizing forces changing the city's historic core and the subsequent emergence of mega-projects. Riyadh provides an interesting counterpoint to these cities in that its development is guided by an institutional authority which, as Al-Naim notes, shaped the character of the city. Both Doha and Abu Dhabi are what one may arguably term typical oil Gulf cities, in that they witnessed a radical transformation from being poor fishing and pearling villages to contemporary metropolises. Yet their emergence has been slow and is only now being experienced, as Adham notes, through the development of 'urban archipelagos' in Doha or the deliberate destruction of old markets and construction of Arabian palaces in Abu Dhabi, as pointed out by me (figure 1.9, 1.10, and 1.11).

Figure 1.9. Doha's Islamic Museum designed by American architect I.M. Pei and the city's emerging skyline.

Figure 1.10. Abu Dhabi's newly refurbished waterfront and its skyline.

Figure 1.11. Kuwait's towers.

Overall the chapters articulate a struggle as pointed out by many scholars (for example, Fuccaro, 2001): the city is viewed both as a recipient of modernity and a focal point for an Arabic-Islamic identity. This is particularly the case in Gulf cities. Furthermore, it is interesting to observe that within these readings the impact of Dubai is quite strong – sometimes articulated explicitly as in the Kuwait, Doha, and Abu Dhabi chapters. Furthermore, these cities are part of the GCC conglomeration and through their mega-projects are in some ways setting themselves apart from the wider Arab/Middle Eastern context – deliberately constructing a separate and independent entity. The following sections provide a more detailed reading of these chapters.

The Chapters: An Overview

Fuad K. Malkawi's prologue calls for a new research agenda pertaining to Arab cities and is prophetically titled 'The New Arab Metropolis'. He rightly notes the absence of the Arab city from global city literature even though the region contains many 'global' religious centres such as Medina, Mecca and Jerusalem – these have significance at a universal level yet the economic focus of globalization has left them 'off the map'. Even centres like Dubai receive minimal scholarly interest (until recently one may add) with writers mostly focusing on its spectacular effects. Echoing the view of many critics of this approach to global cities, he notes that it would be more suitable to use the construct of 'metropolization' as a heuristic device capturing the transformations which the Arab city is currently undergoing. These transformations or changes were identified more than 40 years ago and Malkawi uses his background as a consultant for the UN to identify the problems facing Arab cities, such as rapid urbanization, poverty and the changing core-periphery relation of cities to their hinterland. These issues have intensified and in turn need to be examined in more detail – thus moving away from the typical socio-cultural reading characterizing research on cities in the Arab world. Most significantly Malkawi elaborates on the notion that cities in the region play different roles and their importance varies according to their location within local, regional and international networks. Thus, there are 'degrees of metropolization' in the region leading to a restructuring of the hierarchy of Arab cities. He concludes his chapter by setting an agenda that should be adapted by researchers in the region. This prologue sets the stage quite succinctly for the chapters that follow and which illustrate some of the issues Malkawi discusses. No city should be viewed in isolation or as part of some global network; in their globalizing efforts they interact with a variety of forces at different scales and levels, simultaneously guiding and shaping their development.

The *Struggling Cities* section begins with Rami Daher writing about Amman which he dubs a 'forgotten city' – contrasting it with the likes of Beirut and Cairo – weaving together a passionate and thoughtful narrative which is divided into two parts. First he looks at Amman's history specifically focusing on the increasing interest in its urban and social history. However, the bulk of the chapter is devoted to what he calls 'neoliberal economic restructuring', whereby Beirut and Dubai become models for its recent developments.

Daher devotes considerable attention to the Abdali project, modelled after Solidere's project in Beirut. He suggests that this is part of a larger phenomenon in Amman which includes a proliferation of malls and gated communities; in addition to luxurious towers which represent a form of 'living above the city'. He notes that these transformations are a perfect example of neoliberal urban restructuring – a privatization of public space. He writes that both in its orientation and design it is turning its back on Amman's original downtown. According to Daher 'the State is not absent but heavily involved'. The project has led to a displacement of a major transportation terminal, as well as removal of informal vendors. It will in its current form compete with the existing downtown according to Daher. In addition to the Abdali development Daher also provides us with the results of extensive research whereby he engaged in a process of 'mapping' this new neoliberal landscape. In spite of the general sense of doom prevalent in the chapter a hopeful note is struck at the end by citing examples of projects, supported by Amman municipality, such as the Rainbow Street Project by Turath; and there are examples of other projects also emphasizing inclusiveness and social sustainability.

It would be interesting to place this chapter in a wider context involving the city of Amman which is increasingly being demarcated along economic lines – a rich western area, site of the Abdali project, and various upscale malls, and a poorer eastern part containing slums and refugee camps. Development efforts are increasingly geared towards the former. Furthermore, Daher makes an interesting point related to urban governance – namely the notion of resistance. There is no political awareness in Arab countries in general that would lead citizens to organize public protests if they feel that their interests are threatened. However, with regard to Amman, I observed a thriving blog culture which is criticizing these projects and pointing out the demarcations which exist in the city, dividing it in two parts.[9] These are hopeful signs that citizens are becoming more politically aware – moving from politics with a big 'P' to a small 'p' – to paraphrase Daher.

Closely related to the Amman chapter is Sofia T. Shwayri's depiction of Beirut. A city torn by civil war, it has a very unique position within the Arab world. Her approach relies on the notion of resilience – rebuilding what has been destroyed – which is how she begins her sometimes traumatic but ultimately hopeful depiction. She focuses on the reconstruction of Beirut's Central Business District from 1943 to 2006, identifying three points of transition (Jamila Bargach in her Rabat chapter interestingly uses the word ruptures). These transit points are anchored and defined by the civil war which in many ways shaped the current urban form of Beirut's CBD.

The period before the war is vividly, and perhaps nostalgically, described by Shwayri, noting that this was a time when Beirut was the Arab world's financial centre. Its vivid nightlife and five star hotels are, of course, the stuff of legend for anyone recalling these times. The city was, however, not just the Arab world's amusement centre, but more significantly it provided shelter for intellectuals fleeing oppressive regimes; it also became home for many poor migrants belonging to different ethnic groups. Ultimately this led, according to Shwayri, to 'mosaic landscapes' and a geography of fear. The narrative takes a dark turn with the onset of the civil war. Shwayri's words are evocative of this – using titles and phrases such as 'murder of the capital'. A purposeful destruction of the city's main lifeline – the airport, the port and the CBD – initiated a process that led to the demarcation and fragmentation of Beirut and ensuring of territorial control. In the third transition the city centre is again the target but this time involving an attempt to globalize the city and 'reclaim' its pre-war status. The much discussed Solidere project is revisited, although Shwayri makes it quite clear that this is not just about profit making but that it also has symbolic value – a point largely missed by many critics of the project. She alludes to the current troubles – started by the assassination of Rafik Hariri in the city centre – throwing the city again into a cycle of violence and destruction.

Shwayri's depiction offers many lessons. It shows that when a city is governed by fear it becomes a gated enclave – thus depriving it of becoming an inclusive space for all its citizens. Certainly this notion is prevalent in Beirut. My own experience of walking in the city centre was defined by the presence of security personnel, the constant questioning about my intentions in photographing buildings. More significantly, the Solidere development itself seemed an isolated island. Lebanese colleagues were questioning whether it is a space provided for Beirutis or for rich Arabs. Driving to the airport one is confronted with shabby housing projects and refugee camps – a somewhat disconcerting image – contrasting with the carefully maintained CBD. These marginalized spaces have perhaps been forgotten in the city's drive to become a regional centre once again.

A similar tale involving the role of global capital in re-inventing a city centre is told by Jamila Bargach in her chapter on Rabat. At the very outset she argues that Rabat's history is characterized by ruptures – an apt description applicable to the urban experience of Arab cities. These are closely linked to, and defined by, the colonial experience. Moving swiftly from Rabat's founding in the twelfth century, she begins her narrative in 1914 when Morocco officially became a French protectorate, which initiated a series of transformations in the city's morphology. What makes her depiction so poignant is her observations of the city's shantytowns – a precursor to the infamous *bidonvilles*. The capital has thus been increasingly defined by these ghettos – to a large extent tolerated by the State. In its current transformation these 'pockets of extreme deprivation are being targeted by a palace-led "human development" initiative'. One particular event which transformed the way the government dealt with public housing and slums was the Casablanca bombings in 2003. The perpetrators came from one of the poorest slums in the city. This led to a 're-orientation' in housing policy by inviting private firms to participate in reconstruction and demolition. Bargach also notes the strong involvement of the king in line with a perpetuation of an image of the 'king as builder'.

Bargach's focus then shifts to the current global condition. She shows how one particular Arab Gulf company, Sama Dubai, a Dubai based (government-owned) conglomerate with an extensive international portfolio, is playing a major role in transforming the cityscape of Rabat into a global metropolis and in the process alienating the city's citizens. This transformation includes the Bouregreg River Development Project, developed by a governmental entity. This entity in turn has invited a number of developers – private firms – to propose projects along the river. The centre of the project is Amwaj, a mixed-use, luxurious development by Sama Dubai. Bargach argues that citizen needs are not taken into account in these projects; they primarily serve global capital. In fact they have resulted in displacements and relocations of people living along the river. In an interview with a government official she is told that the government is dealing with the poor by providing a low-income housing project called Tamesna, located far from the city. Because of the separation she writes that 'each city will move in its own orbit'. Ramifications of such policies will include: socio-spatial fragmentation; relocation; and displacement.

The first city in the *Emerging Cities* section is Riyadh. Mashary A. Al-Naim, an academic and architect, provides an invaluable first-hand, local account of Riyadh – a city that has been little written about from an architectural and urban perspective. He describes it as a 'city of institutional architecture' – that is a city that is defined by State sponsored projects. He provides an overview of its changing architectural trends in the twentieth century, situating this within an overall framework that is based on notions of a 'cultural conflict'. It is quite telling that within the Arab world in the 1980s there was a strong trend towards issues of preserving traditional values, a return to Islamic architecture, etc. This trend found further impetus in a variety of conferences and workshops sponsored by the Saudi government and academic institutions.[10] Within this context Al-Naim provides an explanation of why such events took place and the extent to which they were expressed in the city's architecture. His depiction of its institutionalization in a way shows that the State was both controlling architectural and urban development as well as instilling social values. He notes that Saudi society is by nature conservative – that is to say traditional, which is even more evident in Riyadh, the capital and the heartland of that conservatism. As such the city tried to project the image – to the Arab world – that it is resisting modernization while at the same time providing an alternative. The author in particular describes how the Al-Riyadh Development Authority (ADA), set up in the 1970s, played a role in executing and influencing this new image.

To that end Al-Naim provides us with a series of depictions of well known projects and the extent to which they are an effort to preserve traditional architectural values while incorporating modern elements. Of course this trend towards traditionalism – and that it found a particularly receptive audience in Saudi Arabia – needs to be situated in a wider context. Post-modernism and critical regionalism were particularly strong theoretical discourses in the 1980s and 1990s – and as such it was quite natural that these views would find a receptive audience in a conservative society such as Saudi Arabia. However, at the end of the twentieth century and the beginning of the twenty-first things began to change. The various Gulf wars, decline in oil prices, and an exploding population put a strain on Saudi economy – as a result the focus began to shift to other cities in the Gulf, such as Dubai.

In his concluding sections Al-Naim provides some thoughts on the extent to which Riyadh is trying to globalize – whether through its spectacular architecture, deepening patterns of inequality due to arrival of poor migrants, or through its investments in financial zones. He also acknowledges the influence of Dubai although, quoting Riyadh's mayor, he notes that this must be done with 'care'. It is this last point which Al-Naim uses to distinguish Riyadh from other cities in the region; he uses words such as 'hesitant' or 'conservative' to note that the city will retain its traditional roots and thus will not – for lack of a better word – fully globalize. However, Al-Naim's brief incursion into the city's growing slum problem may still prove to be an explosive issue that could result in a fragmented city composed of ghettos of the rich and the poor. The city could thus prove to be an alarming window onto the future for other cities in the region.

Yasser Mahgoub in his chapter on Kuwait relays the familiar story of rapid urbanization in Gulf cities, and the accompanying sense of identity loss due to modernization. He is relying for the most part on an architectural perspective focusing on buildings, but his contribution and the significance of his chapter stems from providing a voice for local architects. These voices are absent from the modernizing discourse of Gulf cities. Mahgoub begins with a historical narrative informing us that the city's history goes as far back as 1760. Its modern urban development began in the 1950s and 1960s characterized by the demolition of old neighbourhoods. Unlike other cities in the Gulf, the notion of a Kuwaiti identity was a prominent factor driving the city's development – perhaps attributable to its precarious political situation. Thus in the late 1960s, according to Mahgoub a panel was set up to 'produce distinctive landmarks'. A series of architects – representing a who's who of the international architectural scene – was selected to accomplish this task of what one may call 'the creation of' an identity. Familiar landmarks are an outcome of this policy – the famed Kuwait water towers; the parliament building and so on.

Kuwait like Beirut underwent a traumatic experience of warfare – in this case invasion by Iraq. Mahgoub tells us that this has further strengthened the desire of local architects to search for that elusive Kuwaiti identity – a kind of essentialist viewpoint. However, another reaction is to become 'completely modern' in a way reflecting general trends in the region. Among these new developments is the 'City of Silk' mega-project – a response to Dubai and others in the region. Mahgoub provides us with examples of buildings produced during that period – reflecting a kind of Disneyesque development.

He also alludes to some problems accompanying these developments, such as the emptying of the downtown area and the proliferation of shantytowns which are a part of the Kuwaiti landscape, such as the Khetan neighbourhood, housing poor labourers mostly from Egypt. There are many others and many media observers have commented on the abject conditions in which these workers live.[11] And it is here perhaps that another tale still needs to be told. Giving voice to local architects should be accompanied by relating how the city's residents live and experience their environment. Here the whole notion of a Kuwaiti identity may not be as important as providing the basic necessities of life.

Manama is a unique city in the Gulf because it was one of the first to benefit from an oil economy but also the first to encounter its depletion. Furthermore, it was a regional capital created by the British following the signing of a Protectorate Treaty in 1892. Mustafa Ben Hamouche examines the city's urban development by identifying three modes of urbanism characterizing its growth and, in turn, impacting its urban form. His planning perspective permeates the chapter, focusing, among other things, on the city's agricultural origins. Another factor setting the city apart from its neighbours is that it became a hub for various transnational communities, resulting in a rich mosaic of ethnic groups and religions. As a result the city developed an urban tradition and urban fabric that comes perhaps close to what one may call a traditional 'Arab-Islamic' city. Hamouche's narrative is supported by extensive research relying in many instances on primary sources and original historical documents, thereby enriching his depiction.

Hamouche also devotes considerable attention to the degradation of the historic core, the dominance of poor expatriates within the city centre, and the existence of slum like living conditions. Seemingly an intentional policy resulting in what he calls 'the dying heart of the old city', new developments – urbanism of globalization according to Hamouche – have further accelerated this process. These new projects – the Bahrain Financial Harbour, for example – are enveloping the old city, in a way masking its deterioration. The focus on such projects, while ignoring the plight of low-income workers and residents, may threaten the fragile social stability in the city. Hamouche advocates a policy of preservation that is not simply focused on reviving a few historical buildings but also a comprehensive strategy that would revive Manama's centre. His elaboration on its rich urban history is a reminder to all of us that there is real value in protecting this heritage.

Khaled Adham's chapter on Doha provides a much needed analysis of a city absent from the urban discourse in the Gulf. His depiction follows the typical tripartite structure of urbanism in the Gulf: pre-oil, oil, and the current global moment, which he describes interestingly as 'scenes'. While providing an overview of various developments taking place, and describing some of the main buildings being constructed he is also trying to understand 'why' these developments are taking place. This is situated within a capitalist framework, which Adham argues has been the driving force in its urban development, starting from pearling until the current condition which emphasizes culture – a form of cultural capitalism.

Thus everything becomes a commodity of sorts, and cities are brands that need to be marketed.

In support of this Adham provides us with a bewildering array of projects which have transformed the city: the Pearl Island reclamation project; the 180 high rises being constructed in the West Bay area; and of course the I.M. Pei Islamic museum project among many others. His brief personal memories of living in the city, the crowdedness of Asian workers in Suq Waqif, are a much needed counterpoint to his general descriptions. It is this last point which I think needs to be further examined. While one cannot dispute the role of capital in driving the growth of cities and effectively becoming an explanation for everything – a view strongly articulated by David Harvey (2006) for example – absent from such an approach are people. Michael Peter Smith (2001) has strongly criticized this and argued for a view that looks at people's daily lives and the strategies that are formed to counteract globalizing influences. Khaled Adham's chapter does, I believe, make an interesting contribution to this debate in global city theory.

In my chapter on Abu Dhabi, which concludes this collection, I set the context of the city's urban development with the help of two case studies: the Central Market project and the Saadiyat Island cultural district. This is anchored in a historical reading illustrating the city's rapid transformation. Unlike its 'noisy' neighbour Dubai, there was a certain reluctance to open to global capital and to transform its cityscape. However, following the death of its late ruler, Sheikh Zayed, in 2004, the city is embarking on a construction drive that is unprecedented in the Gulf region. This is aided by the lack of any significant historical centre that would constrain these developments. The city is trying to distinguish itself by using a development model that is less 'spectacular' than its neighbour, has more emphasis on culture, and is more sustainable.

The first project on which I focus, the Central Market, is a replacement for a *souq* built in the 1970s. While of no historic value it nevertheless represented one of the few authentic settings in the city which was accessible for a large segment of the population. In its place a mixed-use, exclusive mega-project is being constructed. I argue that this project fits with what Harvey (2006) calls a 'geography of exclusion' whereby new developments essentially cater to a select section of the population. Another dimension to this new global orientation is the rather spectacular development of Saadiyat Island – which will house four museums and performance centres designed by the world's 'top' four architects in addition to a museum dedicated to the life of Sheikh Zayed. Both of these projects raise significant issues related to social sustainability, the role of capital in creating spaces of exclusion, and the role of museums and art in a globalizing world – which are discussed in the chapter.

Travellers' accounts, residents' reactions, content analysis of media reports, as well as fictional accounts by Saudi writer Abdulrahman Munif are used as narrative devices to provide a deeper understanding of the city's urban transformation. Many writings on cities in the Gulf give the impression that they are devoid of people.

By using these 'tools' I am trying to offer a parallel reading of the city that would enhance our understanding on 'why' these developments are taking place and 'how' people react to them. In such a way I am showing that the urban experience of such cities is fundamentally similar to other places in the world.

Concluding Thoughts

The cover image for this book shows in the foreground the entrance gate to the exclusive Emirates Palace Hotel in Abu Dhabi with the emerging modern skyline of the city in the background.[12] The image has a sort of menacing quality – by using the symbols of Arab/Islamic architecture these new cities are projecting themselves as the new centres of the region. The chosen symbols suggest power, a new hegemonic condition. They are not 'tribes with flags' anymore (figure 1.12).[13] The back cover image, on the other hand, is in one of Muscat's old *souqs*, dominated by a walking woman in a black flowing robe, clearly defined against the slightly blurred onlookers and stores. Without appearing too nostalgic there is a humanity in this image, reflecting a sense of community, which is something that I believe has strong universal appeal. Muscat, while being part of the GCC, has adopted a different mode of development. It still retains its traditional cityscape, its growth is measured and sustainable – even though it did not escape the 'reclaimed island virus'. However, as a whole, it is a city that is clearly defined by, and geared towards, its citizens and residents (figure 1.13). Gulf cities need to learn lessons from such an approach – artificial neo-Islamic symbols of power should not deflect our attention from the intimate scale of our old markets.

Figure 1.12. Abu Dhabi's Emirates Palace Hotel appears in the background.

Figure 1.13. Muscat's skyline in its traditional area of Matrah.

I have talked at length about the great divide in the Arab world which I believe will have long lasting impact on its urban development. Two cities, which clearly define this problem in unmistakable terms, are not included in this book – Dubai and Cairo. In the first volume of this collection they were discussed in great detail and many of the issues that were raised at that time have intensified and become clearer. For instance, Khaled Adham's chapter in which he discussed the emergence of gated communities in Cairo in the form of the Dreamland project was particularly prophetic (Adham, 2004). Such forms of settlement have become a defining feature of Cairo's cityscape – other Dreamlands have emerged. My own discussion on Dubai and my argument that its developments are fragmented and exclusive has become a central feature of its urban form (Elsheshtawy, 2004b). Increasingly the poor are driven out to invisible labour camps and cities while the city itself is designed to cater for the rich and powerful. At a much more alarming level is the increasing presence of Dubai's real-estate companies in the Arab world's major centres, which elsewhere I have termed 'Dubaization'. Such modes of development deepen the inequality already present in these cities (figure 1.14). Space limitations will not allow me to elaborate on this, but I have written on this subject in a report for UN-ESCWA, titled *The Status of the Arab City*, showing the great rift in the Arab World and the extent to which this is negatively affecting socio-cultural sustainability among other things (Elsheshtawy, 2008a). Also, I discuss Dubai's urban development in an upcoming book whose aim is to ascertain whether it suggests a new form of urbanity (Elsheshtawy, 2008b).

I started this introduction by putting the suggestion that Arabs do not exist anymore. Certainly a reading of these chapters would indicate that, with regard to cities, Arabs are simply hapless recipients of modernism. For example officials in the Gulf are turning towards Western architects and planners to plan, design, form

Figure 1.14. Billboard in Cairo advertising the recent entry of Etisalat, the UAE based telecommunication company, in Egypt. The advertisement reads: 'Etisalat Arrive'. In the background is a middle-class housing project.

and shape their cities. The 'new Middle East' is based on Western conceptions of what our cities should look like. Arabs have disappeared from contributing to the design of their built environment. Another side of the problem is the absence of academics and scholars from any discussion pertaining to urban theory. Archaic institutional rules, which among other things actively discourage scholars from writing books,[14] as well as the lack of any significant research library has led to the absence of the Arab city from the global/world city discourse. I hope that this book will be seen as an effort, a first step, towards overcoming this gap.

And there are signs of hope even within this gloom indicating that there is a way out. Efforts to upgrade slums in Cairo and Tunis have begun to bear fruit, showing that there is a decline in their presence (UN-Habitat, 2007). Or, looking at the urban experiments of Abu Dhabi and Dubai, one can perhaps argue that these are signs of a new urbanity – the emergence of a 'new Arab metropolis' to paraphrase Malkawi. More significant is the growing presence of civic institutions which are effectively beginning to question authorities and planners. Whether in Cairo, Rabat, Amman or even Bahrain, human rights organizations are highlighting the condition of unskilled labourers and the squalor of slums. And an active blogsphere is beginning to give voice to residents of Arab cities; by defying and circumventing official channels they point out growing patterns of inequality in Amman, for example. An alternative discourse is thus being constructed. Arab architects and planners need to take advantage of this unique 'global' moment and begin to adopt a view that unshackles us from the heavy burden of the past and embraces modernity. This is the only way forward and perhaps we can show Adonis that he is wrong and that we do exist after all!

Notes

1.   From an interview with Syrian poet 'Adonis', aired on Dubai TV on 11 March 2006. Transcript on *MEMRI (Middle East Media Research Institute), Special Dispatch Series no. 1121*, 21 March. http://memri.org/bin/articles.cgi?Page=archives&Area=sd&ID=SP112106. Accessed 2 October 2007.

2.   Edward Luttwak, a senior adviser at the Centre for Strategic and International Studies in Washington DC, writes: 'Western analysts are forever bleating about the strategic importance of the Middle East. But despite its oil, this backward region is less relevant than ever, and it would be better for everyone if the rest of the world learned to ignore it'. (Luttwak, 2007)

3.   The report can be found at the following link: http://www.undp.org/arabstates/ahdr2003.shtml. Accessed 12 December 2007.

4.   There have been some studies pertaining to Dubai in particular such as Jumeno (2004), Marchal (2005) and Kanna (2005).

5.   Habibi, Nader (2007) Economic divide among Arabs. *Gulf News*, 13 November, p. 52.

6.   Khalaf, Roula (2007) It's boom time. *Gulf News*, 22 November p. 22.

7.   Al Saqaf, Walid (2007) How to stop illegal aliens. *Gulf News*, 28 September.

8.   This is a point of view strongly articulated by the situationists. Michel de Certeau, for instance, writes: 'The panorama-city is a "theoretical" (that is, visual) *simulacrum*, in short a picture, whose condition of possibility is an oblivion and a misunderstanding of practices. The voyeur-god created by this fiction, who, like Schreber's God, knows only cadavers, must disentangle himself from the murky intertwining daily behaviors and make himself alien to them. The ordinary practitioners of the city live "*down below*," below the threshold at which visibility begins. They walk – an elementary form of this experience of the city; they are walkers, *Wandermaenner*, whose bodies follow the thicks and thins of an *urban* "*text*" they write without being able to read it'. (De Certeau, 1984).

9.   In a blog titled 'Amman, and the filthy rich' an author writes 'I used to roam East Amman with less than 1 JD! can anybody tell me why can't we go to certain places in West Amman using public transportation ?? Abdoun for example ??" In http://abedhamdan.com/2007/05/02/amman-and-the-filthy-rich/. Another blogger: 'The greater Amman Municiaplity (GAM) will advance with a plan to build a city to the east of Amman this year, a step meant to ease pressure off the western and northern parts of the capital… An urban centre called Labour City… In all probability it will be the "Other Amman" i.e. an extension of East Amman, you know, to accommodate all the poor people'. In www.black-iris.com/2006/01/06/introducing-new-amman. Accessed 8 February 2008.

10.   See for example, Serageldin and El-Sadek (1982) in the proceedings of a conference examining the character of Islamic Cities which took place in Saudi Arabia.

11.   Journalist Rania Al Gamal (2007) in an insightful article writes about some of these areas such as Salwa, Fahaheel, Shuwaikh, Jleeb Al-Shuyoukh, Khaitan, Jahra, Sulaybiyah and Bneid Al-Qar. She describes the latter – also known as the bachelors area – as follows:

> The house was decaying with a half collapsed wall. You could clearly see the people living inside the ancient house hanging their worn out clothes to dry. The building looked on the verge of collapsing at any time and all I could do was pray that nobody would be hurt if/when it fell. To go inside the house, you have to walk through a tiny dark corridor where the smell of open sewers and human sweat is mixed with the aroma of spiced cooked rice and summer dampness. The writings on a wall in white chalk welcome you to the home of some of the poorer working classes in the slummy areas of the oil-rich Kuwait: Bneid Al-Qar.

In Al Gamal, Rania (2007) Thousands live in the slums of Kuwait. *Kuwait Times*, 1 June. http://www.kuwaittimes.net/read_news.php?newsid=MjAzMzM0OTcxMw==. Accessed 12 December 2007.

12.   The hotel was recently shown in a movie titled 'The Kingdom' as a stand in for the city of Riyadh; it was supposedly the palace of a ruler.

13.   The quote is attributed to Tahsin Bashir, an Egyptian diplomat: 'Egypt is the only nation-state in the region the others are tribes with flags'. (Quoted in Glass, 1990, p. 3).

14.   Promotional rules in most Arab universities do not count books or book chapters when faculty

members apply for promotion. There are exceptions; for instance UAE University is beginning to apply Western procedures for promotion which, among other things, evaluate a faculty member's general output of research – including journal papers, conference publications, books and book chapters.

References

Abu Lughod, Janet (1999) *New York, Chicago, Los Angeles: America's Global Cities*. Minneapolis, MN: University of Minnesota Press.

Abu-Lughod, Janet (1980) *Urban Apartheid in Morocco*. Princeton, NJ: Princeton University Press.

Adham, Khaled (2004) Cairo's urban *déjà vu*: globalization and urban fantasies, in Elsheshtawy, Yasser (ed.) *Planning the Middle Eastern City: An Urban Kaleidoscope in a Globalizing World*. London: Routledge, pp. 134–163.

AlSayyad, Nezar (2006) Whose Cairo? in Singermann, Diane and Ammar, Paul (eds.) *Cairo Cosmopolitan: Politics, Culture, and Space in the New Middle East*. Cairo: American University in Cairo Press, pp. 539–542.

AlSayyad, Nezar, Bierman, Irene and Rabbat, Nasser (2005) *Making Cairo Medieval*. Lanham, MD: Lexington Books.

Castells, Manuel (1996) *The Rise of the Network Society*. London: Blackwell.

De Certeau, Michel (1984) *The Practice of Everyday Life*. Berkeley, CA: University of California Press.

Elsheshtawy, Yasser (ed.) (2004a) *Planning Middle Eastern Cities: An Urban Kaleidoscope in a Globalizing World*. London: Routledge

Elsheshtawy, Yasser (2004b) Redrawing boundaries: Dubai, the emergence of a global city, in Elsheshtawy, Yasser (ed.) *Planning the Middle Eastern City: An Urban Kaleidoscope in a Globalizing World*. London: Routledge, pp. 169–193.

Elsheshtawy, Yasser (2006) From Dubai to Cairo: competing global cities, models, and shifting centers of influence? in Singermann, Diane and Ammar, Paul (eds.) *Cairo Cosmopolitan: Politics, Culture, and Space in the New Middle East*. Cairo: American University in Cairo Press, pp. 235–250.

Elsheshtawy, Yasser (2008a) *The State of the Arab City: The Effect of Globalization on the Sustainability of the Arab City*. Beirut: UN-ESCWA.

Elsheshtawy, Yasser (2008b) *Dubai: An Emerging Urbanity?* Oxon: Routledge.

Elsheshtawy, Yasser (2008c) The global and the everyday: situating the Dubai spectacle, in Kanna, Ahmed (ed.) *The Superlative City Dubai and the Urban Condition in the Early Twenty-First Century*. Cambridge, MA Harvard University Press.

Friedmann, John and Wolff, Goetz (1982) World city formation: an agenda for research and action. *International Journal of Urban and Regional Research*, **6**(3), pp. 309–344.

Fuccaro, Nelida (2001) Visions of the city: urban studies on the Gulf. *Bulletin of the Middle East Studies Association of North America*, **35**(2), pp. 175–188.

Glass, Charles (1990) *Tribes with Flags: A Dangerous Passage through the Chaos of the Middle East*. New York, NY: Atlantic Monthly Press.

Graham, Stephen and Marvin, Simon (2001) *Splintering Urbanism: Networked Infrastructures, Technological Mobilities, and the Urban Condition*. London: Routledge.

Harvey, David (2006) *Spaces of Global Capitalism: Towards a Theory of Uneven Geographical Development*. London: Verso.

Jumeno, Mathias (2004) 'Let's build a palm island!': playfulness in complex times, in Sheller, M. (ed.) *Tourism Mobilities: Places to Play, Places in Play*. London: Routledge, pp. 182–191.

Kanna, Ahmed (2005) The 'state philosophical' in the 'land without philosophy': shopping malls, interior cities, and the image of utopia in Dubai. *Traditional Dwellings and Settlements Review*, **16**(11), pp. 59–73.

Kanna, Ahmed (ed.) (2008) *The Superlative City Dubai and the Urban Condition in the Early Twenty-First Century*. Cambridge, MA: Harvard University Press.

Kassab, Suzanne (1997) On two conceptions of globalisation: the debate around the reconstruction of Beirut, in Oncu, A. and Weyland, P. (eds.) *Space, Culture and Power: New Identities in Globalizing Cities*. London: Zed Books, pp. 42–55.

Luttwak, Edward (2007) The middle of nowhere. *Prospect Magazine*, May, no. 134. http://www.prospect-magazine.co.uk/article_details.php?id=9302. Accessed 14 December 2007.

Marchal, Robert (2005) Dubai: global city and transnational hub, in Al-Rasheed, Madawi (ed.) *Transnational Connections and the Arab Gulf*. London: Routledge, pp. 93–110.

Marcuse, Peter and Van Kempen, Ronald (2000) *Globalizing Cities: A New Spatial Order?* Oxford: Blackwell.

Robinson, Jennifer (2002) Global and world cities: a view from off the map. *International Journal of Urban and Regional Research*, **26**(3), pp. 531–554.

Rowe, Peter and Sarkis, Hashim (1998) *Projecting Beirut: Episodes in the Construction and Reconstruction of a Modern City*. London: Prestel.

Sassen, Saskia (2001) *The Global City*, 2nd ed. Princeton, NJ: Princeton University Press.

Sassen, Saskia (ed.) (2002) *Global Networks, Linked Cities*. London: Brunner-Routledge.

Serageldin, Ismail and El-Sadek, Samir (1982) *The Arab City: Its Character and Islamic Cultural Heritage*. Riyadh.

Singermann, Diane and Ammar, Paul (eds.) (2006) *Cairo Cosmopolitan: Politics, Culture, and Space in the New Middle East*. Cairo: American University in Cairo Press.

Smith, Michael Peter (2001) *Transnational Urbanism*. Cambridge, MA: Blackwell.

UN-Habitat (2007) *The State of the World's Cities Report 2006/2007*. London: Earthscan.

Chapter 2

The New Arab Metropolis: A New Research Agenda

Fuad K. Malkawi

Sassika Sassen (2001) uses the term global cities to distinguish the contemporary leading cities from the 'past' world cities. They are 'nodes' in the network of globalization, places where the global economy is coordinated and reproduced. Similarly Castells (1996, p. 38) identifies global cities as processes 'by which centers of production and consumption of advanced services, and their ancillary local societies, are connected in a global network'. The main feature of this global network is the fact that it is independent from the State (Smith, 2005) and it indicates the rank of cities in transnational business connections (global cities being the top) as Friedmann (1986, p. 317) noted.

The debate over global (world) cities ignores most cities around the world, including Arab cities. Based on the economic status, the global city discourse focuses mainly on cities in the Western hemisphere. It ignores traditional criteria such as national standing, location of State and Interstate agencies and cultural functions in favour of economy as the primary determinant of a city's status in the global network (Robinson, 2002, p. 534). Cities like Cairo, Damascus and Baghdad can no longer build on the leading status they once acquired to take part in such network. Cities like Mecca and Medina, despite their holy status for all Muslims, and even Jerusalem, despite it being holy for all faiths, are left outside the global discourse. Indeed, even evolving cities that are dominating the regional economic scene (that is, Dubai and other Gulf cities) have little or no significance when it comes to the world economy and its rising network. These cities are at the bottom of the global ladder, if not ignored entirely.

While globalization has left the Arab city behind as a contributor to its evolution, it cannot be denied that the impact of this trend on most Arab cities is significant. Over the past 20 years, cities around the Arab World have been transformed drastically. Nevertheless, we find all too few studies tackling this issue and investigating the current status of these cities and the impact of globalization on their structure. Despite the drastic change, most research still focuses on traditional themes. Indeed, other than a few studies, most research agendas were more concerned with traditionally well studied cities, such as Cairo and Damascus and with issues like their historic evolution and political environment. The interest in rising cities like Dubai remained minimal, let alone the interest in them as places of modernity and global discourse.

Researching the Arab city needs to be transformed to absorb the changes that are occurring in its structure, polity and social life. While one can still subscribe to the idea that no Arab city is seen as a node in the global network, the impact of globalization on the city needs to be assessed. The transformation of the city has to be considered against the background of new concepts and this new approach. In the light of this persistent ignorance of the discourse of globalization of the Arab City, metropolisation would perhaps be a better concept to capture the current transformation of the city. It symbolizes the most recent and most drastic changes that are occurring in major urban centres around the world. It implies a process of change in polity, space, communication, division of labour, economy, etc. It represents the attempts of cities to cope with the change associated with globalization.

A new research agenda may focus on tracing such a phenomenon in the Arab world. It may attempt to define the level of metropolisation in each city. Metropolisation as a theme and a conceptual entry to the problem of the current urban world order will allow us to go further into the definitions of concepts, and to compare them to the same phenomena affecting the other cultural areas. In a sense, it questions the traditional city as a paradigm for contemporary urban life and proposes a new way of understanding and investigating the city. It allows for, and requires, what is conventionally called interdisciplinary treatment.

A Problematic Arab Metropolis

Almost 45 years ago, a group of professionals from most Arab countries met in Cairo to discuss the conditions of Arab cities. They were concerned about the problems associated with the massive urbanization process that swept the Arab world at the time. The Arab city was becoming a metropolis, they concluded. It was growing beyond its traditional boundaries, and becoming a town functioning as a dominating centre with other secondary urban centres on its periphery. The urbanization process emphasized this centralized organization. The features of the Arab metropolis at the time were problematic; urban sprawl, traffic congestion, urban poverty, problems of governance, etc. (Berger, 1961).

The expert meeting reflected the concerns of city managers and planners at the time. Urbanization was the sign of the time and exposed the deficiencies of urban services. The growth of the city was accelerating at a faster pace than the urban structure was able to handle. This problematic status of the Arab city led the planners to rethink its form and structure. Ideas were imported over the years to ease the pressure on the ailing centres. Suburbanization became a trend and new towns, satellite cities or new communities sprang around many of these cities as part of the solution. These ideas may have redirected the growth of the Arab city but did little to ease the pressure on its centre. The centre remained of great importance and the growth of cities remained mainly from inside out. However, the scale of these cities, their division, their interrelations have changed in a drastic and complex manner.

Administrating Arab cities has also been a problem since the 1950s and early 1960s. Solutions, which ranged from creating a single authority for each metropolitan area to having a multi-tier structure, were imported from the West and implemented in the region. For example, it was accepted among planners who were working in the region that what was known then as a *city-region* would be the right basis for local government reform. Following the British experience, many of the former British colonies adopted the idea and implemented it. In 1963 (the same year as a metropolitan authority for Greater London was created) the Greater Amman Region was established. Similarly, Greater Baghdad in Iraq and Greater Khartoum in Sudan both experienced transformations at the hands of British planners, echoing the universal experience.[1] The popularity of the city-region idea and the various calls for creating metropolitan authorities, do not mean that the implementation of these ideas was similar throughout the region. The different experiences in the region varied in terms of the relation between *the central city* and the local authorities within the city-region. This variation made each country's definition of the 'city-region' unique.

The change in the Arab City has become even more drastic over the past 15 years or so. The current status of our cities, under forces of consumption that drive our economy, challenges the traditional definitions of urban life and city form in the Arab world. Perhaps the main physical manifestations of the change in today's economy in the Arab city are the new commercial centres that started to surface on the edges of the traditional city. Today, the Arab World is mainly urban, with more than 58 per cent of the population living in urban areas. By the year 2015, only three countries (Egypt, Sudan and Yemen) will have less than 50 per cent of their population living in cities (UN-Habitat, 2004). With this urbanization, the features of the Arab cities are even more problematic. They have the lowest indicators in terms of governance, lagging behind the Sub-Saharan Africa with respect to accountability and efficient governance. They have a high unemployment ratio (an average of 15 per cent) and a high level of urban poverty.[2] In many of these cities the young have insufficient access to educational and training opportunities.[3]

Urban governance is still problematic as well, and reform movements are limited in most Arab countries. In a World Bank country study of seven Arab countries, it was apparent that they had little decentralization, mostly deconcentration and that their cities' governments were constrained by the lack of policy tools and options. Reform attempts within the countries were focused on structural reforms, without real change in behaviour and efficiency (World Bank, 2007*a*).

The Arab World is becoming urban, but at diverse rates and with diverse characteristics. With this urbanization, the urban-rural gap is widening, so is the gap between capital cities and secondary cities. In general, cities enjoy more attention when it comes to capital spending and fiscal transfers. Rural areas in most Arab countries are lagging behind the urban areas. They are characterized by high levels of poverty, high fertility rates and population growth (adding more pressure on land). In addition, they lack basic infrastructure (roads, irrigation, etc.), often due to the high cost of its provision and maintenance, hindering development in these areas. Rural populations are often marginalized by poverty, location and sometimes ethnicity, religion or tribe.

Not all cities experience the same privileged status, however. Some are also lagging behind in terms of basic services. Capital cities usually enjoy more autonomy and self-sufficiency while secondary cities are still highly dependant on the central government, leaving their governments with limited responsibilities and limited resources. Accordingly, the capital city becomes the national centre of finance and the modern State, and is perhaps more connected to the world outide than to its peripheries. Other cities and rural areas become a liability.

This gap is reflected in urban services as well. A World Bank study of sample households in several cities around the Arab World concluded that while access to services is fairly reasonable, it varies between capital cities and secondary cities. For example, while about 90 per cent of the sample in Cairo had direct water supplies, barely 60 per cent do in secondary cities like Zagazig, and water quality even drops lower, as indicated by a user satisfaction survey conducted by the World Bank. This percentage reaches only 40 per cent in Zagazig when it comes to electricity, while it is above 90 per cent in Cairo. In Morocco on the other hand, while access to water is better in secondary cities, only 20 per cent of the Zem Oud's sample had never experienced problems with water.

In Yemen, garbage collection is weak in Dhamar compared to Sana'a. While all houses in Sana'a have most of their garbage collected, virtually none do in Dhamar. This also applies to street lighting and maintenance of local roads. These services are also rather poor in Egypt in both Cairo and Zagazig, while the gap still exists in the quality of the sanitary system between Cairo and secondary cities.

The condition of Arab cities and their status among world cities vary from one country to another. On the one hand, some cities are closed to the outside world for various reasons, lagging behind when it comes to modernization and world connectivity, while other cities enjoy a prestigious status in the world and lead on many fronts. Some Arab cities traditionally held a regional, if not global, special status. Other cities are emerging as major players on the international scene. Cities which traditionally played a major role in the regional political economy, like Cairo and Damascus, are making room for new arrivals on the international scene (for example, Dubai) that are seeking to posses, and perhaps already possessing, some of the features of world cities and aiming to compete in the global market.

However, all Arab Cities are outside the discourse on global or world cities. Indeed, this applies to most cities of the Third World. Even the largest urban agglomerations are viewed as lacking those characteristics which entitle them to become among the cities placed at the top of the ladder (Smith, 2005, p. 48). Arab cities are rather portrayed as 'gateway cities'. They have interest in world (global) cities, but they themselves attract little or no attention (Beaverstock *et al.*, 2000, p. 10). Consequently, research on these cities focused on either the historic status of cities, or on the current phenomenon of the 'instant cities' developing in association with oil money. The current status of these cities in the world global network, assumed to be at the bottom of the ladder, has been ignored, or only alluded to in passing notes.

The study of global cities focused on surveys of great metropolises of Western Europe, North America and East Asia. Arab cities that had historically dominated trade networks for decades lose any significance and hardly score any points since their contribution to the world economy is trivial, regardless of their importance at the regional level. The authors of the chapters of this book present a new perspective. They show that while the various cities in the Arab World can be interesting in terms of their unique (historic or economic) features, they too posses global qualities that fit the discourse on global cities. Indeed, while none of the authors intends to argue against the global city discourse, the cases presented here could perhaps render the global city restrictive as it is being delimited and enabled by a set of discursive practices, which in the process excludes most cities and applies only to a very limited number of cities in the Western hemisphere.

Although the global network ignores most cities of the world, the globalization of the world economy and the idea of a global city make many of the concepts of urban analysis obsolete. Cities have always been viewed, to a certain extent, as fairly isolated units; 'urban or metropolitan communities within a national structure' (Martinotti, 2002, p. 4). The current emphasis is on the fact that each and every urban place is part of a wider urban system, and can change at any point within the system. Accordingly, cities 'cannot be understood without understanding [their] respective roles within the system' (O'Donoghue, 2002, cited in Anderson and Engelstoft, 2004, p. 64). The study of the city itself is a study of transformation and movement within this network. It is a study of change in the relevant elements of urban centrality; a process by which cities are transformed into metropolises.

Accordingly, the whole understanding of the Arab city should be revisited. The definition, form and structure, and polity of the modern Arab city should be re-examined under the current forces of globalization. Research on the Arab city has to be transformed to absorb two major conditions. First, the existence of multiple networks that perhaps not only link these cities in different degrees to other cities around the world, but also weakens historically established regional networks.

Second, approaches to understanding Arab cities have to change. This becomes even more relevant at the time when these cities vary greatly in their history, economy and space. They no longer fit within the stereotypical Orientalist understanding of the Arab city. The assumption of a traditional Arab city, in which the population living in the city largely coincided with the population working in the city, and the traditional visitors of the city did not affect the social and ecological structure of the city, is no longer valid. Cities are no longer surrounded by walls that separate them from the rest of the land; rather they are centres of urban economic agglomerations intensely connected to their surroundings. They are new metropolises.

Rethinking the Arab Metropolis in the Frame of Globalization

The Arab city of the 1960s was being described as a metropolis in the traditional sense of the word; the idea of polarization by a town over a space that contains other secondary urban centres. Similarly, urbanization, which posed another challenge for the professionals at the time, has been conceived as a process that emphasizes elements of urban centrality featuring conditions of territorialization of the urban economy, high spatial mobility and urban sprawl that is based on functional specialization. The metropolis of the 1960s featured 'internal fragmentations of agglomerations according to a center-periphery opposing core cities surrounding suburban and peri-urban communes'(Kübler *et al.*, 2003).

However, there is more to the question of metropolis than spatial organization and functional coordination. There is the question of leadership among cities and the place of the metropolis in the network of similar cities. Metropolis is thus a title for cities with privileged status in a regional or even local but not necessarily global network of cities. Several cities pretend to this title, reminding of their role as capitals of a united Arab empire (Damascus, Baghdad) or of major part of it (Cairo). Other cities, invoke their role as a spiritual focus of Muslim faith (Mecca, Medina, etc.), or monotheism (Jerusalem). Others are first of all economic metropolises at the national scale (Casablanca), if not international scale (Beirut), while some have recently asserted their position as a focal point of the world economy (Dubai). Lastly, some capital cities base their pretensions on a political influence that reaches beyond their borders. Such is the case of Cairo, which retains the Arab League, and of Riyadh, that fantasizes about being recognized as the leader of the Muslim World.

The 'metropolis' in the Arab World may also describe regional capitals that are submitted to the domination of a national capital, but oversee more or less tightly a network of towns and their surrounding rural environment. This classification identifies the significance of some cities other than the national capitals. Cities like Alexandria in Egypt, Aleppo in Syria, Aden in Yemen, Marrakesh in Morocco, and similar cities in other Arab countries have a major influence on their national economies, but are also critical to regional economic success.

Identifying the new metropolis in the Arab World takes a new relevance at the time of globalization. The focus should, however, be on the process of metropolisation and the transformation of the modes of functioning and of urban networks. Therefore, it is important to identify and set together new criteria that would allow setting up degrees of metropolisation – that is the extent to which urban bodies would cope with the the world economy.

These criteria are of different types. Some are purely economic and usually go beyond urban issues. They encompass the whole set of juridical conditions that facilitate the free movement of capital and goods, investment and production and, above all, the free and easy exchange of intellectual scientific goods and cultural production (that is, information and computerization). Therefore it is important to identify these new activities as well not only in terms of quantity and of description, but also by taking into account the cultural changes they bring with them, through their content and through their methods. Emphasis should thus be placed on the socio-professional categories they mobilize or make present, their own values and the needs that they carry with them, and their ability to influence fashionable and socially correct behaviours around them.

The new Arab metropolis is more than a city and something other than a very large city. It is organized around multiple, highly specialized poles in contrast to the single polar city of the 1960s (Anas *et al.*, 1998) and is characterized by a functional split in service activities, encouraged by the improvements in informational and communications technologies. While coordination of the various economic activities remains the main function of the city, the new metropolis takes on new characteristics which distinguish it from the traditional conception of the city (Bourdeau-Lepage and Huriot, 2004, p. 2).[4] First, the same function of coordination applies to more complex activities and operates at a larger scale, while being concentrated mostly in metropolises and in particular in privileged districts within these cities. This is apparent in several Arab capital cities discussed in this book including the downtown area of Beirut and the new developments in Abu Dhabi, the work of very famous architects.

Second, what keeps the metropolis from disintegrating into smaller units is no longer the State, as would have been the case in the early days, but rather intense interactions in close proximity.[5] For example, the amalgamation of the Greater Amman region into one municipal area more than 20 years ago was forced by the State without any apparent rationale, and despite the fierce resistance from the local communities on the periphery of Amman city. The recent annexation of more land to Greater Amman was a natural conclusion to the extension of the metropolis, and faced little or no resistance from either the local communities or the State. Third, the new metropolis is marked by network interactions, maintaining the global appeal by being located among cities of a similar kind. This form of interaction guarantees the continuous reproduction of the metropolis.

Fourth and lastly, the metropolis is the host to growing internationalism of economic, social and cultural relations. The historic character of cities like Cairo and Damascus, the economic status of cities like Dubai and Abu Dhabi, the special status of Amman in world politics place each of these cities in a prestigious position within the network of similar cities.

In this sense, metropolisation symbolizes the most recent and most drastic changes occurring in major urban centres around the Arab World. It reveals the change that is occurring to the relevant elements of urban centrality. It implies a process of change in polity, space, communication, division of labour, economy, etc. It is a recurrent process of adaptation of cities to the changing technological, economic and institutional form of coordinating complex and long-range economic operations (Bourdeau-Lepage and Huriot, 2004, p. 10). While it cannot be separated from the notion of world cities, it can exist in cities that are ignored by the world city discourse.

A New Research Agenda

Metropolisation is a conceptual research paradigm that is intended to place the Arab city in its proper place in the urban world order. Accordingly, the focus of a new research agenda should be placed on defining the level of metropolisation in each city; the scale under which the change entailed in this process is taking place. Several themes should be scrutinized accordingly to allow the research on the Arab city to go further into the definitions of concepts, and to compare them to the same phenomena affecting other cultural areas. In some sense, this line of thinking questions the traditional city as a paradigm for contemporary urban life and proposes a new way of understanding and investigating the Arab city. The old concepts of urban centrality, concentric hierarchies in which the centre symbolizes power, subside to make room for multiple centralities. A new urban frame is created with attention given in particular to business areas, to communication links and means of transportation internal to the city and linking it to the world outside. The sheer idea of belonging to a unified urban body is brought into question.

The study of the new metropolis should focus on tracing this new urban fragmentation of space in terms of the use of space, of housing models, of public spaces, of living habits and of residential mobility. Segregation within the metropolis and exclusion from its processes are among the themes that need to be questioned. The interactions between the move to develop global systems and their implications for local planning and vice versa should be among the themes in studying the Arab metropolis.[6]

The study of the new Arab metropolis should tackle the various themes outlined above and address several new types of questions in a multidisciplinary fashion. In particular it should consider a new research agenda that submits to new presuppositions.

First, cities are being restructured from internally integrated wholes to collections of units which operate as nodes on regional, if not global economic networks. The forces that are shaping the restructuring of cities can only be understood through their relations to global economic, political and technological changes.

Second, the change that is occurring to our cities is affecting both the social and cultural aspects of the city. With the emergence of global culture our experience of place and the social construction of identities are being radically altered. All previous presuppositions about life in the metropolis are being challenged. A complex mesh of global-local interactions in urban places is emerging. These interactions should be brought under scrutiny.

Third and lastly, the urban structure and form of cities are certainly being reshaped in a way that reflects the economic, social and political changes. Local real-estate markets are increasingly being dominated by global investments. Traditional cityscapes, propagated by advances in transportation and telecommunication, are being drastically transformed to make room for new places of global consumption and material culture; that is, suburban office complexes, business and technology parks, shopping malls, and, even whole 'edge cities'. The *traditional* city centres are being blended into a network of centres forming a multi-tier system with complex relationships that keeps the metropolis from disintegrating.

The new research agenda should also reconsider the question of running the Arab metropolis and revisit the issue of urban governance. If running the city entails the question of political powers and technical bodies to ensure its functioning, governance is a concept that includes all factors that contribute to preserving urban balances, in order to ensure a sustainable and harmonious development of a given space and society. Here, classical questions regarding the administrative and technical functioning of the city, the distribution of responsibilities between public and private sectors, the administrative roles of the State, the region, the municipality, technical agencies and private business, respectively should be raised.

In addition, the study of the Arab metropolis needs to examine the interactions between the move to develop global systems and their implications for local planning and vice versa. The extent of what local planning can or cannot do is highly connected to 'international treaties' and global laws and regulations. Sovereignty, participation, empowerment, and other concepts traditionally understood as specifically local should be re-examined in the Arab metropolis and redefined within the world discourse.

The new Arab metropolis cannot be understood without reference to its relationship and integration with the external world. The degree of this integration, through economic activities and through the internal reshaping of the city and the efficiency of its communications with the outside world is a prominent criterion for its qualification as a metropolis. Each chapter in this book addresses some aspects of the previous arguments. However, the editor of the book, in his chapter on Abu Dhabi, puts forward a question that is relevant to almost every Arab city in this day and age. 'What do these cities offer to the world' he asks. The research on today's Arab metropolis should attempt to answer such a question in its present tense.

Notes

1.   These ideas of city-region and metropolitan authority were not, however, confined to Britain and its former colonies. They were rather universal ideas during the 1950s and the 1960s and were popular in the whole Arab World (see Berger, 1961 and Rodwin, 1961).

2.   Almost 25 per cent of the urban population lives below the poverty threshold with less than US$2 per day.

3.   About 38 per cent of the urban population is under 14 years of age with insufficient access to educational and training opportunities especially in the case of women, while 50 per cent of the urban population is below 18 years of age (UN-Habitat, 2004).

4.   Bourdeau-Lepage and Huriot (2004) argue that coordination has always been the function of the metropolis, but today it is at a more complex level.

5.   While the size of the city is not a crucial issue, the new metropolis is large enough to guarantee complex and perhaps uncertain interactions by larger number of actors and specialized operations.

6.   Traditionally local planning (municipal, district, regional etc.) has been related to State/ Province and Nation-State. Increasingly there is a push for global governance, primarily expressed in *global economic* integration and governance systems. In parallel we have a push for global environmental and social (labour standards, human rights etc.) governance as well.

References

Anas, A., Arnott, R and Small, K.A. (1998) Urban spatial structures. *Journal of Economic Literature*, **36**, pp. 1426–1464.

Andersen, H.T. and Engelstoft, S. (2004) The end of urbanisation? Transformation of the urban concept. *Dela 21*, pp. 53–67.

Beaverstock, R.G. *et al.* (2000) Globalization and world cities: some measurement methodologies. *Applied Geography*, **20**(1), pp. 43–63.

Berger, M. (1961) *The New Metropolis of the Arab World*. New Delhi: Allied Publishers.

Bourdeau-Lepage, L. and Huriot, J.-M. (2004) *The Metropolis in Retrospect: Permanence and Change*, GaWC Research Bulletin 140, pp. 1–28.

Castells, M. (1996) *The Rise of the Network Society*. Oxford: Blackwell.

Friedmann, J. (1986) The world city hypothesis. *Development and Change,* **17**, pp. 69–84.

Kübler, Daniel, Schenkel, Walter and Leresche, Jean-Phillippe (2003) Bright lights, big cities? Metropolisation, intergovernmental relations, and the new Federal urban policy in Switzerland. *Swiss Political Science Review*, **9**(1), pp. 261–282.

Martinotti, G. (2002) Space,Technologies and Populations in the New Metropolis. Position paper prepared for the International Workshop of Project MoVe, Milan.

Robinson, J. (2002) Global and world cities: a view from off the map. *International Journal of Urban and Regional Research*, **26**(3), pp. 531–554.

Rodwin, L. (ed.) (1961) *The Future Metropolis*. New York, NY: George Braziller.

Sassen, S. (2001) *The Global City: New York, London, Tokyo*, Princeton, NJ: Princeton University Press.

Smith, D. (2005) The world hierarchy: implications for cities, top to bottom. *Brown Journal of World Affairs*, **9**(2), pp. 45–55.

United Nations – HABITAT (2004) *The State of the World's Cities: Trends in Middle East & North Africa: Urbanization & Metropolitanization*. Nairobi: UN-Habitat.

World Bank, Middle East & North Africa Region (2007a) Decentralization and Local Governance in MENA: A Survey of Policies, Institutions and Practices. *A Review of Decentralization Experience in Eight Middle East & North Africa Countries*, Report No. 36516–MNA. Washington DC: The World Bank.

World Bank, Middle East & North Africa Region (2007b) Municipal Management & Local Governance: A Service Delivery Perspective. *Giving Voice to End-User Perspectives on Public Service Provision*. Washington DC: The World Bank.

Chapter 3

Amman: Disguised Genealogy and Recent Urban Restructuring and Neoliberal Threats

Rami Farouk Daher

Whenever I open one of the local newspapers in Amman I am astonished by the huge number of advertisements (mostly a whole page) promoting new 'urban' projects – office towers, gated communities or even mega developments such as Abdali[1] in the middle of the city. Furthermore, one cannot help but notice the abundance of new real-estate and business magazines in both Arabic and English, such as *Jordan Business*, *Jordan Property* and *Jordan Land*. They all promote real-estate ventures in the city, on the Airport Highway and in other Jordanian cities as well as providing information on similar ventures in other Arab countries. It is evident that Amman is embarking on a new era of urban/spatial restructuring which is also affecting Middle Eastern cities at large.

In this chapter, I set out to analyse the current urban condition of Amman in particular, and the rest of the Middle East in general. In so doing, I attempt to understand the current neoliberal urban phenomenon and locate it within a regional and global context. My concern is with the politics of place and the different narratives that exist in which the city is realized and understood as a contested reality. Furthermore, I am concerned with urban transformation and change *vis-à-vis* cultural, socio-economic, and territorial changes within the city.

In the first part of the chapter, I present Amman's urban beginnings and past as a marginalized reality that has not been celebrated and recognized by formal State practices and was even excluded from Orientalist/academic definitions of the Islamic Arab cities of the region. My intention is to provide some insight into whether or not Amman suffers from a crisis of identity and also to explain why the State had not until very recently incorporated the urban reality and heritage of the city into its formal definition of the country of Jordan or as a subject of interest for nation building or urban projects in the city.

In the second part of the chapter I address the current transformations in the city in terms of neoliberal urban restructuring and the circulation of surplus global capital. These are exemplified by the Abdali development, described as Amman's new downtown, and by other projects appearing in the city as local and municipal initiatives strive to create a vision for the future of the city.

The chapter will demonstrate that, contrary to the formal rhetoric which promotes the idea that there is no State involvement in such privately-funded urban restructuring, the reality is that the State is subsidizing large-scale real-estate investments, enabling the business elite and transnational corporations to develop mega-projects. Furthermore, important questions are raised not just about Amman, but other cities in the region:

• Where is this surplus capital coming from? And why now in Amman?

• What is this 'moment' of neoliberalism we are part of today? What does it mean? And what are its effects on cities of the Middle East?

• What are the consequences of circulating global capital, urban models and images within the region?

• What are the consequences of the notion of the privatization of planning and empowerment of private transnational capitalist actors in public-private partnerships?

By examining the different urban projects in Amman and elsewhere in the region, we can form a better understanding of current transformations in the production, manufacture and consumption of urban space. These transformations are leading to a new way of visioning and acting on the city, in which the issues of accountability, transparency, democracy, inclusion/exclusion and private/public become highly contested in the midst of continuously changing formal (State and other) practices and emerging 'new actors'.

Part I. Amman: Disguised Genealogy and Swift Transformation

For some people Amman is no more than a new city that offers a comfortable way of life (figure 3.1). But for others it represents a rich reservoir of personal and

Figure 3.1. Panoramic view of the city of Amman showing the relationship between the downtown (Wast al Balad) and the emerging residential hills.

collective memories, where the social memory of place, represented in its streets, alleys, steps and courtyards, is more than a topic of discussion at gatherings and becomes, instead, a 'lived' experience and a true anchor to place, providing symbols of belonging. Yet, for many, Amman is also a city which suffers from a lack of urban identity and a place to which some residents have a weak sense of belonging. As one who was born, and had lived most of his life, in Amman I was, like many others, confronted with the question: 'Where are you from?' And my immediate answer was always: 'I am from Amman'. But my simple answer was seldom satisfactory and was frequently followed by: 'No, really, where are you from?' This used to bother me as a child and teenager and I always wondered why if my answer were that I was from Salt, or Irbid, or any other Jordanian city it would have been satisfactory; and I used to wonder why Amman was not acknowledged as a city which people could claim as their origin. Jawad Anani (1992, p. 4) explained in one of the local Jordanian newspapers that if one asked a student in any local school in the city about his or her origin, the majority would answer that they were from a city or a town other than Amman even if they were born in Amman and had spent their whole lives in the city. Seteney Shami (2005, p. 2), in questioning why the overall consciousness, the set of meanings, and the hegemonic urban discourse concerning Amman is one that negates its identity as a city, suggested that 'the answer partly lies in the ways that Amman's inhabitants construct their identities through references to a multiplicity of cities as well as to alternative identities that work against consolidating an Ammani identity'. Furthermore, Shami goes on to suggest certain justifications or reasons for what she terms the Ammani laments:

> It would appear at first that there are quite easy answers to Ammani laments, and these are readily offered up by many of its inhabitants. First of all, Amman is a recent city. It was re-founded, after some centuries of de-population, as a frontier settlement of the Ottoman state in the late 19th century. Secondly, its population has been formed by numerous waves of displacement and refugee movements. Thirdly, its economy is largely dependent on the fortunes of a rentier state rather than on industry or global financial flows. Finally, Amman has experienced continuous and rapid physical expansion, such that its urban fabric is 'more of a construction site than a city', (*Ibid.*, p. 8)

One of Shami's explanations is that Amman had been too inclusive, its population had developed from numerous waves of displacement and migration starting with Circassian immigrants from the Caucasus as early as the 1870s. They were followed by urban merchants from Syria, Lebanon and Palestine, especially after the establishment of the Hijaz Railroad Line which reached Amman in 1903; Arab nationalists from Damascus seeking refuge from French mandate suppression; a massive wave of Palestinian refugees in 1948 after the Israeli occupation of Palestine and later, in 1967, after the occupation of the West Bank. Later waves of migration and displacement have included Lebanese bourgeoisie after the outbreak of the Lebanese Civil War in 1975, Palestinian and Jordanian returnees from the Gulf after the 1990/1991 Gulf crises, and most recently Iraqis flocking to Amman and other Jordanian cities with their millions causing major crises due to increases in property prices and other commodities. Below, I will attempt to answer the complicated question of the existence (or not) of a crisis of identity in the case of Amman.

Amman: The City (in) Between

To answer the previous question, I seek to understand why Amman's urban beginnings and past existed as a marginalized reality, unrecognized and uncelebrated in both formal State practices and in Orientalist/academic definitions of Islamic-Arab cities. My aim is not only to reveal the latent nature of domination, but also to show the extent to which power mechanisms and relations are present in institutions, regulations and discursive practices. In order to understand the genealogy of such a city, one needs to consider the transformations that the Middle East witnessed over the past two centuries, such as the destruction and replacement of the dynastic religious realm (represented by the Ottoman Empire) by the various post-mandate nation states of Syria, Jordan, Lebanon, Palestine, Iraq, Turkey, and Egypt, during the first half of the twentieth century, and the consequences of such transformations on the definition and practice of nationhood, citizenship, and heritage (Anderson, 1983).

In general, the definition of the region's heritage, through which the newly emerging states were defining themselves, were confined to the classical, religious and ancient monuments (for example, Pharaonic in Egypt, Nabattean in Jordan, Phoenician in Lebanon). Meanwhile, according to Maffi (2002, pp. 210–211) and Schriwer (2002) who have worked extensively on Jordan, the heritage of the recent past (manifested by its rural, urban traditions) was marginalized by official State discourses which attempted to dissociate from the recent Ottoman past and local realities and instead to construct legitimacy for the newly emerging state systems by constructing links with distant origins. Maffi (2000, p. 7) highlights the example of the Jordanian/Hashemite fascination and obsession with ancient Nabattean civilizations which occupied a territory similar to today's modern Jordan.

Official Narrative Discourse. Amman's urban heritage (with some iconic exceptions such as the Roman Amphitheatre) was kept outside the country's official definition of national heritage which was grounded in a dissociation from the recent past and a constructed definition of what Jordan is. Natural sites such as Wadi Rum or the Steppe (*Badiya*) and archaeological sites which link the country to an imagined point of departure (the Nabataean site of Petra) were key 'sites' in constructing a formal Jordanian identity. Urban realities such as that of Amman fell outside this formal definition. Kassay (2006) describes how official Jordanian identity is antithetical to Amman and to its urban reality and how instead 'tribalization' dominated national Jordanian identity.

In addition, the Jordanian State, which had neither major natural resources nor great wealth at the beginning, created its legitimacy through events and spectacles (for example, the public speeches and parades which used to take place in Faisal Plaza in the 1920s and early 1930s) in public spaces rather than through association with certain existing places or a formal programme of public buildings. Rogan (1996, p. 103) stated that:

> beyond the handful of functional buildings commissioned by the British authorities, and the three landmarks of the 'Umari Mosque, Raghadan Palace, and the Residency, or Dar al Mu'tamid, neither the Hashemites nor the British enjoyed the resources to impose their authority on Amman through building projects – no elaborate house of parliament, court of justice, or institution of higher education. Rather than seeking to project the state's power through architecture, the ruling authorities used Amman as a stage on which they enacted elaborate spectacles of ceremonial intended to reaffirm both elements of the colonial state: British trusteeship and Hashemite rule.

Orientalist/Academic Discourses. The urban heritage of Amman dating to the first half of the twentieth century was discredited by several practices which rendered it insignificant and marginal. First, Amman as a city in general, and its urban heritage in particular, had to conform to the stereotypical models of what an 'Islamic' or 'Arab' city should look like.

The Orientalist discourse constructed models and typologies of the 'Islamic' or 'Arab' city, which were adopted and perpetuated by some contemporary academic discourses. Such stereotypes work to discredit a reality which does not fit the criteria and models. Consequently, the application of such models to a city like Amman becomes very problematic. Compared with cities such as Damascus, Cairo or Jerusalem, which do more or less fit the stereotypical model, not only has Amman been little studied but, as explained above, it is a city of a more recent origin whose population developed through different waves of immigration. One of the first to criticize the stereotypical model, which was based on a body of literature produced by Western Orientalists, was the renowned scholar Janet Abu-Lughod (1987, p. 155). According to Abu-Lughod, such generalizations were built on limited examples, mainly Fez in North Africa and Damascus and Aleppo in Bilad al Sham:

> In short, just as we find the first *isnad* to be based chiefly on French North African sources/ studies, particularly focusing on the city of Fez, so we find a second *isnad* based upon the Syrian cities of Aleppo and Damascus, as studied physically by Sauvaget and socio-politically by Lapidus. In each case, a very tentative set of place-specific comments and descriptions appears. These enter the literature and take on the quality of abstractions. With each telling, the tale of authority grows broader in its application. Forgotten is the fact that only a handful of cities are actually described. Forgotten is the fact that only certain legal codes – on which the Islamic form of city is presumed to be based – have been studied. Forgotten is the fact that Islamic cities

have evolved over time and that the socio-political system in Damascus and Aleppo in the 14th century under Mamluk rule cannot possibly provide a convincing description of how Islamic cities *sui generis* were governed. (*Ibid.*, p. 160)

What is very valuable in Abu-Lughod's attempt to deconstruct Orientalist thinking about the Islamic city is that she illustrates 'not only that the idea itself was "created" on the basis of too few cases but, even worse, was a model of outcomes rather than one of process' (*Ibid.*, p. 172). Dieterich (2002) details how this model of outcomes – the stereotypical Islamic and Arab urban features such as the congressional mosque, covered bazaars, public paths, numerous *Waqfs*, and homogeneous organic residential neighbourhoods to which Amman was compared – worked to subjugate and marginalize Amman's distinctive urban features such as its Husseini Mosque, specialty bazaars such as Souq al Bukhariah, the cemetery at Ras al Ain, water *sabils* such as the Hamidian Sabil which was in front of the Husseini Mosque, and coffee houses such as those around the main congressional mosque and in Faisal Street. Many such features were demolished in the name of 'modernity' and 'progress' or because of their uncritical evaluation as obsolete and insignificant.

Qualifying Amman: The City of Many Hats

The fact that Amman did not have a distant origin or homogeneous ethnic composition disqualified the city from being a stereotypical Islamic city and may have led to the crisis of identity to which many of its residents subscribed. I believe that this crisis of identity is gradually diminishing (as will be explained at the end of this section) and that the distinctiveness of Amman and its urban cultural heritage need to be revealed and reactivated. Amman does not have to conform to a discourse that constantly attempts to compare it to cities like Damascus, Jerusalem or Cairo with a distant past and a perceived homogeneous beginning and point of origin. By emphasizing 'homogeneity' such discourses eliminate local difference and, in the process, the distinctive reality, that is Amman.

By enforcing a unified and stereotypical style for Amman's architecture, borrowed from other traditional urban realities, such discourses are degrading the multiplicity and distinctiveness of the city's urban experiences. Amman's multi-ethnic and heterogeneous beginnings in the mid-nineteenth century were very inclusive.[2] The city was considered a refuge place, a city that welcomed visitors of diverse origins. A common scene in the downtown during the 1930s would be men with different head-dresses – the Circassian *kalbaq*, the Lebanese and Syrian *tarboosh*, the Palestinian and Jordanian *hatta* or *kofiah* – climbing Amman's steps to reach the residences on the slopes of the seven hills flanking the downtown.

As intimated above, the multi-layered beginnings of the city have not yet been fully, or even partially, narrated. Furthermore, the inherent uniqueness of Amman's urban heritage has only been recently explored and incorporated into formal State projects of nation building. The city's distinctive urban qualities are present in places like the Hawooz[2] in the residential hills, the urban experience of Faisal Street, the detached single-family dwelling of the 1920s and 1930s, the elegant (yet unpretentious) villas of the 1940s and 1950s with their brilliant modernist logic, aesthetics, and dynamism, the pedestrian steps which connect the downtown area to the surrounding residential hills (figure 3.2) with their distinctive ambiance and experience, or the Ammani public meeting places such as the coffee houses.

In *Shahbandar*, his recent novel set in Amman, Hashem Gharaybeh (2003, pp. 51, 120) says that the essence of the city is that it protects people coming to it from different locations; it is a city which delivers justice to strangers no matter what their origin. He goes on to sketch the urban scene in Amman in the early 1920s by describing how the residents of the city enjoy a continuous celebration of diverse costume and head-dress; costumes from the East or the West mingle with the Syrian and Lebanese *tarboosh*, Circassian *kalbaq*, Iraqi *faisaleiah*, and traditional Arabian *kofiah*, not to mention Western hats and suits with beautiful waistcoats and vibrant designs (*Ibid.*, p. 161). I strongly believe that the significance of this novel is not simply that it celebrates these multi-layered beginnings of the city with its diverse migrants, but that the author chose Amman as his focus. This is a phenomenon which is worth further analysis. For the first time the city of

Figure 3.2. Amman, the city of steps: the Ammani steps of Jabal Amman in Khirfan Street Area.

Amman is the centre of inquiry for Jordanian writers and novelists. Are we finally witnessing a major shift and transformation in this crisis of identity?

This is too large a question to be answered solely on the basis of a series of novels where Amman is the main subject, even though this is not to be discredited if we consider that the writers and novelists of any nation are supposed to reflect the beating heart of society. I strongly argue that we in Amman are gradually witnessing the emergence of a generation/class of Ammanis which is very much interested in the specific characteristics of the city and is even a little nostalgic where the object of this nostalgia is the city of Amman with its downtown, residential hills and the various steps that connect them. But this class is also nostalgic about Amman's urban and social history and its multi-layered beginnings. This interest/nostalgia is manifested in several ways which I will briefly sketch below.

Firstly, one cannot help but notice that a lot of Ammanis from different backgrounds are developing an interest in the city's historic neighbourhoods such as the downtown area (Wast al Balad) and the older parts of Jabal Amman, Jabal al Weibdeh and Jabal al Ashrafieh. This is evident in a return of families who had left earlier, in the proliferation of studies of these urban spaces, and in the formation of residents associations such as JARA (Jabal Amman Residents Association) and Jabal al Weibdeh Residents Association. Furthermore, a lot of cultural bodies and organizations (for example, Darat al Funun, Makan, Dar al Anda, the Association of Jordanian Writers, the Centre for the Study of the Built Environment, the Royal Film Commission, Royal Society for the Conservation of Nature) are choosing to locate in these areas rather than in newer parts of the city. For the first time, the social and urban heritage of the city is being celebrated and recognized for its uniqueness.

Secondly, the urban heritage of Amman and of other Jordanian cities is becoming the focus of several donor agencies projects. I have described elsewhere (Daher, 2005, p. 291) the emergence of urban regeneration/heritage tourism developments in places such as Amman, Salt and Kerak, orchestrated and funded by international donor agencies (for example, the World Bank, United States Agency for International Development (USAID), Japanese International Cooperation Agency (JICA), and the Deutsche Gesellschaft für Technische Zusammenarbeit (GTZ)). These donor agencies emphasized that Jordan should invest in, develop, and promote its tourism sector and cultural heritage; for the first time the urban heritage of Jordanian cities was identified as one of the main assets for the generation of such developments (*Ibid.*, pp. 292–293).

Thirdly, Greater Amman Municipality (GAM) is attempting to reinvent itself and redefine its relationship *vis-à-vis* the city by envisioning its role beyond services and utility provision. This is, perhaps, not the first time that GAM has re-evaluated its mission as it had earlier started to address its role as a patron and facilitator of culture, hence the publication of a special magazine devoted entirely to the city (Saqr, 2003). However this time around the redefinition of roles will have major consequences for the city. Recently GAM initiated several projects addressing

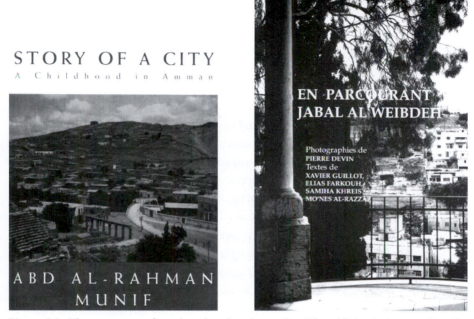

Figure 3.3. The emergence of novels and studies about urban life and living in Amman since the late 1990s. To the right is the cover of a study of urban memory and architecture of Al Weibdeh neighbourhood. To the left is the cover of an autobiographical essay/novel on the city covering the early years up to the middle of the twentieth century.

urban regeneration in locations such as Rainbow Street in historic Jabal Amman, Jabal al Ashrafiah near Darwish Mosque, and in the downtown area of Faisal Street. GAM is also currently involved in putting forward to new vision where heritage protection and the provision of more green and open spaces for Ammani residents are a top priority.

Fourthly, as mentioned above, since the early 1990s there is the proliferation of novels by Jordanian authors, such those by Ziad Qasem, Hasham Gharaybeh, Elias Farkouh, Abd Al-Rahman Munif, and Samiha Khreis (figure 3.3), which focus on Amman. Before this, the settings for Jordanian novels were either mythical spaces or generic Arab-Islamic towns, or even in cities with no specific identity at all, but according to Razzaz (1996, p. 357), Jordanian writers have recently started to acknowledge Amman as a subject for their novels.

This increasing interest in Amman's urban and social history is taking place against a background of neoliberal urban transformations and restructuring which are having a major impact on the people of the city – an impact which will be very different as between rich and poor.

Part II. Neoliberalism at Work:
Circulating Global Capital, Images, and Planning Models

Here I seek to understand the current urban phenomena of the circulation of global capital in search of high-yield, secure investments, of excessive privatization, and urban flagship projects in Amman. The focus will be on contemporary urban transformations in Amman, taking into consideration that such neoliberal urban restructuring could not be understood in isolation from similar transformations within the region at large. Elsheshtawy (2004, p. 6) demonstrates how the literature is filled with work examining the impact of colonialism on the spatial structure of Middle Eastern cities, yet there exists a gap when it comes to the influence of contemporary trends – namely globalization.

Emerging islands of excessive consumption for the elite together with the internationalization of real-estate companies and construction consultancies capable of providing high-quality services signify this neoliberal urban re-structuring in places such as downtown Beirut, Abdali in Amman (Summer, 2005; Daher, 2007a), Dreamland in Cairo (Adham, 2004), Financial Harbour in Manama (see chapter 8) and even in the heart of the Holy City of Mecca through the Jabal Omar Project.[4] Cities are obliged to create the right milieu, a competitive business climate, and first-class tourist attractions in order to lure people to live, invest, and be entertained in them. Developments in Dubai and the Solidere's reconstruction of Beirut's downtown (see chapter 4) are becoming the models to follow in such developments. Adham (2005) noted that circulating images of such neoliberal urban restructuring mimic developments in the West and represent as such an 'Oriental vision of the Occident'.

In 2002 the Gulf Cooperation Council declared the availability of US$80 billion liquidity awaiting investment (Sadiq, 2005). The United Arab Emirates alone enjoys US$26.3 billion in trade surplus, and in 2003 Dubai declared a growth in GDP of 16 per cent per annum. This circulating global capital is searching all over the Middle East for places to invest in real-estate development, in places like Dubai, Doha, Manama, Kuwait, but also in Beirut, Cairo, Damascus, Tunis, and Amman. This will have considerable consequences on the nature of the urban environment as not only is each of these cities competing for international business and tourism, but also for more consumer-oriented services such as themed shopping malls, recreation centres, business towers, and theme parks.[5]

Global Economic Restructuring: Introducing Neoliberalism

Here I believe it is important to introduce the moment of neoliberalism[6] of which we are all part, and affected by, today. Over the past century First and Third world countries have moved from modernity, to postmodernity, to globalization. Under the rationale of economic liberalization and privatization of State enterprises and investments, the world is now part of a neoliberal moment anchored by more conservative politics (Daher 2007b, p. 270). The central tenet of neoliberalism is the notion of competition (competition between nations, regions, firms, multi-national corporations, and even cities). Ley (2004, p. 151) sketches the consequences of this moment for the states of the developing world:

The unexpected collapse of the Soviet empire at the end of the decade seemed to many to consolidate and legitimate these innovations and propelled them with fresh momentum into the 1990s, even as the guard changed at the White House and Downing Street. Privatization, deregulation, partnerships with the private sector, cutbacks to the welfare state, a disciplinary relationship with labour, and promises to downsize government were all part of a new lexicon that seemingly liberated the spirit of free enterprise. This ideology was exported through American political and economic power and punitive action of the World Bank and the International Monitory Fund to debtor nations in the developing world.

Neoliberalism led to excessive privatization, the withdrawal of the State from welfare programmes,[7] the dominance of multinational corporations and, as far as the Third world is concerned, a change from project-oriented international aid to aid in the form of structural adjustments and policy. This was accompanied by the emergence of several agents which assisted neoliberal transformation such as the dominance of the World Trade Organization (WTO), international gatherings such as the World Economic Forum (WEF), the North American Free Trade Agreement (NAFTA), and other similar global organizations and instruments (Daher 2007b, p. 270).

Needless to say, this transformation has a substantial impact not only on cities as a whole, but also on how and for whom urban investment projects are developed. In many cases, the outcome has intensified issues of social equity, inclusion-exclusion, and accountability. Furthermore, with increasing competition between cities, they are gradually becoming places of play and commodities themselves. Fainstein and Judd (1999a, p. 261) illustrate how urban culture is gradually becoming a commodity within the move from modernity to postmodernity, and from internationalism to globalism with considerable effects on cities today.

Middle Eastern Cities Compete for International Business and Investment

Cities across the Middle East are currently competing with one another to attract international investment, and business and tourism development. Cities are 'obliged' to create the right milieu, a competitive business climate, and first-class tourism facilities in order to attract people to come and live, invest, and be entertained. Developments in Dubai and the current urban reconstruction of Beirut's downtown are becoming the models to follow.

As stated earlier, the Gulf Cooperation Council has some US$80 billion in liquidity (surplus capital from oil revenues) which is expected to be spent on real estate, international business, and tourism investments within the next 5 years, especially in countries like the UAE, Qatar, and Saudi Arabia. This vast sum of money, which prior to September 11 was primarily invested in the US and Europe, will seek new markets in the region; some had already found its way into Lebanese, Syrian, and Jordanian[8] markets through multinational hotel and real-estate investments (Sadiq, 2005; Daher 2007b).

Gradually, cities in the Middle East are depending on high-increased rate of mobility within the region where cities are, for the first time, putting their different urban amenities on the market as a tourist commodity to be explored, invested in, and used to entertain tourists, businessmen and, most important of all, affluent clientele from all over the region. As Fainstein and Judd (1999a, p. 261) suggest:

> there does seem to be a degree of consensus that the present epoch involves a different, more flexible organization of production, higher mobility of both capital and people, heightened competition among places, and greater social and cultural fragmentation. Within the city the unity previously imposed by a manufacturing-driven economy has disappeared, and urban culture itself has become a commodity.

Hall (1996, p. 155) explores how cities are being packaged and introduced as products for marketing in an age of 'new urban tourism'. He shows how 'although urban centres have long served to attract tourists, it is only in recent years that cities have consciously sought to develop, image and promote themselves in order to increase the influx of tourists'. Within the context of the Middle East, one observes how, whether it is Beirut or Amman, Dubai or Manama, Cairo or Tunis, cities all over the region are competing for inward business and tourism investment with considerable consequences not only on how these cities are being transformed, or how heritage and urban regeneration is being conceived, but also the way in which tourism and tourist products and experiences are taking a central role in this overall transformation (Daher, 2007b, p. 272).

Observers of the current transformations of the urban scene in the region are likely to conclude that cities are gradually becoming business and tourism spectacles. For example, Reiker (2005) explains how, over the last decade, there has been considerable research examining neoliberal urban projects and tourism ventures in a metropolitan context in the West, but that 'much less attention has been given to these developments in the region'.

In order to understand current urban transformations in the region, one has to reflect on the present urban restructuring, and the role of different actors and agents *vis-à-vis* these transformations. Actors and agents range from multinational corporations to regional investors (for example, from Saudi and the Gulf), to local Jordanian investors who are also playing a significant role in such urban transformations. It is fascinating to examine the effect of the circulation of global capital, excessive privatization, the rise of a new Arab elite, and circulating urban/tourism flagship projects in Jordan and throughout the Arab region.

The Abdali Project and the Solidere Phenomenon: Conspicuous State Subsidies and the Privatization of Planning in Amman

Here I focus on formal shifts in the creation of 'public' urban space in Amman, which is orchestrated by partnerships between multinational corporations and the State through the establishment of new regulating bodies, such as the National

Resources Investment and Development Corporation (MAWARED).[9] Several of these neoliberal corporate visions, reinforced by the State's concentration on economic prosperity and encouragement of international investment in the country, are leading to urban geographies of inequality and exclusion and spatial and social displacement of second-class citizens, functions, histories, in favour of first-class tourism developments and real-estate ventures.

Solidere's Beirut downtown reconstruction (see chapter 4), which was presented to the public as the main post-war reconstruction effort, has been criticised as being simply a real-estate development project where history and heritage are merely themes incorporated through Disneyfied pastiche representations. It is true that the project also includes the preservation of older buildings and urban spaces from the traditional Lebanese and French Mandate periods (Summer, 2005), but it is important to note that the final outcome is a very exclusive urban setting where the whole notion of urban memory and property ownership has disintegrated. This reconstruction is creating a collaged urban morphology designed for consumption by tourists and the Lebanese people alike.

The Solidere model of urban restructuring became the adopted approach within the region. Not only was it was copied in Amman in the Abdali Project, but there are plans to apply it elsewhere within the region. This neoliberalization in the creation of public urban space circulates urban images, spectacles, and models and is leading to the dilution of local differences and the circulation of 'corporate' urban forms and images.

In Jordan, State policies are gradually moving away from 'regional politics' (for example, an emphasis on Arab nationalism and unity) and social agendas (for example, in agriculture, health, or education) towards neoliberal agendas of privatization and a situation where most vital assets and sectors are rented or sold to the outside (for example, water, telecommunication, power). The Solidere phenomenon in the shape of the Abdali Project is just one realization of the change in State policy in the Kingdom which are symbolized by the socio-economic transformation programme centred on alleviating poverty, creating job opportunities and partnerships with the private sector.

According to Bank and Schlumberger (2004), this new approach is made possible by a new economic team around the King and by the regime's one-sided discourse: economic and technological development. A shift in Jordan's policy priorities has been evident from the first days of King Abdallah's reign: from regional politics and the effects of the peace process to far reaching reform of Jordan's economy, widespread privatization, and economic competitiveness and activism. The emergence of the new guard – the Economic Consultative Council (ECC) – facilitated the structural adjustment programme, Jordan's accession to the World Trade Organization, the Free Trade Agreement with the United States, and paid lip service to privatization (for example, telecommunication, power, water, tourism, and planning). Bank and Schlumberger (2004, pp. 40–41) added that during November 1999, the King had invited more than:

150 leading representatives of the private and public sectors to the Dead Sea Retreat, a two-day seminar. In December, he created the Economic Consultative Council as an advisory body for economic policy planning. The ECC has 20 members, and the King presides over it. For an economy in which the State has been the main employer and most powerful economic agent for decades, it is remarkable that the ECC was in its initial composition dominated by 14 representatives of the private sector.

It is interesting to note the common traits between these appointees in terms of their educational and professional background and work views. According to Bank and Schlumberger (*Ibid.*), they include individuals like Ghassan Nuqul (Vice Chairman of the Nuqul Group), Fadi Ghandour (co-founder and CEO of Aramex), Suhair al Ali Dabbas (General Manager of City Bank in Jordan) and international lawyer, Salah al Bashir. They are all aged between 35 and 45, almost all hold a degree in business or economics from universities abroad, primarily from the US or the UK, and speak English fluently. Furthermore, they are all successful business people oriented towards the international market.

They represent Jordanian economic (success stories) symbolizing young, self-dash confident 'winners' in globalization and have internalized the currently fashionable neoliberal jargon. Their agenda is thus primarily economic – the far-reaching economic and technological transformation of Jordan and its integration into the globalized world economy. (*Ibid.*)

The Abdali project represents a clear realization of neoliberal urban restructuring and is facilitated by the State's socio-economic transformation programme. The project, boosted by the State's concentration on economic prosperity and encouragement of international investment and turning its back on Amman's original downtown just 1.5 km away, is likely to lead to urban geographies of inequality and exclusion and spatial and social displacement. The remodelled area, previously the site of the General Jordan Armed Forces Headquarters, consists of 350,000 m² in the heart of Amman and will contain a built-up area of approximately 1,000,000 m². In order for this project to succeed, the investors together with the State realized that it could not be facilitated through regular governmental bodies and that a new organization had to be established. Thus MAWARED was created by the King and is similar to other neoliberal institutions in the region such as Solidere in Beirut and ASEZA (Aqaba Special Economic Zone Authority). These organizations are replacing older governmental bodies such as municipalities and governorates which have either been disbanded entirely or have taken on a more technical role such as service and infrastructure provision, permits and land appropriation, and traffic and transportation management. Nina Robertson in an interview for *Jordan Business* (one of the new leading venture capital and real-estate magazines in Jordan), attempts to understand this newly constructed entity which is neither private nor public but actually both:

Behind arguably the most ambitious of these projects is the state-owned National Resources

Investment and Development Cooperation (MAWARED). Established in 2000, the company's original mandate was to redevelop several inner-city military plots and turn them into income-generating mix-use sites as well as to relocate the military out of densely populated areas with investment potentials to new facilities. Just 5 years after its inception, MAWARED has become Jordan's leading urban regeneration entity and its largest real-estate developer. It has several affiliates, including the Development and Investment Projects (DIP) Fund, essentially the investment arm to the military; The Urban Workshop, a non-profit independent urban studies center; and the newly-established Amman Real-Estate Management & Services (AREMS), specializing in real-estate consultancy and management. (Robertson, 2007, p. 45)

In an exclusive interview for *Jordan Property Magazine*, Baha Hariri (son of the late Lebanese Prime Minister Rafiq al-Hariri, Chairman and CEO of Saudi Oger and Chairman of the Abdali Investment and Development PSC) explained how the project would 'endeavor to create out of Amman's new downtown, Abdali, which will redefine urban living in the city' (Al-Hindi, 2007b, p. 19). Al-Hindi had also interviewed Jamal Itani who is the CEO of the private shareholder company Abdali Investment and Development. He explained that:

> the Project is a plan to create a new center for the City by coordinating between investors in order to execute around 45 unique development designs resulting in a number of harmonious buildings which maintain a high level of quality for both developers and investors. (*Ibid.*, p. 20)

In the case of Amman and the Abdali project, it is obvious that there is a tendency for this neoliberal investment to turn its back on the city's existing downtown (which is in need of major urban and economic regeneration). It is obvious too that the project is declaring itself as the 'new downtown' for the city, and this is evident not only through the pronouncements of the chairmen and CEOs of the main developers but also through MAWARED's interface with the general public, which is restricted to smart graphics on billboards around the construction site, and through its brochures and website (figure 3.4). These all enjoy slick marketing slogans that tap into the property consumers' mindset. Al-Masri (2007, p. 180) commented on how the project is being announced as the new downtown for Amman by stating that today the development of such new areas in the Middle East is paralleled in most cases by neglect of the historic urban quarters within the same cities. The Arab world is currently notorious for letting historic city centres deteriorate, while in other parts of the developed world attention has been given to the historic parts of cities through area conservation and revitalization, transforming derelict downtowns into places where people wish to live and work.

Analysing the details of the investments in the Abdali project, one realizes that the bottom line is that the State is subsidizing large-scale investment for the business elite of the region to create such flagship projects of urban restructuring. Contrary to the State's declarations and propaganda which advocate an absent State

Figure 3.4. A stretch of billboard about the Abdali urban regeneration project as the only source of information for the community at large about this major neoliberal urban restructuring project in the city.

in such projects, it is very clear that it is not absent, but is 'there', heavily involved, and there to stay. The financial contribution of the State is considerable. Prime urban land made available for investment forms the greater part of the subsidy, but other subsidies include tax exemption, infrastructure provision, elimination of all barriers and red tape, and special building regulations making the development possible.

It is also important to shed light on the nature of the shareholding of this neoliberal investment. The privately owned (private shareholder) Abdali Investment Company (AIC) was created in 2004 to develop and manage this mixed-use urban development with just two investors: MAWARED and Saudi Oger (Summer, 2005).[10] As a private real-estate developer, it is responsible for implementing the project, and is in charge of its management and master planning. This is similar to Solidere in Beirut, but the shareholder setup in Abdali is very different.[11] Initially, AIC was set up with a capital JD39 million on a 50/50 partnership basis between MAWARED and Oger Jordan (the Jordanian subsidiary of real-estate giant Saudi Oger Ltd). The Saudi based Oger group is owned by the family of Rafiq al-Hariri. This joint venture was altered in 2005, however, when the United Real Estate Company, under the Kuwait Projects Company (KIPCO) group, joined as partners. KIPCO bought 12.5 per cent of Abdali Psc shares which left MAWARED and Saudi Oger with 43.75 per cent each (Al-Hindi, 2007*a*, p. 20).

It is interesting to note that regardless of the similarities between the different neoliberal urban restructuring projects in diverse contexts in the Arab world, each takes shape within a completely different local context and is consequently reshaped by it. Elsheshtawy (2004, pp. 18–19) confirms that while certain processes in globalization may seem to come from outside (for example, multinational corporations setting up regional headquarters), these processes are in fact activated from the inside by local actors. Furthermore, Swyngedouw *et al.* (2002, p. 545) explain how such neoliberal urban restructuring projects are incorporated in localized settings, hence the term 'glocalization.'

In the case of Amman, beneath the rhetoric of MAWARED lies a public (State) subsidy for private real-estate development for very selective urban business regional elites from Lebanon, Jordan, and the Gulf. Robertson (2007, p. 46) states that:

> Unsurprisingly, investors (mainly from the region) have been scrambling to get a piece of the pie. As a state-owned, financially independent company, MAWARED is able to offer them unique advantages that other corporations cannot: access to huge tracks of land in prime locations with the infrastructure in place. Being state-owned also makes MARWARED an attractive partner for the private sector, offering fast and smooth processing of official dealings with relevant authorities.

This conservative liberalism, according to Swyngedouw *et al.* (2002, p. 547):

> seeks to reorient state interventions away from monopoly market regulation and towards marshaling state resources into the social, physical, and geographical infra- and superstructures that support, finance, subsidize, or otherwise promote new forms of capital accumulation by providing the relatively fixed territorial structures that permit the accelerated circulation of capital and the relatively unhindered operation of market forces. At the same time, the state withdraws to a greater or lesser extent from socially inclusive blanket distribution-based policies and from Keynesian demand-led interventions and replaces them with spatially targeted social policies and indirect promotion of entrepreneurship, particularly via selective deregulation, stripping away red tape, and investment partnership.

Al-Sayyad (2001, p. 14) refers to the 'transfer of design and political control from local governments and citizens to large corporations and the design professionals they hire'. Based on interviews conducted at the Greater Amman Municipality (GAM), it appears that MAWARED has been created to take on the role formerly played by GAM in such sensitive projects. Interviews and fieldwork clearly show that in Jordan, and in the Abdali project in particular, the boundary between regulator and investor and even public and private are becoming very blurred. In short, in Jordan's neoliberal urban restructuring, the boundary between 'State' and 'civil society' is very blurred, transparency is non-existent, and public information about the Abdali project is minimal.

Abdali, modelled after Solidere and with some of the same investors, is promoted by MAWARED's brochures, website, short video, and other promotional materials as the 'New Downtown for Amman'. However what is clear is that the project will intensify the socio-economic and spatial polarization not only between east and west Amman but between a new 'elitist urban island' and the rest of the city. The Abdali development will result in the displacement of the nearby Abdali transport terminal, together with its drivers, informal vendors and occupants, to the outskirts of the city. An IT park, luxury offices and also some residential space will be introduced in addition to a newly created civic 'secular' plaza bounded by the State Mosque, the Parliament, and the Law Courts. This will present fierce competition to the existing downtown which is gradually decaying and suffering from a lack of economic vitality. This is reinforced through a combination of physical, social, and cultural boundary formation processes. Hall (1996, p. 159) describes how 'the creation of a "bourgeois playground" in the name of economic progress may create considerable tension in the urban policy-making environment', while Shami (1996, p. 45) suggests that 'relocation frequently accompanies urban modernization and is linked in many ways with the idea of mobility as a valued characteristic of urbanness. However, while mobility may mean freedom and new opportunities for some, for others it may mean the very opposite'.

Another contested dimension of this neoliberal investment is the forced gentrification and selling out of private property for private development because part of the land acquired by the investors is owned by private people. Furthermore, in a part of the proposed development area, known locally as the Za'amta neighbourhood, there are residential apartments. Here, residents are being asked to sell to the investor and leave their properties. One of these properties at the edge of the development area is the Talal Abu Ghazaleh Organization (TAGorg) headquarters. Indeed TAGorg has publicly announced that the Greater Amman Municipality is acting as a mediator to convince the organization to sell its land while threatening to expropriate it if it refuses. In general they are all being asked to sell to the developer, but obviously through the Greater Amman Municipality (GAM) which is left to deal with the difficult work of MAWARED and Saudi Oger (appropriation of private land for private development) and is being put in the position of regulator and infrastructure provider without actually being part of these neoliberal projects or even benefiting from them financially. For the average Ammani citizen, whose only source of information about the project is the billboards around the construction site, it is GAM which is at the forefront and is blamed for the relocation of the Abdali transportation hub (which caused major problems for those using public transport). Interviews in the former transport hub suggest that these ordinary Ammani citizens are not even aware of the existence of MAWARED or Saudi Oger.

It is interesting to research how these new autocratic bodies are created, how they function, who is employed and how they are supported by a very powerful and chic image, promotion campaign, graphics, and the whole paraphernalia that centres on image and late capitalist consumerism advertising.

The Creation of Gated Communities, the Malling of the City, and the Quartering of Urban Space

The Abdali project is not a unique phenomenon in Amman; there are several projects either being built or proposed for the capital. Some of these are exclusive high-rise offices, others are well-protected gated communities along the Airport Highway catering for the wealthy and the upper middle class. Table 3.1 below presents a critical analysis of these different projects in terms of the nature of their real-estate company; the origin of their capital; project type and associated lifestyle; in addition to targeted clientele.

In the late 1990s the city was plagued with a series of shopping malls, some even in the eastern, less affluent part of the city. This accentuated a growing consumer society with adverse effects on smaller businesses, neighbourhood corner shops and local grocery stores. One mall, Mecca Mall, located in the western part of the city, has been labelled the 'most popular public Ammani space' by Jordanian critics in local newspapers (figure 3.5). These malls are very selective in the way they choose their clientele. Not only do they have rigid security with multiple sensors, CCTV and check points, but they exercise a no entry policy for those they claim to be unwelcome participants in the mall space – predominantly young Ammani males who feel excluded from this gated consumerist community.

In Amman, the effect of such socio-economic transformation on the creation of new public urban space produces 'a privatized public space' based on a highly

Figure 3.5. Interior of Mecca Mall showing the sales centre for GREENLAND Project (The Shrine of Neoliberalism where 'property' is the new consumer good par-excellence in the Arab world).

Table 3.1. Real-estate developers' discourse in and around Amman.

Name of Real-Estate Company	Origin of Circulating Capital and Transitional Capitalists' Class	Location of Real-Estate Project	Project Type, Lifestyle and Architectural Style	Name of Project and Marketing Slogans	Targeted Clientele (Catering for Closed/Open Community)
Discourse I: Selling 'Paradise' on the Ground					
TAAMEER Jordan/Jordan Company for Real-Estate Development (PLC)/ www.taameerjordan.com	UAE and Jordan CEO: Ahmed Dahleh Amman, Airport Highway		Villas Cost/m²: 600 JD Facilities and lifestyle: centralized underfloor heating; maid's room with laundry; interior customization; 24 hour security and maintenance; indoor and outdoor swimming pool, spas and health clubs.	*ANDALUCIA* 'The grass is greener at ANDALUCIA'	Upper class Gated closed community
Kurdi Group www.greenland.jo	Jordan CEO: Obaidah al Kurdi	Marj al Hamman, near Amman, close to the Airport Highway	Mostly villas, but also apartments Architects: Kurdi & Ashdak Cost/m²: apartments: 657–796JD; villas: 700–784JD Sales centre: Open area in Mecca Mall	*Green Land* 'The joy of living'	Middle- and high-income Open community
AMAAR Properties in partnership with Triad Investments www.amaar.net	Jordan and UAE	Al Hummar, Amman	Villas Architectural style: modern smart home system; centralized AC and heating system; centralized satellite and internet; 24 hour security and maintenance; health clubs	*Al-Hummar Hills* 'A new oasis for dwelling in Amman' 'Provides distinctive homes that will redefine everyday life' 'Elite Products for the Elite Community' 'Al Hummar Hills is an ingeniously fresh approach to gated communities compound living' www.hummarhills.com	Upper middle-class and high Gated community; compound living

Bayan Holding (developer); Gulf Finance House (financing); Al Hamad Construction & Development Co (construction)	UAE	Near Airport Highway on the way to Marj al Hamman, Amman	Villas and apartments Architectural style: modern/contemporary Facilities: cable TV; central gas distribution; central irrigation system; VRV system Architects: Consolidated Consultants Sales centre: under construction	*Royal Village* 'The Royal Village, the joy of living in the City away from life worries and noise' 'The Royal Village, the address of contemporary life'	Middle and high Closed gated community

Discourse II: 'Living above the City in the Clouds'

Abdali Investment & Development PSC (a private shareholder company). A public-private-partnership between the State-owned investment corporation MAWARED and Saudi Oger as the main developer and contractor, plus the Kuwaiti investment group KIPCO	Saudi Arabia and Jordan Chairman Bahaa Hariri/ Chairman and President of Saudi Oger: Sheikh Sa'ad Hariri Director General of MAWARED: Akram Abu Hamdan Prominent Board Member: Ali Kolaghassi US$1.5 billion investment	Abdali, in the heart of the city of Amman A 3.5 million foot² development	The Towers sector of the project is a mix of high- and mid-rise developments designed to accommodate corporate offices and offer integrated building management systems to ensure state-of-the-art services for corporate tenants. The residential area will be mixed-use space with luxury apartments	*Abdali Urban Regeneration Project* 'A new downtown for Amman' 'The planting of a heart for an old City is the essence of the Abdali Project'	Corporate businesses; upper middle-class residents and expatriates Closed community
EMMAR partnered with the Bin Suaidan Group of Saudi Arabia	Jordan and Saudi Arabia	Amman, 5th Circle area, Zahran Street 40,000 m² development	The commercial towers; high end corporate offices	*EMMAR Towers* 'Best place to practise commercial activity' 'A comprehensive security system'	Closed community
Bayan Holding (developer) / Gulf Finance House (financing); Al Hamad Construction & Development Co (construction)	UAE	Amman, 6th Circle area	Two Towers (commercial and hotel) Architects: Consolidated Consultants Sales centre: under construction	*Jordan Gate* 'Share the vision, embrace the future' 'Energizing Jordan and beyond' www.jordan-gate.com	High end

continued on page 58

continued from page 57

Dubai Properties DDC; Dubai Development Cooperation (project managers)	UAE GEO: Jordan Branels	Abdali, in the heart of the city of Amman	Residential and mixed-use offices Architects: Cladio Nardi Lifestyle: underground parking; wireless internet; under floor heating; voice over IP based security; shops; cafes; gym; library; private cinema	Two Towers: 1. Vertex Towers and Residence www.vertexjordan.com 2. Commerce-One 'A unique jewel in a special site' 'Enjoy an urban and prestigious life style in Amman' 'The most glamorous and luxurious address for living in Amman	Upper middle and high Closed community
DAMAC Properties	UAE Main shareholder: Mr. Sijwani of the UAE CEO: Peter Riddoch Regional (Jordan) Office Director: Wisam Atqi	Abdali, in the heart of the city of Amman	*The Heights* Studios and one-bedroom apartments Cost per m²: 1400–2500JD *The Lofts* Studios and apartments. Cost per m²: 1400–1600JD *The Courtyard* Residential and commercial tower 22 floors with four offices on each. Cost per m²: 2200 JD for residential space and 3100JD for commercial space In general: serene landscape; gateway to the Abdali Master Plan; over-looking malls, offices, and the new downtown Amman; ample parking on three levels; video phone entry; advanced cabling system for telephone internet lines; 24 hour concierge and help desk facilities; standby power generator; water storage tanks and garbage rooms; exotic sauna/jacuzzi; state-of-the-art gym; temperature-controlled swimming pool; a variety of high class retail outlets and specialty restaurants.	Three main towers: *The Heights* (35-storey offices) *The Lofts* (8-storey residential) *The Courtyard* 'Lofty views, open terraces, and deluxe living in the city center' 'Luxury lifestyle providers'	Upper class Gated community

Sources: This table was constructed based on field work conducted by the author in Amman between 2006 and 2007 by visiting different project locations, real-estate investors sales centres, exhibitions, and by consulting different local business and real-estate magazines such as *Jordan Business, Jordan Property,* and *Jordan Land.*

selective definition of the public (Crawford, 1995) and triggers a new meaning of public/private and inclusion/exclusion. It is important to understand local/global relationships *vis-à-vis* the processes of urban inclusion/exclusion and the power mechanisms embedded in such 'urban restructuring' projects and corporate visions.

This notion of 'island planning', where certain urban development projects turn their back on adjoining districts and areas or even create a privatized, controlled, and protected environment, becomes a contested reality which deserves further attention. Referred to by Sassen (cited in Elsheshtawy, 2004, p. 18) as the 'quartering of urban space', the same problem is expected in Abdali; the result will be a 'fragmented city', a 'patchwork of discrete spaces with increasingly sharp boundaries (gated business centres, leisure, tourism and community spaces)'. According to Elsheshtawy (2004, p. 8), these 'protected enclaves of the rich' will also increase the gap between the rich and the poor within the same city. Fainstein and Judd (1999*b*, p. 9) claim that:

> carefully bounded districts have been set aside as 'tourist bubbles' isolated from surrounding areas of decay. Within these districts, historic and architecturally significant structures are integrated with the new generation of tourist facilities that, instead of evoking images of an urban golden age, are quite contemporary.

Gated communities and privileged shopping malls are invading the urban landscape of several Middle Eastern cities today, and unfortunately:

> many places are being put into play due to the increasingly global character of these contemporary mobilities. The 1990s have seen remarkable 'time-space compression', as people across the globe have been brought 'closer' through various technologies. There is an apparent 'death of distance' in what is sometimes described as a fluid and speeded-up 'liquid modernity'. (Sheller and Urry, 2004, p. 3).

Sheller and Urry elaborate on the concepts and lifestyles associated with these 'places to play'. They believe that tourism is not only transforming the materiality of many 'real' places, but is also having a deep impact on the creation of virtual realities and fantasized places. 'These are enormously powerful and ubiquitous global brands or logos that increasingly feature tourist sites/sights as key components of the global culture that their brand speaks to and enhances' (*Ibid.*). These brand companies include many in 'travel and in leisure: Disney, Hilton, Nike, Gap, Easyjet, Body Shop, Virgin, Club Med, Starbucks, Coca Cola, and so on. These brands produce "concepts" or "lifestyles": liberated from the real-world burdens of stores and products manufacturing' (*Ibid.*), and these lifestyle concepts revolve around generic types of places to play: the hotel pool, the waterside café/restaurant, the cosmopolitan city, the hotel buffet, the theme park, the club, the airport lounge, and the shopping mall.

An important question emerges from this: within these places of play of intense mobility, who gets the opportunity to be mobile? And what is the relationship between the local and global within this mobility? It is only global money and a chosen few who are granted this privilege. The rest of the world cannot join 'the play'; entry to these global places of play is restricted for the majority and is only permitted through their involvement in the provision of services and infrastructure (for example, Indian and Pakistani workers in Dubai hotels and resorts; domestic workers from Indonesia and the Philippines in Beirut and Amman) (Daher, 2007*a*). Junemo's (2004, p. 181) work on Dubai is informative as it describes the socio-economic, spatial and demographic transformation taking place in this extraordinary place of constant 'play'.

Yet these 'playscapes' whether in Dubai, Amman, Cairo or Beirut are simply gated communities with practices of inclusion and exclusion. They are usually guarded and are closed off for many to ensure the type of people allowed to participate in these places of leisure and consumption. Junemo (2004, p. 190) illustrates how these places maintain and enforce a symbolic distinction between those with access to the networks and those without. This distinction is crucial for the formation of a distinct social identity for the upper middle class where monetary capital is turned into some accepted form of social capital in order to gain access to such upmarket social networks.

The Transnational Capitalist Class and Their Real-Estate Development Discourse: Selling Paradise on the Ground; or Living above the City in the Clouds

Between 2005 and 2007 I researched current real-estate ventures by visiting different project locations, sales centres of main real-estate companies and exhibitions, interviewing the CEOs and deputy managers of such companies, and consulting a huge variety of literature published in magazines such as *Jordan Business*, *Jordan Property*, and *Jordan Land*. One of the outcomes of this research is table 3.1 which presents a critical analysis of the different projects in terms of the nature of their real-estate company; the origin of capital and the transnational capitalist class; project type and associated lifestyle; marketing slogans; and targeted clientele and cost. I suggest that the real-estate projects can be divided into two main categories: Type 1. Gated communities in the form of residential compounds; and Type 2. Exclusive office space in the form of high-rise towers. The following is a discussion of the these two types of neoliberal investment in Amman.

Type 1, such as Andalusia, Greenland, Hummar Hills and the Royal Village, represents gated communities and housing enclaves for the very rich, which I dub 'selling paradise on the ground', because a quick glance across the different marketing slogans and discourses of the developers (for example, 'The Joy of Living', 'Provide distinctive homes that will redefine everyday life') suggests that the projects are promising a utopian existence and a completely transformed individual once he or she becomes part of this exclusive community. The architecture attempts to offer a traditional envelope for these villas and apartments by the use of traditional materials and colours and certain historicized elements (for example, wooden pergolas, *mashrabiyahs* and so on). The architectural style represents, in most cases, a poor and unsophisticated understanding of a mythical Orient. But once one attempts to reveal and peel off this Disney-like and superficial layer, it is very obvious that these projects represent an oriental vision of the Occident, where the Occident is American-style suburban living with its single-family house, front yard, garage, and basketball ring.

Type 2 projects like the towers sector of the Abdali project (including the Vertex, the Heights and the Lofts), Jordan Gate, and many others constitute exclusive office space and luxury apartments which I call 'Living above the City in the Clouds'. The wealthy residents strive to be part of the city, but in reality they are living in a privileged position above the city. In their marketing slogans these projects promise a distinctively luxurious lifestyle and a protected and safe environment (for example, 'Lofty Views, Open Terraces, and Deluxe Living in the City Centre'; 'Luxury Life Style Providers'; 'A Comprehensive Security System'). As Sklair (2001, p. 6) says:

> global capitalism thrives by persuading us that the meaning and value of our lives are to be found principally in what we posses, that we can never be totally satisfied with our positions (the imperative of ever changing fashion style), and that the goods and services we consume are best provided by the free market, the generator of private profit that lies at the heart of capitalism.

It is obvious that the new service good of neoliberalism today is property.

Table 3.1 reveals the different actors and agents behind these neoliberal projects, they include people like Bahaa al-Hariri (Chairman and President of Saudi Oger), Akram Abu Hamdan (General Director of MAWARED), Jordan Branels (CEO of Dubai Properties), and Mr. Sijwani (major shareholder in DAMAC Properties) to mention a few. These people play a crucial role in the politics and dynamics of these investments and also in the direction of capital flow within the region, let alone the lifestyles prevailing within the projects.

I suggest that further research on neoliberal urban restructuring should focus more on the human agent behind global capital flow and ethnographies which target these transnational capitalist individuals so as better to understand the nature and future of these investments. Ley (2004, p. 152) pinpoints the importance of studying the different discourses of these transnational capitalists while attempting to bring the issue of human agency to a globalizing discourse which 'has frequently been satisfied with speaking of a space of networks and flows devoid of knowledgeable human agents'. Sklair (2001, p, 4) suggests that this 'new class is the transnational capitalist class, composed of corporate executives, globalizing bureaucrats and politicians, globalizing professionals, and consumerist elites'.

Local/Municipal Initiatives in the Midst of Neoliberal Transformation in the City

Shami (2005, p. 16) recognizes the city as a product of people 'who make space and place, discursively and materially; negotiating macro-level forces in culturally specific ways'. I also believe that the city is a complicated organism of different power mechanisms and contested narratives. Thus while gated communities are being built on the Airport Highway and luxurious apartments and office towers in Abdali, the city is, and will continue to be, the stage for different agents or actors such as the municipality, a local community group, a philanthropist, an NGO, or even a private investor with an alternative vision or approach.

A particularly important actor in the city is the Greater Amman Municipality which is changing how it sees itself, especially in terms of its role in the city. GAM today considers its role to be more than services and infrastructure provision and attempts to address the future of the city through a vision which 'seeks, in partnership with Amman's citizenship, to provide exceptional municipal services that far exceed the expectation of service-recipients, while keeping up with modern conveniences and preserving the city's heritage and spirit'.[12] The new mayor of Amman, Omar Al-Maani, explained how GAM is looking for Amman to be a modern, efficient, green city and one that is pedestrian-friendly and has a lot of activities. During a 2006 lecture to the International Affairs Association entitled 'Amman Present and Future', Al-Maani emphasized that GAM went beyond the traditional role of municipal administration in serving the city, and that it plays an effective role in developing society and achieving sustainable development.[13] Yet, as mentioned above, GAM is also being put in a difficult position by being asked to be the regulator (or better, the rationalizer) for the neoliberal urban restructuring in the city. As a regulator of future developments, GAM's role, so far, centres on envisioning the new master plan for the city in addition to researching appropriate locations for new high-rise developments, and drafting guidelines for future growth.

GAM is also undertaking different heritage management projects and addressing the creation of public spaces within the city. One of these projects is the urban regeneration of Rainbow Street located in a historic part of the city, close to the downtown area. The project aims to create more spaces for the public (in the form of small urban gardens and panoramic lookouts) in addition to 'giving voice' to this distinctive Ammani urban reality. At the same time as GAM's project started at Rainbow Street in 2005, transnational capitalists were buying historic properties in the area, which they saw as a golden opportunity for real-estate investment as it is becoming popular with the thirty-something crowd of Ammanis.

The project designers (TURATH Consultants) saw a chance to counter current neoliberal threats to the area and to foster a successful public space which is more inclusive. They were seeking to present a model to counteract the fact that public spaces today are part of a neoliberal strategy of gentrification and late capitalist investment. Their main objective was to maintain the healthy character and socio-economic make-up of the area which is composed of small and medium size businesses, middle and upper middle class residents, and different public amenities such as cultural and research centres, mosques, churches, schools and a vibrant mix of other functions such as retail and restaurants. Shop owners were striving to stay in business in an area with continuous pressures of increased property values and rapid transformation. It was very evident that different narratives were operating simultaneously at Rainbow Street.

Wakalat Street, in the new shopping district of Sweifieh, is the focus of another GAM project and represents an attempt to reinvent public life in the city. The project is part of a wider public space strategy put forward by GAM to address the reality of existing public spaces and the quality of urban life in Amman. The main design objective is to produce an 'anti-Mall space' by creating a 'walkable street', and a recreational promenade which encourages pedestrian life in Amman. The aim is to create a street that is inclusive, welcoming people from all parts of Amman and, at the same time, is a vibrant urban space which will win back public life from shopping malls to the 'real' streets of the city. It is hoped that Wakalat Street will become a demonstration project for other areas to follow. Other GAM projects proposed for the city include the urban regeneration of Faisal Street in the downtown area, the revitalization of Darwish Mosque Plaza in the historic

Figure 3.6. The new JARA (Jabal Amman Residents Association) Flea Market where Ammanis are flocking to historic urban quarters of the city for a touch of urban history and a different Ammani experience.

neighbourhood of Ashrafieh, and collaboration with different newly-emerging neighbourhood associations such as JARA (Jabal Amman Residents Association) and Jabal Al Weibdeh Residents Association to improve the urban quality of life in their respective environments (figure 3.6).

Concluding Remarks: Resistance in a One-Dimensional Society

It is interesting to attempt to understand the nature and scope of public debate over the neoliberal urban transformations in Amman. In the city, critical debates are more sporadic, concentrating on 'technical' matters of investment (for example, traffic congestion, spatial considerations in terms of where to locate high-rise buildings). In addition, and in many contexts, there is a huge overlap between the State and the public sphere represented by its various civil institutions and NGOs (which might form communication structures facilitating critical public debate). In Jordan, the borderlines between the State and civil society are very blurred. For example, many NGOs receive State funding or engage in State-run projects while others are linked to the Royal Family who patronize such civic institutions which are seen as extensions of the State and where the possibility of critical resistance is impossible or very difficult. There is hardly any scholarly or even popular writing on such transformations.

Swarbrooke (2000, p. 275) describes how in certain developed countries such as the United Kingdom one can find public protest against the use of public resources (funds, subsidies) to support flagship projects and tourism developments. Protest is made because it is thought 'wrong for poor communities to, in effect, offer subsidies, to wealthy private companies' and that the money invested in such mega urban projects should be devoted to more worthy causes. It is often suggested that in depressed urban areas, social infrastructure – health, education, and housing – should be the priority for the allocation of public funds.

In the Middle East, questions of politics of place, urban development, and heritage definition have predominantly remained outside the domains of political and public consciousness. In general, politics and matters subject to public debate (and open for public scrutiny) are confined to a *traditional* conception of the term (for example, matters of the *Shari'a*, and the Palestinian issue; in other words, politics with a big 'P'). Meanwhile, questions of politics of place, identity construction, contested pasts, and appropriate development modes (politics with a small 'p') have predominantly remained outside the domains of politics and critical debate. In the different Middle Eastern contexts discussed, critical public debates by different actors and agents (regardless of their nature and different concerns, mechanisms of contestation, and areas of emphasis) do not culminate in any action on the ground, they remain at the level of the discourse leading to further frustrations. Discourse emancipation should perhaps concentrate on different sub-cultures of residence at the level of the 'individual' (initiating resistance at the individual level through continuous networking).

The issue of resistance at the level of the individual maybe one of very few solutions where the self is considered an active particle of resistance capable of networking and contestation in an age of neoliberalism, State and monopoly organized late capitalism, media and the dominance of the image, and the increasingly powerful positions of large-scale transnational corporations and big businesses in public life in Jordan and maybe elsewhere in the region. Sklair (2001, p. 297) believes that 'capitalism can only be successfully challenged through social movements that target global capitalism through its three main institutional supports, the TNCs, the transnational capitalists class, and the culture-ideology of consumerism'.

My purpose in this research is not so much to critique as to contribute to the understanding of this new phenomenon of 'neoliberal urban restructuring' and to elevate the level and essence of the discourse and public debate about key crucial transformations in my city, Amman. I realize that this 'neoliberal' urban phenomenon is very difficult to challenge. I simply want to lobby for a public request, on behalf of the city, to the transnational capitalist class, who are the beneficiaries of this phenomenon, to pump at least a small fraction of profit and 'royalties' into the real downtown of Amman. This could be considered as overdue taxes or charity, or even as a reversal subsidy.

Such neoliberal urban transformations in Middle Eastern cities will definitely lead to adverse effects on the urban realities of these cities and also on the gap between the different socio-economic groups which make up the urban setting. For Amman, and since most of these projects not only target a high end clientele but are also located in western Amman, it is evident that these neoliberal endeavours will increase the divide between the poorer east and the more affluent west of the city. Our relationship with the city has always been, and will always be, a contestation between social classes, different groups, and mechanisms of inclusion and exclusion. More recently, this relationship has become ephemeral and superficial, and our sense of belonging to place is very transient in nature. We think that we live in the city as our craving for urbanity increases; but rather, we live 'above' the city in gated realities.

Notes

1.   The *Abdali* Project is a new large urban development project being constructed on former army land (most of which was empty) in the middle of Amman. Funding for the project is made available through partnerships between the State and transnational real-estate development companies. The Towers Sector of the Project is a mix of high- and mid-rise buildings designed to accommodate corporate offices and offer integrated building management systems to ensure state-of-the-art services for corporate tenants. The residential area will be mixed-use space with luxury apartments.

2.   Public lecture by Seteney Shami, entitled 'Amman is not a City', presented at the Center for Middle Eastern Studies at the University of California, Berkeley. The lecture, part of the Center's Spring Lecture Series, was held in March 2001.

3.   *Hawooz*: is originally a main source of water (e.g., well, spring, other) and gradually, formulated a

nucleus in the form of an urban node (*green* circle in certain cases) in Amman's residential hills.

4.   www.jabalomar.com. Accessed 7 September 2007.

5.   The circulation of Gulf and Saudi capital into cities such as Amman or Beirut was amplified mainly after the incidents of 11 September when that Arab surplus capital was no longer welcomed in the United States or Europe, and the only places left for investment were cities of the Arab world and the Indian subcontinent.

6.   According to Wikipedia (http://en.wikipedia.org/wiki/Neoliberalism. Accessed 9 September 2007), the term neoliberalism is used to describe a political-economic philosophy which has had major implications for government policies from the 1970s, and has become increasingly prominent since 1980. This philosophy de-emphasizes or rejects positive government intervention in the economy (which complements private initiatives), and focuses instead on achieving progress and even social justice by encouraging free market methods and fewer restrictions on business operations and economic 'development'. Its supporters argue that the net gains for all under free trade, free market, and capitalism outweigh the costs in all or almost all cases.

7.   The boundary between the 'State' and 'public' is becoming very blurred with major consequences where the State is pulling out of support for vital sectors (for example, education, agriculture and health) and is becoming simply just like another corporation or institution amongst many, making issues such as accountability very problematic.

8.   Saraya project in Aqaba. *Al-Rai'* Newspaper, No. 12659, 19 May 2005, p. 13. New projects in Amman. *Al-Rai'* Newspaper, No. 12661, 21 May 2005, p. 17.

9.   MAWARED: National Resources Investment and Development Corporation.

10.   Saudi Oger (Oger Jordan) is an international developer. Saudi Oger entered the partnership as the main investor and also brought the expertise of its foreign master planners (Millennium Development & Laceco).

11.   In Beirut, for example, Solidere's capital initially valued at $1.82 billion consisted of two different types of shares: type A shares issued to holders of expropriated property in the city's downtown relative to the value of the expropriated property; and type B shares (with an initial stock offer of US$100 per share) issued to external investors. Solidere's own rhetoric sugars the type A shares and rationalizes their facilitation by stating that 'most lots in the Beirut Central District are owned by tens, hundreds and in some instances (the *Souq* areas) thousands of people'. Therefore, the type A shares are being presented as the only 'just' solution for such a dilemma.

12.   http://www.ammancity.gov.jo/English/vision/v1.asp. Accessed 27 April 2007.

13.   http://www.ammancity.gov.jo/english/news/n.asp?news_id=727. Accessed 27 April 2007.

References

Abu-Lughod, Janet (1987) The Islamic city, historic myth, Islamic essence, and contemporary relevance. *International Journal of Middle East Studies*, **19**(2), pp. 155–176.

Adham, Khaled (2004) Cairo's urban déjà vu: globalization and urban fantasies, in Elsheshtawy, Yasser (ed.) *Planning Middle Eastern Cities, An Urban Kaleidoscope in a Globalizing World*. London: Routledge, pp. 134–168.

Adham, Khaled (2005) Urban Boundaries and New spaces of Capital in Cairo. Social Science Fourteenth Annual Symposium 'The Transformation of Middle Eastern Urban Landscapes: From Modernism to Neoliberalism', The American University of Cairo (AUC), Cairo, Egypt, 12–15 May.

Al-Hindi, Rania (2007a) Real estate investments. *Jordan Property Magazine*, No. 5, pp. 18–19.

Al-Hindi, Rania (2007b) Abdali: the countdown begins. *Jordan Property Magazine*, No. 9, pp. 16–32.

Al-Masri, Wael (2007) The phenomena of large Arab investment in the Gulf area. *Jordan Land Magazine*, No. 9, pp. 187–181.

Al-Sayyad, Nezar (1995) From vernacularism to globalization: the temporal reality of traditional settlements. *Traditional Dwellings and Settlement Review*, **7**(1), pp. 13–24.

Al-Sayyad, Nezar (2001) Global norms and urban forms in the age of tourism: manufacturing heritage, consuming tradition, in Al-Sayyad, Nezar (ed.) *Consuming Tradition, Manufacturing Heritage: Global Norms and Urban Forms in the Age of Tourism*. London: Routledge, pp.1–33.

Anani, Jawad (1992) Who are the Ammanites? *Ad-Dustour*, 28 October, p. 4.

Anderson, B. (1983) *Imagined Communities: Reflections on the Origins and Spread of Nationalism*. New York, NY: Vintage Books.

Bank, A. and Schlumberger, O. (2004) Jordan: between regime survival and economic reform, in Perthes, Volker (ed.) *Arab Elites: Negotiating the Politics of Change*. Boulder, CO: Lynne Rienner, pp. 35–60.

Bourdieu, Pierre (1998) *Acts of Resistance: Against the Tyranny of the Market* (Translator Richard Nice). New York, NY: The New Press.

Crawford, M. (1995) Contesting the public realm: struggles over public space in Los Angeles. *Journal of Architectural Education*, **49**(1), pp. 4–9.

Daher, Rami (2005) Urban regeneration/heritage tourism endeavors, the case of Salt, Jordan: local actors, international donors, and the State. *International Journal of Heritage Studies*, **11**(4), pp. 289–308.

Daher, Rami (2007a) Re-conceptualizing tourism in the Middle East: place, heritage, mobility and competitiveness, in Daher, Rami (ed.) *Tourism in the Middle East: Continuity, Change and Transformation*. Clevedon, Somerset: Channel View Publications, pp. 1–69.

Daher, Rami (2007b) Tourism: heritage and urban transformations in Jordan and Lebanon: emerging actors and global-local juxtapositions, in Daher, Rami (ed.) *Tourism in the Middle East: Continuity, Change and Transformation*. Clevedon, Somerset: Channel View Publications, pp. 263–307.

Dieterich, R. (2002) What is 'Islamic' about the City of Amman? Paper submitted to the Conservation and Regeneration of Traditional Urban Centers in the Islamic World: Learning from Regional Experiences and Building Partnerships Conference, Amman, Irbid, Salt.

Elsheshtawy, Y. (2004) The Middle East city: moving beyond the narrative of loss, in Elsheshtawy, Y. (ed.) *Planning Middle Eastern Cities: An Urban Kaleidoscope in a Globalizing World*. London: Routledge, pp. 1–21.

Fainstein, Susan and Judd, Dennis (1999a) Cities as places to play, in Judd, Dennis and Fainstein, Susan (eds.) *The Tourist City*. New Haven, CT: Yale University Press, pp. 261–272.

Fainstein, Susan and Judd, Denis (1999b) Global forces, local strategies, and urban tourism, in Dennis Judd and Fainstein, Susan (eds.) *The Tourist City*. New Haven, CT: Yale University Press, pp. 1–17.

Gharaybeh, Hashem (2003) *Shahbander* (Novel in Arabic). Beirut: Dar al-Adab.

Hall, Colin (1996) *Tourism and Politics: Policy, Power, and Place*. Chichester: Wiley.

Junemo, Mattias (2004) 'Let's build a palm island!': playfulness in complex times, in Sheller, M. and Urry, John (eds.) *Tourism Mobilities: Places to Plat, Places in Play*. London: Routledge, pp. 181–191.

Kassay, Ali (2006) The Absence of an Ammani Identity. Paper presented to the Cities and National Identity in Jordan Conference, Institut Français du Proche-Orient, Amman.

Ley, David (2004) Transitional spaces and everyday lives. *Transactions of the Institute of British Geographers*, **29**(2), pp. 151–164.

Maffi, Irene (2000) Le statut des objects dans la mise en scène muséographique du passé en Jordanie: le discours historique, la narration mythique et la tradition. Les Documents du CERMOC (CERMOC DOCUMENT), No 10: Patrimony and Heritage Conservation in Jordan (Maffi, Irene and Daher, Rami). Beirut, Amman: CERMOC (Center for Studies and Researchers on the Contemporary Middle East), pp. 3–16.

Maffi, Irene (2002) New museographic trends in Jordan: the strengthening of the nation, in Joffe, George (ed.) *Jordan in Transition 1990–2000*. London: Hurst, pp. 208–224.

Qasem, Zeyad (1998) *Abna' Al-Qala'* (Novel on Amman), 3rd ed. Beirut: Arab Institute for Publishing and Studies.

Razzaz, Mo'nes (1996) Amman in Jordanian novels (in Arabic), in Hourani, Hani, and Dabbas, Hamed (eds.) *Amman: Realities and Expectations, Issues on Culture, Environment, and Construction*. Amman: Al-Urdun Al-Jadid Research Center, pp. 349–357.

Reiker, Martina (2005) Symposium Thematic Introduction. Social Science Fourteenth Annual Symposium 'The Transformation of Middle Eastern Urban Landscapes: From Modernism to Neoliberalism', The American University of Cairo (AUC), Cairo, Egypt, 12–15 May.

Robertson, Nina (2007) Blueprint for the future: Akram Abu Hamdan builds new heights. *Jordan Business*, April, pp. 44–51.

Rogan, Eugene (1996) The making of a capital: Amman 1918–1928, in Hannoyer, Jean, and Shami, Seteney (eds.) *Amman: The City and Its Society*. Beirut: CERMOC, pp. 89–108.

Sadiq, Rula (2005) Dazzling Dubai: The 'Invisible' Hand of Global Competitiveness. Social Science Fourteenth Annual Symposium 'The Transformation of Middle Eastern Urban Landscapes: From Modernism to Neoliberalism', The American University of Cairo (AUC), Cairo, Egypt, 12–15 May.

Saqr, Yasir (2003) The Cultural Amalgamation of Greater Amman: A Quest for an Identity. Unpublished paper.

Schriwer, Charlotte (2002) Cultural and ethnic identity in the Ottoman period. Architecture of Cyprus, Jordan and Lebanon. *LEVANT: The Journal of the Council for British Research in the Levant*, **34**, pp. 197–218.

Shami, Seteney (1996) Researching the city: urban space and its complexities, in Hannoyer, Jean, and Shami, Seteney (eds.) *Amman: The City and Its Society*. Beirut: CERMOC, pp. 37–54.

Shami, Seteney (2005) Amman is not a City: Middle Eastern Cities in Question. Unpublished paper, Social Science Research Council, New York.

Sheller, M. and Urry, J. (2004) Places to play, places in play, in Sheller, M. and Urry, John (eds.) *Tourism Mobilities: Places to Plat, Places in Play*. London: Routledge, pp. 1–10.

Sklair, Leslie (2001) *The Transnational Capitalist Class*. Oxford: Blackwell.

Summer, Doris (2005) Neoliberalizing the City: Transitional Investment Networks and the Circulation of Urban Images in Beirut and Amman. Master Thesis in Urban Planning, American University of Beirut (AUB).

Swarbooke, John (2000) Tourism, economic development and urban regeneration: a critical evaluation, in Robinson, M., Long, P., Evans, N., Sharpley, R. and Swarbrooke, J. (eds.) *Reflections on International Tourism*. Houghton-le-Spring, Tyne and Wear: Business Education Publishers, pp. 269–285.

Swyngedouw, E., Moulaert, F., and Rodriguez, A. (2002) Neoliberal urbanization in Europe: large-scale urban development projects and the new urban policy. *Antipode*, **34**(3), pp. 542–577.

Chapter 4

From Regional Node to Backwater and Back to Uncertainty: Beirut, 1943–2006

Sofia T. Shwayri

'It will be rebuilt; Lebanon will be back', read a poster commonly seen on the roads around Beirut in late summer 2006. It detailed the date of every Israeli attack on Lebanon, including the latest in July that year (figure 4.1). With the end of each devastating incursion came reconstruction; the poster was just one among many flanking the major roads and highways as Lebanon was still being pounded by the Israeli Defence Forces. Neither the call for reconstruction nor the motivation of the authors of these messages would have surprised passers by. After all, the process of reconstruction has rarely awaited the end of hostilities. In fact, plans for reconstruction are often drawn while wars are still being fought. In France as early as 1941, reconstruction plans were formulated by professionals and published in architectural journals (Roger, 1941; Vincent, 1943). The situation was not very different in Britain at the same time, where architects not only developed plans and published them but also put them on public display. In some cases, reconstruction frameworks are formed and finalized prior to the starting of the actual fighting, as was the case with the US-Iraq war launched in March 2003 where reconstruction contracts were handed out in February of that year (Rosenberg *et al.*, 2003).

It is the private sector that clamours for reconstruction. This has been the case with every destructive incursion since the formation of the modern State of Lebanon in 1943. Banks, now as then, are credited with playing an instrumental role. They were prominent in the making of the Lebanese economic miracle of the years up to 1975, a period when Beirut's Central District became the financial capital of the Middle East. This fuelled the overspill of banks from their traditional home on Banking Street into neighbouring Hamra Street in the 1960s. A year into the Civil War in 1976, following the destruction of the downtown area, this process accelerated further with various businesses relocating to the immediate and distant suburbs, creating alternative centres. With the end of the Civil War in 1990 and the subsequent return to the traditional Central District, the banks, like

Figure 4.1. 'It will be rebuilt; Lebanon will be back.'

other groups of the private sector, returned to take part in various aspects of the reconstruction. This most recent billboard call for reconstruction was about the rebuilding of the infrastructure that had supported the re-emerging globalized centre; Beirut International Airport, the Port of Beirut, and the highways linking the city centre to various parts of the country and to the world (figure 4.2).

The urban transformation of Beirut is largely the story of the expansion and development of a central business district into the role of a regional node between 1945 and 1974, its contraction to a backwater from 1975 to 1990, and its subsequent uncertain steps from 1991 towards a reconstructed globalized city centre. Each of these periods went hand-in-glove with a concept for the central business district. In the period from 1945 to 1974, the Central District was viewed as a 'unitary centre', the centre of political, economic and social life of the country. This point of convergence, in 1975, turns into a vector for the dispersal of all activities that shot outwards to the immediate and distant periphery, turning it into a deserted island, cut-off from its immediate domestic environment and the wider world as all its traditional core activities were ripped away. This, however, did not stop it from remaining an 'attractive real-estate market' for individuals who planned for the future. As the immediate and distant suburbs became highly urbanized, the Civil War ended and planning for the reconstruction of the Central District was well in hand. This development followed contemporary ideas: since

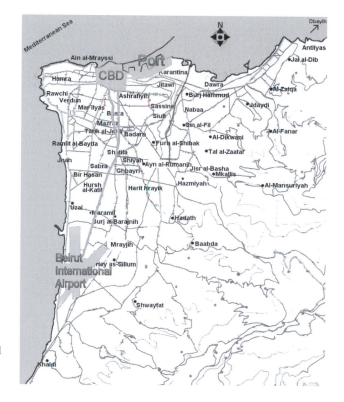

Figure 4.2. Map of the Metropolitan Region of Beirut indicating the Central District, the international airport and Port of Beirut.

the mid-1980s, downtown areas of cities in the Western world, especially North America, were viewed by planners and architects as the 'nodes in the global economy' (Abbott, 1996). Sharing these views, the Lebanese government and the private sector embarked on the reconstruction of the Central District in an attempt to reclaim its pre-war role as a regional economic node while, at the same time, planning for a future in which they hoped to 'place Beirut on the global economic map' (Huybrechts, 2002).

The periodic shift from one conception of the central business district to the next was dictated by the repositioning and reorganization of the private sector in each of these moments, shaped by a confluence of local, regional, national and supranational factors. The making of Beirut's Central District as the political, economic, and social centre of the Lebanese capital will be the focus of the first section of this chapter covering the period from 1943 to 1974. Just a few days into the Civil War, in April 1975, the fighting extended from the periphery into the Central District, gradually ripping the heart out of the capital and turning it into a ghost town. This process of change will form the second section. The last part will focus on the current era of reconstruction in a globalizing Central District as it is once again becoming a battlefield for regional and global actors.

A Capital City: Modernity and Uneven Development

In the century from 1843, Beirut turned from an insignificant port town to the capital of a newly independent state (Fawaz, 1983; Kassir, 2003; Hanssen, 2005). It was an era in which the foundations of a modern capital were laid, enabling it to expand its role from being yet another capital city to become a regional economic node. One crucial moment in this transformation came in 1923 when Beirut was declared the seat of the French High Commission and its administrative services. The focus from then on was making Beirut an economic and cultural centre of France in the Levant (Davie, 2001). This role was not totally novel as, since the nineteenth century, the city had been a trading post connecting France to its partners in the Levant as well as in the Far East. However, to keep up with this role and make it a showcase of France in the Eastern Mediterranean, a new centre was envisioned to replace the traditional one. A programme was devised to improve and develop its infrastructure. This included improving the road network within the capital and highways connecting the Central District to the hinterland and to neighbouring Syria, for example the Beirut–Damascus Highway; installing street lighting and telephone lines. Upgrading land links to neighbouring countries, however, was not sufficient. To widen its horizon in the whole region and beyond meant improving the existing port and building a modern airport. Work on the port started in the 1920s and continued over decades to keep up with the increasing traffic. By 1934, the expansion of the port included paving the quay, building a new basin, new warehouses, shops, and a free zone; an improvement that 'gave Beirut the edge over competing ports' along the Mediterranean like the Port of Haifa, and saw Beirut become 'a major regional port of the Eastern Mediterranean' (Saliba, 2004, p. 39). Work on the airport started in parallel, and before the end of 1927, construction was completed; Beirut had its modern airport in Bir Hassan, south of the centre (Saliba, 1998). When both port and airport were completed and connected via a network of roads to the Central District, a new compressed economic space was created that made Beirut a strategic node during the Mandate period.

These changes proved timely. Beirut, the capital of the newly emerging independent Lebanese State, took centre stage in a region about to be plunged into turmoil. With the foundation of the State of Israel in 1948 came the migration of several hundred thousand Palestinians, some of whom arrived in Beirut. The Palestinian disaster led to the effective loss of the port of Haifa and saw the transfer of its activities north to the Port of Beirut, making it virtually the only portal to the rest of the Arab World. This enforced role required further work to be done on the Port of Beirut with the expansion and development of a jetty and a fourth deck. In fact, prior to the arrival of the Palestinians, the relative stability that characterized Beirut made it a sanctuary to Armenian refugees fleeing Turkish persecution, arriving in waves as early as 1911 and continuing until the 1930s, forming an important labour force in the extensive construction work both in the port area and the city. In addition to the refugees, a large number of middle-class intellectuals fled unstable political and economic conditions in Syria, Egypt, and Iraq. All made Beirut their home (Kassir, 2003).

These regional factors, compounded by local policies, lay at the heart of the phenomenon that was the transformation of Beirut, and more specifically its Central District, into a regional node between the early 1950s and the mid-1970s. Significant were the bank secrecy laws of 1956, enacted with the aim of promoting Lebanon as the financial hub of the Middle East, with Beirut at the centre of circulation of foreign and local capital. This, coupled with a service economy based on a *laissez-faire* policy, free enterprise, and market forces, attracted Arab, Western and expatriate monies. The success of this node depended on developing a modern infrastructure including the expansion of the Port of Beirut located along the north coast of the Central District and an international airport south of the city, all connected via a network of modern highways; these projects formed a fundamental component of the government's agenda of this period. The refashioning of the capital made it attractive to those seeking a better life, Lebanese and non-Lebanese alike. Some of the newcomers settled in poverty in miserable conditions in two concentric rings of slums and refugee camps around the capital. The different types of flows crossing the Lebanese capital from the mid-1940s to the mid-1970s resulted in the creation of a deeply divided landscape which is the focus of the rest of this section.

The spatial proximity of the Central District to the waterfront and to the port area was instrumental in transforming Beirut from the coastal town of the nineteenth century to the mid-twentieth-century's regional maritime gateway. Its competitive role was enhanced with the building of the airport that connected the capital by air to cities in the Middle East and the Gulf, as well as Africa, and the wider world. This spatial reconfiguration allowed the Central District, the port, airport and connecting roads to operate as one entity while turning the city into a regional economic node, a status that increasingly depended on maintaining the most modern modes of transportation to supplement the capital's transformation into other nodes for tourism and culture. The result was a partnership between the private sector and the Lebanese State for a period of almost three decades, when the transformation of the Central District went hand in hand with the continuous expansion and development of the airport and Port of Beirut. Physical change was enforced by government policies designed to create an environment conducive to these regional flows but which eventually led to its demise.

The building of a modern airport was the first major construction project of the newly-independent Lebanese government and more specifically of its Ministry of Public Works and Transportation. Construction work started in 1948 and in less than 3 years, the government inaugurated the first runway which was followed almost two months later by the addition of a second. As expansion work of the new airport was being completed, the Lebanese State launched Air Liban in 1951 to serve neighbouring Arab and Gulf Countries and to encourage tourism and business (*AsSiyaha*, 1963, p. 55).[1] Established in 1945 by Saeb Salim Salam, Middle East Airlines (MEA) was another airline whose success allowed it to establish a partnership with the erstwhile Pan American World Airlines (Pan Am). The expansion of its services and operations allowed it, in the 1960s, to absorb Air Liban and thus become the national carrier (Kassir, 2003) (figure 4.3).

Underlying the city's growth were government policies that compounded the flow of the capital and the expansion of the banking sector and turned the capital into a safe haven for depositing and investing Arab money. This reached its peak in the 1960s and early 1970s. These banking policies led to a number of transnational corporations selecting Beirut as the seat of their regional headquarters. Most chose to locate along Riad as Sulh Street, which until World War II formed the western edge of the city of the Mandate period and its business activities. Major remodelling work in the late 1940s saw the transfer of the Post Office and the relocation by Lebanese banks scattered throughout the city to this one street which became Banking Street characterized by its proximity to administrative services as well as to maritime businesses (Ruppert, 1999). Beirut now acquired regional financial centre status; from a maximum of seven foreign banks existing in Beirut up to 1945, the number rose to ninety-three in 1966, sixty-eight of them Lebanese (Hudson, 1968, p. 63). This figure does not include discount houses or agencies for foreign exchange.

The development of the banking sector was paralleled by the growth of the tourist sector, the spatial manifestation of which was in the Central District but more westerly as the downtown area grew beyond its traditional boundaries. New areas of development spread over a hilly landscape to form the high-rise hotel district overlooking the Mediterranean. It comprises a series of five star hotels such as the Phoenicia Intercontinental, Holiday Inn and Hilton, in addition to some

Figure 4.3. Middle East Airline summer timetable from 1953.

built in the late nineteenth century and the early decades of the twentieth century, and office buildings like Starco and St. Charles City Centre designed mostly by foreign architects in partnership with locals. Some sat directly along the bay (Saint Georges and Phoenicia Intercontinental), while others, like the Holiday Inn, were further uphill (figure 4.4). The result was the image of a modern urban landscape increasingly seen as Western (Arbid, 2002).

The expansion westward continued apace reaching Hamra. Its location west of the traditional city centre, in the heart of Ras Beirut and a few hundred metres from the campus of the American University of Beirut, made this expansion an immediate competitor to the Central District, attracting big businesses. The main commercial growth occurred in the 1960s with big name businesses such as Red Shoe, Domtex, Zahar, ABC and others opening branches there (Boudisseau, 1993). At the same time, an important commercial relocation took place; Lebanon Central Bank left the downtown area for Hamra, a move that was soon accompanied by foreign banks moving in the same direction, transforming the place into a financial zone. Hamra was also a meeting place for tourists, intellectuals and citizens from the more well-to-do walks of life, famous for its picturesque shop fronts with their elaborate ornamentation, the coffee shops, nightclubs, amusement centres, cinemas and its general bustle of activity. The growth and development that Hamra Street enjoyed was part of a process of urban transformation instigated by cultural and commercial connectivity to the Western world that appeared to be exclusive to Ras Beirut and the hotel district. In December 1971, a Lebanese Ministry of Tourism brochure likened Hamra Street in Beirut to the Champs Élysées in Paris, Regent Street in London, Via Veneto in Rome, Jose Antonio in Madrid, and Fifth Avenue in New York City, giving it the official name of 'Tourist Road' (*AsSiyaha*, December, 1971, pp. 8–9).

It is estimated that tourists using the airport reached more than 1.5 million in 1969 from around a quarter million in 1954. The growth was monitored by the Lebanese Council for Civil Aviation, formed in 1956, for the purpose of maintaining the airport's competitive regional status. Less than two decades after

Figure 4.4. An aerial view of the Hotel District from the early 1970s.

its construction a project of expansion was begun (Hayek and Rizk, 1968, p. 35). In mid-1968, a committee headed by the Minister of Public Works and Transportation was formed for this purpose. In March 1969, the Council of Ministers approved the project planned to be executed in two phases. The first phase focused on expanding the existing runways to accommodate the new generation of Jumbo jets. The second phase consisted of constructing a new runway to be completed in April 1971. Both phases were financed by the Lebanese private banks.[2] The continuous improvement and expansion work allowed Beirut International Airport (BIA) to register 46,505 take-offs and landings, and 1,156,565 passengers in 1966; to expand from thirty-eight airlines in 1962 to seventy-five international airlines by 1970 (*AsSiyaha*, August, 1971, p.15). BIA by the early 1970s functioned not only as the gate of Lebanon to the world but as a distribution aviation node for the region, increasing further Beirut's commercial importance. As work was being done on the airport, the Port of Beirut was itself the focus of expansion in the 1960s, the goal being to turn it into the largest *entrepôt* of transit in the region. Ownership was transferred from the French to the Lebanese, becoming the *Compagnie de Gestion et d'Exploitation du Port de Beyrouth*. Two basins were upgraded, a third basin completed, and a fourth planned, while the length of its wharf extended further, the number of warehouses grew and the free zone expanded (Babikian, 1997).

Many factors paralleled this transformation of the Central District from a local trading post into a regional economic node and led to Beirut being labelled the 'Paris of the Middle East'.[3] These included its first class luxury hotels complimented by a wide range of more moderately priced ones, the majority of which lined the waterfront and 'its flourishing banks [that] hide the secrets of international numbered accounts'. Possibly even more important was Beirut's nightlife. 'Beirut … is a very attractive and unusual city … if you arrive by air at night the lights of Beirut scintillate like stars thrown in the sea…'. Its 'gay nightlife' was highly prized. Varied were the nightspots that included 'stereo' clubs exclusively for dance and drink. Some even replicated the Parisian boulevard style with sidewalk seating, such as those seen on the Rue de la Paix.

> Beirut – outside its few museums – is a city enslaved by the ephemeral present, like New York or Tokyo, Maison Top Ten, Venus-Le Night Club a Grand Spectacle, Restaurant Lucullus, nearby Maameltein's Casino du Liban, the Crazy Horse Saloon, El Morroc and the Moulin Rouge: such discotheques, clubs, cabarets and restaurants… (Ward, 1971, p. 21)[4]

By the early 1950s, Beirut contained a total of almost 1,000 nightclubs, discos and pubs. The story of its nightlife stretches back as far as 1920 with the Zaytouni area near the hotel district being famous for the 'French Restaurant', 'Alfonse', and 'Lido'. Between 1955 and 1960, Beirut began leaning more and more towards noisier nightlife. Nightclubs in the Zaytouni district were either established independently or were included in the fancy hotels on the ground floor or on the roof. It was not long before the glorious days of Zaytouni gradually waned to be replaced in the early 1960s by new districts like Raouche, Jnah and Hamra Street (*AsSiyaha*, 1963, pp. 64–65). An area of approximately a square kilometre extending from Zaytouni to Phoenicia to Hamra Street, Ras Beirut and Raouche included twenty-one *plages*, fourteen nightclubs, 1,063 pubs, coffeehouses and restaurants, sixty cabarets and 156 cinemas (*AsSiyaha*, September/October, 1963, pp. 28–29).

Despite all the local efforts at promoting and maintaining Beirut's regional status, the Arab-Israeli conflict that had proved a blessing in the two decades following the formation of the State of Israel, came back to haunt the city, as the situation deteriorated once again in 1967 and 1973, slowing the flow of tourists into Lebanon. For a country that relied heavily on tourism this was of great concern to Lebanese officials and professionals in the tourist industry (Prost-Tournier, 1974, p. 369).[5] Being innovative, Middle East Airlines and British Overseas Airways Corporation (BOAC) collaborated with four major hotels – Al Bustan, Saint Georges, Vendôme and Phoenicia – to promote Beirut in the United States and Europe as 'the oldest and newest convention city'. The concept was born of Peter Rosini in London, a representative of BOAC and the person responsible for promoting London as the city of conventions. Beirut had all the potential to play this role, from a climate that allows the tourist to enjoy its coastal morning sun and in less than an hour ski on its snowy mountains, a shopping district for a variety of European, Asian and African products, banking facilities and exchange offices, and no restrictions on money imported to or exported from the country. Soon, Beirut hosted thirty-six conferences including international, regional and Arab medical conferences and hotel conventions (*AsSiyaha*, May, 1970, pp. 74–75). Other ideas were also considered such as 'Beirut, the city of festivals', and 'Beirut, the city of exhibitions'.

As the private sector worked tirelessly to redefine Beirut's role, during the Presidency of Fouad Chehab (1958–1964) the State promoted a climate of economic prosperity and diversity – the Golden Years. This term not only applied to the 6 year term of Chehab's presidency but to the entire period prior to the outbreak of the Civil War in 1975. The President and his administration focused on planned development and spatial management, particularly in the poorest areas of the country – areas that were largely ignored at the expense of the capital's economic and social dominance (Verdeil, 2003). The goal was to promote social justice and national unity. Two large-scale programmes were launched. One was concerned with tackling the country's development problems and the other the establishment of a number of institutions like the Directorate of Statistics, Council for the Implementation of Construction Projects and the Council for the Implementation of Large Scale Projects for the City of Beirut (Chami, 1962).[6] The former programme was initiated by a French research team from the *Institut International de Recherches et de Formation en Vue de Developpement* (IRFED) who produced a long-term plan that included a set of recommendations. However local and regional pressures blocked the implementation of these programmes and before long the study was shelved.

The impoverishment of the Lebanese countryside due to a decline in the agricultural sector was paralleled by a continuous process of growth and development in the service sector, largely concentrated in the capital. There were large waves of rural-urban migration and a subsequent rise in inequality among social and religious groups in Beirut, as the migrants settled on the urban periphery. These migrations continued apace well into the war period of 1975 to 1990 as Israel occupied Southern Lebanon. By 1970, these villagers, mainly Shiites, constituted 22 per cent of the total population living in Beirut and its suburbs. These internal movements occurred in parallel with regional transformation both within the Lebanese borders and neighbouring countries. Most important of these were the Arab-Israeli wars (1948, 1967) which threw up a large wave of Palestinian refugees (153,814) (Massabini, 1977, p. 153). In 1958, another wave of immigrants came into Lebanon, mainly Syrians (232,403), leaving their homes following the agricultural reforms there by the Baathist regime. During this phase, the total population of the city had almost doubled from 450,000 in the 1960s to 940,000 in the 1970s (Khalaf, 1973). Whether fleeing wars, autocratic regimes, or simply seeking a better life, the large numbers of Arabs and non-Arabs alike who claimed Beirut as a temporary home made it plausible to refer to the Lebanese capital as an immigrant centre as attested by Mahmud Darwish, the Palestinian writer, in his book, *Memory for Forgetfulness*.

> Beirut was an island upon which Arab [and non-Arab] immigrants dreaming of a new world landed. It was the foster mother of a heroic mythology that could offer the Arabs [and non-Arabs] a promise other than that born of war. (Darwish, 1995)[7]

But the immigrant city did not extend its benefits to all those newcomers and the promises of the modern city were enjoyed only by the privileged few; the migrants and refugees became marginalized. For a long time no official recognition was made of their presence in the hope or belief that they would eventually return to their original homes. An unstable security situation in certain parts of Lebanon in combination with continuous regional upheavals prolonged the stay of the 'temporary' Lebanese residents and Palestinian refugees living in slums, shantytowns and refugee camps surrounding Beirut. Although refugee camps and shantytowns are two distinct physical forms of settlement, they both came about through similar processes of struggle during the Independence era and up to 1982. The refugee camps are first and foremost legal settlements, often set up by an international body and the host country for a specified period of time. As for the Palestinian refugees in Lebanon, the United Nations Relief and Work Agency UNRWA leased several plots of land from the Lebanese State for a period of 99 years.[8] The location and the physical form of these settlements were determined by the Lebanese State. While the host country determined the socio-political status of the refugees, their means of survival remained the responsibility of UNRWA. This included delivering services such as education, health, relief and social services. The physical form of the camps was planned as a space of containment policed by the Lebanese State externally and managed internally by UNRWA. In parallel, squatter settlements of mainly village migrants were gradually appearing on the urban fringe, largely on agricultural or unattended public land, some near the refugee camps. The upward mobility that some refugees enjoyed saw them move out of the camps into the city, allowing them to lease their former homes to poorer new arrivals, Lebanese or otherwise. The result was 'mosaic' landscapes, each revealing the saga of a group of people, their struggles across time and space the outcome of which constituted the formation of two concentric 'rings of misery', one on the edge of municipal Beirut and the other within the Metropolitan Region of Beirut.[9] This exposes the contradictions of 'stability' that governed Beirut at the time, real instability which some decades later was blamed in part on the continuous influx of immigrants that not only transformed certain parts of Beirut into 'transitional homes' but also became the 'spaces of struggles' with the signing of the Cairo Agreement on 2 November 1969. From then on, the status of the refugee changed to that of resistance fighter.

The Cairo Agreement was reached between the Lebanese army general commander and Palestinian representatives, granting the Palestinians the right to carry weapons in the camps and attack Israel across Lebanon's southern border. The changing power relations among the refugees and the Lebanese State further complicated the development of their physical environment. The migrant residents transformed marginal spaces into homes from where they could start a new life, while the refugees used the camps to redefine their relationship with their former homeland and their host state. The result as described by Samir Khalaf (1993, p. 87) was a:

> burgeoning geography of fear [which] swiftly expanded. A feeling of enclosure, reinforced by ideologies of enmity towards the 'other', were the harbingers of darker days ahead. Indeed, the 'turf wars' between disenfranchised and threatened groups vying to protect, claim or reclaim their contested spaces within the inner city or the urban fringe, which had characterized the early rounds of civil strife, were largely a byproduct of such fears.

Only a few months after the agreement was reached, in March 1970, clashes erupted in Southern Lebanon resulting in Israeli raids that intensified over time, forcing the local inhabitants to abandon their villages and seek shelter in the southern suburbs of Beirut. Meanwhile, members of the Palestinian Liberation Organization (PLO) in Jordan fought the local military from September 1970 for a ten month period resulting in their elimination and expulsion to bases in Lebanon, an act which resulted in the influx of several hundred thousand refugees (El Khazen, 2000). The situation between the Palestinians and Israelis prior to the Cairo Agreement was already worsening. In response, the Israelis retaliated by attacking and destroying key Lebanese infrastructure including Beirut International Airport and MEA, the Lebanese national carrier. The first of these attacks happened in 1968 soon after the 1967 war, Israeli forces homing in on a

Figure 4.5. Aftermath of the Israeli attack on Beirut International Airport in 1968.

busy airport full of Arab and Western tourists and businessmen (*AlNidaa*, 19 May, 1991, p. 4).[10] The attack lasted 45 minutes, leaving behind more than a dozen MEA planes and hangars destroyed and fuel dumps in flames (figure 4.5). This attack came two days after a number of armed members of the Popular Front for the Liberation of Palestine opened fire in Athens on an El Al Boeing bound for New York, resulting in the death of one passenger. Although the physical damage caused was substantial, the greater harm was to the reputation of the airport, especially as the litany of aircraft hijackings carried out by PLO members in September 1970 saw the airport as one of the sites of these operations. The Lebanese State was quick to add security measures to its rebuilding and expansion project to counter the negative international media attention that the airport was receiving but it was not long before Israeli forces struck again, just 3 years after the first, this time destroying three MEA planes. The deterioration in the security situation at the airport was of grave concern to foreign airlines despite the measures taken by the Lebanese authorities to address these concerns such as the banning of taxis from parking in front of the departure and arrival building (*AsSiyaha*, 15 December, 1972/15 January, 1973, p. 57). It was the immediate environment, comprising illegal migrant housing and Palestinian refugee camps, that was viewed as posing the serious threat. Consequently, these shutdowns, perceived as isolated incidents became the norm both during the war (1975–1991) and after (1991–2006). From the outbreak of the Civil War in 1975 the airport started witnessing periods of total shutdown as a direct result of being targeted by local warring factions. Very quickly airlines boycotted the airport, from seventy-five international carriers, only one – the national carrier – remained. Once a hub for tourists, even the local population came to fear it, choosing alternative means of travel where possible. And so began a long dark chapter of three decades of shaken confidence in the role the capital used to play, as destruction extended from the airport to engulf the port and the Central District; Beirut became a theatre of intense fighting among warring factions who savagely targeted the symbols of its success.

A No-Place: Murder of the Capital by Militia

The Civil War began on 13 April 1975. It started on the periphery of Beirut and moved very quickly to the centre with the intention of destroying a homogeneous landscape that was the capital city's political, social and economic spatiality shared among the eighteen religious and sectarian Lebanese groups. These shared spaces occupied both the low ground of the traditional city centre and the high ground of its modern addition to the west. This process of deliberate destruction of the Central District unfolded in the first 2 years of the war. Heavy weaponry targeting larger areas, forced the retreat of fighting militias behind broader fronts and ultimately led to the drawing of the 'Green Line' that split the Central District into two and denuded it of its activities. Although the destruction of the infrastructure of the Central District saw the ruin of a regional economy, it failed to destroy totally the national economy, as this survived on the margins and witnessed the emergence of a militia economy in this first phase of the war (1975–1982) (Picard, 2000).

Following these acts of wide-spread destruction that included both the city's airport and the port, militia groups moved to control these key nodes to support their newly formed 'mini-states'. They also built and maintained their own infrastructure such as illegal ports that spread all along the Mediterranean coast. Turning the Central District into a backwater was largely completed in these first two years of the 16 year long war. This was achieved through a series of battles fought among members of militias organized under two umbrella movements polarized around the Left and Right wings of politics; the predominantly leftist group, together with the Palestinians, formed the National Movement; their rightist foes the Lebanese Front.[11] The transformation of the Central District was consolidated in two main ways. One, the separation was formalized along the 'Green Line', a division between East Beirut (predominantly Christian) and West Beirut (predominantly Muslim). Second, the political, social and economic life became decentralized. Although the process of destruction and control of Lebanese State institutions was completed only in the second half of the war (1983–1991), the focus of the rest of the section is on the first two years of the war, as the phase during which the Central District was turned into a no-man's land, and the subsequent process of destroying its regional role by militias, fronted, incidentally, by people who were senior in the official government.

The extension of control over the capital was achieved by key actions in the Central Business District (CBD) whereby assaults were directed at the *souqs* (the traditional markets), the quarters housing the legislative and executive power bases, and the hotel district where damage was greatest. The first of these actions took the form of a street battle in Martyrs' Square, in the centre of the CBD.[12] This was the people's premier public space in the capital, a point of convergence for rich, poor, Christian, Muslim, Lebanese and foreigner, alike. It was also the site of key governmental, commercial, financial and tourist activities. Additionally, Martyrs' Square was the hub for the transit system that linked most of the residential, commercial and industrial areas of the city. This mix of activities allowed it to become the most celebrated urban space in the CBD, serving as both a social and business space (figure 4.6).

Figure 4.6. Beirut's Central District 1975–1976.

Gunmen, carrying mostly small arms, stormed the square only four days after clashes erupted on the periphery. Buildings were set on fire. The first targets were the Opera House, the Police Central Offices, and the Rivoli Cinema. The battle extended west of the square to a number of *souqs* (the *souqs* of Sursock, Al-Nuriyah, Abu-Nasr)[13] and a modern office complex (Al-Azariyeh). First came looting and then fires that raged for four continuous days leaving the *souqs* in almost total ruin. The government was immediately hounded by the local merchants who accused it of failing to protect their interests. As a response to this outcry and in an effort to limit further destruction, the Governor of Beirut imposed a night-time curfew in some parts of the Central District (*AnNahar*, 20 September, 1975, p. 1).[14] This move had the opposite effect to that intended. The CBD became the private domain of the gunman and led to more devastation, particularly in areas previously unaffected by the bombing, as the fighting extended west to the site of Parliament. The Place de l'Etoile housed the legislative power and was the second on the list of contentious spaces. Gunmen set up 'mobile' checkpoints in Beirut, while random kidnapping and killing spread fear among people and politicians alike.

Despite a plan by the Leader of Parliament to ensure the safe arrival of the deputies in order to maintain an effective government, it was not long before parliamentary sessions were interrupted as the fighting intensified in the vicinity, thus making it difficult to reach Place de l'Etoile. This situation became an issue of concern for the majority of the deputies; some saw the solution as remaining in their traditional location, defying the gunmen with a sit-in. Others, however, suggested finding an alternative, more secure site. The majority rejected this latter proposition because approval would have not only meant giving up a specific place but also waiving parliamentary immunity. The consequences would have been the collapse of the legislative body of the State authority – the one authority with any possible hope of restoring sovereignty. The resistance by the deputies was met only by the gunmen attacking the parliamentary building, a situation described by the Speaker of the House as an attempt to:

assassinate the parliament as the premier democratic institution in Lebanon … part of a general destructive scheme to destroy all the public and state institutions … it is not going to succeed … that is why we decided to keep on meeting. (*AnNahar*, 20 September, 1975)

(Ironically, it was six months later that the parliamentary building received the direct hit that caused its ultimate surrender (*AnNahar*, 5 April, 1976).) An alternative place then had to be found. Villa Mansur located along the Beirut-Damascus Highway, or part of what became the Green Line, dividing East Beirut from West Beirut, in the vicinity of the National Museum, was selected to play the role of temporary parliament building.

The pressure of conflict was not consistent, however. After a few months of fighting, in September 1975, a cease-fire allowed life to become seemingly normal once again, with the traditional traffic jams on the streets and squares of the CBD. However, these jams were not caused by conditions normal to pre-war life. They were due to businesses removing their remaining assets, ironically enacting the unwritten policy of the warring factions to constrict the flow of the economic lifeblood in the heart of the capital. Snipers shooting anyone who moved then turned the CBD into a no-man's land. By night gunmen deployed to the older section of the town and the assault on the vital economic and social organs of the city was extended to the main shopping district known as Bab Idriss (*AnNahar*, 9 and 11 October, 1975). Bab Idriss included some of the famous *souqs* (Souq al-Tawileh and Souq al-Jamil) which were used not only by Lebanese of different religious and ethnic backgrounds but also by Europeans. Souq al-Tawileh housed the most fashionable boutiques in Beirut carrying the latest Parisian creations, Scottish tweeds and gowns from the famous *haute-couture* houses. Gunmen blew up some shops and set others on fire (figure 4.7). The destruction of the market area affected Christian and Muslim merchants alike.

While the battle in Bab Idriss lasted for two and a half months until December 1975, punctuated by a number of ceasefires, the fighting also extended west from the Central District to the residential areas of Ras Beirut. Characterized by tall buildings, this residential area would add a new dimension to the battle. Until that point in the war, the militias' control of space had been limited to the streets and neighbourhoods, but this soon changed as they were able to cash in on the value of there being no effective government control over their activities. They began the move from a horizontal to a vertical warfare. By now they had acquired longer range missiles. They moved to the higher ground, to the high-rises of the Western addition to the Central District. The first building to be seized was Burj al-Murr, a 32-storey tower block under construction, which dominated the capital's skyline. This was located only a few hundred metres from the seat of government (the Serail), which was subjected to direct hits as it became a prime target in the battle between two factions. One faction was able to control its burnt-out shell (after a fire claimed most of the structure and consumed all its historical documents including microfilm, the minutes of historic sessions and a collection of the official

Figure 4.7. Tackling the fires in the *souqs*, September 1975.

gazette). With that the capital lost its last remaining symbol of power, the executive (*AnNahar*, 22 January, 1976; 22–23 March, 1976).

Thereafter the warring factions moved to the hotel district located just a few hundred metres down the road where five star hotel complexes were concentrated along Minet al Husn, at the waterfront and west of the Port of Beirut (*AnNahar*, 8 December, 1975). For four months (December 1975 to March 1976) the hotel district remained one of the most active battlefronts centred around four major hotels, Saint Georges, Holiday Inn, Phoenicia and Hilton, the last being under construction at the time, all in an attempt to control the high ground. Forces of the Lebanese Front and the National Movement attacked and counter-attacked, taking and losing ground, but all the time draining more life from the city with the destruction of the hotel district, one building at a time. The subsequent retreat of the Lebanese Front back towards Bab Idriss and finally Martyrs' Square, caused more destruction to the downtown and the port area. The result of the fighting in this area extended the reach of the Palestinians and Murabitoun[15] from the southern suburbs to Martyrs' Square in the centre of the city. From this time, the infamous Green Line was drawn.[16] Economic and commercial life in the CBD was now effectively dead.

It was estimated that the fighting in the Hotel District caused the full or partial destruction of thirty-six luxury hotels including the Holiday Inn, Phoenicia Intercontinental, Saint Georges, Vendome, Martinez, Palm Beach, Kadmos,

Melkart, Beirut International and the Hilton. After just one month of battle, still localized around the three main hotels of Saint Georges, Phoenicia and the Holiday Inn, 18,000 jobs were estimated to have been lost (*AnNahar*, 19 December, 1975). The destruction spread to countless numbers of night-clubs, restaurants and coffee-shops in the area. In addition to the hotels that came under direct attack, of equal significance was the damage that extended to a number of major international hotels that were under construction with the result that some of these projects stopped indefinitely. Others, such as the Hilton, were complete and ready to start operations but, with just two weeks to go to the scheduled opening ceremony in early May 1975, the fighting meant that instead of welcoming its intended clientele of foreign businessmen and tourists, first through its doors were the militants.

Realizing that just destroying the Central District would not lead to the creation of homogeneous territorial entities, the warring factions battled each other on the periphery. On the eastern side, members of the Lebanese Front attacked Palestinian Refugee Camps and Shia Muslim slums, while members of the National Movement and Palestinian militants shelled the Christian areas in the southern suburbs (figure 4.8). The multiple small wars during 1975–1976 caused large waves of displacement, estimated at about 50 per cent of the population. Individuals crisscrossed the city, the region and the world. Lebanese of the Shiite Muslim majority and Palestinians moved from East Beirut to West Beirut and to the suburbs, abandoning the refugee camps and surrounding areas which included Tal al-Zaatar, Jisr al-Basha, and Burj Hammud, Naba, Ras adDikwani, Harit alGhawarni and Fanar. The majority of the displaced Lebanese headed for communal land (*musha'*) around Beirut Airport (Raml al-Ali, Uzai), deserted beach resorts (Jnah), and land in Hayy al-Sulum, Laylaki and Al-'Amsuriyyah; a minority returned to the south of the country and to the Biqa (Faour, 1993). Meanwhile counter movements by Christians took place between West Beirut (Ras Beirut, Hamra and Ramlat al-Bayda) and the southern suburbs (Harat Hrayk, Burj al-Barajni) (Faour, 1988, pp. 98–99). Their ultimate destination varied from East Beirut and its suburbs, to Europe or North America.

With the destruction of shared residential spaces, the fragmentation of the capital appeared complete with each group establishing control over a defined territory and key infrastructure nodes such as the airport and port. For both these two nodes, this was to mean a decade and a half of destruction and loss. For the Port of Beirut, this dark chapter began with the first round of fighting on the evening of 19 April 1975 when flames engulfed its warehouses. The damage caused was estimated in billions of Lebanese pounds, especially as operations at the port stopped for over a year. Before long, the fifth basin at the port was controlled by members of the Lebanese Front, and soon thereafter competition would emerge from the growth of illegal ports that spread all along the coast both south and north of the capital. The beginning of the end came in 1989, when the military government of General Michel Aoun declared war on the illegal ports, shutting them down by violent means (*AlHayat*, 7–8 October, 1989).[17]

Figure 4.8. Street warfare in the battle for the control of the periphery 1975–1976.

The airport remained the sole aerial connection to the world, sustaining direct attacks from both local warring factions and from Israeli forces from the early days of the war. These attacks caused its shutdown from June until end of December 1976. Repeated attacks and more destruction became the trend with every round of fighting, thereby making the swift resumption of activities very difficult. Sometimes it totally shut down to commercial traffic; it became a military base for the Israeli Forces during their three month siege of Beirut in the summer of 1982. Despite these events, Beirut International Airport was an important economic and public space for the militia of the southern suburbs; there was no alternative source of financial support for them and the airport provided jobs for thousands of Shiite migrants and the displaced. More than 500 individuals closely tied to Amal[18] were known to have held security jobs at the airport (Picard, 2000, p. 304). The control of this space was also important in that it further empowered their presence in the city, allowing them to make claims on the Lebanese State and on the world at large. None of this, however, prevented the government from devising reconstruction plans for these key nodes, most of which were shelved as another round of fighting broke out.

The Reworking of a Globalizing City Centre

The end of 15 years of Civil War in 1991 meant that physical reconstruction could 'officially' begin. This, however, was simply the latest round because reconstruction was very much a feature of the war period as well as the destruction. In fact, the end of every round of fighting marked the beginning of another round of reconstruction; some of these processes were led by the State and others left to private initiatives. Two such moments in particular saw the design of large-scale plans for the rebuilding of the Central District: the first following the first two years of conflict in 1977 and the second in 1983 following the Israeli invasion of Beirut the previous year. As with every ceasefire-inspired endeavour, the focus was to rebuild the city centre to its pre-war status in the Middle East and the Gulf. Unlike earlier attempts of reconstruction, the latter case saw one key question dominate the debate among professionals and the Lebanese public: could the decline that Beirut witnessed over the course of the war years be reversed? In other words, was it a priority to rebuild the Central District, especially as the emerging post-war State was a shambles and needed reorganization down to the core of every institution. The social landscape was in a far worse condition, with more than half the population displaced. That was at the local level. At the regional level, while Beirut was in decline, other capital cities in the region were expanding and taking over the role that the Lebanese capital once played. Key sectors of the economy fled during the war. For example, some of the international financial institutions, firms, insurance companies and banks left Beirut for Amman, Cairo and Dubai (Hanf, 1993, p. 349). Others simply closed, particularly those in the tourist sector. An even more important factor is the volatile political and military situation between Israel and Lebanon as has been witnessed in the decade since the launch of the nation's reconstruction programmes. Israeli forces have repeatedly targeted key infrastructure including the international airport and major power stations. The last round came in the summer of 2006, where, along with the airport and power stations, the Israeli Defense Forces targeted all the major highways and bridges linking Beirut to the rest of the country and beyond to the Arab World.

Despite everything, the Lebanese State opted for reconstruction of the war-torn Central District. After all, the presence of a central business district in a city has significance symbolically and has, since the mid-1980s, been viewed 'as the command post in the global economy' (Abbott, 1996, p. 405). If Beirut was to be put back on the regional map, the argument in favour of rebuilding its financial and administrative centre was indisputable. The launching of such an endeavour depended on a range of issues; key among them was acquiring the money to jump-start the project and to devise a strategy to deal with the complex patterns of ownership. But the recreation of this node also depended on its link to other nodes in the network and that would only be possible through infrastructure which was itself in almost total ruin due to the heavy damage sustained during the Civil War years. This meant that the reconstruction of the Central District was also about the redevelopment of Beirut International Airport, the Port of Beirut, and the development and expansion of a road network that would connect these three nodes; a framework that the Lebanese Company for the Development and

Reconstruction of Beirut (*Société Libanaise pour le développement et la reconstruction de Beyrouth*), known as Solidere from its French acronym, used to promote its project for the reconstruction of the Central District.

The absence of funds for reconstruction and especially those required to kick start the first phase was a challenge that would be resolved through a partnership between the government and the private sector with the aim of establishing a private real-estate company which would oversee the reconstruction. In fact, the legal framework of such a company was formed in 1962 (Kabbani, 1996).[19] The most innovative aspect of the project was the strategy devised by the real-estate company to come up with the funds necessary to start the process: land ownership was converted into shares in the company. As to how planners envisioned the role and form of downtown Beirut, this had changed little from those prevalent in the half century since independence from France in 1943 when Beirut changed from a showcase of France in the Levant to become a regional node. The process of reinserting Beirut into the global circuits from the early 1990s to the summer of 2006 will form the story of the rest of this section. This is not only a story of the physical reconstruction of the three key spaces – the Central Business District, the airport and port – but is also one of reclaiming the Central District by its 'traditional' actors or groups with visions of Beirut as a future global node.

The major reconstruction programmes were launched as soon as the guns fell silent in 1991 and the physical barriers between East Beirut and West Beirut were removed. A Master Plan was prepared by Dar Al-Handasah Consultants (DAR)[20] and commissioned by the Lebanese Council for Development and Reconstruction (CDR), a public authority formed in 1977. The 1991 Master Plan, prepared by Henri Edde, imagined the city as a mixed-use centre with open spaces and modern infrastructure. The plan called for a total demolition of the historic core and replacement by modern buildings. Three major north–east axes shaped the design of the new city centre, a reinforcement of those historically present in the city. Martyrs' Square is the site of the most striking of those axes. Edde proposed the replacement of the square by an avenue '10 meters wider than the Champs Elysees' (Sarkis, 1993, p.115). Moreover, the plan featured references to different places around the world. For instance, marking the edge of the CBD were to be twin towers representative of the World Trade Center in Manhattan, while other parts hinted at Florence, Washington and London.

Underlying this project were several assumptions, such as the creation of a real-estate company that was to be in charge of financing and implementing the project. Opponents of the plan saw the establishment of this company as sidestepping the role of the public sector to form a monopoly by the private sector over what was considered to be the largest project in the history of the country. More importantly, one outcome of the project would be the 'increased fragmentation of property rights'. The new company would expropriate all the land in the Central District, exchanging ownership rights for shares in the enterprise. Supporters, on the other hand, saw the company as the 'only realistic' solution to the then political situation, the widespread corruption, and the distrust in the public sector. Perhaps the most controversial aspect of the Master Plan was its treatment of the Central District as a clean slate requiring the bulldozing of all buildings, private and public, and monuments, ruined or not, to be replaced by modern buildings. This led eventually to DAR's plan being ditched and work starting on a new master plan.

The new plan was approved by the Lebanese Cabinet in October 1992, a more detailed one in February 1994 and implementation in September of the same year. This approval was only the beginning of a legal and administrative battle for the real-estate company that would be incorporated in May 1994. So the private share-holding company, Solidere, was created by the Lebanese government to manage the entire process of reconstruction and renewal of infrastructure of the CBD. In turn, the company was granted exemption from taxes for 10 years as well as exclusive development rights in the reclaimed zone (figure 4.9). Its operations were divided into four main functions: supervision of the government-authorized reconstruction plan;[21] financing and rebuilding the infrastructure; rehabilitation work and development of the real estate; and the management of property (Solidere, 1993).

Solidere expropriated all property in the Central District, transforming these parcels into shares that formed the capital of the company. Shares were of two types. Type A was issued to the original property owners in the Central District, for an equivalent value of their property, as determined by Solidere's board of founders. Type B shares were issued to potential investors to draw in additional funds. Purchase of shares was limited to Lebanese citizens and companies, Lebanese state and public institutions, and people of Lebanese descent, and Arabs. Non-Arabs could not buy shares unless they were original property holders. They could only buy in after construction was completed. Predictably, the property for shares scheme caused uproar, as did the process of assigning share value to the land. Not only did physical ownership turn into an abstract commodity but both the value of the share and location in the city of the future was to be determined solely by the company. Opposition was widespread, including intellectuals, planners, architects, landowners, property owners and Beirutis in general.

Figure 4.9. The waterfront and reclaimed land in 2007.

Solidere countered this opposition with a very sophisticated multimedia campaign. For this purpose, the company organized public talks, information sessions, and conferences. Two of the major slogans that dominated the promotional campaign were 'Beirut is for you, ask for it', and 'Beirut the ancient city of the future' (Makdisi, 1997). The opposition was won over and share issue was over-subscribed by 142 per cent. Reconstruction could begin.

Initially, the reconstruction of the 'finest city centre' was to be completed in three phases to span over a period of 25 years. The first phase started soon after the creation of the company in May 1994 with the focus on infrastructure, underground parking, marine works and landfill treatment. Plans were devised for the development of the hotel district, the residential areas of Saifi and Wadi Abou Jamil, and the traditional *souqs*. Once considered a core feature of the Central District, Solidere used the reconstruction of the *souqs* to help Beirut regain its place on the world stage by launching an international competition, with its theme being 'the design of the new Souqs of Beirut'. The main objective was to design for a mercantile community that characterized pre-war Beirut and which during the war migrated to different districts within the metropolitan area or beyond. This migration resulted in a loss of its function as a commercial space and hub, signifying the loss of the CBD's identity.

The design of the new *souqs*, according to Solidere, is a project for the reconstruction of a physical and social environment that would allow for diversity and interaction, helping to rejuvenate the heart of the war-torn city. Among the most important elements the programme called for is the preservation, rehabilitation, and reconstruction of specific buildings on the competition site and also a street network that follows the traditional Hellenistic street grid uncovered by the archaeologists. However, while Solidere was calling for such a programme, demolition was in progress after the archaeologists completed their dig. In the company's promotional campaign, archaeology was a primary tool. Claiming to uncover Beirut's past, Solidere funded archaeological digs. However, following a blaze of initial publicity before local and international media, economic considerations took over and the excavation for foundations and the ensuing construction destroyed the archaeological remains. The physical remains of a history spanning the ancient world, the medieval period and the Ottoman Empire have been lost forever. In exceptional cases, remains were retained to avoid potential conflict such as the preservation of a shrine that was excavated in the traditional market place.

However, the renovation and rebuilding work of a globalizing city centre cannot be divorced from the supportive infrastructure, an aspect that time and again was emphasized by the company's glossy publication which focused on the location of the Central District being less than 5 kilometres from Beirut International Airport, and adjacent to the port. With the completion of a series of highways and underpasses linking the Central District to the airport and to the peripheral suburbs, a trip from the Central District to the newly expanded

Beirut International Airport could be completed in seven minutes. In fact, the renovation and expansion of the airport started as soon as the war ended in 1991. As mentioned earlier, both the Central District and the airport had been the focus of repeated attempts at reconstruction during the war and, more importantly, had both been the subject of much debate regarding the usefulness of rebuilding for the purpose of restoring them to their pre-war role. The pre-war airport operated as the airport for Arabs who came to Beirut as tourists or were in transit between the Gulf and Europe. However, while the Civil War was raging in Lebanon the region moved on with, for example, the construction of more modern airports that would draw even more business from beleaguered Beirut. Furthermore, the project of developing and expanding the airport was an expensive endeavour that seemed to lack justification in light of the local domestic and regional political uncertainties: the State was in debt and lacked the financial means to fund reconstruction and there was a volatile political situation created by the continued occupation of Southern Lebanon by Israeli forces. The latter would prove the biggest headache in the decade that followed the end of the war as the Israeli Defense Forces were repeatedly to target key infrastructure nodes, with the airport forming a primary target as evidenced most recently in July 2006.

In spite of these challenges, the Lebanese State opted not only to renovate but to expand and develop the airport. Symposia were held for this purpose and attended by public officials, representatives of engineering companies, consultants, engineers and architects, and sponsored by private groups, banks and engineering firms (*AlDiyar*, 6 September, 1993).[22] In fact, just as Solidere started reconstruction in the Central District in 1994 so did the work on the airport. A master plan was devised with an initial goal to increase the annual passenger capacity to 6 million, to be achieved in its first phase (1994–1998). The goal thereafter was a gradual increase to 16 million passengers by 2035 (CDR, 2005). In the first 4 years, a new passenger terminal and two new runways were built. Since 1998, the work has mainly been concerned with the construction of various supporting facilities.

The second phase of reconstruction began in 2004, a few years later than anticipated, with work focused on the planning of large-scale real-estate projects, designs of the new waterfront district and completion of restoration work in some of the residential districts. Local and regional challenges have forced a slow down in some of the company's work, causing a modification to the anticipated phasing for the completion of the project. For instance, the tremendous support Solidere enjoyed in the first few years came from the Lebanese cabinet and more specifically from its Prime Minister Rafiq al-Hariri, believed to be the largest shareholder. This changed when Hariri was replaced by Salim Al Hoss in 1998, who was to lead the cabinet until 2000, a period that witnessed a slow down in Solidere's work. The return of Hariri as Prime Minister in 2000 reinvigorated the company and its work, which thereafter became more imaginative and creative by launching various competitions; the latest of which was announced in June 2004 for Martyrs' Square and the Grand Axis of Beirut. But before the results of the competition were announced, Solidere suffered a blow so fundamental that it was felt far beyond the Central District and which revived dormant questions about the ability of Beirut ever to dust off the taint of war and destruction. On 14 February 2005, almost a decade and a half after the hotel district was swept clean of shells, 1,000 tons of explosives blasted its heart out and killed the prime minister, causing extensive damage to surrounding hotels and, more importantly, shattering the image of the city still rising from the ashes. However, life went on in typical Lebanese fashion; Solidere quickly resumed its activities, launching new construction projects, welcoming new businesses as well as old, organizing or hosting conferences and exhibitions, concerts, sport events, and scores of visitors including businessmen seeking investment opportunities, tourists and locals alike simply seeking to enjoy the downtown area.

Conclusion: What Next?

As I conclude this piece, it is the summer of 2007, one year on from the beginning of a new chapter in the transformation of the Beirut landscape, especially its Central District. From early 1991 the Central District was the site of major post-war reconstruction, reaching the apogee of stability by mid-2006 as seen in the levels of tourism and foreign investment. In the first half of 2006, investment in the real-estate sector in the Central District alone amounted to at least US$7,200 million as evidenced by the Damac Properties residential tower on the waterfront and the US$600 million Beirut Gate from Abu Dhabi Investment House, the single largest private investment to date in the Central District (*Le Commerce du Levant*, May, 2006, pp. 78–79).

On 12 July 2006 all new-found optimism evaporated. A full scale war broke out with Israel. The International Airport and the sea ports were bombed to closure, resulting in an effective siege that cut the city off from the outside world. Hotels emptied as tourists fled the country, foreign business and investment froze and the heart of the capital came to a total standstill.

The end of the war just a few weeks later, however, did not see a return to the new-found 'normality'. In fact, the end of hostilities signalled the start of a year long internal struggle for the spaces of the Central District that was once more under siege. Its two major squares (Martyrs' Square and Riad as Sulh) are occupied by protestors bidding to topple the pro-Western government, the seat of which is located a few miles distant in the hilltop Serail (figure 4.10). This conflict, while currently free of violence, is more complicated than the previous ones fought in this space but retains the regional and global hues from those past struggles. This current protest has once again sucked the lifeblood out of the heart of the capital: eight months into the protest, bankruptcies directly related to the protest accounted for the demise of more than 120 institutions, both tourist and commercial (*AlMustaqbal*, 10 July, 2007, pp. 1 and 12).[23]

Instead of toppling the government, however, the protestors have contributed to the paralysis of the Lebanese State and seen a populace that welcomed a third of those displaced by the war in its schools and public spaces turn hostile. The controlling of public space is not exclusive just to the Central District; it has become the norm for the whole of Beirut. Politicians, fearful of assassination, have turned their residences into gated camps secured by roads shut off to traffic and various other forms of defence. Similarly, the Serail, the seat of government, has become a fortified castle on the hill overlooking the city. Since the beginning of the protest in late 2006, it has become the permanent residence for the prime minister and members of his cabinet. Concrete walls have become a necessary part of the landscape as their presence now is on streets around hotels, as well as public and commercial buildings.

As Beirut turns its back to the local and non-local alike, the future of the Central District is again in question. These recent events have revealed that the political divisions are deep, a sharp reminder that a flourishing Beirut is as dependent today on the volatility of the region's politics as it always has been. So what is the significance of all the development and reconstruction since 1990 today? Will the expectations of Solidere and its backers be met and Beirut become once more prominent on the regional map? The history of Beirut, the topography and the geographical location of the Central District, in addition to being the hub of tourist and business activities, coupled with *laissez-faire* economic policies that favour business, are all promising factors. If the various Lebanese factions can resist treating Beirut as the main battlefield in the 'War for the Others' then stability will reign for the long haul. Despite the current profound political divisions and the

Figure 4.10. Riad as Sulh Square in the Central District occupied by anti-government protestors.

deteriorating security situation, there is growing foreign interest, both regional and global, in Beirut's real-estate market. According to various media reports, it is estimated that over 2 million square metres were sold to foreigners in the first half of 2007 (*AlSharq AlAwsat*, 21 July, 2007).[24] This is not too surprising considering the real-estate market of the Central District remained attractive even during the darkest days of the 1975–1990 war when it was commonly seen as a backwater and alternative business centres were springing up elsewhere. Back then there were moments when the square metre price skyrocketed, such as in November 1981 when the price increased over 350 per cent above its 1978/1979 price. In Souq Idriss alone, thirty-three transactions were recorded in 1981 and seven in 1980 (*AlDustour*, 30 November, 1981, pp. 35–37).[25] It is the persistent refusal of both the Lebanese State and professionals not to give up on reconstruction in the heart of the capital during periods of calm that has been instrumental in maintaining the concept of the Central District. There is no reason to doubt the continuance of this historical trend.

Despite the long struggle ahead for Beirut to reclaim its regional role, there are clear signs that it has the potential to rise once again. The changes at the Port of Beirut as well as the airport, in addition to the branching out of Lebanese banks across the Arab world, all attest to this. The Port of Beirut has been the focus of rehabilitation and construction work on its five basins since the mid-1990s so that it is positioned to reclaim its pre-war role of regional maritime hub, an investment that is starting to pay-off. In August 2005, the Port Authority signed a deal with the Swiss Mediterranean Shipment Company to use the port as a trans-shipment centre for goods coming from the Far East to the Arab World. According to the President of the International Chamber of Navigation, many more companies approached the port authority for similar deals, but these had to be declined until further expansion work was completed (*Daily Star*, 11 August 2005, p. 8).[26] No physical development will be sufficient, however, unless policies are enacted to open up the economy and allow these spaces to compete with other nodes in the region. More legislation, such as the 'open skies' policy of 2001, is required. This encouraged foreign airlines to 'increase the number of flights they operate point-to-point between Beirut and another city' (*Daily Star*, 12 July, 2000) and resulted in more passengers, mainly tourists, using the airport: this reached 1.3 million travellers in 2005. In spite of the assassination of Prime Minister Hariri that same year, the government has been actively promoting Lebanon as a tourist destination, spending over a million dollars on a worldwide advertising campaign for this purpose in 2006 (*Daily Star*, 17 March, 2006, p. 7). Just as this investment was starting to show a return, the latest conflict with Israel erupted. Although the post cease-fire political situation is still in turmoil, one bright spot is Lebanon's banking system. More and more Lebanese banks have adopted expansionist policies, branching out to the Arab world and introducing new services. This is very encouraging as it was always the banking sector that underpinned Beirut's reputation as the region's premier financial locale in the pre-war era.

As Beirut is shaping itself for the future, it is relying as much as ever on its traditional pillars of strength.

Notes

1. *AsSiyaha*, or *Tourism*, was an independent weekly photographic magazine, concentrating on tourism, the economy and immigration. It was published by Adib Mroueh between 1963 and 1975 and distributed in the Gulf States, Syria, Iraq, Jordan, Sudan, Libya and Tunis, in addition to Lebanon.

2. Bank Lyonnais paid for the acquisition of the surrounding land on which the new runway was built, turning it from private to government ownership.

3. Beirut, like many other capitals, acquired a range of unofficial names, some whose sources are known while others remain unknown like 'Paris of the Middle East'. Some of the known names are 'Switzerland of the East' by Lamartine as quoted by the authors of *La Revue Phenicienne* in 1919. And a guide from the 1930s, predicted the future of the city as the 'Nice of the Levant' as the image of the capital was marked by high society occupying the salons, impressing the visitors with their elegance and multilingual abilities. It was a world that offered the visitor plenty of desired resources during their stay (Kassir, 2003).

4. 'Casino du Liban' was built in 1959. It is made up of gaming rooms, a theatre and spectacular dinners, making it one of the biggest casinos in the world. Since it opened, the casino has played a major role in the development of tourism in Lebanon. Nine months after it opened its doors, it has captured 29 per cent of the tourists and by 1966, 72 per cent of its clients were tourists.

5. It is estimated that tourism counted 16 per cent of the total GNP in 1972, while in 1965, tourism made up 20 per cent of the total GNP.

6. The long-term plan was commonly known as the *Plan Perspectif* spanning between 4 to 6 years. The recommendations included improvements in the following areas: hydraulic engineering, roads, transport, ports, airports, energy, agriculture, industrial and craft education, applied research and tourism. Based on these recommendations, the government set a new development planning policy such as 5-year irrigation plans, potable water and infrastructure in remote areas.

7. Mahmud Darwush is a Palestinian writer, born in 1942 in the Upper Galilee village of Birwe. Destroyed in 1948, the inhabitants of the village fled north. Mahmud and his parents made their journey north into South Lebanon eventually arriving in Beirut. It was not long before his parents returned to what became the new State of Israel, staying until 1972 when they again made their way to Beirut. This time, Mahmud stayed long enough to live the horrible days of the 1982 Israeli aggression on Beirut. *Memory for Forgetfulness* is the product of the agonizing days of the invasion as lived one hot summer day in August of that year. Originally written in Arabic *Dhakirah lil Nisyan: al Zaman.* (Bayrut: al-makan, yawm min ayyam Ab, 1982).

8. UNRWA was formed in 1949 to assist Palestinian refugees in the Occupied Territories and the Arab World by providing educational, social and healthcare services.

9. According to the last major planning study (*Schéma Directeur 1987*) approved by government, the Beirut Metropolitan Region or the BMR extends over an area of 218 km² equivalent to 2.1 per cent of the whole country. It extends along the Mediterranean coast and rises up to a height of 400 m to the east. From the north it is bounded by the Dog River and from the south by the Damour River.

10. *AlNidaa* was published by the Lebanese Communist Party in 1970 as a local political newspaper.

11. The National Movement included Arab political parties such as the Iraqi Baath Party and the Egyptian Nasserites, while the Lebanese Front was composed of a coalition of Christian militant groups, dominated by the Kata'ib, the National Liberal Party, the Marada brigade, the Tanzim and the Guardians of the Cedars.

12. Originally a garden, it was replaced in 1884 by a square dedicated to Sultan Abdel Hamid II, becoming Al Hamidiyeh. In 1916, the execution of Syrian Lebanese nationalists on the square led to its being renamed Martyrs' Square (Tuwayni, 2000).

13. Souq Sursock was a street on which textiles were traded, mainly by Muslim merchants; Souq Al-Nuriyah was a meat and vegetable market; Souq Abu-Nasr was the local and oriental spice market.

14. *AnNahar* was founded in 1933 as an Arabic daily newspaper. It follows an independent political line, although at times it was seen to be pro-Western in its views during the war years of 1975 to 1990, as well as being viewed as pro-government in the current political standoff in Lebanon.

15. Murabitoun is the militant wing of the Movement of the Independent Nasserites. It was founded in 1958 as a neighbourhood group that was a strong supporter of the Palestinian Liberation Organization (PLO) and, consequently, a strong opponent of members of the Lebanese Front, a coalition of right-wing groups. The PLO was both the main financial beneficiary and military backer of the Murabitoun until the latter's collapse in the mid-1980s.

16. The location of the Green Line neatly divides the city geographically and was the point at which the Muslim and Christian communities met. It was also a point of equilibrium strategically and militarily.

17. *AlHayat* is a leading international Arabic daily, published in London with a worldwide distribution since re-launching in 1988. Conservative in its views, it is sympathetic to pro-Western governments in the region. Like the *Daily Star*, *AlHayat* was founded by Kamel Mroueh in 1946 in Beirut, where it was published until its enforced suspension in 1976.

18. Amal (Hope) is a Shiite Muslim militia formed in 1974 by the Imam Musa Sadr, a Lebanese cleric educated in Iran and a member of the National Front.

19. Article 19 of a law enacted by the Lebanese government to establish the Higher Commission of Urban Planning laid out the parameters of forming a real-estate company. Since then several decrees have been issued adding to the original HCUP, detailing both administrative aspects and modes of operation of the company.

20. Dar al-Handasah is a major consulting firm in Lebanon and the region.

21. The authorized approved Master Plan includes: 1. public and religious buildings; 2. the preserved historic core of the city; 3. new developed financial district; 4. the traditional souqs area; 5. mixed-used area; 6. residential area; 7. public parks and squares; 8. archaeological excavation area; and 9. marinas (Solidere, 1993).

22. *AlDiyar* is a local Arabic daily newspaper. Founded in 1988 by Charles Ayoub, previously a member of the Syrian Nationalist Party, it postures a pro-Syrian Regime view.

23. *AlMustaqbal* is a local daily Arabic newspaper founded by the former Lebanese Minister Rafic Hariri in 1999.

24. *AlSharq AlAwsat* is a local Saudi Arabian newspaper founded in 1978.

25. *AdDastour* was an international Arabic political weekly magazine published in London during the early 1980s.

26. *Daily Star* is a local English language Lebanese newspaper founded in 1952 by Kamel Mroueh. Although its publication was stopped during the war of 1975–1990, it returned very briefly in 1985, only resuming full publication once more in 1996. From then it became the leading English newspaper in the region. In 2000, it partnered with the *International Herald Tribune*, representing it in the Gulf States, Syria, Egypt, Yemen and Iraq. It is perceived as a conservative, pro-government, pro-Western newspaper.

References

Abbott, Carl (1996) Five strategies for downtown: policy discourse and planning since 1943, in Corbin Sies, M. and Silver, C. (eds.) *Planning the Twentieth-Century American City.* Baltimore, MD: The Johns Hopkins University Press, pp. 404–427.

Arbid, George (2002) Practising Modernism in Beirut: Architecture in Lebanon, 1946–1970. Unpublished dissertation, Harvard University, Cambridge, MA.

Babikian, Christine (1997) Développement du Port de Beyrouth et hinterland, in Arnaud, J. (ed.)

Beyrouth, Grand-Beyrouth. Beyrouth: Centre d'Etudes et de Recherches sur le Moyen Orient Contemporain.

Berman, M. (1996) Falling towers: city life after urbicide, in Crow, D. (ed.) *Geography and Identity*. Washington DC: Maisonneuve Press, pp. 172–192.

Boudisseau, Guillaume (1993) *L'évolution des fonctions de la rue Hamra (Beyrouth, Liban) de 1975–1992*. Tours: Université François Rabelais.

Castells, M. and Mollenkopf, J.H. (1991) *Dual City: Restructuring New York*. New York: Russell Sage Foundation.

CDR (2005) *Progress Report*. Beirut: Council for Development and Reconstruction.

Chami, Jean (1962) Le Ministère du Plan fait peau neuve. *L'Orient*, 31 May–1 June.

Coward, M. (2004) Urbicide in Bosnia, in Graham, S. (ed.) *Cities, War, and Terrorism: Towards an Urban Geopolitics*. Malden, MA: Blackwell Publishing, pp. 154–171.

Darwish, Mahmud (1995) *Memory for Forgetfulness: August, Beirut 1982*. Berkeley, CA: University of California Press.

Davie, May (2001) *Beyrouth 1825–1975: un siècle et demi d'urbanisme*. Beirut: Publications de l'Ordre des Ingénieurs et Architects de Beyrouth.

El Khazen, Farid (2000) *The Breakdown of the State of Lebanon*. London: I.B. Tauris.

Fa'ur, 'Ali (1993) *The Geography of Displacement*. Beirut: Dar al-Mu'assasah al-Jughrafiyah (in Arabic, *Jughrafiyat al-tahjir al-sukkani: dirasat maydaniyah waqa'i'wa-hulul*).

Faour, Ali (1988) Al-Harb wa al-Tahjir al-Sukani fi Lubnan. *Al-Mustaqbal al-Arabi*, **114**, pp. 98–99.

Fawaz, Leila (1983) *Merchants and Migrants in Nineteenth-century Beirut*. Cambridge, MA: Harvard University Press.

Freiha, Asma (1992) *Les Libanais et la vie au Liban: de l'independence à la guerre, 1943–1975*. Beyrouth: Dar al-Sayad.

Gavin, Angus (1996) *Beirut Reborn: The Restoration and Development of the Central District*. London: Academy Editions.

Graham, S. (2004) *Cities, War, and Terrorism: Towards an Urban Geopolitics*. Oxford: Blackwell.

Hayek, A. and Rizk, R. (1968) *Al-Mouhandess: Lebanese Engineering Achievements*. Beirut: Edited Magazine of the Order of Engineers and Architects.

Hanf, Theodor (1993) *Coexistence in Wartime Lebanon: Decline of a State and Rise of a Nation*. London: Centre for Lebanese Studies in association with I.B. Tauris.

Hanssen, Jens (2005) *Fin de Siècle Beirut: The Making of an Ottoman Provincial Capital*. New York: Oxford University Press.

Hudson, Michael (1968) *The Precarious Republic*. New York: Random House.

Huybrechts, Eric (2002) Beirut: building regional circuits, in Sassen, S. (ed.) *Global Networks, Linked Cities*. New York: Routledge, pp. 237–246.

Kabbani, Oussama. (1992) *Prospects for Lebanon: The Reconstruction of Beirut*. London: Centre for Lebanese Studies.

Kabbani, Oussama (1996) Solidere: the case of Beirut Central District, in Barakat, Sultan (ed.) *Urban Triumph or Urban Disaster? Dilemmas of Contemporary Post-war Reconstruction*. York: University of York Press, pp. 63–72.

Kassir, Samir (2003) *Histoire de Beyrouth*. Paris: Fayard.

Khalaf, Samir (1973) Urbanization and urbanism in Beirut: some preliminary results, in Brown, Carl (ed.) *From Madina to Metropolis: Heritage and Change in the Near Eastern City*. Princeton, NJ: The Darwin Press.

Khalaf, Samir (1993) *Beirut Reclaimed: Reflections on Urban Design and the Restoration of Civility*. Beirut: Dar An-Nahar.

Khalaf, Samir and Khoury, Philip S. (eds.) (1993) *Recovering Beirut: Urban Design and Post-war Reconstruction*. Leiden: Brill.

Lambourne, Nicola (2001) *War Damage in Western Europe: the Destruction of Historic Monuments during the Second World War*. Edinburgh: Edinburgh University Press.

Ley, David (2004) Transnational spaces and everyday lives. *Transactions of the Institute of British Geographers*, **29**(2), pp. 151–164.

Makdisi, Saree (1997) Laying claim to Beirut: urban narrative and spatial identity in the age of Solidere. *Critical Inquiry*, **23**, pp. 661–705.

Massabini, Micheline (1977) Contradictions urbaines et guerre civile: la destruction du bidonville de 'la Quarantaine' à Beyrouth. *International Journal of Urban and Regional Research*, **1,** p. 153.

Picard, E. (2000) The political economy of civil war in Lebanon, in Heydemann, S. (ed.) *War, Institutions, and Social Change in the Middle East.* Berkeley, CA: University of California Press, pp. 292–321.

Prost-Tournier, Jean Marc (1974) Le Liban: premier pays touristique du Moyen-Orient Arabe. *Revue de Geographie de Lyon*, **49,** pp. 369–376.

Roger, Jean (1941) Reconstruction. *Urbanisme*, October–November.

Rosenberg, E., Horowitz, A. and Alessandrini, A. (2003) Iraq reconstruction tracker. *Middle East Report*, **227,** pp. 28–31.

Rowe, Peter G. and Sarkis, Hashim (eds.) (1998) *Projecting Beirut: Episodes in the Construction and Reconstruction of a Modern City.* New York: Prestel.

Ruppert, Helmut (1999) *Beyrouth, une ville d'Orient marquée par l'Occident.* Beyrouth: Centre d'Etudes et de Recherches sur le Moyen-Orient Contemporain.

Safier, Michael (2001) Confronting urbicide. *City*, **5**(3), pp. 416–429.

Saliba, Robert (1998) *Beirut 1920–1940: Domestic Architecture Between Tradition and Modernity.* Beirut: The Order of Engineers and Architects.

Saliba, Robert (2004) *Beirut City Centre Recovery: The Foch-Allenby and Etoile Conservation Area.* London: Thames & Hudson.

Sarkis, Hashim (1993) Territorial claims, in Khalaf, S. and Khoury, P.S. (eds.) *Recovering Beirut: Urban Design and Post-war Reconstruction.* Leiden: Brill.

Short, J.R., Breitbach, C., Buckman, S. and Essex, J. (2000) From world cities to gateway cities: extending the boundaries of globalization theory. *City*, **4**(3), pp. 317–340.

Solidere (1993) *Information Brochure. The Development and Reconstruction of the Beirut Central District.* Beirut: Solidere Communications Division.

Tuwayni, Ghassan (2000) *Bourj Place de la Liberté et Porte du Levant.* Beirut: Dar al-Nahar.

Verdeil, E. (2003) Politics, ideology and professional interests: foreign versus local planners in Lebanon under President Chehab, in Nasr, J. and Volait, M. (eds.) *Urbanism: Imported or Exported? Native Aspirations and Foreign Plans.* Chichester: Wiley-Academy, pp. 290–315.

Vincent, Jean (1943) *La reconstruction des villes et des immeubles sinistres après la guerre de 1940.* Paris: Impr. Bishop.

Ward, Philip (1971) *Touring Lebanon.* London: Faber and Faber.

Chapter 5

Rabat: From Capital to Global Metropolis

Jamila Bargach

In the final chapter of *Rabat: Urban Apartheid in Morocco*, Janet Abu-Lughod (1980), having completed an empirical analysis confirming the patterns of poverty to have marked the modern history of Rabat, asks whether the urbanism to be adopted in the city would tend towards egalitarianism and a sense of equity or whether it would continue trotting the same path of fragmentation and segregation it had done before. Although the choice seemed theoretically evident, the consequences of the city planners' decisions in subsequent master plans have led to an increase in the fragmentation of the city, the serious ghettoization of its social classes and the decrease in socially-mixed public spaces. Neighbourhoods display a given range of living standards, be they high or not, becoming therefore places for the aggregation of similar social classes and levels of income from the extremely affluent Rabat Mega Mall to the numerous low-income housing projects. This situation was exacerbated by continuous production of informal housing which was a source of profit for unscrupulous promoters but led to more social fragmentation.

The concern behind these questions is that of the equitable distribution of resources which has always been the apparent heart of the politics of urbanism and city planning in Rabat. In this chapter I argue that since its 'colonial-modern' re-founding in 1913 by Maréchal Lyautey, Morocco's first *Commissaire-Résident Général*, Rabat's history is marked by moments of *deep rupture* in the 'lived space' (Lefebvre, 1970) where the urban reality calls into question ideologies of spatial distribution and the political edifice that justifies it. While I locate the first rupture as the 1952 *Ecochard trame*,[1] when the reality of the ever-increasing Moroccan 'poor' within the city had to have a solution, the second ends with the year 2000 and the last of a series of five-year city plans adopted since Morocco's independence in 1956, all of which revealed the limits of technocratic management of space and the piecemeal vision underlying it; the third is the ongoing construction within the heart as well as the ever-expanding peripheries of the city.

I argue that while the first two ruptures were the outcome of *real* socio-economic processes and were the byproducts of local changes, the third one is the byproduct of global capital at work in which the driving force is profit. This third rupture brings us to a sort of new imaginary city; a global city which meets international standards and reproduces codes of consumption that could be located anywhere in the world; to huge building sites which alter the morphology and identity of the city; to an urban planning that serves its own interests before it does that of the city's inhabitants. The architectural focus is on the prestige and desirability of the place as commodities of modern capital. To demonstrate this I focus on two projects: the development and revalorization of the Bouregreg Valley (SABR Management, Caisse de Depôt et de Gestion and Sama Dubai) and the Saphira Project (Emaar), which give rise to questions concerning urban governance and participation, to the sense of entitlement of all citizens to the space they inhabit and shape, that is their city, Rabat.

Introducing Rabat

Rabat, Morocco's capital, is located on the eastern shore of the Atlantic with Mohammedia to its south and Kenitra to its north. With a population of little over two million according to the 2000 State figures, the city today occupies an area greatly increased since its institution by royal decree as the country's capital, following the decision of the French colonial authorities in 1913. As *Commissaire-Résident Général,* Hubert Lyautey indelibly marked his vision of the destiny of this city on all Morocco's so-called 'imperial cities' (namely, Marrakech, Fez, and Meknes) and on urban planning in general. A learned man, sensible to art, he believed the 'Orient' to have been a place of great civilization and that there should be respect for this heritage. Further, in Morocco, he wanted also to avoid the pattern and consequences of the Algerian experience (Rabinow, 1989). The changes and the technical progress needed for the development and the economic exploitation of Morocco should not be implemented within the existing *medina* (traditional old cities), argued Lyautey, but required new spaces created specifically for them. The decision to build new French quarters (then called *les villes Européennes*) located outside the ramparts of the old cities (described either as *les villes musulmanes* or *les medinas*) generated the polarized contemporary urban landscape of the 'traditional versus the modern' city.

To understand the magnitude of the change that was to take place in the *medina*, a brief historical summary is needed.[2] Ribat al-Fath is the correct name of Rabat – *ribat* in Arabic means knot or the act of knotting, evoking an image of protection. *Fath* means conquest and the combination of the two – protection and conquest – in a way sums up the history of this city. The ambivalence of the name, as Abu-Lughod would have it, suggests a sort of continuous tension between an impulse of concealment and one of disclosure, of conservation and innovation, and of enclosure and openness that characterized the succession of rulers and residents.

The city was officially founded in the twelfth century by the Almohad king, Abu Yusuf Ya'qub al-Mansur (who ruled from 1184 to 1199) as a fortress from which to launch his campaign in Spain. But the famous buildings of the city (the Hassan mosque, for instance) and the grandiose plans this king had for Ribat al-Fath were never completed (they remain today unfinished) and with his death Rabat rapidly declined, becoming little more than a simple *qasba*. It was not until the early seventeenth century, when Muslims expelled from al-Andalus settled there, that Rabat began to grow and flourish again. It became, with Salé, a base for the famous corsairs who waged war against Christian Spain on the high seas. In the eighteenth century when trade replaced piracy as Rabat's economic base, goods passing through the port made the *medina* a relatively rich place. The *medina* boasts some architectural wonders from this period whose ornamentation carries influences from Spain and the innovation of artists and artisans.

Morocco maintained its independence during the eighteenth and nineteenth centuries while other states in the region succumbed to Turkish, French and British domination. Over this period Rabat continued to be an important trading post. However, in 1912 with the signing of the Treaty of Fez by Sultan Mulai Abdelhafid of the Alaouite Dynasty, Morocco became a French protectorate, with Maréchal Lyautey as Resident General. The *medina* of Rabat, at that time, had between 20,000 to 25,000 inhabitants and was a dynamic centre even though its port had declined in importance in the face of competition from Casablanca.

With the implementation of the protectorate, profound cultural differences between the Muslim and the European populations were translated and sustained spatially through the creation of two separate living spaces opposed to each other in their formal as well as their internal dynamics. Landscaping played an important part in demarcating the frontiers between the two areas, often with the more elaborate forms facing towards the *ville Européene* while the other side was simpler, merely hiding from view the 'Muslim', the more 'disagreeable' sections. On the one hand, the logic of this spatiality echoes the governing style of French colonialism in the case of Morocco, that is, no direct intervention in the indigenous affairs of the local people, but only ruling in their name; while on the other hand, it would firmly ensconce the pattern of the 'caste city' (Abu-Lughod, 1980, p. 217).

The Main Neighbourhoods of Rabat

At this point I present, very schematically, the main neighbourhoods of Rabat as this will help locate the ongoing projects and the sense in which the city is growing.

Centre City/Hassan. This was the administrative centre of the kingdom during the Protectorate. Most ministries and the head offices of banks are to be found here. The main avenue of the Badr Mosque leading to Hassan is the site of luxury hotels which have stunning views on the Bouregreg Valley.

Medina/Oudaya. Like other *medinas* in Morocco, the one in Rabat is the place for small and informal businesses, but it also houses artisans of all types. The Rue des Consuls which leads up to the Oudaya is where the famous blue and white houses overlooking the mouth of the river are to be found.

Takadoum. This is perhaps one of the most degraded neighbourhoods in Rabat. Some often deride its name (*takadoum* in Arabic means development and some call it *ta'akhur*, underdevelopment). This neighbourhood, far from the centre of Rabat, is rather poor though it has developed a sort of autonomy mainly in all types of traffic (including drugs, with the slum of Douar al-hajja next to it).

Agdal. A neighbourhood of villas under the Protectorate, it is the area which has witnessed the most incredible and profound changes of all the city. The high-rise apartments which replaced the old villas have skyrocketed in value and the Avenue Fald Ould Oumeir is now home to established names in the world of fashion and consumption.

Hay Riad/Souissi. The well-off families of Agdal and greater Rabat will slowly desert their neighbourhoods and live in this new haven for the upper and middle classes. The wealthier will opt for Souissi, while Hay Riad also houses apartment buildings. Avenue Nakhil has offices and restaurants on each side and the area is not just a dormitory city as one might imagine at first.

L'Océan. This was the old Spanish neighbourhood from the colonial era, a poor relation compared to Agdal. With the end of colonialism, it became the home of the petty bourgeoisie, successful artisans and small businessmen. It has, however, witnessed a serious decline and become quite poor, especially as it was adjacent to the seashore where there were (and continue to be) slum communities squatting in degraded buildings.

Rabat: A First Phase

Maréchal Lyautey had the power to appropriate land all around the Rabat *medina* (article 7 of a decree signed by Sultan Moulay Youssef in 1914 allowed the expropriation of land for communal and public utility use and this still applies even today). He surrounded himself with a group of young, committed architects whom he had personally selected, and most notably hired architect/planner Henri Prost to design a master plan for the city. His plan for the modern city of Rabat was composed of sharply drawn quarters and defined zones. There was an important administrative centre adjacent to the Moroccan king's palace, a downtown with a train station, a series of neighbourhoods with apartment buildings where the European population resided, and roads for cars. The municipality set to work as early as 1912 in order to establish the infrastructure for urban living (merchandise, information, water, sewage and so on) making Rabat an enormous building site, according to contemporary writers. The architectural style adopted in this first phase allied a sort of re-interpretation of Islamic style architecture by Prost and his cohort and the more contemporary style of Art Nouveau, Art Deco and external ornamentation of buildings. While this plan boasted technical proficiency (width of avenues, alignments and heights of buildings) and a beautiful system of parks and public gardens, it stifled the traditional *medina* where density was bordering the limit of danger with a doubling of its residents since 1912. The Rabat master plan provided neither for the growth of the Moroccan population nor for land speculation by Moroccans as well as Europeans. As early as the 1930s uncontrolled building development began appearing along the seafront areas beyond the limit of Prost's plan, this was to become Quartier de l'Océan where the poorer French, but also Spanish and Italians lived. Around these appeared yet even poorer quarters inhabited by waves of destitute rural migrants attracted to the city in hope of work. These were the precursors of the *bidonvilles* (shanty towns), lacking in hygiene or aesthetics, and were seen as breeding all sorts of danger for themselves and for the general public order. This idea that poorer areas were dangerous was to gain prevalence with time and to become inalienable, a sort of permanent disruption in a seemingly homogeneous and 'peaceful' ordering of space.

Prior to and during the second World War, there was a massive influx of Europeans in Morocco for whom a new office, the *Office Chérifien de l'Habitat Européen*, was created in order to guarantee good, if not the top-rate, living conditions. At the same time, the conditions of the poorer Moroccan population were at their worst. An eloquent example was that of Rabat's Douar Dabbagh (a slum on the road to Casablanca and an extension of Quartier de l'Océan) which was renamed Cité Yacoub Al-Mansour after the Almohad founder of Rabat in the twelfth century. Here some work was initiated in 1943, though it relocated only a token 700 families out of a population of some 18,000. It was only in 1946 when the Resident General Erik Labonne invited French architect/planner Michel Ecochard, an admirer of Le Corbusier, to Morocco that there was recognition of the local population's housing needs (Rabinow, 1989). Ecochard was granted practically unlimited power to prepare new urban plans for Morocco. Not unlike Henry Prost, Ecochard had little regard for ethnographic and historical realities and, as a modernist, he believed in universal human needs. He advocated the mass production of housing units based on these needs, which were translated into plans with 8 x 8 m units with two rooms, a toilet, a kitchen and a patio. These units were to be part of the *Ecochard trame* or layout, with services (schools, hospitals, etc.), leisure facilities and pedestrian zones. The plan was, however, a failure not only because it was never completed, but also because it did not account for difference or for possible growth and it further consolidated the 'caste city', as Abu-Lughod labelled it. I would like to stress particularly the idea that the *Eccochard trame* made no room, either literally or figuratively, for families to grow. Large families lived overcrowded in two rooms; separate sleeping arrangements for males and females were hardly possible, while the address itself carried, and still carries, a stigma.

Ecochard's plan to accommodate the poorer population was a turning point in the modern urban history of Rabat. It was a rupture in a story of high modernism, itself heir to nineteenth-century French urbanism with its hygienist, regularizing mode *à la* Haussmann. For the colonial regime to be faced with the need to build housing units for the ever-growing urban Moroccan population has to be considered in terms of a historical continuity where the *indigène* or local population was, in reality, at the bottom of the list of the regime's concerns. The *Ecochard trame* failed in the case of Rabat (he was successful to a certain extent in Casablanca), but the small number of units (1500) that were eventually built in Rabat's Cité Yacoub Al-Mansour (out of an original plan needing to accommodate between 35,000 to 40,000 residents) initiated a socio-spatial pattern that was to be reproduced in other parts of the city and then throughout the country. This pattern, an aggregation of social groups sharing the same ethnic and socio-economic profile, led to a fragmentation and a coding of physical space: one neighbourhood is affluent and another simply a labour pool, one is for the Europeans and another for the *indigènes*. However questionable, this coding is not in itself so much a problem as is the stigmatization of the poorer spaces and the consequences of such stigmatization on the wider social space and the scarcity of services. The Cité Yacoub Al-Mansour was a precursor of this in that it embodied a difference *vis-à-vis* the *medina* and *vis-à-vis* the *ville moderne*. It possessed neither the historical weight of the *medina* nor the aesthetic ingredients or access to services of the *ville moderne*. Located on the periphery of Rabat, it is a sort of *banlieue*, far away from both urban realities but with its own processes and patterns. The Cité became a kind of embodiment and precursor for the further disruption and disarray of Rabat.

Rabat: Second Phase

Transition towards independence was difficult, and it was all the more so in cities because they had become places of ferment both for and of change; change, certainly in governance matters, but also in the distribution and access to resources. Following Morocco's political independence in 1956, the growth of Rabat continued unabated; it was a mosaic of neighbourhoods each with its apparent socio-economic standing and mode of living. The legacy the French had left to the Moroccan technocrats continued not only because some of the programmes were firmly entrenched, but because the Moroccan officials had themselves studied in France and so employed the same conceptual tools that the French had used. Generally speaking, the Moroccan government worked with both 3 and 5 year plans in the early period extending from 1957 to 1974. During this time, the State built some 45,000 housing units for rent. This period was one of very rapid urbanization but a significant percentage of the development (42 per cent) was illegal, non-regulated housing. By the end of the last 5-year plan in 1974, the construction of State-sponsored rental housing came to an end and new politics emerged. The Moroccan State could no longer invest in building mass housing (in fact even in rich countries, constructing for the poor is costly and often insufficient for the entire poorer population) and had to design some other solution which came in the form of relaxation of the regulations for (or closing the eye to) non-regulated or self-built housing, re-integrating it by providing sanitation, roads, electricity, etc. Slums or *bidonvilles* and non-regulated or *non-réglementaire* housing are two different housing types. The first are built with make-shift materials, the second are built with bricks and mortar and both were produced in large numbers during this period. Described by some scholars as new types of countryside within the city, termed rura-banization by Bahi *et al.* (1986), slums and unregulated housing became an integral part of the wider landscape of Rabat and Salé. By the 1980s, segregation by economic status had clearly replaced the caste system which dominated the city during the colonial period. The new reality was that the capital city was divided along lines of income and social status. The Souissi neighbourhood, for instance, was and continues to be an 'exclusionary' space for those able to afford it, while the 1982 riots all originated in poorer neighbourhoods such as parts of the Océan, Takadoum, Yacoub al Mansur, G5 and others qualified as housing 'poorer' and low-income people.

By 1984 when slums had become such an urban reality, particularly in Salé, the government decided to take action by creating the ANHI (*Agence Nationale de Lutte contre l'Habitat Insalubre*), a national agency to develop programmes to counter insanitary housing. These programmes went through a range of forms due not only to difficult logistics, but especially to the reality on the ground. That reality is that individuals and families invest all they possess in building what amounts to a shack, turning it into more than housing: into a symbol for better living, for a more promising tomorrow. Eradicating this type of housing was close to 'murdering' the dream while in reality these people would become homeless overnight. Much closer to damage control than genuine planning, the programmes went from the total physical eradication of slum housing, to the *recasement* or *relogement*, whereby slum dwellers would be relocated elsewhere while the space vacated was put to other uses, to finally *restructuration*, that is improving the non-regulated housing so as to meet a minimum standard of urban norms. This technocratic approach to physical space created social tensions because the norm of 'hygiene' was too strong, too structuring. This situation was further fed by a high rate of unemployment and a dire economic situation. In 1994, King Hassan II decreed the building of 200,000 housing units for the poorer social strata as Rabat-Salé had grown exponentially. However, like the shortfall of the Ecochard plan, only some 92,288 were completed and the promises made to the poor were not kept.

Originally only higher social classes had lived in Rabat's suburbs but, by the mid 1990s, civil servants and increasingly professionals also started fleeing the city to what have now become Rabat's expanding suburbs, such as Hay Riad and Trik Zaer. Thus I would argue that Rabat has lived through its second rupture in that most of the state-run programmes had shown some limitation. In this second rupture multiple realities have shattered the totalizing vision of the city that the State had worked with, and the social system glided slowly towards a *laissez-faire* that practically bordered on chaos. The question remains: to what extent was there a genuine interest in serving the best interests of slum dwellers and in creating a city that aspires to some form of equity? Perhaps this is merely a rhetorical question, perhaps the question should not look for a 'genuine interest' but at housing becoming a national concern. The reality of slum dwellings, that appeared overnight within vacant lots and/or on the peripheries of the capital, happened with the quiet agreement, if not support, of sections within the Ministry of Interior for, among other reasons, harnessing votes. The blatant political instrumentalization of city programming and plans that was to become evident once the *Direction de l'Habitat et de l'Urbanisme* ceased being part of the Ministry of Interior that had been since 1962, left a capital city which has grown inequitably, with ghettos for the rich, ghettos for the poor and very few mixed spaces where the two meet. It is a fact that security-oriented urbanism exacerbated social cleavages and also created new ones.

At the dawn of the twenty-first century, yet another 5-year plan was adopted by the government in which there is a more liberal approach and in which private promoters are encouraged and are given financial benefits in order to provide decent housing for the ever-growing population. The era of global capital has appeared and firmly established itself. Banks give extremely interesting rates and the slogan of 'buying is better than renting' is to be found everywhere in advertising campaigns. 'Adequate housing' (*a-ssakan al-la'iq*) has become a leitmotif in mass marketing of one's 'dream-house'. The importance of *a-sskan al-la'iq* invaded also the official discourse, particularly in the aftermath of the suicide bombing which took place in Casablanca on the night of 16 May 2003. Although no official or clear statement was ever made as to a direct relationship between living conditions (namely, the most abject slum of Cariane Toma where the bombers originated) and beliefs/behaviour (namely, 'terrorism'), the massive building programmes launched throughout Morocco spoke eloquently as to an unquestionable and implicit causality. Peripheral and poor neighbourhoods were spoken of in the media as breeding grounds for all sorts of ideologies of extremism. Poverty, destitution and misery were portrayed as engulfing these 'marginal and banished' spaces, excluding housing, work, and all other services. Though radicalism can be located anywhere, it seemed obvious to earmark such environments as radical and especially dangerous. Though this is another topic in its own right, the fact that Cariane Toma in Casablanca was destroyed overnight and its residents relocated to special shelters, is an indicator as to the social engineering underlying the building and construction programme.

To invite large-scale companies such as Al-Omrane, Al-Doha or Chaabi Lil-Iskane to become State partners in building the housing needed confirms this re-orientation of the politics of housing. Behind this, as stated before, lies a sort of social reform and, of course, huge benefits for the companies. It is, once again, the reality of the event, the bombing, that acted as a trigger for reconsidering, re-evaluating and shifting the gears of the politics of housing. The technocratic governing of space, which I identified earlier as the second rupture in the history of the city, confirmed its limitation in that it could not account for the complexity of social space as it had focused mainly on the physical space. As Henri Lefebvre (1970) argued, urban space is a totality that is made up of the practices and the representations of those who live in it and those who are informed by it. Reducing such complexity to one or two elements is bound, sooner or later, to reveal its shortcomings.

Today Rabat continues to be a building site: quaint villas dating back to the peak of colonial period being replaced by four- and five-storey buildings (Agdal entirely and parts of Océan), new massive projects along the coast, and a totally new city on the periphery (Tamesna, inaugurated by King Mohammed VI in March 2007). However, beyond these developments, Rabat is now the scene of another type of project: the Saphira project funded by the United Arab Emirates company Emaar, and the massive scheme for the development of the Bouregreg Valley carried out by various groups (Sorouh d'Abu Dhabi with US$750 million and Sama Dubai with about a 50 per cent of the financing amounting to US$2 billion) in partnership with the Groupe Caisse de Depôt et de Gestion (CGD), the State financial institution devoted to the economic and social development of the country. Rabat is now beginning a new stage in its history, that of being a site for the investment of global capital. It is no longer the local reality that interpellates politics – at least downtown while mass housing development continues unabated – but it is delocalized capital that searches for means of creating profits while serving to endorse the image of the king as a builder. Architecture is becoming a mere commodity, an instrument enhancing the imageability and representability of the project while there is little that transpires as its essence. The focus of the rest of this chapter will be on these two new projects and the way space, history and memory are appropriated and manipulated even when the official slogans read 'environment, citizenship, memory of the lieu, and betterment of transportation'.

Rabat: The Current Phase

Before becoming the capital, Rabat could hardly be evoked without its centuries' old rival and sister, Salé and the river that separates them, the Bouregreg, the site of over twenty-three centuries of recorded history. Salé, a Phoenician trading centre, Sala Colonia, during the Roman period; an independent city-state after the invasion of the Arabs in the sixth century; the hub of pirates following the fall of Muslim Spain; and a respected centre of religious knowledge and mystics. Following Morocco's independence in 1956, the old *medina* of Salé was deserted by its native population who moved either *extra-muros* or to Rabat to accommodate modern lifestyles. Salé had strong economic ties with its hinterland but these changed due to colonial infrastructure and to the rural migrants who poured into the city, building shanty towns around the modern neighbourhoods and making Salé today one of the greatest concentrations of this kind of habitation. Salé's historical prominence has been replaced by the reality of a dormitory city, suffering from serious infrastructural shortages and urban poverty. At the end of the twentieth century, the State launched a new urban programme of a planned city, Sala Jadida (New Salé), which has since created a new urban landscape. Sala Jadida, though a research topic in its own right, is deemed half-failure, half-success; success because it has helped solve the housing shortage, and failure in that it has merely become a dormitory city whose residents lack a sense of belonging.[3]

Rabat and Salé are located on opposite sides of the River Bouregreg which flows immediately into the Atlantic (figure 5.1). The mouth of the river forms a beautiful natural frontier between the 'rival sisters' and separates their *medinas*. Each bank has its prestigious sites: the esplanade and the Tower Hassan, the Mohammed V mausoleum, the Kasbah des Oudayas, the cemetery, the relics of Chellah on the Rabat bank; the tomb of Sidi Ben Acher, the aqueduct, and the Salé *medina* with its history going back to Phoenician times yet to be excavated, on the Salé bank. The king, Mohammed VI, bears a personal responsibility for the *'Projet d'aménagement et de la mise en valeur du Bouregreg'*. The implication of this is that the king, as the highest authority in the country, is symbolic on many counts, the most important of which is that the project cannot fail because of the 'moral' guarantee he represents. Some argue that this truly gigantic project (as will become evident in what follows) carries on the tradition of 'the king as a builder'; the king leaving his mark to posterity; the leader wanting to embellish his capital city; to demonstrate what the order and organization of a well-governed State should be. Given such implications, there is not only a sense of secrecy hovering around the project, but also that whatever has been decided or chosen should not, cannot, be subject to change. The description which follows is gathered from a promotional CD (Franck Beugniet, Sigma, 2004), various architecture magazines and journals as well as interviews with professionals, mostly administrators within the Ministry of Urbanism (of which later). This project is supposed to transform the identity

Figure 5.1. Different perspectives of Moulay Hassan Bridge connecting Rabat and Salé over the River Bouregreg. This is a construction dating back to the French colonial period and until the late 1970s was the only road connection between the rival sisters.

of an 'administrative' capital, quaint and boring to one of high modernism and dynamism. But these will remain contained within the delimited space as the total periphery of Rabat cannot grow outside the 'green belt' that surrounds it. All projects can only work within the space which is legally available.

An extremely potent discourse has been woven around this project: it aims to rehabilitate and to hoist the city to the level of the big metropolises of the Mediterranean. It will become a hallmark for tourism which in turn will create the wealth sorely needed by this Third World country, and especially, the capital city which has always suffered from its administrative weight. Such a project promising revenue is, therefore, a 'citizen-project', serving fundamentally one and the same citizen entitled to his/her city. Tourism being one of the major sources for currency, Morocco hopes to receive 10 million tourists and this project is planned to become its main driving force in attracting them. Said to be the beacon for the twenty-first century in terms of size as well as budget, this truly gigantic project is to be completed by the year 2015. It will occupy 5000 hectares and has a budget of 10 million dirhams (about US$1.3 million). Completion will be in two phases: Bab Al Bahr (Gateway to the Sea), and then Amwaj (Waves), which is located more inland and hence justifies the name in that the waves roll in. The latter is made of Sahat Al Kabira (the Great Agora), Kasbat Abi Raqraq (Kasbah of the River), Sahrij Al Oued (the River's Bowl), Al Manzah Al Kabir (the Great Promenade) and Bouhairat Assouhoul (the Green Lakes). These names share a common sense: they reflect the physical attributes of the place, but also operate a sort of union between contemporary political slogans (citizenship, the agora, the promenade) while laying claim to the past. The names play on nostalgia, of supposed openness and inclusion. But is this idea of public space, practiced as such today, to remain or will there be an inversion of this logic? This question can be partly answered as we continue investigating this titanic project (figure 5.2).

The first sequence, Bab Al Bahr, is an opening, a view towards and an embracing of the sea. While traditional architecture of the *medina* has always turned its back on the sea, and cemeteries have often been placed between the *medina* and the sea as a sort of symbolic frontier, Bab Al Bahr embraces this space. The preliminary work consists mostly of dredging the area and erecting flood defences. It is only after completing this sequence, that work will begin on the Atlantic harbour and marina. The marina and the two ports are intended to re-establish the link with the maritime history of the area, when Salé and Rabat provided haven for ships which attacked the Spanish and Portuguese fleets as a retaliation to the expulsion of Muslims' from Andalusia and when corsair booty was the basis of economic activity of the region. In this area of about 3.5 hectares, a new neighbourhood will be built in the form of a village for artisan arts and crafts. However, and in none of the presentations of these projects, has the cemetery been included or discussed. Bab Al Bahr cannot possibly take place without a mention of the cemetery which has always been on the outskirts of the *medina*, a sort of buffer between the sea and the world of the living. It seems that the presentation of the project, the stress on

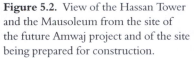

Figure 5.2. View of the Hassan Tower and the Mausoleum from the site of the future Amwaj project and of the site being prepared for construction.

aesthetics, on the grandiose, even on the monumental, has been oblivious of the space of death (figures 5.3 and 5.4).

Amwaj, the second sequence of which is Sahat Al Kabira (the Great Agora), is the centre of the project. A recreational space will be created in the form of an artificial island which is said to be the hyphen between the two cities. This site which will spread over 100 hectares and will cost more than US$2 billion to develop was conceded to Samai Dubai. There will be a museum, suspended gardens, an international conference centre, in addition to various tourist facilities and services: a yacht marina, five star hotels, pleasure beaches, luxury offices, hundreds of boutiques and stores, shopping centres and open-air amphitheatres. Kasbat Abi Raqraq (Kasbah of the River) close to Chellah, an archaeological site dating back to the Roman period, and the Mausoleum will have an artificial lake and will apparently have a small residential area. On the other side of the river, a Technopolis will be built and a highway will lead to it. This village will occupy 300 hectares and will be the leading place in communications and multimedia services. It is structured around three different poles: one for hosting conferences, the second 'offshore' for call centres and other multimedia activities, and finally a third for teaching and research. The Sahrij Al Oued (the River's Bowl) will be exploited for nautical activities of all sorts, with a focus on ecological tourism. Al

Figure 5.3. Views of the River Bouregreg where the marina will be built.

Figure 5.4. Images of the eastern area to which some of the project will extend.

Manzah Al Kabir (the Great Promenade) and Bouhairat Assouhoul (the Green Lakes) will be devoted to tourism activities with the necessary hotels and services. It also envisages thousands of units of accommodation, luxury offices, all equipped with state of the art technology, on an area of 200,000 square metres with hundreds of boutiques and stores of different types and sizes occupying 100,000 square metres (figure 5.5).

Figure 5.5. Views showing the context of the Amwaj development.

The general presentation of the project stresses the importance of transportation and therefore there will be a tunnel through the Oudayas as well as a tramway between the two cities. The entire project boasts of its public spaces including hanging gardens, squares, cultural sites, and beaches. The billboards separating the construction site today parade slogans about the *lieu de mémoire*,[4] and this being a 'project for citizenship'. The architectural plans show a scheme in harmony with the natural environment, and the designers profess to respecting and safeguarding the historical characteristics of the valley despite the apparent modernism within the models. As it stands now, this site is naturally beautiful on a large scale but, the architects argue, at the smaller scale it is spoiled by clumsy developments and inadequate forms of occupation: an inconvenient rail and waterways network, anarchic occupation of the land on the Salé bank, impairment and deterioration of the buildings on the borders of both *medinas*.

The PAG (*Plan d'Aménagement Général*), the overall plan, aims at creating patterns that will make the area more welcoming to visitors, to embellish both banks of the river and revalorize the historical monuments. Promoters describe the project as combining an 'authentic Moroccan' architecture (reduced to the reproduction of certain forms of tile and archway) with the modern spirit, but it seems that such style and the extent of the plans do not respect the historical monuments as cultural landmarks. The focus is too much on spaces of 'consumption' rather than on the 'agora', which the project is so eager to promote. This is the third major project for Samai Dubai in just five months. It follows first the Dubaï's Towers, Doha with an estimated cost of US$300 million, and then the construction of a seaside resort in the Omani capital, Muscat, with an investment of US$820 million. At this juncture in the history of Rabat, it is no longer the spatial needs of the resident that are at stake as much as global capital. The fact is that arguments about citizens' rights, the *lieu de mémoire*, and a project for all, are incessantly repeated, but have turned into hollow slogans that join the long list of failed promises and projects both under the French and the Moroccans. However, and as one official in the Ministry of Urbanism argued when I presented such ideas to him, 'the contemporary world market compels us to give priority to what will be financially beneficial. This is not to say that the needs of citizens is ignored' (Belbachir, 2007) and he continued by showing me the model of Tamesna and many of the previous mass-housing projects.

Tamesna will be a new city about 20 kilometres south of Rabat. Its name in Berber means 'vast plains' and the plans aim not only to respond to the housing shortage, but also to make it possible for low- and middle-income families to acquire a home. With the ongoing projects in Rabat, prices have become beyond the reach of even well-off classes. In other words, Tamesna is a sort of compensation when faced with the simple impossibility of acquiring a home within the city of Rabat. But unlike Sala Jadida, the plan for Tamesna has university centres and commercial places in order to encourage a social mix (*Ibid.*). According to the same official, Tamesna will be built on the principle of an internal centrality; in other words, it is not only a 'satellite' of another city but one in itself. But if Tamesna is part of the larger Rabat, created as a solution for the housing problems within Rabat and its vicinity, how does this argument of centrality help us to understand the future relation between these two cities? Only time will allow us to answer this question with any kind of specificity, but I can speculate from the experience of Sala Jadida that each city will move in its own orbit – whither then Rabat's citizenship project?

This project is well underway and will certainly be economically beneficial to the city as an interview with the Mayor of Rabat illustrates (*Labyrinthes*, May/June 2006), but this is only the tip of the iceberg and the services which the project will provide will only be available to those able to pay. In some sense, what has so far been a space for all will perforce become a semi-private if not totally private space for those who are able to afford it. The logic of the marina, the practice of equipment-oriented nautical sports, the very high-standard housing units as well as luxurious offices will mark the Bouregreg Valley as a space belonging to the wealthy, shaped by international and transnational movement of capital. Even when it is presented as a citizenship project, it is a select sort of citizenship. Further, the very idea of an 'arts and crafts village' on an island, will make of it a sort of folklorization, if not Disneyfication, that has been depleted of its essence even when the form is perpetuated and reproduced.

The second project, Saphira, like the Bouregreg Valley, is gigantic. The Atlantic coastline of Rabat has been selected by Emaar to implement its other massive project. And in the words of Emaar themselves:

> Saphira with its bustling marina and beachfront development will successfully reopen Rabat not only to the sea but also to the world. Eleven kilometres alongside the Atlantic coast is the piece of land specified for the project of renovation, and highlighting of the natural beauty of Rabat and its rich heritage. The Saphira project – Jewel of the Atlantic, will give birth to 9 districts that will evoke the past of Morocco and the beauty of its shore. The nine districts of Saphira combined will create for Rabat a vibrant beachfront, tourist, residential, business and leisure community that will revive and rejuvenate Morocco's pride – Rabat.[5]

This coastline of about 12 km, extending from Bab al Bahr to Harhoura, a small seaside resort to the south of Rabat, is characterized by steep cliffs. Its natural layout necessitates high-cost, high-competence and massive investment. What is known of the project so far is that it will be spread over 330 hectares and has a budgeted cost of US$3.1 million. The agreement signed between King Mohammed VI and Emaar stipulates that the Saphira project includes housing and commercial complexes, luxury hotels, recreational and leisure spaces, a private hospital with 250 beds, an office tower of 50 floors, in addition to high-quality villas and yet another marina. Within the presentation of the project, the same arguments surface once again: raising the capital to the status of an international metropolis and connecting it to its historical past. The link with the past comes mainly in the form of the conversion of the Marie-Feuilly hospital built during the French protectorate into an exclusive five star hotel and also the rehabilitation of some old military spaces as leisure places. Similarly to the Bouregreg project, what social segment will be able to access these very high-class buildings? Of course, only a limited few.

Rabat will of course change and become radically different (figure 5.6). As one of my interviewees commented 'they'll change so much that one will ask if Rabat is still Rabat!!'. In other words what will remain in terms of continuity after so much has changed? Going back to the question Abu-Lughod asked nearly 30 years ago, it seems that the answer is here now. Rabat will be different in terms

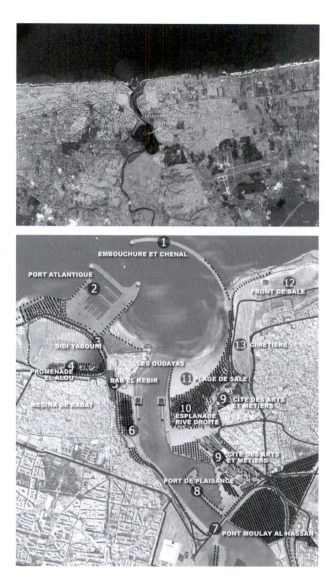

Figure 5.6. The ambitious Rabat project.

of its morphology, but it will keep on reproducing its pattern of socio-spatial fragmentation. These two truly major projects leave very limited, if no space at all, for the poorer social strata. Where will they go? Some will remain in dilapidated housing units, some will move to Tamesna and other peripheral areas that are affordable. But chasing away the poor, certainly not the intention of the designers, is in essence a contradiction of these projects' arguments and slogans, but can it be otherwise when they continually put forth a standard and level of livelihood that can be afforded only by the better off? Even today, as the projects are underway, property prices close to the sites of the two projects have skyrocketed. It is a primary process of elimination, of natural selection as the ecological urbanism of the Chicago School would have it. This third and final rupture is not, therefore, so different in its outcome from the first two except in its scale. While the first two failed to keep their promises, this last one will produce even more social fragmentation and pain because of its sheer size and because an important population living in the Kasbah or in the Océan areas (where the Saphira project is to take place) will be relocated somewhere else. No one could answer my questions for sure, but rumours do, as I found when interviewing in the Océan neighbourhood. The urban imaginary will certainly become richer because of the sheer volume to be built, but it will also be affected in other ways when true mixed social spaces will be reduced to a minimum if not eliminated. Perhaps it is cautionary to err on the optimistic side and hope that Al-Manzah al Kabir or Sahat al-Kubra (Agora and Promenade) will be truly faithful to their original meaning, the answer as to how remains to be seen!

Notes

1.   Michel Ecochard (1905–1985), the French architect/planner, proposed a policy for housing the Muslim population of Rabat, based on the use of a *trame sanitaire* which became known as the *trame Écochard*, and allowed the densification and upgrading of these quarters. He stated clearly that he wanted to replace the *bidonvilles* or shanty settlements.

2.   This review is based on the following references: Bencheikh, 2000; Kharoufi, 2000; Le Tourneau, 1957; Royaume du Maroc, 2000; Terrasse, 1949.

3.   For a more detailed review of Sale's history see: Brown, 1976; Chastel, 1997; Naciri, 1963.

4.   A *lieu de mémoire* is any significant entity, whether material or non-material in nature, which by dint of human will or the work of time has become a symbolic element of the memorial heritage of any community.

5.   http://www.emaar.com/International/morocco/Index.asp. Accessed 23 May 2007.

References

Abu-Lughod, Janet (1980) *Rabat, Urban Apartheid in Morocco*. Princeton, NJ: Princeton University Press.

Bahi, Hassan *et al.* (eds.) (1986) *Habitat Clandestin au Maroc*. Casablanca: Imprimerie Arrissala.

Belbachir (2007) Interview 16 January.

Bencheikh, Ahmed (2000) Gouvernance des villes au Maroc: éléments d'une réflexion prospective, in Kharoufi, Mostafa (ed.) *Gouvernance et société*. Casablanca: Afrique Orient.

Brown, Kenneth (1971) An urban view of Moroccan history: Salé, 1000–1800. *Hesperis-Tamuda*, **12**.

Brown, Kenneth (1976) *People of Salé*. Cambridge: Cambridge University Press.

Chastel, Robert (1997) *Rabat-Salé: vingt siècles de l'Oued Bou Regreg*, 2nd ed. Rabat: Edition la Porte.

Kharoufi, Mostafa (2000) Espaces urbains, pouvoirs et mouvements sociaux au Maghreb, in Kharoufi, Mostafa (ed.) *Gouvernance et sociétés civiles: les mutations urbaines au Maghreb*. Casablanca: Afrique Orient.

Le Tourneau, Roger (1957) *Les villes musulmanes de l'Afrique du Nord*. Algiers.

Lefebvre, Henri (1970) *La révolution urbaine*. Paris: Editions Gallimard.

Naciri, Mohammed (1963) Salé: étude de géographie urbaine. *Revue de Géographie du Maroc*, Nos. 3–4, pp. 39–72.

Nora, Pierre (1996) From lieux de mémoire to realms of memory, in Nora, P. and Kritzman, D. (eds.) *Realms of Memory: Rethinking the French Past*. Vol. 1. *Conflicts and Divisions*. New York: Columbia University Press.

Rabinow, Paul (1989) *French Modern*. Cambridge, MA: MIT Press.

Royaume du Maroc (2000) *Recueil des circulaires relatives à l'urbanisme.* Publication de l'Etat Marocain.

Royaume du Maroc Ministère de l'Aménagement du Territoire, de l'Environnement, de l'Urbanisme et de l'Habitat (2000) *Le territoire Marocain: Etat des lieux.* Rabat: Editions Okad pour la Direction de l'Aménagement du territoire.

Terrasse, Henri (1949) *Histoire du Maroc des origines à l'établissement du protectorat français*, 2 vols. Casablanca: Atlantides.

Chapter 6

Riyadh: A City of 'Institutional' Architecture

Mashary A. Al-Naim

Modernity and Conflict with Tradition in the Saudi Built Environment

The origin of contemporary architecture in Saudi Arabia stems from the first half of the twentieth century when Aramco (Arabian-American Oil Company) built its first housing projects in the eastern region of the Kingdom between 1938 and 1944 (figure 6.1).[1] These projects introduced a new concept of space and a new image of the home (Shiber, 1967). It is possible to argue that this early introduction had a deep but not immediate effect on the local people. It made them question their knowledge and how to react to these developments. In other words, this early change can be seen as the first motive for a social resistance to the new forms and images in the contemporary Saudi built environment (Al-Naim, 2006).

The significant impact of this experience was manifested in conflicts between the old and new in local society. The threat of external interference and its impact on social and physical identity created for the first time a reaction to the physical environment. Resistance to the new is to be expected in the early stages of change, but it is critical to assess how people reacted to the changes and how deeply they were influenced by them.

The conflict between traditional cultural values and the introduction of Western physical images was very limited at the beginning of modernization; the local people followed what they knew and tried to implement it in their daily lives in their homes. However, the contrast between the traditional and the new in their minds can be considered the beginning of physical and social changes in Saudi cities (Al-Naim, 2005). The first indication of a conflict between local and Western culture can be ascribed to Solon T. Kimball, who visited Aramco headquarters in 1956. He described how the senior staff (American) camp in Dhahran was completely imported from the United States. He said:

> No one westerner would have difficulty in identifying the senior staff 'camp' as a settlement
> built by Americans in our South Western tradition of town planning. It is an area of single-story

Figure 6.1. The new housing image of Aramco in the 1930s and 1940s. (*a*) The early American camp in Dhahran (1930s); (*b*) American camp in Ras Tanunurah (1950s).

dwellings for employees and their families. Each house is surrounded by a small grassed yard usually enclosed by a hedge. (Kimball, 1956, p. 472).

The local people still persisted with their own spatial concepts and images and resisted the imported ones which were considered 'strange things'. Therefore, when Saudi workers and their relatives 'moved in, they took over any empty land available and erected basic shelters and fences of locally available material, separated from each other by narrow irregular footpaths' (Shiber, 1967, p. 430). This created 'a community of mud-brick and timber houses, built in a traditional and comfortable way' (Shirreff, 1979).[2]

Kimball noticed this community and described the Saudi camp which was built adjacent to the senior staff camp as 'neither planned nor welcomed' (figure 6.2). He added that 'these settlements represent the attempt by Arabs to establish a type of community life with which they are familiar'. Kimball recognized the insistence of the native people on their own identity through his description of the Saudi camp as 'an emerging indigenous community life' (Kimball, 1956, p. 472).

In the first two decades of change the attitude of local people towards their homes also changed somewhat. What Kimball described is the position of local people on their first direct contact with Western culture. At this stage they refused change and stuck with what they knew. This is not to say that the new images had not influenced them; however, they were in the process of developing a new attitude towards their homes. This attitude was not yet fully formed as they were still in a process of understanding the extent to which these new images represented a break with the traditional idea of a home.

The government and Aramco were not happy with the growth of these

Figure 6.2. Saudi camp in Dhahran in 1930s and 1940s.

traditional settlements (figure 6.3). Therefore, in 1947, the government asked Aramco, which employed American engineers and surveyors, to control the growth around the oil areas. This created the first planned cities in Saudi Arabia, Dammam and Al Khobar, which followed a gridiron pattern (Shiber, 1967).[3] The spatial concepts and house designs which were introduced in these two cities accelerated the impact of a new image of housing on the local people, not only in these two new developments, but also in the surrounding old cities.

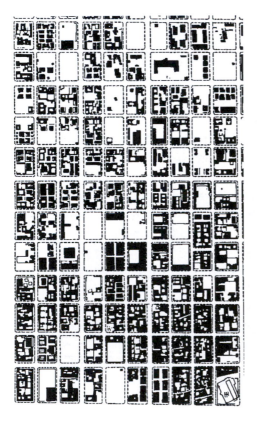

Figure 6.3. Planning system of Al-Khobar. The first planned city in Saudi Arabia (1947).

This can be considered the story of modernization in Saudi Arabia, the country which was unified in 1932 and moved rapidly towards building a modern nation with huge urban settlements. The city of Riyadh started on the road to modernization in the second half of the last century; in the process it has attempted to preserve its original identity, which was difficult due to its position as capital of Saudi Arabia. However, one can argue that the story of Riyadh's urban development represents the process of urbanization in Saudi Arabia in the twentieth century. Furthermore, such a narrative is linked to major milestones of Saudi society.

Riyadh's Experience of Urban Change

Riyadh's importance dates back to 1824 when 'Turki bin Abdullah Al-Saud (1824–1834), the founder of the second Saudi State (1824–1891) moved to Riyadh from Al-Dariyyah, a small town nearby, 20 Kms. Northwest Riyadh' (Sadleir, 1866). In the centre of Riyadh, Turki built a mosque and a palace. Over the next four decades no major changes occurred to the central area of the town except for an extension made to the mosque and the palace by Faisal bin Turki who succeeded his father in 1834. Another important addition was a bridge between the mosque and the palace for security (Al-Naim, 1996). When Palgrave visited Riyadh in 1862, it had established the urban form which remained decades later (figure 6.4). The city had been the capital for almost 40 years and different quarters with their own specific characters had evolved within the area bounded by the walls of 1824.

Figure 6.4. Three-dimensional map of Riyadh in 1862.

Three years later, Lewes Pelly visited Riyadh and wrote that 'it appeared a considerable and neat looking place, without, however, any pretensions to beauty; but built of sun dried bricks, and its suburbs enlivened by a few date groves' (Pelly, 1866, pp. 44–45). He also said of the palace:

> the Fort was at no great distance, and situated in the center of the town. There was a large open space in its front; no part of the building had the slightest architectural pretension; and reception place was a long low room, supported on rough-hewn wooden pillars, approached by a dingy staircase (*Ibid.*, p. 46).

The Formation of Modern Riyadh (1902–1953)

Following that, the city became one of institutional buildings, especially after King Abdulaziz regained Riyadh in 1902. Initially the king was chiefly concerned with unifying the country and, during the 1910s and 1920s, little was initiated in Riyadh except rebuilding the city wall and the old palace to be used as a royal base. The population of the city grew from 8,000 in 1902 to 19,000 in 1918 (Philby, 1922). The first car was seen in the city in 1919 and was dragged by camels from the desert. By 1913 King Abdulaziz had conquered Al-Hasa and the whole Eastern Region, and by 1923 there was an indication of oil reserves in this region, which in 1938 proved to exist in commercial quantities. In this sense, Riyadh in its modern form can be considered a twentieth-century city.

At this time, and with an area of not more than 1 km^2 (figure 6.5), the city remained free of any major modernization and was considered traditional and very conservative. However, following unification of the Kingdom of Saudi Arabia in 1932, Riyadh started to expand and the first building outside the wall was commissioned by the king's brother Mohammed who built his palace in Atiqah (Alangari, 1996). During two decades prior to the death of King Abdulaziz in 1953, the city grew slowly and prepared itself as the kingdom's capital. The population increased from 40,000 in 1935 to 83,000 in 1949. The first government institutions were established: the Ministry of Finance (1932); a core for the municipalities (1937); the first airport (1942); the Ministry of Defence (1944); and the Ministry of Interior and inauguration of the railway line connecting Riyadh with the eastern coast (1951).

It was clear that Riyadh was preparing for major changes. King Abdulaziz took a major step that influenced the urban development of the city, when he moved his residence from the walled city to Al Murabba'a Palace (1937). He started a plan to modernize the city, but change was slow because of World War II, while the economic environment, which was traditional and very local, reduced the government's capability to implement its plan.

Al Murabba'a Palace was located 2 km north of the centre of Riyadh and spread over 16 hectares. The name Al Murabba'a (the Square) stemmed from its form, 400 by 400 metres (figure 6.6). Al-Hathloul (2002) notes that the construction of

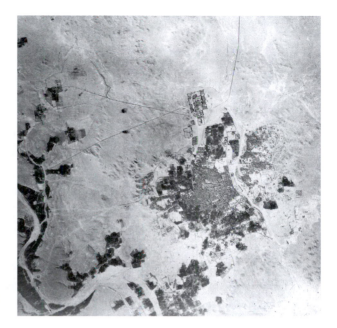

Figure 6.5. A map of Riyadh showing the old city and the beginning of the urban expansion in the 1930s and 1940s.

Figure 6.6. A new extension in the north of Riyadh showing Alsuwaidi farms and the new palace.

Al Murabba'a encouraged the development of Al-Futah, an area located between Al Murabba'a and the old city. This development took place in the 1940s when a number of the king's sons decided to build their palaces there. Also with the palace in the northern part, northwards became a primary direction for the city's expansion. It indicated to citizens that living within the walls was no longer necessary. Some modernization was introduced as early as the 1930s, including electricity, water closets and a drainage system. While other signs of modernization were evident with the arrival of cars and telephones in Riyadh, with 300 cars in 1939 and 50 telephones in 1936.

Urban growth was strongly influenced by the economic growth due to the oil boom after World War II. For example, oil income grew from US$10.4 million in 1946 to US$210.7 million in 1952, which encouraged the extension of urban and architectural activities outside the city wall. From 1944 the city wall started gradually falling apart because of the urbanization and the expansion outside the old city and the government initiated the first organized planning when it divided the Manfuha district into residential lots of 8 m by 8 m and a street width not less than 8 m. This was because of the introduction of the automobile and the need for wider streets.

Compared to what happened in the Eastern region, few changes occurred in Riyadh in the 1930s and 1940s. However, an indication of social change can be found in the suburbs constructed at that time. For example, for the first time in the city, new neighbourhoods were classified according to economic and social status (Facey, 1992),[4] but the construction methods and style remained completely traditional. Facey described the changes in Riyadh in the 1940s as:

> Despite the mushrooming development of the city outside the walls, traditional methods of construction continued to be employed. The local architecture had to be adapted to the creation of buildings for government and the royal family on a scale hitherto unimagined by local craftsmen. (*Ibid.*, p. 302)

While the urban and architectural activities during the 1930s and 1940s were taking place in the Eastern Province due to oil and industrial activities, Riyadh remained away from any major urban change (except Al Murabba'a). However, it was preparing itself as an administrative centre as seen from the new governmental district (Al Murabbaa'), the increase in the number of cars and growth of telecommunications activities. Riyadh was ready for the urban boom in the following decades and this happened when the city began significantly changing its urban environment by shifting from traditional structures and forms to modern concrete buildings which were introduced in the late the 1940s.

A Step towards Modernization (1953–1975)

The situation changed completely when, in 1953, King Saud succeeded his father and decided to modernize Riyadh.[5] The king built the royal residential district, known as Annasriyyah in 1957, which introduced reinforced concrete to Riyadh for the first time (Abercrombie, 1966).[6]

Annasriyyah was started in 1950, the grid pattern was introduced in 1953 and in the same year the first asphalted road was built to link it to the existing city. The conflict between new and old in the minds of local people became an important issue in Riyadh because the city was facing radical physical and social change. This was manifested in the construction of Al-Malaz neighbourhood which was also completed in the late 1950s (figure 6.7) (Fadan, 1983).

A new era opened for Riyadh. The process of modernization accelerated with major demolition of the historic core where the old palace, mosque and surrounding buildings were cleared out. The introduction of large construction

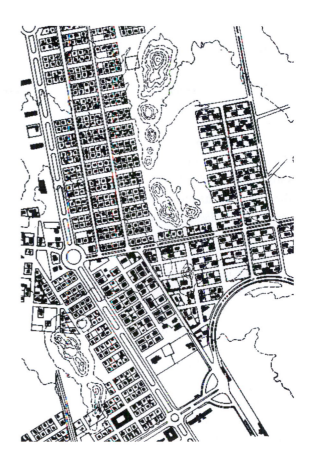

Figure 6.7. AlMalaz Master Plan.

companies to the city began with the American company, Bechtel, which constructed the airport terminal. However, the new king's most important decision which transformed the city was to transfer government institutions and agencies from Jeddah and Makkah to Riyadh. This opened the door for Riyadh to become the city of institutional buildings as the government started to construct buildings and residential neighbourhoods to accommodate those agencies and their employees.

King Saud opened Riyadh to modernization and during the first year of his reign (1953) he started to build the Alhamra Palace in southern Al Murabba'a to which he moved in 1957. Also in 1953 he moved his residence to the new concrete Annasriyya Palace. He carried out administrative reforms following the establishment of the Council of Ministers in 1954. One could say that the 1950s were a turning point in the urban history of Riyadh: new ministry buildings which opened along the Airport Road were designed by Egyptian Architect, Sayyed Kurayem, and the new Al-Malaz neighbourhood, sponsored by the Ministry of Finance, introduced a new house type (the villa).

These developments created cultural discord among Riyadh residents, since they resulted in a major conflict between old and new effectively splitting Riyadh into new and old districts, mirroring their residents' attitudes (Al-Hathloul,

1981). In the same year King Saud University was established. These changes also paralleled a significant increase in population, which grew from 106,000 in 1955 to 300,000 in 1968.

Riyadh became attractive to many Saudis and people migrated to the city from other regions. New neighbourhoods appeared, taking the name of the people living there, for example, Hilat Alqisman (occupied by those from Qasim) and Hilat Aldawaser (occupied by those from Wadi Al-Dawaser). It was thus expected that the population of Riyadh would grow and that urban activities would expand. The impact on the city was clear: the need for housing and infrastructure encouraged the government to re-think the urban planning of the city and to initiate major steps to regulate the urban growth of Riyadh.

Al-Malaz was a result of this and, as mentioned earlier, it was a milestone in the urban history of Riyadh because it brought a new lifestyle to the city, changing local people's perception of the meaning of home. The new type of house introduced in Al-Malaz, the villa, was originally imported in the 1930s, but was developed in the 1950s when the Aramco Home Ownership Program forced people in the Eastern Province to submit a design for their houses in order to qualify for a loan (Lebkicher *et al.*, 1960). People relied on Aramco architects and engineers to design their houses, because there were few architects in Saudi Arabia at that time. In order to speed up the process, Aramco architects and engineers developed several design alternatives for their employees to choose from. However, all these designs adopted a style known as the 'international Mediterranean' detached house (figure 6.8) (Al-Hathloul and Anis-ur-Rahmaam, 1985).

Figure 6.8. A number of villas constructed in the 1950s by the Aramco Home Ownership Program in Dammam.

The urban concepts implemented in Riyadh were similar to those in Dammam and Khobar.[7] Nevertheless, there was an initial difference between the two experiences. In the case of Annasriyyah and Al-Malaz, the entire project, including planning, designing and construction, was completed by government agencies. People who occupied the residential units were given no opportunity to express their opinion about their houses. Generally, with Aramco and Riyadh housing projects:

> ... a completely different conception of a house, cluster, and neighbourhood has been introduced. It starts from the tiny details of the house construction, and spreads to the internal spatial organisation of the rooms and finally to the external appearance and the relationship of the house to those in the neighbourhood. (Fadan, 1983, p. 97)

Exposure to this new image was still limited to government and Aramco employees, many of whom had experienced different cultures, either because they were not natives of Saudi Arabia or because they had studied abroad. However, these two major changes in Riyadh raised questions about the meaning of the home. This can be seen by the way first Annasriyyah, and then Al-Malaz, became known as New Riyadh (Al-Hathloul, 1981).

The increasingly obvious contrast between old and new, and a general sense that their identity was under threat from continuing urban change, raised a series of issues among residents. Should they preserve their own traditional identity or adapt to change? Should they stick with what they knew or make use of new concepts and technology? Certainly, people are usually more enthusiastic about experiencing the new, especially if it is associated with a distinguished social class, such as government employees, who appeared as a highly educated elite in an illiterate society (Alangari, 1996).[8]

Similar to the situation in the Eastern region, many people living in the traditional areas in Riyadh kept their traditional buildings and remained in their traditional houses until the late 1960s. The impact of the new designs was very clear but society was not yet ready to step towards the social and physical changes. Nevertheless, people in traditional areas did make a few changes to imitate the image introduced by the new houses in Al-Malaz.

The mud surfaces of traditional houses were plastered with cement and the edges of the house parapets were topped with a thin layer of cement to reflect the sharp and neat edges of the concrete. These changes extended to the old style wooden external gates which were replaced by steel ones with concrete canopies on the top, similar to those of the Al-Malaz houses. It is apparent, then, that concrete structures with their neatness and sharp form became a very common symbol used by people in Saudi Arabia to communicate modernity (figure 6.9).

Consequently, a haphazard spread of urbanization was noticed in the 1960s. Urban expansion was everywhere and from all directions due to the increasing numbers of immigrants coming to Riyadh from other cities in the kingdom,

Figure 6.9. The mud surfaces of the traditional houses in Riyadh plastered with cement and the traditional house gate replaced by a concrete one because it reflects modernity.

searching for work. This encouraged the government to hold an international competition in 1968 to plan the city. Doxiadis Associates of Athens won the competition and started their survey immediately. Their plan influenced the urban morphology of Riyadh and reinforced the north–south axis of the city which still characterizes its urban identity (figure 6.10). On completion of the plan in 1971, and its approval by the Council of Ministers in 1973, Riyadh became a huge construction site financed by the oil boom (oil income was $22.6 billion in 1974).

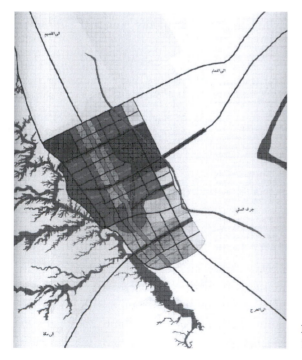

Figure 6.10. Doxiadis Master Plan, 1968.

Modernity vs. Tradition: Questioning the Urban Form of Riyadh

Modernity as a philosophical concept is widely linked to the concept of Westernization in Saudi Arabia. They were ambiguously connected in both literature and people's minds and this increased resistance to physical change in Saudi Arabia's contemporary built environment (Al-Naim, 2005). Jomah (1992, p. 325), for example, confused the processes of modernization and Westernization in his study of the houses in the Western region of Saudi Arabia. He states 'The environmental stress that took place in Hedjaz in the middle 1900s is usually described as "Westernization" or "Modernization"'.

Because the clash was between two completely different cultures and lifestyles, modernization in Saudi Arabia is widely interpreted as Westernization. This enhanced the sense of threat to Saudi identity and the internal social resistance towards the introduced concept (Abercrombie, 1975).[9] Abercrombie on his visit to the kingdom in 1966 said 'wherever I went, I found the Arabians welcoming the 20th century, but never with open arms' (Abercrombie, 1966).

King Faisal replaced King Saud in 1964. The new king, who was Prime Minister in the King Saud era (1953–1964), took two major steps which changed the perception of modernity in Saudi Arabia: female education (1962) and TV broadcasting. Although society was not completely ready for change at that time, the resistance which existed was not strong enough to stop it. The impact of the TV was crucial because it brought new images of cities and houses to the Saudi people and lessened their resistance to change. However, some people in Arabia reacted strongly against modernization. In every aspect of life they thought about the impact of imported values and technology on their morals and social values. As Abercrombie's Saudi friend said 'modernization we want, we need, and we will have ... but on our own terms' (*Ibid.*, p. 5). As a result, the change was limited to physical issues rather than values; the people of Riyadh remained traditional in their living patterns even if they appeared physically very modern.

This resistance did not change even when the whole of Arabia was exposed to extensive change in the 1970s.[10] Dalley[11] indicates the resistance of Saudis to Western influences in the 1970s. He states:

> A matter of great concern to the Saudis is the influence of foreigners on the morals and social habits of the people… The Saudis are probably quite right not wanting to be influenced by our ways, but it is difficult to see how it can be avoided if they are insistent on paying for hundreds of years of 'development' in decades. (Dalley, 1976, p. 166)

Al-Awaji also indicated in 1971 that traditional values still dominated social life in Saudi Arabia. He stated 'The dominant social value system ... is still traditional. Not only [has it] continued to dominate, but also [it has compelled] institutions to adapt their behaviour to its demand' (cited in Anderson, 1984, p. 160). In the 1970s and 1980s, several researchers indicated that Saudi society was still persisting in its traditional way of life. Costello (1977) indicated that, among Middle Eastern countries, Saudi Arabia was subject to minimal European influence. Shirreff (1979) also shared this view when he stated that 'in Riyadh, the conflict between traditional and modern, ethnic and foreign is most marked'. He discussed the possibilities of change in the social traditions of Saudi Arabia and concluded that 'the resistance is strong, and in 1978 it was felt to be tightening up'. Anderson (1984, pp. 159, 163) supported this view when he stated 'traditionalism still pervades Saudi Arabian society'. Also, he indicated that traditions found a way to continue in modern Saudi society. He stated that 'the traditional forms of social interaction which ensure cohesion within tribal society had found accommodation in modern Saudi Arabian Organizations' (*Ibid.*, p. 163).

Thus, the issue of identity arose as a result of the association between the modernization process and Westernization. It is argued here that the need for identity in Riyadh was widely associated with the threat that people felt as a result of the rapid changes that traditional Saudi society had experienced in the previous three decades.

This modernity 'situation' influenced Riyadh's urbanization in the 1960s and 1970s, which was characterized by a construction boom and a rapid expansion of the city. As a result Riyadh was nicknamed by its mayor as a city of 'Streets and Buildings'. The residents were still conservative and modernization was only in the physical environment not in the way of living. People were rarely seen in public places or walking on the streets. Men and women were segregated at all levels which reflected on the whole atmosphere of the city. It is possible to argue that the people of Riyadh were not yet ready for modern life, even though they welcomed the physical change of their city.[12]

Loss of Belonging and the Search for Architectural Identity

As a result of the rapid change in the 1970s a sense of not belonging became the main issue in the developed environment of Riyadh as people suddenly found themselves in a completely different physical environment. For example, Ben Saleh (1980) indicated the loss of traditional identity in the Saudi built environment. He said:

> Recent buildings have lost their traditional identities and have become hybrids of exotic character in their architectural form, main concepts, arrangement of spaces, organization of elements, and building techniques employed. (cited in Al-Gabbani, 1984, p. 275)

Konash (1980) agreed with this view; he criticized the lack of knowledge of local culture amongst the Western firms which practised in Saudi Arabia and suggested collaboration between Saudi and foreign architects. Al-Hathloul (1981) also studied the impact of Western urban concepts on contemporary Saudi cities. He suggested that Arab-Islamic traditions which formulate the needs of Saudi families should be respected in any future building regulations.[13] Fadan (1983, p. 15) went further in his criticism and attributed the loss of traditional identity to the social changes in Saudi society. He stated that the 'attraction to Western life-style has drawn Saudi attention away from developing a clear and concise understanding of the evolution of a traditional living environment'. These studies agree on the negative impact of Western images on Saudi cities.

At the time concerned, however, people were fascinated by Western design. For example, Boon (1982) mentioned that contemporary homes in Saudi Arabia were strongly influenced by colonial villas in the Middle East. Al-Gabbani (1984, p. 275) found in his study of Riyadh that 'most of the housing units constructed follow western models which symbolize prestige and use costly imported materials'. Abu-Ghazzeh (1997) indicated that modern architecture in Saudi Arabia seemed to be 'culturally destructive'. He criticized the desire of Saudi architects to reflect images of economic and technological development through the adoption of 'Western design'. He attributed this situation to the 'disassociation of the privileged business elite from their cultural roots'. These people tried to express themselves in the built environment by designs mainly borrowed from the West. This then encouraged the middle classes to imitate Western images which were created by the business elite. That is not to say that people did not express their socio-cultural values and express themselves in their homes, but that people experienced new things for the first time, and hence were attracted to them. Later, personal and social identities were expressed through extensive alterations to those buildings.

In the 1980s a mix of Western, traditional, and historical (mostly Arab-Islamic) images were found in the Saudi home environment.[14] This reflected the consciousness of designers and people to create visual identity in the built environment.[15] Mofti (1989), for example, criticized new buildings which derived their physical forms from different sources. Some buildings were strongly influenced by the prevailing trends in architecture worldwide, such as postmodernism and regionalism. Other examples are extremely formal and far from local cultural images, such as Greek or Roman classical images. In the best cases, we can see some buildings imitating traditional forms or borrowing from Arab-Islamic architecture such as Mamluk design.

Most studies of the built environment in Riyadh have focused on the lack of identity – specifically, on the impact of borrowed forms on visual identity rather than paying more attention to the relationship between people and the surrounding physical environment. Therefore, most of the suggestions to maintain identity in the contemporary home were centred on re-using traditional images. Boon (1982), for example, suggested that in order to have an identity it is important to revive traditional urban images. Al-Nowaiser (1983) reached the same conclusion when he indicated that, in order to reflect 'a genuine sense of identity', it is necessary to find 'valid features of architectural heritage' to incorporate into the design of contemporary Saudi housing.

These views helped and accelerated the emergence of an architectural trend in

Saudi Arabia in the 1980s and 1990s,[16] which concentrated on external images and specifically on recycling traditional images in new buildings. However, this trend was still far from the real need of people in Saudi Arabia. Ten years ago, one of the local newspapers[17] discussed this matter under the title 'Issue: our contemporary buildings have no identity'. The editor stated that 'the architectural crisis of our contemporary buildings increases day after day ... a confusion of images is the only description for our contemporary buildings'.

Thus, what happened, and is still happening, in the built environment in Riyadh is a reaction to this sense of loss of identity (Al-Naim, 1998).[18] Borrowing from the past is used as a tool to maintain visual identity in Saudi Arabia. This is clearly understood from Al-Shuaibi's statement that 'designers of various disciplines always borrow from the past, whether ancient or recent' (cited in Salam, 1990, p. 38).[19] Abu-Ghazzeh (1997) also encouraged those buildings which he called 'hybrid regional architecture'.

It was clear that yearning for identity in Saudi Arabia was very much related to its position and role in the Arab and Islamic worlds. One of the causes in my view was an Islamic revivalism after the holy mosque incident in 1981 (when a group of terrorists invaded Alharam in Makkah). Reviving the Arabic/Islamic identity became an objective in itself, even if it happened through physical forms. Also, Saudi academics educated in the United States, particularly those who graduated from MIT and Harvard and were influenced by the Aga Khan programme in architecture, came back to Saudi Arabia in the early 1980s and found themselves in an environment ready to absorb their ideas.

Riyadh under Urban Pressure

Riyadh did proceed to establish itself as a capital for a modern country by constructing a series of institutional buildings. One of the first, and very significant, was inaugurated in 1973: the General Organization for Social Security. It was designed by the Saudi architectural firm, Omrania & Associates. Another phase of the project was added in 1982. In fact, this building indicates how Riyadh was seeking modernity even if its society was still very conservative. It seems that most Arab cities at that time were interested in physical development more than reform of social values (Jarbawi, 1981). The social security building was influenced by Boston City Hall which was built between 1963 and 1968 (Al-Hathloul, 2002). What one can conclude here is that in the 1970s there was a clear movement towards modernity because of the 1960s reform and the flourishing economy which enabled the government to sponsor large-scale projects and rebuild the city.

Later in the 1970s, a number of developments contributed to the expansion of the city, one of which was the establishment of the Real Estate Development Fund (REDF) in 1974 to help Saudi families build their own homes by giving them interest free loans. This new institution was one of the main factors which changed the meaning of residential image in Saudi society resulting later in the decline of all traditional areas. This led, in 1975, to the establishment of the Ministry of Municipal and Rural Affairs and the Ministry for Housing and Public Works (which was closed recently) to control urban development.

In the mid 1970s, the Minister's Council established the Higher Executive Committee to supervise major developments in Riyadh. The committee was involved in three major projects, the Diplomatic Quarter, Foreign Ministry Staff Housing, and Qasr Alhokm district (Justice Palace district). These three projects changed the image of the city and drew attention to the identity of Riyadh and to the question of architectural identity. Riyadh's continued loss of local character led, in 1979, to the establishment of the Qasr Alhokm Area Development Office (QAAD). Prior to this, in 1973, steps were taken by the government to develop the area by inviting Franco Albini to prepare a Master Plan. Albini submitted his feasibility study in 1974 and completed his design and drawings in 1976 (figure 6.11). However, QAAD revised Albini's scheme and assigned Albeeah Group (a local architectural firm) to review the scheme. This led to the establishment of Arriyadh Development Authority (ADA) in 1983, which became the most important urban management institution in Saudi Arabia.

In 1976 the government assigned the French SCET International to review the Doxiadis Master Plan, because the city had expanded beyond the plan. The purpose of this revision was to make short-term implementation proposals. This took 6 years to be approved which meant that Riyadh continued to implement Doxiadis's plan until 1982 when the government approved the SCET proposals. Indeed, Doxiadis's plan institutionalized the urban development of the city, and

Figure 6.11. One of the main plazas in Qasr Alhokm.

still defines Riyadh's urban character. The city after this project implemented the grid system and became a city with clear planning patterns. A north–south axis was introduced in the city and the inner historic part was subject to enormous urban pressure which ended up with decay and the demolition of major traditional buildings including the old Qasr Alhokm and the grand mosque.

The 1980s can be described as the era of large projects due to the decision by the government to revive the historical part of Riyadh. Revenue was inflated by the oil and rose to US$102.10 billion in 1981. In 1984, the first phase of Qasr Alhokom construction started and was completed in 1985 (designed by Franco Albini). It included three buildings: Emara (city government headquarters), the Mayoralty and the Police Headquarters. Also, ADA reviewed the Albeaah plan and started implementing it (figure 6.12). Riyadh was searching for a local and regional identity, which led to an emerging trend called 'new traditionalism'. Major projects supported this and made the city attractive to architects. King Saud University campus (1984) and King Khaled International airport (1983) which were designed by the American firm, Hellmuth, Obata & Kasabaum (HOK); the Ministry of Foreign Affairs, which opened the same year, was designed by the Danish firm, Henning Larsen. The Diplomatic Quarter was inaugurated in 1987 and a year later the second phase of the Qasr Alhokm was started; it opened in 1992 (including the Justice Palace, Grand Mosque, AlMeqillyah shopping mall, and a number of plazas) (figure 6.13). These buildings were among those that characterized the new traditionalism and presented it as an intellectual trend not only in Saudi Arabia but in the Arab world.

Figure 6.12. An image showing part of Albini's scheme (on the right).

Figure 6.13. One of the internal courtyards in Qasr Alhokm.

What is astonishing is that by 1992 the population of Riyadh had jumped to 1.5 million and spread out over 2,000 km².[20] This indicated the amount of urban development that had taken place. The Second Gulf War delayed development as a result of expenditure related to the conflict. However, the rise in oil prices after the war gave Riyadh another chance to reinstitute urban activities. To this end in 1994 a new real-estate company, Arriyadh Development Company, was established to complete the remaining parts of the Qasr Alhokm district. The company immediately started on the third phase of Alhokm district and the construction of Alta'ameer shopping mall was started in 1996 (designed by the Jordanian architect Rasem Badran and Egyptian architect Abdulhalim Ibrahim).

Riyadh as a Setting for Regional Architecture

Riyadh has tried to emphasize the authentic traditional characteristics of its local architecture in its institutional buildings. Arriyadh Development Authority was established to enhance the city's built environment and to emphasize the government's objective of representing the image of power and authority. The notion of 'Institutional Architecture' is used here to reflect both process and product. On the one hand the city of Riyadh is characterized by its institutional buildings (governmental), while on the other those buildings are mostly designed and constructed by ADA, itself a significant institution. It will be demonstrated below how the institutional process and product created the identity of contemporary Riyadh.

The cultural consciousness which ADA developed reflects the new trend in Saudi Arabian architecture. From its position as a strong cultural and professional institution it started to exercise its power by recycling the traditional heritage of Riyadh in new projects. This section will concentrate on four projects designed and controlled by the Authority including: Qasr Alhokm district, the Diplomatic Quarter, the Foreign Ministry Staff Housing and King Abdulaziz Cultural Center. These projects contributed to institutionalizing the image of Riyadh and consolidated its regional identity in the 1980s and 1990s.

The Dilemma of Architectural Identity in Riyadh

The meanings we give to physical forms in reality do not exist in the forms themselves, but in our minds and they are generated from our past experience and significant events related to the forms. In that sense, culture, history and architecture are interrelated concepts and we cannot understand any one of them in isolation from the others.

I am concerned with the 'cultural consciousness' that has developed in contemporary Saudi architecture over the last three decades. What I mean by 'cultural consciousness' is an awareness either by specific groups of people, or national institutions, of the need for architecture to reflect specific cultural goals and images. Recent attempts to employ the Arab-Islamic traditions in Riyadh's contemporary architecture aimed at implementing this objective. This emphasized the high level of resistance society has shown to the incompatible images that have been introduced in the Saudi built environment.

In the search for a new terminology reflecting historical and contemporary architecture, we should differentiate between two types of architecture in Riyadh. First, there is the traditional architecture which can be considered part of what we call 'architecture of Islamic cultures'. This term will reflect both the constant and the variable characteristics of the architecture that existed in the different Islamic historical periods. It reflects the continuity of Islamic principles and values as well as the evolution that may have occurred in the technological environment. The second type of architecture is contemporary, which should continue as a communicative mediator between Islamic principles and values and the values upheld by Saudi society and modern technology.

Consolidating the Cultural Image of Riyadh

Despite the impact of the perceptual language of Western architecture in Saudi Arabia, some recent structures reflect local cultural significance. These projects reveal an ability to generate design principles from traditional architecture and recycle them in contemporary practice. Such structures include the Ministry of Foreign Affairs (Riyadh), the National Commercial Bank (Jeddah), the Island Mosque (Jeddah) and the Diplomatic Club (Riyadh). However, the most distinctive project is the Qasr Alhokm district in Riyadh. This complex is an interesting example of the significance of culture, history, and architecture in contemporary Saudi Arabia.

The Qasr Alhokm district reflects the height of tension between continued traditional values and the desire for modernity in Saudi Arabia. In its development this project has passed through two historical phases. The first phase can be called the 'preconscious' stage where the project and the whole of central Riyadh were viewed in a cultural context and the architecture was to reflect cultural significance.

The cultural significance of Qasr Alhokm can be seen through the change in attitude to the message to be embodied in Riyadh's architecture. In this sense the scheme submitted by Franco Albini between 1976 and 1979 was reviewed and drastically altered by Arriyadh Development Authority in the early 1980s. The Albini scheme was revised due to the conflict between tradition, which the Authority sought to mobilize in Riyadh's architecture, and modernity, which formed the basis of the Albini scheme.[21] Fortunately, only a few buildings were constructed. Later, the Authority held an international competition for the design of the main buildings in the district, the Qasr Alhokm, the Grand Mosque and the surrounding plazas.

ADA was established to enhance the city's built environment and to emphasize the government's objective of representing the image of power and authority. The district was considered one of the most important projects through which the Authority aimed at realizing this goal. It binds the Kingdom's capital with the rest of the country through the adoption of certain perceptual images from all regions of Saudi Arabia. The goal of the project was to revitalize the centre of Riyadh and enable it to resume its historic role as a political, cultural and commercial hub.

The cultural consciousness which Arriyadh Development Authority developed reflects the new trend in Saudi Arabian architecture. From its position as a strong cultural establishment it started to exercise its power by recycling the traditional heritage of Riyadh in these new projects. David Morley and Kevin Robins discussed the importance of such strong institutions in mobilizing the cultural images in any society. They write that:

> tradition is not a matter of a fixed or given set of beliefs or practices which are handed down or
> accepted passively. Rather, as Wright has argued, tradition is very much a matter of present-day

politics, and of the way in which powerful institutions function to select particular values from the past, and to mobilize them in contemporary practices (Morley and Robins, 1995, p. 47).

The authority, then, is aware of its role as a mobilizing force for the cultural goals in Riyadh's contemporary architecture.

Riyadh in the early 1980s desperately needed to rebuild its heart. The loss of identity and the feeling that the city was not reflecting the religious and political image of the country propelled many who were involved in the city's management to adopt traditional forms. This started the era of 'New Traditionalism' as a preferred architectural style for the city which had been influenced by the rise of Postmodernism in the 1970s and by the idea of Regionalism in the 1980s.

The old city had changed significantly from its original layout and form; several parts were demolished and new streets introduced, so altering the morphology and separating the Grand Mosque from other parts including the Palace. Therefore, the Qasr Alhokm district project aimed at enhancing the urban centre of the city and recreating its old spirit, historical image and traditions. This is also linked to the beginning of the Aga Khan Award in 1977 which encouraged traditional Islamic practices in the contemporary architecture of the Islamic World. It seems here that historicity is an integral part of the contemporary Arab mind, which made it easy to encourage most of the prominent Arab architects to adopt the new traditionalism as the only architectural trend.

The main concept of the project was to reflect the cultural and historical significance of central Riyadh. It was to achieve this not only by establishing a strong relationship between the Alhokm Palace and the Mosque through the surrounding buildings and public spaces, but also functionally by finding a clear and direct relationship between them through their forms. In the same way, the spaces and courtyards between the two structures are seen as part of the Mosque's court, reflecting the position of the Mosque as the centre for all spiritual and human activities in the area. In addition, the designer tried to emphasize the spiritual and physical relationship between the ruler, the legislator and the cultural mores of society.

The historical location of the Mosque and the Qasr Alhokm was considered the most important determinant in selecting the site. Moreover, the strong relationship between the Mosque and the Palace, which characterized the old Riyadh, was recreated in the new design. The location of the Alhokm Palace between the Mosque and the Emirate building encouraged the designer to establish a clear axial relation between the Mosque, the Palace and the Emirate, one of the basic principles of Muslim cities. This axis joins the main open squares and emphasizes the relationship between these structures and the Almasmak (the old fort in Riyadh). In addition, the distribution of the entrances to the Mosque and the Palace were influenced by the main spine established on the site. It enabled the absorption of crowds by situating the plazas close to the main entrances.

As to the Palace, the royal and ceremonial entrance was situated on the

Assafat Square opposite the Mosque's south-east elevation. The presence of Assafat Square between the Mosque and the Palace emphasized the spiritual and physical connection between the two buildings. The spatial characteristics were enhanced by the reconstruction of the two bridges connecting the Mosque with the Palace which create a sense of entry to the square as well as providing the whole composition with a feeling of unity.

One of the most important plazas in the district is Imam Mohammed Bin Saud Square, which connects similar key public buildings, namely the Emirate, Municipality, the Police Headquarters and other commercial activities with the Mosque and the Palace. It works as a main distribution point in the site. The square has also become a transitional area connecting the existing structures and new constructions to enrich both. As a general principle, all exterior walls are treated uniformly in local limestone of earthen colour. Therefore, the façades of the Palace and the Mosque are emphasized by strong surfaces with small openings. This feature reflects both sensibility to the hot dry climate and the importance of privacy and power. In general, the visual message of the external appearance of the district reflects the history and the great events that occurred in these places.

Regarding the Grand Mosque, the prayer hall contains numerous rows of columns, as in the old mosques, such as the Prophet Mosque. In addition, an element from Riyadh's local architecture is used in the prayer hall and the passageways surrounding the Mosque's court. The columns are each connected by a wooden rod used as a decorative element. The wood is covered with brown leather and light fittings. Another principle was developed from the adjacent historic building, Almasmak, namely the ribs which support small towers in the roof. These towers were successfully employed to increase spirituality in the mosque by providing indirect sunlight to the prayer hall.

Searching for authenticity is a highly intellectual matter. Nevertheless, the rejection of the Albini scheme during the early 1980s reflected the consciousness of the role of architecture, especially in those public buildings, to communicate the cultural and historical meanings of the site. The meaning of architecture, in this sense, extends beyond denotative and instrumental meanings to connotative meanings, where the aesthetic and symbolic qualities of the place can be reproduced.

New Traditionalism and the Spread of a Local Image in Riyadh

Contemporary architecture in Saudi Arabia during the 1980s and 1990s can be described as striving to be inclusive rather than exclusive. The terms inclusive and exclusive were used by Venturi in 1966, when he criticized the selective approach of modern architecture. On the one hand, he argued that modern architects tend to exclude several problems in their designs. Mies van der Rohe's phrase 'less is more' clearly defines the term 'exclusive'. To define the concept of inclusiveness Venturi said that 'less is a bore'. He argued that Mies's projects excluded a number of problems and therefore could be repeated at any site irrespective of its individuality or spiritual significance. On the other hand, Venturi used the term 'inclusive' to explain two concepts. First, it refers to the employment of the historical configurations in contemporary design to reflect some symbolic meanings. Second, it refers to the consideration of the site's characteristics and of all the issues involved in the design problem instead of selecting among them. He argued that if, however, the problems prove irresolvable the architect 'can express this in an inclusive rather than an exclusive kind of architecture'.

The concept of 'inclusive' can be related to the Islamic principle of 'inclusiveness', which means, 'Every thing is allowed unless there is a verse from the holy Qur'an or Tradition from the Prophet which prohibits it'. In this sense, the inclusive trend in Saudi architecture should be characterized by its ability to absorb the perceptual and associational quantities of traditional culture and mobilize them in contemporary practice. It should communicate the people's images and preferences and link them with their culture and historical events.

The architecture of the Qasr Alhokm district can be categorized as inclusive. The degree of inclusiveness is reflected in its cultural, historical, spatial and visual significance. As an urban project, it recalls a traditional human and spiritual sense. This is achieved by providing the project with the ability to reflect the personal image within the cultural image or what is called 'diversity within unity'. The diversity of spatial qualities and architectural details is contained within the principles of hierarchy of spaces and homogeneity of visual quality. The provision of pedestrian paths, open squares and various cultural and commercial activities recalls the traditional feeling and increases the sense of place. One of the most important features in the layout of the district is the main spine which was created throughout the site. This spine implies religious and cultural meanings. The analogy can also be made between this spine and the Al-Qasaba, which characterized the commercial centres in Muslim cities throughout history. In fact, the original historical site was developed on a spinal layout with a series of open spaces arranged in a longitudinal organization to link the Palace with surrounding buildings, especially the grand mosque which was located on the opposite side of the palace.

Qasr Alhokm district can be considered as one of the best examples emphasizing the characteristics of the inclusive approach in Saudi Arabian contemporary architecture and urbanism. However, architecture is very dynamic, and such an approach may change. Saudi architects may use it as a starting point towards defining their own practice and direction.

Institutional Buildings and the Need for Institutionalizing Traditions

The Qasr Alhokm district is not the only one that institutionalizes the new traditionalism trend in Riyadh. In fact there is another which started at the same time: the Diplomatic Quarter was developed to satisfy the decision of the government in 1975 to move foreign embassies from Jeddah to Riyadh. An area of 800 hectares about 8 km north-west of the heart of Riyadh was selected for the new project. The quarter was designed to accommodate 30,000 people and 120 embassies (figure 6.14). The Master Plan was prepared by the German firm Albert Speer & Partner (AS&P) and the Albeaah Group was responsible for the urban design of the central area.

The project introduced two major ideas to the city. First, it is a semi-gated community which was unknown in Riyadh; second is the introverted development of the central area and creation of Sahat Alkindi Plaza. The decision to build a massive wall, which comprises the Arriyadh Development Authority headquarters and numerous other buildings, to surround the Alkindi Plaza and the Jumaa Mosque brought the sense of a traditional Muslim town which is usually built around a mosque and main plaza (figure 6.15). The analogy with the old centre of

Figure 6.14. Qasr Tiwaiq in the Diplomatic Quarter.

Figure 6.15. Alkindi Plaza and the Jumaa Mosque in the Diplomatic Quarter.

Riyadh is very clear here. The central area of the Diplomatic Quarter is sending messages that Riyadh is still holding its cultural identity even if the city is moving steadily towards modernization.

Numerous projects in the Diplomatic Quarter have won Aga Khan Awards, such as the Tuwaiq Palace (Diplomatic Club), the Embassy of Tunisia (designed by Mimita bin Mahmoud, and Faraj), the Embassy of Japan (Designed by Kenzo Tange) and the landscape project which was designed by the German landscape architects Bodeker, Boyer and Wegenfield. In fact the Quarter is a unique case in the urban development of Riyadh because it changed the whole image of the city's residential and public environments. Now Arriyadh Development Authority is trying to reshape the housing environment by organizing international competitions and symposia in neighbourhood design (2004 and 2007 competitions). The main objective of these competitions is to generate new ideas for the city and learn from its past experience, especially from the Diplomatic Quarter.

This can be linked also to the Ministry of Foreign Affairs Staff housing project which was designed in the same period also by Albert Speer & Partner (AS&P). It covers an area of 40 hectares and consists of detached and semi-detached villas

Figure 6.16. Ministry of Foreign Affairs staff housing project.

(figure 6.16). In fact the importance of this development stems from the urban concepts used. Reinterpreting the traditional design and generating a contemporary traditional Arab town were seen as messages of the identity that Riyadh wanted to express. Culs-de-sac and clustering of houses were used to express this identity. This project influenced most of the regulations used by the Ministry of Municipal and Rural Affairs in planning and directing housing development in Riyadh.

Arriyadh Development Authority also began the construction of King Abdulaziz Cultural Center in the 1990s. The area covers 37 hectares and includes the Almurabba'a Palace, the new National Museum and Darat Amalak Abdulaziz (the cultural organization dedicated to the history and culture of Saudi Arabia and the Arabian Peninsula) (figure 6.17). The project was planned by Arriyadh Development Authority and a number of architects contributed to the design of its components, including the Canadian firm, Moriyma & Teshima Architects, and UK structural engineers Buro Happold, who designed the National Museum; Rasem Badran and Omrania & Associates who were involved in the Darat Amalak Abdulaziz; Omrania & Associates who designed the historical centre of King Abdulaziz Library. The project was completed in 1999 and demonstrated a new experience in managing architectural and urban projects. Arriyadh Development Authority confirmed in this project its capability as an institution to mobilize its vision, coordinate all parties and work as a master planner.

In fact Riyadh has been striving to maintain its regional identity for the last three decades. Arriyadh Development Authority, which was created to secure this objective, seems to have succeeded in achieving this through its role in the institutional buildings whose construction it initiated and supervised. This enabled Riyadh to become the most active Arab city in the 1980s and 1990s especially in reviving traditional architecture and maintaining a regional architectural language. A number of leading Arab architects worked in Riyadh, including the Iraqi

Figure 6.17. King Abdulaziz Cultural Center.

architect Mohammed Makkiya, Egyptian architects Abdulwahed Al-Wakeel and Abdulhalim Ibrahim, and Jordanian architect Rasem Badran. All are considered new traditionalists and Riyadh gave them a chance to express their visions.

Post Traditionalism and Globalizing the City of Riyadh

Riyadh in the last 10 years has been trying to become a global city. The idea of identity and image are no longer defined by local parameters. The city now is composed of a number of 'towns' within its boundaries and these naturally reflect plural images. This can be seen when Riyadh absorbed the smaller villages around it such as Dir'yya, also when the city expanded beyond the expected limit, which resulted in different areas having their own character and identity. For example, the historic centre of Riyadh has a very distinctive identity exemplified by the new business district (which is located in a longitudinal zone between King Fahad Road and Al'Ullaya Road and characterized by its steel and glass high-rise towers). In addition to the presence of a modern central business district, other factors may contribute to achieving a global city status, such as the city's rapidly expanding area (2000 km^2) and increasing cosmopolitan population (4.5 million).

Riyadh has become attractive to people from all over the Kingdom and this has resulted in a kind of clustering within the city where newcomers, usually consisting of poor young families, live in deteriorating areas such as the historic centre. Characterized by low rent these areas are affordable – and thus the city has both rich and poor areas.

Realizing the bad image caused by the presence of low-income neighbourhoods, the government initiated a series of policies to deal with this problem. For example, a few years ago King Abdullah (when he was crown prince) visited one of the poor areas in Riyadh and announced that there needed to be a national plan for poverty. Prior to that Prince Salman (the Riyadh Governor) took action by initiating his project for charity housing. Three clusters were built and more are coming. However, in spite of these efforts, increasing migration to the city will not eradicate poor areas and they will continue to coexist with the richer parts.

To maintain the image of the city, ADA developed a strategic plan to 2020. This plan is flexible and aims to control urban development and manage the physical and environmental problems in the face of the city's rapid growth. It indicates that if the population grows to more than 10 million in the next 15 years there will be a problem in maintaining the living standards in the city. Recently, ADA said the growth will be limited to only 7 million. However, Riyadh is now a globalizing city in the sense that it is preparing itself as a regional and international financial centre.

Before the turn of the century there were few projects that indicated the move towards globalization. Alfaysaliyyah Tower (completed in 2000), designed by the British firm Foster & Partners, became a sign of a new era. The plan was to develop the whole area between Al'Ullaya Road and King Fahad Avenue as a new financial and administration centre. Another project was the Almamlka Tower (completed in 2003) designed by Omrania & Associates in association with the American firm Ellerbe Becket (figure 6.18). Further projects are under design such as the King Abdullah Financial Center and IT City. These developments will change the image of the city and reorient it as a global centre.

The city of Riyadh is very conservative and it was not easy to move from one status to another because of the deep rooted cultural image within its society. However, Alfaysaliyyah and Almamlka reshaped people's perception not only in Riyadh but in the whole Kingdom. This could be attributed to the media, which played a major role in constructing the new image of the city by using the two towers extensively as a sign of progress and belonging to the global world. People now believe that the only way to express globalization is through high-rise towers. For example AlRajhi tower is one of the more recent developments, designed by W.S. Atkins & Partners Overseas, who also designed Burj Al-Arab in Dubai (figure 6.19).

In spite of such developments it would be incorrect to argue that traditionalism no longer exists. Riyadh is still considered a conservative city not in its architecture but in its urban life. Generally, there is no opposition to globalization, especially its financial and technological aspects. However, the city and its people resist cultural globalization. There is a belief that they should 'think global' but also 'act local'.[22] The term 'global' is, however, very much valid if we really want to assess the architectural and urban situation in Riyadh.

Riyadh is influenced by the global phenomenon of 'marketecture', a composite of 'market' and 'architecture'. Many architects now practice in the region primarily to satisfy their clients' economic interests. This influences the quality of urbanism by making cities move towards 'theme architecture'. It cannot be denied that Riyadh is looking to Dubai as a model, even if it is with conservative steps.[23] The Dubai experience became very attractive for many people in the region. Many cities in the Gulf consider Dubai as a model that they should follow not only in

Figure 6.18. Kingdom Tower and the business district.

Figure 6.19. The new AlRajhi tower.

its physical development but also from the economic point of view. Doha, Kuwait, Manama and the main Saudi cities became more oriented to liberating their economy and opening their market for global activities. In Saudi Arabia, Emaar from Dubai became an important player in the King Abdulla Economic City in Rabeq (Western Saudi Arabia) and we believe that the involvement of Dubai in Saudi Arabia's urban development is increasing.

Conclusion

Searching for an identity takes different forms. The dilemma is whether or not Riyadh should have a specific identity. This question opens the door for criticism of the whole urban process in the city. Global cities should be open to all ideas and should interact with all cultures, but this means that the idea of 'one identity' or 'one image' does not exist any more. What really matters here is whether Riyadh is ready to accept these global conditions. Striving for a unique cultural identity drove Riyadh in the 1980s and 1990s to adopt and reinforce traditional images. The question now is what will happen to the city and what are the images that will express its new global role.

Riyadh will remain as the city for institutional architecture, but will practice this role from a different perspective because it is now an urban site not only for

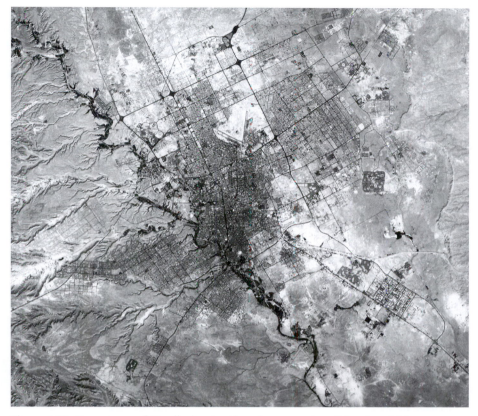

Figure 6.20. Recent map of Riyadh showing the urban expansion of the city which now covers more than 2,000 km².

governmental buildings but also for private sector activities. In the last decade, numerous shopping malls and office towers have been erected to serve private sector activities which in effect will transform the city to a site of global capital where notions of identity become secondary. Twenty-five per cent of the national revenue comes from this city and it is a major hub for financial and commercial activities. It thus has all the ingredients for integrating into the global system which needs to be enhanced by attracting foreign capital and creating an environment conducive to investment.

Whether Riyadh will continue to be the city of institutional architecture or will change to a city of financial and commercial architecture will depend very much on the next few years when it grasps the consequences of globalization. Hesitation towards globalization is very clear in the first decade of the new millennium because it was predicted before the turn of the century that the skyline of Riyadh will be transformed into a massive wall of high-rise buildings. This has not happened and we have considerable doubt whether this will happen in the future. What we strongly believe is that Riyadh will continue as a hesitant city and the impact of globalization will be limited. Riyadh is considered the heart of Saudi society which is naturally conservative and resistant to accepting major social changes.

The strategic plan for the city maintains its conservative attitude and is not trying substantively to open up Riyadh to global investment. It is not easy for a city like Riyadh to be a global city in the literal sense of the phrase, but we do expect it will become a global city, different from all others – 'a very conservative global city'.

Notes

1.   Aramco built its first camp in Dhahran in 1938, then in Ras-Tanura in 1939, and by 1944 in Abqaiq.

2.   Also, Al-Hathloul (1981), has said: 'The initial growth of Dammam and Al-Khobar in the late 1350s[H]/1930s and early 1360s[H]/1940s was not planned in an orderly fashion. As the population grew, people took over any available land and erected basic shelters and fences of local materials. Following the traditional pattern of Arab-Muslim cities, the streets were narrow and irregular' (pp. 145–146).

3.   Shiber (1967) describes the plan of Al-Khobar as: 'It covered only about one quarter square mile North of the company pierhead storage yard. The blocks averaged 130 by 200 feet with separating streets of 40 and 60 foot widths'. Moreover, he indicated how the new plan ignored the existing Saudi settlements. He states 'Here again, the gridiron pattern was oriented north-south. No consideration was given to the mushroom growth of temporary structures and those were demolished to open the new streets' (p. 430).

4.   Facey (1992) states that 'The growth of suburbs in the 1930s and 1940s took, broadly, two forms. Low-income groups, such as the bedouin labourers and mechanics, congregated in concentrated suburbs to the east and south of the old city. The royal family and the well-to-do, by contrast, built their palaces and residences to the north and west, and adopted more spacious pattern settlements' (p. 300).

5.   Facey (1992) indicates that 'Riyadh during the reign of King Saud underwent prodigious growth. The King was determined that the new fabric of the city should reflect its status as capital of a modern nation. Traditional, local methods and styles of architecture and planning gave way entirely to imported ones. Henceforth cement and reinforced concrete took over. Grid-plan streets and arterial roads appeared ...' (p. 317).

6.   Abercrombie (1966) describes Annasriyyah as: 'The mile-square palace complex was a city within a city, complete with mosques, schools, shops, and playgrounds. Rows of sumptuous villas lined the four-lane avenue leading to the giant pink reception hall' (p. 10).

7.   'The physical pattern of Al-Malaz follows a gridiron plan with a hierarchy of streets, rectangular blocks, and large lots which in most cases take a square shape. Thoroughfares are 30 metres in width, main streets 20 metres, and secondary or access streets 10 and 15 metres' (Al-Hathloul and Anis-ur-Rahmaam, 1985, p. 208).

8.   Alangari (1996), argues that the Al-Malaz project 'inspired the populace to imitate and copy the new residential prototype (the villa) for several reasons: firstly, the project was sponsored by the Government, so it was an authorised scheme by the decision makers showing how modern [Riyadh] should be; secondly, it was the first residential public project to be executed in the capital with modern facilities and landscape boulevards in contrast with the dusty and unhygienic traditional residential quarter'. Therefore, 'to the society it became the dream living environment' (p. 267).

9.   Abecrombie (1975) states 'Certainly the Middle Easterners do not want from us cultural – and certainly not religious – missionaries. In general, their beliefs, their dress, food, decorations, prayers and ways of behavior are infinitely more firmly established and devoutly practiced than our own' (p. 12).

10.   We can link this social resistance with what the Ministry of Labour and Social Affairs aimed to preserve in the 1960s. Assah (1969), mentions that the Ministry aimed 'to assist in directing

balanced social development in the kingdom with the aim of raising the standard of the citizens, improving their living conditions and providing them with the necessities for happy and dignified life, at the same time preserving and reinforcing spiritual and moral values with the object of building a progressive integrated community' (p. 252).

11.   One of the British architects who worked in Saudi Arabia for several years.

12.   Recently changes occurred in understanding urban space in the city of Riyadh. The present mayor, Abdulaziz Al-'Ayaf (he is an architect and urban planner), encouraged the slogan of 'human city'. To encourage Riyadh to be more human he built a number of roads for walking and encouraged the idea of neighbourhood gardens. Also, we can mention here three major projects which will change the face of Riyadh's urban space. First, and the most critical, is the rehabilitation of Wadi Hanifa which is 70 km from the north to south, on the west side of Riyadh. Second, is the King Abdulla Park which is 700,000 m² in the west of Riyadh which includes botanical, scientific, international etc, gardens. The third is King Abdulla Garden in Al-Malaz (in the first modernized part of the city). These developments will redefine the meaning of public space and, hopefully, will change the relationship between the people and their physical environment.

13.   The study by Al-Hathloul (1981, p. 266) introduces for the first time the impact of Western urban concepts on the Saudi built environment. Also, it suggests that 'urban form within the Arab-Muslim city is to be found not within the physical elements themselves but within their system of arrangement (the rules of conduct), then these elements can be adapted or can even change so long as their system of arrangement or their relationships remain constant'.

14.   Musa'ad Al-Angari (the former Mayor of Riyadh) mentioned in 1983 that Riyadh had several architectural styles such as European, Islamic, and vernacular (*Assyasa* (Kuwaiti Newspaper), 6 February 1983).

15.   We can link the consciousness of the traditional and historical forms in Saudi Arabia in the 1980s to the criticism of modern architecture by many architects and historians. For example, Venturi (1966) in his book *Complexity and Contradiction in Architecture* paved the way for postmodern architecture. Malcolm (1974) attributes the failure of modern architecture to its inability to understand the relationship between the physical space and social space and its ignorance of the traditional pattern and historical continuity. Frampton (1980) shares these views and he stresses that modern architecture isolated itself from society due to its rational and industrial tendency.

16.   We can go back further and attribute this trend to the 1968 Doxiadis plan for Riyadh. This plan suggested that 'in any new comprehensive planning legislation, special building rules and regulations should be drafted to ensure the maintenance of the basic principles of local architecture (i.e. internal courtyard, etc.) without necessarily mimicking old and absolute architectural forms and construction techniques' (cited in Al-Hathloul, 1981, p. 174).

17.   *Al-Yaum* (Arabic newspaper), No. 8698, 2 April 1997.

18.   Early attempts to re-use traditional images in contemporary buildings started in the late 1970s, especially in government buildings. This can be attributed to the raised consciousness worldwide of local cultures.

19.   Saudi Architect and the head of Albeaah group.

20.   For more detail refer to the strategic plan final reports prepared by the ADA, 2004.

21.   This can be related to arguments within contemporary architectural theory pertaining to the failure of modern concepts in architecture in addressing the relationship between physical and social space. One of the main consequences was ignorance of the importance of traditional patterns and historical continuity (Malcolm, 1974). This promoted the technological and economical development over local culture. Frampton (1980) criticized modern architecture because it isolated itself from society due to its rational and industrial tendency. Thus modern architecture 'in its most abstract form, has played a certain role in the impoverishment of the environment … particularly where it has been instrumental in the rationalization of both building types and methods, and where both the material finish and the plan form have been reduced to their lowest common denominator, in order to make production cheaper and to optimize use'.

22.   The awareness about the impact on urban life became an intellectual issue in Saudi Arabia. The First Saudi Umran Forum held in Riyadh (2–4 April 2007) was about the new economic cities in Saudi Arabia. The author presented a paper 'The new cities in Saudi Arabia: one identity or multi identities'. The presentation was about globalization and its impact on Saudi cities. Most of the papers presented at the conference were about this issue and how the cities will respond to it.

23.   In many meetings with the Mayor of Riyadh, Prince Abdullaziz Al-'Ayaf (he was a faculty member in the Department of City Planning, King Saud University), he mentioned that he liked Dubai and he consider it as a 'model'. This is not to say that he is aiming to imitate the Dubai experience but he is very much interested to learn from it and direct Riyadh to be itself.

References

Abercrombie, S. (1975) The Middle East: design, politics and policy. *Design and Environment*, **7**(4), pp. 11–13.
Abercrombie, T. (1966) Saudi Arabia beyond the sands of Mecca. *National Geographic*, **129**(1), pp. 1–53.
Abu-Ghazzeh, T.M. (1997) Vernacular architecture education in the Islamic society of Saudi Arabia: towards the development of an authentic contemporary built environment. *Habitat International*, **21**(2), pp. 229–253.
Alangari, A. (1996) The Revival of the Architectural Identity: The City of Arriyadh. Unpublished PhD thesis, University of Edinburgh.
Al-Gabbani, M. (1984) Community Structure, Residential Satisfaction, and Preferences in a Rapidly Changing Urban Environment: The Case of Riyadh, Saudi Arabia. Unpublished PhD thesis, University of Michigan.
Al-Hathloul, S. (1981) Tradition, Continuity, and Change in the Physical Environment: The Arab-Muslim City. Unpublished PhD thesis, Massachusetts Institute of Technology.
Al-Hathloul, S. (2002) Riyadh Architecture in One Hundred Years. Public Lecture presented in Darat Al-Funun, Amman, 21 April.
Al-Hathloul, Saleh and Anis-ur-Rahmaam (1985) The evolution of urban and regional planning in Saudi Arabia. *Ekistics*, **52**(312), pp. 206–212.
Al-Naim, M. (1996) Culture, history, and architecture: Qasr Al-Hokm district in Riyadh. *Ahlan Washlan* (Saudi Arabian Airline Magazine), **20**(9), pp. 12–17.
Al-Naim, M. (1998) Continuity and Change of Identity in the Home Environment: Development of the Private House in Hofuf, Saudi Arabia. Unpublished PhD thesis, University of Newcastle upon Tyne.
Al-Naim, M. (2003) Dynamism of the Traditional Arab Town: Case of Hofuf in Saudi Arabia. Paper presented in the 35th Seminar of Arabian Studies, British Museum, London, 17–19 July.
Al-Naim, M. (2005) *Political Influences and Paradigm Shifts in the Contemporary Arab Cities: Questioning the Identity of Urban Form*, CRiSSMA Working Paper No.7. Milan: Pubblicazioni dell'I.S.U. Universita Cattolica.
Al-Naim, M. (2006) *The Home Environment in Saudi Arabia and Gulf States*. Vol. 1: *Growth of Identity Crises and Origin of Identity*. Vol. 2: *The Dilemma of Cultural Resistance, Identity in Transition*. CRiSSMA Working Paper No. 7. Milan: Pubblicazioni dell'I.S.U. Universita Cattolica.
Al-Nowaiser M. A. (1983) The Role of Traditional and Modern Residential Urban Settlements on the Quality of Environmental Experience in Saudi Arabia: Unyzeh and New Alkabra in Alkasseem Region. Unpublished PhD thesis, University of Southern California.
Al-Soliman, Tarik M. (1991) Societal values and their effect on the built environment in Saudi Arabia: a recent account. *Journal of Architectural and Planning Research*, **8**(3), pp. 235–255.
Anderson, G. (1984) Differential Urban Growth in the Eastern Province of Saudi Arabia: A Study of the Historical Interaction of Economic Development and Socio-Political Change. Unpublished PhD thesis, Johns Hopkins University.
Assah, A. (1969) *Miracle of the Desert Kingdom*. London: Johnson Publications.
Boon, J. (1982) The modern Saudi villa: its cause and effect. *American Journal for Science and Engineering*, **7**(2), pp. 132–143.

Costello, V.F. (1977) *Urbanization in the Middle East*. Cambridge: Cambridge University Press.

Dalley, K. (1976) The current state of play in Saudi Arabia. *RIBA Journal*, May, p. 166.

Doxiadis Associates (1977) Formulating a housing program for Saudi Arabia. *Ekistics*, **44**(261), pp. 105–108.

Facey, W. (1992) *Riyadh the Old City: From its Origin until the 1950s*. London: Immel Publishing.

Fadan, Y.M. (1983) The Development of Contemporary Housing in Saudi Arabia (1950–1983). Unpublished PhD thesis, Massachusetts Institute of Technology.

Frampton, Kenneth (1980) *Modern Architecture: A Critical History*. London: Thames and Hudson.

Jarbawi, A.B. (1981) Modernism and Secularism in the Arab Middle East. Unpublished PhD thesis, University of Cincinnati.

Jomah, H.S. (1992) The Traditional Process of Producing a House in Arabia during the 18th and 19th Centuries: A Case of Hedjaz. Unpublished PhD thesis, University of Edinburgh.

Kelly, K. and Schnadelbach, R.T. (1975) Dry prospects in Saudi Arabia. *Landscape Architecture Magazine*, October, pp. 442–444.

Kimball, S.T. (1956) American culture in Saudi Arabia. *Transaction of the New York Academy of Sciences*, Series II, **18**(5).

Konash, F. (1980) Evaluation of Western Architecture in Saudi Arabia: Guideline and Critique. Unpublished Master thesis, University of New Mexico.

Lebkicher, Roy, Rentz, George and Steineke, Max (1960) *Aramco Handbook*. Netherlands: Arabian American Oil Company.

Lipsky, G.A. (1959) *Saudi Arabia: Its People, its Society, its Culture*. New Haven, CT: HRF Press.

Malcolm, M. (1974*) Crisis in Architecture*. London: RIBA Publications, pp.16–17.

Mofti, F.A. (1989) Transformation in the built environment in Saudi Arabia. *Urban Futures*, **2**(4).

Morley, D. and Robins, K. (1995*) Spaces of Identity*. London: Routledge.

Palgrave, W.G. (1865*) Narrative of Year's Journey Through Central and Eastern Arabia (1862–3)*. London.

Pelly, L. (1866) *Report on a Journey to Wahabee Capital of Riyadh in Central Arabia*. Byculla, Mumbai: The Education Society's Press.

Philby, B. (1922) *The Heart of Arabia: A Record of Travel & Exploration*. London: Constable.

Sadleir, G.F. (1866) *Diary of A Journey Across Arabia (1819)*. Bombay. (Reprinted with an Introduction by F.M. Edwards, Cambridge: The Oleander Press, 1977).

Salam, H. (ed.) (1990) *Expressions of Islam in Buildings*. Proceedings of International Seminar sponsored by the Aga Khan Award for Architecture and the Indonesian Institute of Architects, Jakarta and Yogyakarta, Indonesia.

Shiber, S.G. (1967) Report on city growth in the Eastern Province, Saudi Arabia, in *Recent Arab City Growth*. Kuwait.

Shirreff, D. (1979) Housing ideas differ on what people want. in Andrews, J. and Shirreff, D. (eds.) *Middle East Annual Review*. England: World of Information, pp. 59–62.

Venturi, Robert (1966, 2002) *Complexity and Contradiction in Architecture*. New York: Museum of Modern Art.

Chapter 7

Kuwait: Learning from a Globalized City

Yasser Mahgoub

This chapter focuses on the process of globalization as experienced by the city-state of Kuwait. It traces the development of architecture and the built environment in the city during the second half of the twentieth century, focusing on the impact of economic, political and cultural aspects of globalization. The analysis covers the development of public buildings designed by large multi-national firms for government institutions and large companies as well as private houses designed by small offices influenced by individual clients' needs and ambitions. It attempts to illustrate the development of these distinctive built environments under the pressures of globalization.[1]

The Arabic for globalization is *Aawlamah* and was first used to describe the increased global economic activities which characterized the second half of the twentieth century. It is derived from the origin-word *Aalam*, which in Arabic/ Islamic culture constitutes an important cornerstone of Islamic belief as a religion that addresses the whole globe and people (*Aalameen*) and not only the residents of the Arabian peninsula. This notion motivated the spread of Islam to the rest of the world's nations and places. A cultural globalization movement facilitated the spread of Islam from India to Spain towards the end of the first millennium.

In today's Arab world, globalization is often viewed as 'another term for capitalism and imperialism' and that 'all Arabs and Muslims need to consider it an imminent danger that is endangering the political, social, cultural and economic stability' (Za'za', 2002). This attitude arose because the impact of globalization was more rapid and dramatic in most Arab and Muslim countries than in other parts of the world as it followed the footsteps of colonialization. Many feel they are on the receiving end of globalization and not participating in its making, but others point to the advantages of globalization and argue that worries about domination are exaggerated and that there is no threat to sacred beliefs.

Critics of globalization in the Arab world suggest that globalization is a new form of colonialization and that a Western view is being imposed on the East, and on Arab and Islamic cultures. Participants and observers of daily life in the

Arab world can immediately realize its impact on individuals and society at large. Globalization can be seen in everything from the introduction of the latest telecommunications technology to the spread of international fast-food franchises and shopping centres. What is more difficult to observe from the outside is the transformation of culture in the face of these pressures because culture changes more slowly than the individual.

This chapter illustrates the process of globalization which Kuwait has been going through since the mid-twentieth century, both as process and product. While the product is more visible and easily identified, the process is more discreet and differs from one context to another.

Urban and Architectural Development in Kuwait

Before the Discovery of Oil

The city-state of Kuwait is located at the northern tip of the Arabian Gulf, occupying 17,818 square kilometres. It is bordered by Iraq to the north and Saudi Arabia to the south (figure 7.1). According to the Urban Indicators published by UN Population Division, Kuwait is the second most urbanized country in the world with 97.6 per cent of the population living in urban areas – only surpassed by Singapore with 100 per cent (United Nations Population Division, 2003). Kuwait falls in the fourth position among Middle Eastern countries – after UAE, Qatar and Israel – in the per capita GDP list (World Factbook, 2002). This status was achieved in less than 50 years, during the second half of the twentieth century.

Figure 7.1. Map of Kuwait and the Gulf.

According to Al-Mutawa (1994):

> more than three centuries ago, there was a small 'kote', 'a small castle', near the sea, established
> by 'Barrak', the Prince of Beni Khalid, for his rest during the spring that was the beginning of
> buildings in the old Kuwait city. It is said that the name of Kuwait was derived from the 'kote'.

Before the discovery of oil during the 1930s, Kuwait was an isolated, traditional settlement beside a small creek, overlooking the Arabian Gulf. During the sixteenth century it was 'part of the Ottoman Empire, although there never was a real Ottoman presence' (Slot, 1998). Despite being part of the Ottoman, and later the British, Empire, lack of natural resources and a harsh climate meant that Kuwait was never really fully colonized (Vale, 1992). The country was a trading place for nomadic tribes and sea traders; the inhabitants depended on the Gulf for their livelihood through fishing, pearling and travel. However, after the discovery of oil, Kuwait emerged as an important country in the world economy and recently in world politics because of its location at the crossroads from the Gulf to Iraq and Iran (Anderson and Al-Bader, 2006).

Kuwait's vernacular settlement was made up of mud brick courtyard houses built along narrow alleys. The town was surrounded by a semi-circular defensive wall constructed in 1920 to protect it from tribal attacks. Al-Bahar (1984) said of the houses that 'they responded to human, social, cultural and environmental needs'. They were built by traditional master builders, called *Al-Ustaz*, who understood the form the houses should take. As Rapoport (1987) put it, 'in the past designers and clients shared culture, they were typically members of the same group'.

Al-Bahar (1984) explained that the many design features of the older houses of Kuwait was the cultural concept of separating male and female quarters and the notion of privacy and security. The courtyard was an important feature that provided shelter from the harsh climate as well as safety and privacy for the family. Islam and Al-Sanafi (2006) concluded that, in addition to the climatic factors and the availability of building materials, the specific guidelines which influenced the design of Kuwait's traditional courtyard houses were: privacy of the occupants, especially women, in relation to outsiders and male visitors; the treatment of guests; responsibility to neighbours; and modesty in life.

The First Master Plan

Kuwait has been through a rapid process of modernization since the discovery of oil in the 1930s. The city's urban planning began in 1951 with the first master plan by the British firm Minoprio, Spencely and McFarlane. Their main objectives were to set down the improvements which they considered necessary for the development of Kuwait in accordance with the highest standards of 'modern town planning' (Minoprio, Spencely and McFarlane, 1951). The issues which they regarded as being of primary importance were:

Figure 7.2. Old house, Bait Al Badr, courtyard.

Figure 7.3. Old mosque, the Sailors' Mosque, renovated.

- ◆ the provision of a modern road system appropriate to the traffic conditions in Kuwait;

- ◆ the location of suitable zones for public buildings, industry, commerce, schools, and other purposes;

- ◆ the choice of zones for new houses and other buildings needed in residential areas, both inside and outside the town walls;

- ◆ the selection of sites for parks, sports grounds, school playing fields and other open spaces;

- ◆ the creation of a beautiful and dignified town centre, particular attention being given to the treatment of Safat and the siting of public buildings;

- ◆ the planting of trees and shrubs along the principal roads and at other important points in the town;

- ◆ the provision of improved main roads linking Kuwait with nearby towns and villages.

They emphasized that the plan was a broad outline to a comparatively small scale, and that more surveys and larger scale drawings would be required before building could start. Their accompanying report also referred to the layout of residential areas, the siting and design of individual buildings, public services including water supply, sewerage and electricity, building bylaws, administration, and a programme of development.

The late 1950s and early 1960s witnessed the implementation of the first master plan by the Ministry of Public Works under the supervision of the Kuwait Development Board established in 1950 and headed by the Emir of Kuwait. Demolition of the city walls and old houses in residential areas to provide land for the construction of new public buildings paralleled the construction of new roads and residential neighbourhoods south of the old city, in the desert.

These neighbourhoods were self-sufficient entities with schools, shops, mosques and other services. As Gardiner (1983) put it, 'there was no need to come into the city except for work because everything was there'. As part of the government's policy for the distribution of wealth, low-income families were given public housing while rich families were compensated with plots of land and money if their houses were demolished or their land acquired. Building regulations proposed by the master plan allowed for the construction of individual 'villas' on these plots. Buildings and houses erected during the 1950s and 1960s reflected the modernist style of architecture which dominated that era.

The first master plan was an example of town planning theories of the early twentieth century which aimed at producing an 'ideal environment' for modern societies. As described by Minoprio, 'it was a difficult commission. We didn't know anything much about the Muslim world and the Kuwaitis wanted a city – they wanted a *new* city, hospitals, schools, housing and good communications… All we could give them was what we knew' (quoted in Gardiner, 1983).

The plan called for the demolition of the old houses inside the city wall to make way for new roads and public buildings. The plan followed the original form of the city which was an oval overlooking the Kuwait bay to the north and surrounded by a semi-circular defensive wall to the south. The wall was the third in a series of concentric walls that were built during different periods to defend the city from tribal attacks. The first wall was built in 1760 with an approximate length of 750 metres when the town area was about 11.275 hectares. The second wall was built in 1811 and was approximately 2300 metres long and the town area was about 72.4 hectares. Finally, the third wall was built in 1921 and was approximately 6,400 metres and had five gates. The town area was then about 750 hectares (Kuwait Municipality, 1980).

The car was a major factor in the planning of the new city. As described by Gardiner (1983):

> the city plan was primarily a road plan that arose from the five gateways of the wall; the roads radiated out from these gateways and, together with three intersecting ring roads, formed the boundaries of the new townships (or neighbourhood units).

Figure 7.4. Demolished old houses.

A green belt replaced the semi-circular defensive wall and a system of roads was developed to create new neighbourhoods. The neighbourhoods were designed as 'self-supporting entities, fully equipped with schools, shops, mosques, community centres and police stations' (*Ibid.*). Each neighbourhood accommodated up to 12,000 inhabitants and was surrounded by freeways on four sides. Arterial roads led to the neighbourhood centre while collector and local roads led to the houses. The first neighbourhood was called after the Emir of Kuwait Sheikh Abdullah Al-Salem Al-Sabah and is referred to as Al-Dahia, or 'the neighbourhood'. Here the first villas and palaces of influential families were built.

Criticisms of the Early Stages of Development

Saba George Shiber (1964) observed that, 'Kuwait literally exploded from a small village to a fast-urbanizing regional metropolis in just over twelve years'. He claimed that the speed of this unique urban explosion, the momentum propelling

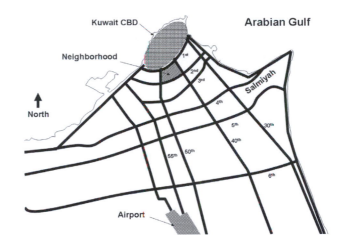

Figure 7.5. Analysis of Kuwait's built environment structure.

it to a chain of explosions, the ambitious drive behind the fast urbanization and the vast revenues making all this possible were, perhaps, unprecedented in urban history. This rapid urbanization created a built environment that is criticized by specialists and the public as being unfriendly, hostile and lacking a sense of belonging. In his keynote address to the First International Conference on Architecture and Design in Kuwait, the renowned Kuwaiti architect Hamed Shuaib (1999*a*) criticized the fact that architecture in Kuwait was being produced by architects from different parts of the world. He asked the question posed at many conferences and seminars held in the Gulf area: 'When will we, in Kuwait and other Gulf countries, have modern architecture suitable for our community, environment and heritage?' '*Asimatna, Laysh Jazia?*' – meaning 'Why is our capital unsightly?' – is a question posed by observers and critics of the quality of the urban environment in Kuwait (*Al-Anbaa*, 2001). The 'lost identity in the built environment' is another observation made by the laypeople, professionals and specialists (*Al-Qabas*, 2003).

Shuaib (1999*b*) argued that Kuwaiti architecture had passed through three distinctive phases between the end of the 1950s and the end of the twentieth century. The first phase witnessed a mixture of houses built, some according to Kuwaiti traditions – courtyard houses closed from the outside and open to the inside area, known as *alhoush* – while others were modern Western villas. The second phase, during the 1960s and 1970s, witnessed the introduction of villas whose design followed the Mediterranean architecture found in Egypt, Syria and Lebanon from where their architects came. The Kuwaitis were inspired by the cultural development of these Arab Mediterranean countries, where they used to spend their summer vacations. The villas were designed using strange shapes and forms which did not reflect the type of life which existed within them. The third phase encompasses the 1980s and the 1990s when an interest in the revival of Kuwaiti traditional architecture evolved.

In his book *History of Architecture in Old Kuwait City*, Kuwaiti architect Saleh Al-Mutawa (1994) criticized foreign architects for their insensitivity to cultural needs and traditions:

> the architects that came from abroad did not take the time to study the cultural needs of the people of Kuwait such as having a separate entrance to the male guests' room, the 'Dewania', and the future family expansion. They did not try to satisfy these needs through their designs, nor did they study the climate of Kuwait: hot and dry from April to November; cold and humid from December to March; dust and sandstorms; and high levels of solar radiation.

He claimed that Kuwait suffers from these unfortunate architectural mistakes which failed to produce housing to meet the societal needs of the local people. The foreign architects created a mixture of architectural styles, depending on their different nationalities and backgrounds.

Another Kuwaiti architect, Abdullah Qabazard (1999) observed that, as 'oil flowed, the population boomed and the city sprawled'. He criticized the rapid expansion that was based on hastily made plans disregarding the needs and traditions of the local population and the tearing down of old structures. The city centre, he added:

> once a place where families lived, shopped, worked and played, was foreordained a commercial district and residents were shifted to Western-style suburban and family homes and apartments, boxy designs of these flats and villas internally inappropriate for traditional, orthodox Kuwaiti lifestyle and externally unsuited for the nation's harsh climate. (*Ibid.*)

The city continued to expand as further master plans were developed and implemented. More neighbourhoods were added and roads expanded. More ring roads were constructed to annex more desert land to the urban area. An industrial area was established in Shuwaikh to the west and a shopping and entertainment area was established in Salmiyah to the east. The city stretched along the coastal strip limited by the water of the Gulf to the north and east and oil fields to the south and west. The neighbourhoods assigned for private housing lacked entertainment activities during the evening, while the commercial neighbourhoods of Salmiyah, Farwaniya and Hawalli, which contain shopping and housing for expatriates, are more lively and full of activities during the evening (figure 7.6).

In the southern neighbourhood of Khetan, thousands of low-income, expatriate manual workers, including some 60,000 Egyptian Saiidis – the villagers of Upper Egypt – reside in what is virtually a shanty town. The inhabitants live in crowded living conditions in converted courtyard houses with 20 to 25 workers in

Figure 7.6. Shopping at Salmiyah – Al-Fanar Shopping Center.

Figure 7.7. Expatriate workers' houses.

each house. The room rent varies between 15KD to 45 KD (US$54 to US$162) per person per month depending on the size, location and number of tenants in the room. Most rooms are shared by more than five persons which makes the rent from each house very profitable for the owner. The living conditions of this marginalized group have been deteriorating rapidly, especially since the Second Gulf War. The government developed plans to clear the area and move the inhabitants to a new location, but implementation of this plan is very slow.

Mastering the Development of Kuwait's Urban Environment

The urban environment in Kuwait has passed through significant stages. During each stage a master plan, or a review of a master plan, was produced:

◆   The first master plan (KMP1) was prepared by Monoprio, Spencely and Macfarlane in 1951 (see above).

◆   The Municipality Development Plan was an assembly of planning studies for different areas in Kuwait prepared by Kuwait Municipality staff during the period from 1952 to 1967.

◆   Colin Buchanan & Partners developed a second master plan (KMP2) from 1967 to 1968 in which they suggested improvement of the road system and the construction of new cities outside the urban area.

◆   The first review of the second master plan (KMP2R1) by Shankland Cox in 1977 suggested the construction of Subiya city and Khiran city to the north and south of Kuwait city.

◆   Colin Buchanan & Partners re-examined the second master plan (KMP2R2) in 1983.

◆   In 1990, Kuwait Municipality commissioned the Kuwaiti firm SSH and the international firm W.S. Atkins to develop a third master plan (KMP3). Work stopped during the Iraqi invasion but was completed in 1997 after the liberation of Kuwait.

◆   In 2003 Kuwait Engineering Group in collaboration with Colin Buchanan & Partners were commissioned to develop a new master plan review in 2003.

The second master plan developed in 1968 by Colin Buchanan & Partners stretched the city north and south along the Gulf shores. It also called for the dispersion of the city centre by creating new centres so as to overcome the growing traffic congestion problems. With the rise of oil prices after the 1973 Middle East War, the country had sufficient income to support its ambitious plans.

In 1977 the British planning firm Shankland Cox proposed the establishment of two new cities: one in the north at Ras Subiya and the other in the south near Al Khiran. The towns were planned to be self-sufficient in employment and services and were to be designed to a high environmental standard (Kuwait Municipality, 1980), but the plans were not implemented during the 1980s and 1990s due to economic and political circumstances which increased pressure on the existing urban areas.

However, the compact traditional design of the city was replaced by urban sprawl. Attached courtyard houses were replaced by detached villas, narrow shaded alleys for pedestrians were replaced by wide streets for cars. This automobile oriented planning created an automobile dependent society where the car is the primary means of transport and almost all private cars are occupied by the driver only. Public transport is used only by poor expatriate workers from Asia and Middle Eastern countries. Car dependency raised the levels of air pollution and increased traffic problems, while lack of adequate parking within house plots resulted in vehicles parked on sidewalks, creating visual pollution and people unable to use them for walking and social interaction. Different types and colours of sheds were installed to protect cars from the burning summer sun so increasing the visual pollution. This is a result of changes in the building bylaws permitting larger areas within the plots and preventing cars from parking outside the plots (Mahgoub, 2002).

As Shiber (1964) observed:

the first wave of new buildings to occupy the cleared area were fairly mundane structures

Figure 7.8. The contemporary housing environment.

designed primarily by Egyptian architects and Arab contractors, as Kuwait had virtually no trained designers, engineers, or town planners.

The first master plan introduced many of the Western world's ideas and ways of living to Kuwait: the transformation of housing form from traditional courtyard house to detached villa; dependency on cars for transport instead of walking through intimate shaded narrow walkways; the replacement of indigenous communities by planned neighbourhoods and so on. It also introduced new building types in the downtown business district, as opposed to the mixed-use traditional arrangement, and zoning regulations that separated work and residential areas (*Ibid.*).

Modern Architecture in Kuwait

Al-Bahar (1985) was very critical of the architecture produced during the 1970s and 1980s. She thought that it was 'comparable to visiting a Disneyland of residential manifestations'! She attempted to provide a realistic picture of changes and transformations that have led to the birth of what she called 'hodge podge' architectural forms. She focused on the architecture of private villas in Kuwait during the 1980s emphasizing its eclectic character and asserted that:

the overall affluence allowed the increased acquisition of motor cars, the introduction of new technologies, the importation of architects, engineers, other professionals and labourers from various parts of the world, in an effort to build the modern Kuwait. (*Ibid.*)

Al-Bahar attributed the sense of freedom in designing the shapes of the new villas to a lack of understanding of the various aspects of Kuwait's environment by both citizens and architects alike. She criticized the attempts of 'mediocre architects' who were:

> in search of a new identity that had no link with the past, and rather than develop, enhance and refine the traditional character in the context of the new, they simply discarded the old and started to build the new on very shaky and superficial grounds. (*Ibid.*)

Architecture produced during that period introduced the use of new materials – concrete, aluminium, and coloured rendering – and technology – air-conditioning and communication systems. It also ushered in modern architectural elements such as cantilevered balconies, large picture windows and angled elevations. Sloping roof canopies at acute, oblique, skew or deformed angles, functionless decorative slabs of concrete punched with various openings, and multi-coloured rendering loudly reject any association with the past. 'Jetlike structures and flying rockets became a symbol of modern living' (*Ibid.*).

The external appearance of these houses did not reflect the slowly changing cultural and social needs of the inhabitants. Balconies were seldom used and whenever possible were closed to provide more usable space. Windows were always closed and covered by heavy opaque curtains to prevent outsiders from looking into the house. The poor performance of these buildings both climatically and environmentally under severely hot conditions during the long summer months resulted in the later pursuit of more modest and functional structures. Yet, the house was transformed from a place for living to a showcase of wealth and social status. As Al-Bahar put it:

> people perceived their houses as a symbol of their affluence and status in society and each individual was compelled to state uniqueness in architecture. This in turn generated the eclectic forms that are so much part of the Kuwaiti residential architectural scene today [1985]. Neo-classical, Baroque, Neo-Islamic, Bungalow style, Spanish, North African, Cubist, Neo-Bedouin, outer space you name it, you will find it … and even more! (*Ibid.*)

The most troubling aspect of this eclectic style period is that these diversely styled:

> dwellings stand side by side in Kuwaiti's residential neighbourhoods to display an architectural extravaganza, a carnival, a showroom of copied styles and motifs, results of confused aesthetic values and a lack of understanding of a need to develop one's own architectural identity. (*Ibid.*)

Yet this new lifestyle did not completely eradicate the traditional one. As Vale (1992) put it, 'the very rapidity of change left an important residue, a concern for traditions and values of the past'. Some elements of the traditional life before the discovery of oil have persisted. Most of the villas are designed with two separate entrances: one for guests and one for the family to provide privacy and the customary separation between males and females. The *diwaniya*, a gathering

Figure 7.9. Villas from the 1970s.

room for male guests in the houses of the affluent in the society and a symbol of social status and influence, is constructed as a room attached to the villa. Rich merchants in old Kuwait built large *diwaniyas* on the Gulf, usually located close to the outside main entrance so as to provide direct access for male guests without passing through the rest of the house. The return of the *diwaniya* started with the erection of a tent in the villa garden and was then replaced by a temporary structure and finally by a permanent room attached to the villa.

Another important stage followed the implementation of the first master plan. The architecture produced during that era was completely alien. It required the development of architectural landmarks which would relate architecture to the region. A panel of four advisers – Sir Leslie Martin (English), Franco Albini (Italian), Dr. Omar Azzam (Egyptian), and Hamid Shuaib (Kuwaiti) – chaired by the Kuwaiti Prime Minister, Shaikh Jaber Al Ahmad, was set up in the late 1960s to find solutions to the emerging problems (Gardiner, 1983).

The advisory commission invited several internationally known architects to design landmark buildings in Kuwait. They instructed them regarding the types of buildings and design approaches they expected. They selected four firms of architects from different countries to propose solutions for the emerging problems: Candilis, Josie and Woods of France for residential neighbourhoods, Belgoigose (BBPR) of Italy for the old *souq*, Peter and Alison Smithson of England for governmental buildings and climatic problems, and Reima Pietilä of Finland for the waterfront development.

Figure 7.10. Old and new *diwaniyas*.

During the 1980s several remarkable buildings, designed by internationally recognized architects, were constructed in Kuwait. They included: the National Airport by Kenzo Tange, the Parliament Building by Jorn Utzon, the Ministry of Foreign Affairs by Raili and Reima Pietilä, the Central Bank by Arne Jacobsen, and the Kuwait Water Towers by Lindstorm, Egnell and Bjorn (Kultermann, 1999). This practice facilitated the dissemination of global trends into the urban environment in Kuwait.

Danish architect Jorn Utzon is best known for his design of the Sydney Opera House. His Parliament Building, home to the National Assembly, occupies 120,000 m² on the Gulf Road. Construction began in 1978 and was completed in 1985. The building resembles an Arabian tent – the symbol of hospitality to all visitors – open at the front to catch the cooling breeze from the sea.

In 1973 the Finnish architects Raili and Reima Pietilä were commissioned to design a new complex as an extension for the old Sief Palace. The complex, completed in 1983, comprised three structures; the Old Sief Palace extension, the Council of Ministers building and the Ministry of Foreign Affairs building. The advisory committee required the architects to design the complex to 'demonstrate

Figure 7.11. The Parliament building by Jorn Utzon.

new Islamic architecture' (Randall, 1985) and to harmonize with existing structure. The architects developed an innovative solution providing a stylistic progression from the traditional to the postmodern forms. They respected the height and style of the existing building and used the 'soft, yellow colour of indigenous housing for the buildings' for the exterior walls (*Ibid.*). They applied several climatic solutions to provide shaded exterior spaces while admitting air to interior spaces. It was their hope that the 'architectural characteristics of the Sief Palace Area Buildings can harmonise and relate to those more universal, natural denominators of Kuwait Bay – its sky, sands and sea' (*Ibid.*).

While the architects' intentions were legitimate and professional, the complex's humble scale and character did not satisfy the ambitions of the government. In 1984, a new project for the extension towards the west of the old Sief Palace was initiated with a much larger area and more complex contents. It contains three main buildings; the Emir's office, the Crown Prince's office and the Prime Minister's headquarters. Each building is as large as the 1973 group of buildings. The exterior uses detailing and geometric designs, such as Islamic *mushrabiyas* and pointed arches as well as influences of Najd and other Gulf styles. The display of these influences was meant to relate these important buildings to other countries in the region. The interiors display the aesthetic and formal elements of Arabic and Islamic architecture and heritage.

Kuwait Towers are the most important landmark on the Gulf Road. They were designed by the Danish architect Malene Bjorn and inaugurated on 26 February 1977; they won the Aga Khan Award for Architecture in 1980 (figure 7.12). As Kultermann (1981) put it,

In her Kuwait Towers Malene Bojrn has provided a symbol not only for the emerging urban environment of Kuwait, but for the Middle East in general.

In this project, water is contained in a sculptural form which imitates traditional Arabian perfume containers. The towers are located at the tip of the Ras Ajouza peninsula across from the palace of the late Emir of Kuwait, Sheikh Jaber Al Ahmad Al Subah, and according to his personal wish. Of the three towers two are used as water containers and the third is a lighting pole. The tallest is 180 metres and contains a 4,500 m³ water reservoir, a ninety seat restaurant and a rotating observatory. The second tower is 140 metres high and is used only as a water reservoir. The spheres are:

> covered with enameled plates of steel painted in colour scheme of blues, greens and greys in harmony with the traditional ornamental forms of the Gulf architecture of the past, creating a brilliant impression in daylight and light spectacle at night. (*Ibid.*)

The towers have become a symbol for the city and the State of Kuwait with their huge spheres hung on pointed towers.

The 1980s witnessed an economic crisis and the collapse of the Kuwaiti stock exchange, known as Azmat Souq Al Manakh (figure 7.13).[2] This affected both

Figure 7.12. Kuwait Towers.

public- and private-sector spending. Kuwait was also influenced by political conflicts in the region which had persisted since the early 1980s when the Islamic revolution in Iran succeeded in assuming power. This was followed by the Iran-Iraq war which lasted 8 years and threatened the security of the whole Gulf region. Kuwait supported the Iraqi side financially during the war, however a conflict 'fabricated' by Iraq over that support ended with Iraq's invasion of Kuwait. As Vale (1992) put it,

> even before it was invaded in August 1990 by Iraq, Kuwait was known to the world for three things: its oil, wealth, and its precarious position in the war-torn Persian/Arabian Gulf. Nestled between Iraq and Saudi Arabia and across the Gulf from Iran, Kuwait struggled to remain officially neutral in the Iran-Iraq war during the 1980s though it gave an estimated $1 billion a year in financial assistance to its Iraqi neighbors. Such aid did not ease perennial border disputes and other tensions with Iraq, however, as the Iraqi invasion of Kuwait soon made clear.

During the 1970s, the government of Kuwait became very concerned about the 'paucity of Kuwaitis living in the center of the city' (Erickson, 1980). Kuwaitis were residing in the neighbourhoods and abandoned the downtown after working hours. To balance the overwhelming presence of expatriates in the downtown, the government initiated a project to provide housing for Kuwaitis there. The Canadian firm of Arthur Erickson was appointed to design a residential complex of large 300 m² apartments with the general requirement that if they were to be

Figure 7.13. The Kuwait Stock Exchange – Souq Al Manakh.

high-rise, 'no apartment should look into another for reasons of privacy'. They:

> opted for a scheme of stacking the apartments, which were really enclosed villas with an outside courtyard. The staggered stacking offset that courtyard so the light came in vertically, and the only view out was through a controlled retractable screen opening into the courtyard. The apartments were organized into neighborhoods of ninety to hundred families. Each neighborhood was clustered around a small shopping complex and shared with others a number of mosques, schools, a large central club, a park and roof gardens. The stacking of the villas resulted in a configuration which provided a sheltered, shaded space in between; this neighborhood common space was reminiscent of the souq. The landscaping had a series of trellised walkways which connected the various components, so that automobiles were relegated to the outside and the central area became entirely pedestrian. (*Ibid.*)

The project is a landmark in Kuwait's downtown with its distinctive form, yet it is currently facing several problems which reflect the inability of Kuwaitis to adapt to living in vertical housing. Most tenants rented out their apartments and resided in the neighbourhoods. Problems are mostly related to the maintenance of shared facilities and infrastructure. Detached villas in the neighbourhoods provide total control of land and the occupier's responsibilities are clear. In the case of the complex, maintenance of elevators, staircases, water tanks and other shared facilities was expected to be provided by the government. Furthermore, shared entrances, staircases and elevators did not provide adequate privacy for the residents, and villas were regarded by Kuwaitis as more socially prestigious and appealing.

Al-Duaig (2004) suggested that the public attitude during the 1980s was 'toward evaluation and assessing architecture in Kuwait and people started feeling the diverse effects of the architectural problems'. He asserted that 'revival' was the main feature of this stage. 'People started thinking about the past and traditional

Figure 7.14. Villas from the 1980s with traditional elements.

architecture' (*Ibid.*). It was a reflection of the postmodern attitude which dominated the architectural movement at that time. In most of the Arab world, architects started to look back at the pre-modern period and historical references to develop an architecture appropriate for each locality. The revival of the past focused on the use of traditional design for architectural elements such as windows, doors, roof parapets, arches, arcades and courtyards.

The Invasion, Liberation and Reconstruction of Kuwait

On 2 August 1990, the Iraqi regime of Saddam Hussein decided to invade Kuwait and annex it to Iraq. This event initiated international collaboration as 'allied' forces from different countries arrived to liberate Kuwait in 1991. As Al-Bahar (1991, p. 14) put it:

> the Gulf conflict has had a shattering impact on Kuwait's economy, its environment, service infrastructure, industries and intellectual, cultural and academic institutions. The cost of reconstructing and repairing the damage to Kuwait during the occupation has been estimated at between US$25–30 billion.

During the invasion many architectural landmarks were damaged or vandalized. The well-known Kuwait Towers, the National Assembly Building, the Sief Palace and the International Airport were among the buildings which suffered. Hotels, office buildings and private villas were also burnt or vandalized. A task force was established even before the liberation of Kuwait to develop plans for the reconstruction of Kuwait (*Ibid.*).

After the liberation by the allied forces, led by the US, on 26 February 1991, the plans for recovery and reconstruction were put into action. These included tackling the burning oil wells, clearing mines and explosive dumps as well as the repair of public buildings and infrastructure. New architectural design and planning projects came to a halt. As Al-Bahar noted:

> no new design projects are expected to be commissioned during this period as emphasis will be directed primarily towards the reparation of the damage inflicted on existing buildings. Although architects could participate in some capacity in the rebuilding efforts, Kuwait's post-war construction market will mainly require the professional services of structural surveyors, civil engineers, construction managers, and interior as opposed to architectural designers. (*Ibid.*)

The post-invasion reconstruction requirements resulted in a downgraded architectural service, a lack of appreciation of the importance of the architectural design discipline and an environment bereft of high-quality architecture and expertise.

Architectural Developments during the Twenty-First Century

The invasion by Iraq and liberation by international forces had a dramatic impact on Kuwaiti culture and polarized the opinions of Kuwaitis. One side attributed this trauma to the illusions of Arabism and the other to the secular trends away from true Islam. The first became more interested and supportive of Westernization, Americanization and globalization and the second became more interested in reviving Islamic traditions and customs. This is reflected in the architecture produced in the post-war period, especially private villas. Public buildings exhibit more Islamic architectural features (arches, motifs, and patterns) but villas follow either Islamic or Western design (figure 7.15). Many Kuwaitis resided outside Kuwait during the year of Iraqi occupation and when they returned they brought with them designs and styles from their temporary homes.

The continuation of the Iraqi regime during the 1990s did not allow the level of security required for rapid development. The fall of Saddam Hussein's regime in 2003 brought with it a more optimistic atmosphere for development and construction. Yet it did not materialize because of the long bureaucratic procedures required to implement projects. Kuwaitis feel the loss of their State's leading role in the region due to the rise of other regional economic and financial centres, especially Dubai, during the 1990s when Kuwait was recovering from the impact of the invasion trauma.

This led to an extreme polarization in the production of architecture in Kuwait. On one hand it reflected the need to construct new modern buildings which

Figure 7.15. A 1990s villa built after liberation.

link Kuwait with the global world and on the other hand buildings that reflect Kuwait's history and belonging to a particular place. As described by Khattab (2001), 'particularly in the case of Kuwait, reasserting the local identity has lately become a matter of great importance especially after Iraq's claims on Kuwait and the Second Gulf War'. This was reflected in the architecture being produced by Kuwaiti architects in their attempts to recognize and acknowledge the heritage of traditional Kuwaiti architecture during the 1990s (Mahgoub, 2007).

Figure 7.16. A modern villa revealing 'multiple identities'.

Figure 7.17. Contemporary public buildings reflect a globalized identity.

The work of Saleh Al Mutawa represents a trend by several Kuwaiti architects to express a cultural identity in their projects (figure 7.18). His book *History of Architecture in Old Kuwait City* was published in 1994 and the same year the Emir of Kuwait awarded him with a prize for his distinguished work on preserving traditional Kuwaiti architecture and he is the subject of Godfrey Goodwin's 1997 book, *Saleh Abulghani Al-Mutawa: A New Vision in Kuwait.*

(a)

(b)

(c)

Figure 7.18. Projects by Saleh Al Mutawa.
(a) Salmiyah Palace Hotel;
(b) Jabriyah housing;
(c) Al Zumuruda Hall.

In his projects, Saleh attempts to represent his vision of a Kuwaiti identity in architecture by employing the traditional elements illustrated in his book. One of his important projects is the Salmiyah Palace Hotel. Located in the middle of the shopping and commercial district of Salmiyah at the crossing of Salem Al-Mubarak and Amro Ibn Al-As Streets, the building is one of the most eye-catching in Kuwait. According to Saleh, the elements used in the building are derived from traditional Kuwaiti architecture: arches and wooden *mushrabiyas* (*Amaar*, 2002). A short tower is located at the top of the roof symbolizing the traditional wind catcher (*badjeer*). The building is composed of six floors used as a hotel above five commercial floors. The hotel has 80 rooms designed according to the traditional Kuwaiti room called a *kashtaban*. Each has a suspended floor that contains the bed.

Saleh applies his vision consistently in all his designs and buildings. His other projects include Al Zumuruda Hall which became a landmark with its suspended towers of palm trees and wind catchers. His Kuwaiti style apartment buildings in Jabriya and Salwa are attractive especially to European expatriates who call them 'the Spanish villas' believing that they are designed according to the Spanish style!

Adjacent to Saleh's Salmiyah Palace is the Central Plaza shopping centre which employs a completely different architectural style. The building comprises two seven-storey towers consisting of offices and residential apartments and was designed by the architect John Seller, in a postmodern classic style with a large atrium in the middle and classic style columns on the elevation. Another Saleh building is located on the other side of the Central Plaza and together the three buildings create a composition which I would call 'the clash of styles'.

Figure 7.19. The clash of styles: Salmiyah Palace Hotel and Central Plaza.

Figure 7.20. Marina Mall.

Marina Mall, with 30,000 m² of shopping, entertainment and dining, is part of the waterfront development of the Gulf Road (figure 7.20). It is connected via a bridge crossing the Gulf Road to Marina Crescent, a complex hosting a variety of international restaurants and cafés (especially Starbucks), an exclusive marina for yachts, and the five-star Marina Hotel. As its slogan suggests, '*The Mall offers more of everything*': more shops, more new brands, more food variety, more entertainment options, more parking space, more convenient services, and more. Opening in stages between 2002 and 2005 it has become popular with all ages and nationalities for its easy parking beneath the shops and spacious air-conditioned corridors and central atrium. According to a post-occupancy study, only 47 per cent of the visitors go there for shopping, the rest come for other activities – dining, movies, meeting friends, and so on. The success of Marina Mall encouraged the rapid development of other grand shopping malls in Kuwait, such as Al Kut, The Avenues and The Dome.

The Third Master Plan

In 1990, Kuwait Municipality commissioned SSH (Salem Al Marzouk and Sabah Abi Hannh Consulting Office) to develop a third master plan for the city of Kuwait. The work stopped during the invasion of Kuwait, was resumed in 1992 and completed in 1997. The third master plan projected that the total population of Kuwait would reach 3.8 million by 2015 and that the capacity of the urban area is only 2.3 million inhabitants. The plan therefore recommended the distribution of the additional 1.5 million inhabitants to the new towns of Khiran and Subbiyah. It also called for the addition of new towns to the west.

Five years after the third master plan, and following recent changes in the region, Kuwait Municipality commissioned the Kuwaiti consultant KEG (Kuwait Engineering Group) in association with CBP (Colin Buchanan & Partners) to review and update all data and information to accommodate new plans and projects and develop a new master plan to the year 2030. The third master plan review (KMP3R1) concluded that 99 per cent of the population resides in urban areas which cover only 8 per cent of the total area of the country. The population reached 2.644 million in 2004 with an annual increase of 4.8 per cent. Kuwaitis make up only 4.8 per cent of the population, while of the 65 per cent non-Kuwaitis, 83 per cent are aged between 15 and 60. The KMP3R1 projected a population of 5.4 million by the year 2030.

The KMP3R1 raised several red flags. It warned against Kuwait's dependency on oil as a single source of income. It also warned of shortages in drinking water and electric power supplies if the power stations that produce power and distilled drinking water were not upgraded. The expected increase in the number of vehicles and continuing dependency on private cars, coupled with lack of an attractive public transport system, posed a real challenge. The study concluded that several sectors of the roads had reached 85 per cent capacity. In conclusion, the KMP3R1 warned of extreme infrastructure problems by 2008. Traffic congestion, especially during peak hours, water and electricity shortages, especially during the summer season, have been experienced in Kuwait since 2005. The population according to the latest statistics is approaching 3 million and a new construction boom is sweeping the downtown area.

One of the most noticeable changes above ground is the construction of new high-rise buildings in the CBD made possible by changes in the building regulations which increased the floor area ratio and maximum allowed number of floors. It is feared that this will have a negative impact on traffic congestion, parking and infrastructure (Mahgoub, 2006). These new high-rise buildings do not reflect the character and forms of traditional architecture as much as the use of state of the art materials and technology. They are rising in downtown Kuwait amidst a network of buildings representing other periods of modernization. For example, the slick tower of Burgan Bank is located across the street from the State Grand Mosque. Its curved façade covered with glass and metal cladding is in extreme contrast to the Islamic character of the mosque. The State Grand Mosque, started in 1979 and completed in 1986, was designed in accordance with Islamic and traditional architectural heritage. Rakan Tower, with its patterned glass façade, was completed in 2006 and is located across from the first complex of Al Muthana constructed in 1978 which is faced with precast concrete panels. This is only to contrast these new towers with the high-rise buildings of the 1970s and 1980s which reflected Islamic and local identity. In the design of tall buildings there is a trend to move away from the expression of national identity towards one of globalization.

Figure 7.21. New high-rise towers.

Future Mega-projects in Kuwait

On 30 March 2006, Kuwait announced plans to build a new city on the north side of Kuwait bay area. The new city, called Madinat Al-Hareer or City of Silk, is expected to cost more than 25 billion KD.[3] The vision statement for the city stresses the emergence of competing centres in the Middle East, such as Dubai, Abu Dhabi, Riyadh, Manama, Muscat, and Doha and how they have transformed themselves from quiet trading ports into international cities of commerce, leisure, and hospitality. As proclaimed by the statement, the city is: 'founded on the rich heritage of Arab gardens, towns, palaces, and markets. It balances Centres of Faith with Centres of Commerce as a rich garden city on the Arabian Gulf'. It will comprise four new city centres: Finance City, Leisure City, Culture City, and Ecological City. 'It is a new cosmopolitan city for a new century' (Eric Kuhne Associates, 2006).

At the centre of the city stands Burj Mubarak Al Kabir, 'the Tower of a Thousand and One Nights'. The tower is designed to be higher than all known tall buildings in the world, especially the Burj Dubai which is expected to rise to more than 800 metres:

Standing 1001 meters tall, it will house 7 vertical villages combining offices, hotels, leisure, and residential into a vertical city centre that reaches for the heavens. The design is inspired by the defiant flora of the desert as much as the rich folklore of Arabic heritage described in '*Kitab Alf Layla wa-Layla*'.[4] (*Ibid.*)

The metaphors used in planning and designing the City of Silk are borrowed from historical moments when Arab civilization was at its glorious pinnacle at the end of the first millennium. These are the moments of glory that all Arabs are proud of and eager to live again.

Figure 7.22. The City of Silk.

Another mega-project expected to be built within the next 10 years is the New University City in Shidadiyah. Kuwait University is the only public university subsidized by the State of Kuwait. Established in October 1966, 5 years after Kuwait became a sovereign state. Kuwait University has expanded from a small institution comprising Colleges of Science, Arts and Education, and a Women's College with 480 students and thirty-one faculty members, to a diversified institution with multiple campuses and more than 17,000 students and 1,200 faculty members. On 20 April 2004 the National Assembly issued law number 30/2004 regarding the construction of the New University City by the year 2014 and the transfer of all facilities from the current campuses. It is expected that the total enrolment will reach approximately 30,000 full time students by the year 2025.

The New University City will have three affiliated campuses, one for female students, one for male students, and a medical campus. Male's and female's campuses will be separated by a wide oasis – a 'Palm Forest' over a kilometre in length with 10,000 palm trees. Faced by faculty offices and graduate research centres, it will be a quiet space of academic repose, a sanctuary and place for contemplation which will become an icon for the university. Each campus is organized along a 'galleria' – a grand scale outdoor weather-protected street, urban in character and animated by student activities that link all major functions of each campus (figure 7.23). The galleria will give an identity to each campus, creating a sense of place that will be memorable for all its students. Within the University

Figure 7.23. The new university campus master plan.

City, college clusters will form neighbourhoods bringing scale and identity to each part of the university. The landscape work includes development of the open space system in terms of sustainability, microclimate design, planting technology and the establishment of naturalized areas around the site. Significant focus has been placed on the design of the 'oasis', which is greatly enhanced by the introduction of a water course which extends the length of the oasis and with clusters of palm trees and landscaped berms creating a more naturalistic setting.

While the new university campus is expected to resemble that of any modern Western university, its identity will be influenced by cultural and social conditions. One of the significant factors in shaping the campus is the separation of male and female students – a stipulation of the parliamentary decree for the initiation of the new campus which has resulted in designing two separate adjacent campuses with many duplicate facilities.

Another project under construction is the Heritage Village. After the implementation of the first master plan, only a handful of historic buildings were preserved. The government announced plans to construct a traditional village in part of the old city. The site contains several old buildings which will be preserved and integrated in a new scheme that intends to 'rebuild' that part of the old city as it was more than 50 years ago. The planning follows the lines of the old streets and houses while introducing new functions and uses. The designer used traditional elements such as *alfarej* (narrow streets) and *alhoush* (courtyards) in the design of the Heritage Village which is expected to be a major tourist attraction.

Conclusions: Contextualizing Globalization

Thus, the story of Kuwait is a rich and long story written within a very short span of time. It is the story of a humble, organic desert Arab village that exploded into a haughty, over-extended desert Arab metropolis according to a geometric paper-plan, finding itself today a full fledged State embroiled in scientific planning and world affairs. (Shiber, 1964, p. 2)

Kuwait was influenced by rapid economic development during the mid-twentieth century which started after the discovery of oil. This economic prosperity initiated the development of its modernization through the first master plan in 1952. The 1973 Middle East War which created a sharp increase in oil prices initiated a second phase of its development. The stock market crash during the 1980s and the decline of oil prices slowed the process. Political conditions in the area were always a major concern because of their impact on the price and supply of oil to the world as is evident throughout recent decades. These economic and political conditions promote cultural changes that impact people's ways of life by introducing new building types, technologies, etc. People's view of themselves and their past experiences affects how they interact with these new conditions. As Vale (1992) put it:

> Kuwait's great wealth has not come about without consequences. A half-century of oil-sponsored riches led a tribally oriented sheikhdom to confront issues of global scope.

The case of Kuwait supports Christopher Alexander's argument that 'the biggest problem in architecture in the second half of the twentieth century is the connection between people and the physical world – the building of streets and so forth'. Essentially, what we miss now, Alexander (1994) argues, is the sense of belonging or possession in the true emotional sense. Kuwait also highlights the impact of globalization and, as Anderson and Al-Bader (2006) put it:

> There are many possible consequences should the forces of globalization in architectural design remain unchecked in Kuwait and other Gulf States. One possibility could be the general debilitation or eventual disappearance of the 'sense of place' that most had proffered in their 'pre-petroleum' years. Despite the awe-inspiring scale and extravagant building forms that most of the Gulf States exhibit today, there is an overarching sadness and sameness reflected in the pervasive 'Las Vegas' veneer that has been lacquered upon them. Such actions tend to endorse an impetuous rush to 'super modernity' for architects in other developing countries for fear of being left behind, as well as a possible squandering of critical resources that might be better spent in producing more appropriate and sustainable architecture.

The future carries more uncertainties than certainties for the region. Kuwait is located at the cross-roads of conflicts in the Middle East. While the elimination of Saddam Hussein's regime created a sense of security for Kuwait, the security situation in Iraq is overshadowing that sense of security. Also, the increasing tension between the US and Iran over Iran's nuclear activities is posing another serious threat to all countries in the Gulf.

Kuwait's dependency on oil as the only source of income poses a danger for its economic sustainability. Other Gulf countries started investing in long-term sources of income, yet Kuwait is still dependant on one single source of income. The US and EU are initiating serious attempts to create alternative fuels to replace their dependency on oil. They also encourage research into developing methods of improving renewable energy sources. This may lead oil prices to drop to levels that cannot sustain the current expenditure patterns. Already the country is experiencing increased traffic congestion and a shortage of electricity and water supplies, especially during the summer months. Many projects are on hold due to lack of adequate utility supplies. Delay in implementing vital infrastructure projects is affecting other major urban, housing and industrial projects.

Globalization is finding its way through shopping centres, mobile phone and other electronics technologies, and fast-food chains. However, it has been a force for good for the unfortunate expatriate workers as it has brought pressures from international human rights groups to improve their living and working conditions. Globalization is also being transmitted by the numerous foreign firms practising in Kuwait. As Erikson (1980) put it:

> it is impossible for anyone from the West to do any more than attempt to understand the environmental and social conditions and the ideas that have given rise to architectural styles in the Muslim countries. The final expression of those ideas and factors has got to come from within the Islamic world.

Gail Satler (1999) argues that:

> in most existing analyses, we find the Western 'eye' or traditional frameworks being imposed on Eastern (other) forms so that their intention and structure are, at best, rendered *other* or *complementary*, their meanings are dismissed as less significant and are evicted or subsumed into more familiar and therefore understandable frameworks.

The role of the outsider is important in transmitting the latest knowledge and technology, and criticizing from a distance the outcome of the process. Yet, as the case of Kuwait illustrates, the absence of the local architects and planners, especially during the early stages of development, contributes to the creation of an alienated place.

Notes

1. The term 'globalization' appeared during the second half of the twentieth century to describe the state of intense interaction and interdependency of the world economies. It is credited to Theodore Levitt, who in 1983 coined the term in the article he wrote at the Harvard Business Review entitled 'Globalization of Markets', which appeared in its May–June issue that year. The term has been used since the end of the Cold War to refer to the rapid spread and exchange of information, technology and ways of living which was facilitated by transportation, communication and trading.

2. *Souq Al Manakh* is the name of the Stock Exchange Building which was constructed on the spot where traditional trading caravans used to rest near the market.

3. 1 KD equals approximately US$3.60 at November 2007 exchange rates.

4. *One Thousand and One Nights*.

References

Al-Anbaa (2001) Asimatna, laysh jazia? (Why is our capital unsightly?). *Al-Anbaa* Newspaper, 24 August, No. 9081.

Al-Bahar, H. (1984) Traditional Kuwaiti houses. *Mimar*, No. 13, pp. 71–78.

Al-Bahar, H. (1985) Contemporary Kuwaiti houses. *Mimar*, No. 15, pp. 63–72.

Al-Bahar, H. (1991) Kuwait's post-war reconstruction, *Mimar*, No. 40, pp. 14–17.

Al-Duaig, Osama (2004) Kuwait contemporary architecture, in Abed, Jamal (ed) *Architecture Reintroduced: New Projects in Societies in Change*. Geneva: The Aga Khan Award for Architecture.

Al-Hassan (1992) *The Iraqi Invasion of Kuwait: An Environmental Catastrophe*. Kuwait: The author.

Al-Mutawa, S. (1994) *History of Architecture in Old Kuwait City*. Kuwait: Al-Khat.

Al-Naim, M. (2005) *Architecture and Culture: Critical Studies on Arab Architecture*. Riyadh: Al-Yamama.

Al-Qabas (2003) Architecture commentary. *Al Qabas* Newspaper, 10 August, No. 10834.

Alexander, Christopher (1994) Domestic Architecture. Paper presented to Mediamatic Conference, 'Doors of Perception 2', Amsterdam. Available at http://www.mediamatic.nl/Doors/Doors2/Alexander/Alexander-Doors2-E1.html. Accessed 9 November 2007.

Amaar Magazine (2002) Kuwait Palace Hotel: excellence in design. *Amaar Magazine*, No. 58, pp. 18–28.

Anderson, Richard and Al-Bader, Jawaher (2006) Recent Kuwaiti architecture: regionalism vs. globalization. *Journal of Architectural and Planning Research*, **23**(2), pp. 134–146.

Dandekar, H. (1998) Global Space meets Local Space in the Twenty-First Century. Proceedings of an International Symposium 'City Space + Globalization: An International Perspective', College of Architecture and Urban Planning, The University of Michigan, 26–28 February.

Eric Kuhne Associates (*Madinat Al Hareer*) City of Silk Vision Statement, 22 March 2006. http://www.civicarts.com/civicarts.php. Accessed 26 July 2007.

Erickson, A. (1980) Projects in Kuwait and Saudi Arabia, in Safran, Linda (ed.) *Places of Public Gathering in Islam*. Philadelphia, PA: Aga Khan Award for Architecture, pp. 87–92.

Gardiner, S. (1983) *Kuwait: The Making of a City*. Harlow: Longman.

Goodwin, G. (1997) *Saleh Abulghani Al-Mutawa: New Vision in Kuwait*. London: Alrabea.

Islam, A. and Al-Sanafi, N. (2006) The traditional courtyard house of Kuwait, in Sibley, Magda (ed.) *Courtyard Housing*. London: Taylor & Francis, pp. 83–93.

Khattab, O. (2004) Reconstruction of traditional architecture: a design education tool. *Global Built Environment Review*, **2**(2), pp. 29–39.

Kultermann, U. (1981) Malene Bjorn's work in Kuwait. *Mimar*, No. 2.

Kultermann, U. (1999) *Contemporary Architecture in the Arab States: Renaissance of a Region*. New York, McGraw-Hill.

Kuwait Municipality (1980) *Planning and Urban Development in Kuwait*. Kuwait: The Municipality.

Mahgoub, Y. (2002) The development of private housing in Kuwait: the impact of building regulations. *Open House International*, **27**(2).

Mahgoub, Y. (2004) Globalization and the built environment in Kuwait, *Habitat International*, **28**(4), pp. 505–519.

Mahgoub, Y. (2006) Contemporary architecture in Kuwait. *Al Binaa Magazine*, January, pp.106–111.

Mahgoub, Y. (2007) Architecture and the expression of cultural identity in Kuwait. *The Journal of Architecture*, **12**(2).

Minoprio & Spencely and P.W. Macfarlane (1951) Plan for the Town of Kuwait: Report to His Highness Sheikh Abdullah Al-Salim Al-Sabah, The Emir of Kuwait, November 1951.

Qabazard, Abdulla (1999) Contemporary homes of Kuwait: building on a tradition of utility. *The Kuwait Digest*, April–June, pp. 20–25.

Randall, J. (1985) Sief Palace area buildings. *Mimar*, No. 16.

Rapoport, A. (1987) On the cultural responsiveness of architecture. *Journal of Architectural Education*, **41**(1), pp. 10–15.

Satler, Gail (1999) The architecture of Frank Lloyd Wright: a global view. *Journal of Architectural Education*, **52**, pp. 15–24.

Shiber, Saba George (1964) *The Kuwait Urbanization: Being and Urbanization Case-Study of a Developing Country*. Kuwait: Al-Madianah Al-Kuwaitiyyah.

Shuaib, Hamed (1999*a*) Key Note Address to the First International Conference on Architecture and Design in Kuwait, Kuwait Regency Palace Hotel, 24–27 October.

Shuaib, Hamed (1999*b*) Towards a modern Kuwaiti architecture developed from the tradition. *AMAR*, No. 38, November, pp. 24–26.

Slot, B.J. (1998) *The Origins of Kuwait*. Kuwait: Center for Research and Studies on Kuwait.

Sultan, G. (1978) Designing for new needs in Kuwait, in Holod, Renata (ed.) *Toward an Architecture in the Spirit of Islam*. Philadelphia, PA: The Aga Khan Award for Architecture.

Taylor, Brian Brace (1990) Kuwait City waterfront development. *Mimar*, No. 34.

Vale, L.A. (1992) *Architecture, Power and National Identity*. New Haven, CT: Yale University Press.

World Factbook (2002) http://www.wri.org/wri/wr-98-99/pdf/wr98_ud1.pdf p.274.

United Nations Population Division (2003) Demographic trends. http://earthtrends.wri.org/pdf_library/data_tables/pop2_2003.pdf. Accessed 26 July 2007.

Za'za', Bassam (2002) Arab speakers see threat to culture by globalization. *Gulf News*, 21 March.

Chapter 8

Manama: The Metamorphosis of an Arab Gulf City

Mustapha Ben Hamouche

Bahrain is an archipelago of thirty-six islands surrounding a main island protruding from the Arabian land mass into the Arab/Persian Gulf. The total land area of all the islands is about 700 km² of which the main island accounts for 90 per cent. Manama, the capital, is located close on the northern coast of the main island, overlooking the Gulf.

Despite the region's generally harsh climate, in the northern part of the island there is evidence of human settlement dating back to the Bronze Age. More than 100,000 burial mounds, some 5,000 years old, have been found in the north and centre of the island but, unlike early settlements in Mesopotamia, there is little sign of intense urbanization.

Before the evolution of the present twin cities of Manama and Muharraq in around 1783, the island's inhabitants were spread amongst some fifty small settlements,[1] mostly villages and hamlets, located both along the coast and in the interior of the island (Larsen, 1983; Khuri, 1980). Until oil was discovered, the economy depended mainly on the reasonable fertility of the land and the rich coral which enabled fishing and pearling to flourish.

This chapter is chronological so as to present the successive development stages of Manama of which three may be identified:

1.   Autonomous urbanism, in which the city was the outcome of natural and man-made factors.

2.   Bureaucratic urbanism, in which the State, through political, administrative and financial powers, became the major actor in the city.

3.   Global urbanism, in which the rising multi-national and financial organizations became the major urban player in the city.

Each of these stages has a specific urban pattern that co-exists with the others; together they form the present structure of the city. The first, which to a large

Legend

- 2006
- 2002
- 1980
- 1970
- 1951
- 1933
- 1903

Figure 8.1. Development of Manama from 1903 to 2006.

extent distinguishes the old core, is characterized by incremental forms and fractal geometry; the second, mostly found in the new extensions, is characterized by Cartesian geometry; and the third, which represents the recent trend of mega-projects, is marked by coarse urban forms and monumental architecture (figure 8.1). The aim of this chapter is to show how these three stages are reflected in the morphology of the present city.

Autonomous Urbanism

Early maps and photos indicate that the city of Manama grew by accretion (M675.05: 1828; M675.10: 1862; and M675.30: 1933).[2] Despite the presence of a royal quarter in the city, known as Fareej al-Shuyukh (Abuzid, 1998), the fortress and later the governor's palaces, the city does not appear to have developed in the same way as other royal cities of earlier Islamic eras, such as Baghdad during the Abbassid and Cairo during the Fatimid periods. Environmentally, Manama's development was influenced by the conditions of site, such as climate, coastal location, topography and water supply. Socially, residential quarters reflected the different tribes and ethnic groups who enjoyed a high degree of freedom and autonomy in their internal affairs. In fact, the organic development and complex urban fabric of this city during the early stage of its development was an interaction between these factors which are described below (figure 8.2).

The City and Its Setting

Although Manama and Muharraq appear to be twin cities founded simultaneously,

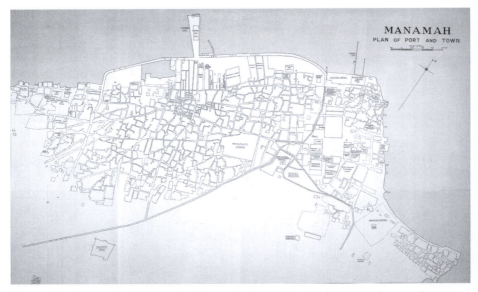

Figure 8.2. Manama in 1933 showing the morphology of the old city during the pre-oil era.

Muharraq took the lead because of its defensive location and thus became the capital city. Thus Manama developed as a subordinate settlement and a gateway to the main island. Its location on the north-east tip, together with the Hidd and Abu Maher fortresses, was part of an efficient defensive system controlling the marine commercial trade in the Arab/Persian Gulf, which frequently passed through the Bahrain bay (Walls, 1987, pp. 13–19). The old port, the place on which the present Bab-al-Bahrain building was erected, thus seems to be the embryo of the city.

Besides this strategic location, the site shaped the city in various ways which are still present in its morphology even today. With the waterfront as the baseline, early growth took the shape of a rough oval which extended incrementally east and west along the coast, and more slowly, southwards into the interior of the island.

Land, Water and Property System

Besides fishing and pearling, daily life in Manama depended on agriculture and an abundance of surface water resulting from the geological characteristics of its setting (Larsen, 1983). Its urban morphology seems therefore to have been shaped by the gradual development of the irrigation system, land subdivision for agriculture and the tenancy system. Despite the lack of rain, many springs and shallow wells provided the local communities with sufficient water for drinking and irrigation. The original urban nucleus evolved close to these sources such as at Ain Mubarak, Ain Ali, Ain Quful and Ain Muqbil, Ain Muqsim,[3] or along their streams (M675.05: 1825; M675.16: 1937) (Lorimer, 1908, p. 1161; Al-Araiyadh, 2006).

Two types of irrigation system existed. The first, known in the Gulf and Persia as the *falag*, consisted of underground channels which worked by gravitation to drain water from an upper source to the lower cultivated land. When describing Manama, Lorimer (1908, p. 1159) commented that a date grove towards the American hospital appeared to be watered by a *falag* from a spring in the Manama Fort. However, due to the abundance of springs, it seems that surface irrigation, known as *seeb*, saved local population from the heavy reliance on the more sophisticated *falag* method (BGWO, 1916, p. 312; Belgrave, 1960, p. 130; Tailor, 1818; Durand, 1878/1879, p. 535). This second method consisted of lifting water from wells in goat skins either by animals or a counterpoise thus irrigating the numerous palm groves. In the absence of major topographical constraints and the presence of a smooth slope towards the sea, water channels ran parallel, all leading to the coast and so shaped the future street network. Streams from Ain Muqbil and Umm-Shuoom were a case in point. Similar traces could still be seen on the 1970 map of Manama (M675.53: 1970).

The lines in figures 8.3*a* and *b* represent water channels that would have separated agricultural plots, and so formed the property boundaries which developed into pathways.[4] Some of these lines extended as paths connecting the city with the remote palm groves to the south and south-east. Other paths, which have now become major roads, linked the city to the remote villages along the northern coast, such as Jid-Hafs and Budaiyye, and in the hinterland, such as Riffa and Zallag, as shown on the map developed by Lorimer (1908). In other words, Manama, like other pre-industrial cities, would have been the market to which farmers from remote villages transported their crops. It thus grew as an urban centre on which a system of roads converged (Larsen, 1983, p. 119).

As the main crop was dates, space allowances for planting of palm trees, known as *hareem*,[5] could also have regulated the width of plots, lines of properties and the distance between two streams. In 1956, a land unit, locally known as *maghras*,

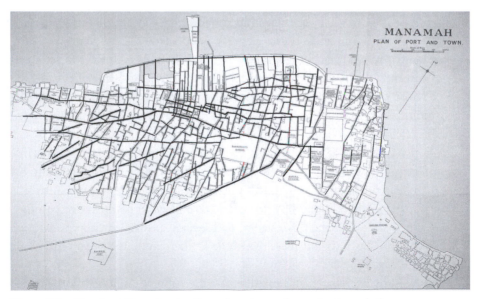

Figure 8.3*a*. Dominant lines showing the early water canals running towards the sea.

Figure 8.3b. A topographic map of Toubli area, Bahrain, in 1970, showing the remaining canals separating the land properties and running towards the sea.

measuring 18×18 ft^2 (about 5.5×5.5 m^2), was used to define the area for cultivating one palm tree (BAR, Vol. VI, 1956, p. 77).

In Search of a Micro-climate

Street layout was determined by the need to provide shade and shelter from the heat and humidity. Tunnel-like streets oriented north–south helped remove the smells of dried fish in the bazaar, a feature also found in old Kuwait (Broeze, 1997, p. 171). The predominantly north-westerly wind of the region, known as the *shamal*, blew through these streets and so reduced the effects of the long hot and humid summer. Shade was achieved through narrow and winding streets. In the case of wider streets and open spaces such as the market, shade was provided by cloth and other light fabric, so on a really hot day they were the coolest places in the town (Belgrave, 1960, p. 444).

In houses, the use of wind towers, the famous technique to reduce thermal discomfort imported from Persia, continued until the late 1960s as old images of Manama show (figure 8.4).[6] These, together with the wide use of courtyards within houses, enabled domestic activities to take place in comparative comfort. Palaces and wealthy houses, for instance, had several specialized courtyards, such as the reception court, the business court, the kitchen court and the animal court (Broeze, 1997, p. 176).

Only wealthy merchants and members of the ruling family had houses built in stone. Poor people lived in huts with sloping roofs, whose walls were of woven

Figure 8.4. The old district of Manama during early 1970s showing the compact urban fabric characterizing the traditional pre-oil city.

palm fronds, known locally as *barasti*. *Barasti* were not only low cost, but provided good interior cross ventilation (Belgrave, 1960, p. 192; BGWO, 1916, p. 321). As early maps show (1933), Manama was surrounded by a ring of these dwellings which accommodated low-wage labourers and new migrants. In 1959 there were 2,464 *barasti* out of a total of 9,637 houses in Manama. By 1965 the number had decreased to only 1,000, while the total number of houses had increased to 11,909 units (BAR, 1965, p. 122). For the purposes of privacy, each *barasti* stood within a courtyard and was surrounded by fences of upright palm fronds. Gradually, with the increasing living standards, but also because of frequent fires, these huts were replaced by stone structures, cemented with mortar. Besides these technical responses, people in very hot seasons used to move away from the city to high lands such as Aali and Riffa or to cooler places such as Adhari lake, and palm groves.

Trade, Fishing and Economic Subsistence

A regional economy based mostly on maritime activities determined Manama's destiny as a port town and then a port city; several mutually supportive activities – fishing, pearl-diving, shipping, shipbuilding, and trade – reflected this (Broeze, 1997, p. 152; Khuri, 1980, p. 36, Rumaihi, 1976, p. 39).

Pearl fishing was the backbone that made Manama one of the major poles in the Persian Gulf for pearls and trading (Datta and Nugent, 1985 pp. 25–40). In 1907, there were 917 pearling boats and employment for 17,500 men. Bahrain was also famous for its boat building, an industry that gave employment to about 200 carpenters (Belgrave, 1960, p. 440). In 1903–1904 nearly 130 boats were purchased by Qatar and Oman. Describing the port in the early 1900s, Lorimer (1908, p. 1266) stated that it was very active, as nearly 100 ships entered and left daily.

Thus Manama had a mercantile tradition which developed the institutions and commercial experience of its local population. Institutions, such as *Majlis al Urfi* (Customs Council) or *Majlis al-Tijarah* (Trade Council), which were established to settle disputes among merchants, reflect this.

The relationship with the sea and marine activities has thus strongly influenced Manama's urban structure, and does much to explain the city's form. Early maps, for instance, show the strong link between the quay extending into the sea and the bazaar, both of which are located on the same axis. Besides the linear development of the city along the coast, its north–south streets are directed perpendicularly to the coastline.

The bazaar or *souq* contained about 450 shops, a central open area and a closed market for valuable goods, called Qissariya (Lorimer, 1908, p. 1162; BGWO, 1916, p. 320).

Manama's economic growth, as shown by the records of ruler's taxes on revenues from pearl trade and the number of boats from the late nineteenth century onwards (Rumaihi, 1976, pp. 44–45), was reflected in continuous expansion along the coast, which reached the villages of Ras-Rumman and Naeemon on either side of the city. In 1905, its oval form extended 2.5 km along the coast and reached 300 m inland. Maps of Hemming (M675.10: 1901–1902) and Lorimer (M675.18: 1904–1905) are very informative in this respect. To the south and beyond the sandy belt, on which the present cemeteries are located, land was predominantly used for palm grove cultivation. A network of footpaths crossed these groves to link the city to other coastal villages and water sources, such as Juffair, Halat Bin-Anas, Al-Saqiyah, Al Gharayfa, Al Adliyya, Al-Mahuz, Al-Jufair, Umm-al-Hasam on east, and Al-Quful, Al-Zinj, and Al-Salihiyah on south, all now part of today's city (Khuri, 1980, pp. 250–251).

Agriculture was another important economic sector for the local population. Historical sources provide the distribution pattern of palm groves and the number of trees in each settlement. For example, about 500 date palms belonged to the town proper and another 800 to the adjacent Naeem village; further to the south-east, Hoora and Juffair had 300 and 2,230 palms, respectively; and to the west, Jid-Hafs, Bani Jamra and Bilad Al-Qadim had 16,500, 1,300, and 12,000 palms, respectively (Lorimer 1908, pp. 212–230, 1161; BGWO, 1916, p. 318). Despite the collapse of agriculture, palm trees continued to shape the landscape of Bahrain until the early 1980s. In 1974, for instance, the government counted 892,000 trees, which represented 47 per cent of the total number that formed the green belt along the northern coast (Al-Khalifa, 1994).

Social Structure and Spatial Organization

Despite the periodic ravages of epidemics and diseases, such as cholera and malaria, the population of Manama grew steadily over time (Faroughy, 1951, p. 20). From 1818 to 1905, the city passed from a small village of 8,000 people to a sizeable town of 25,000 (Tailor, 1818, p. 120; Lorimer, 1908, p. 1160). Its role as a port city within the Gulf region made it a hub for transnational communities most of which are now represented to differing extents in the social fabric. Connections with other cities and inland localities and the in-migration of labourers in search of a better living continually shaped Manama's population which was thus always characterized by cosmopolitanism (Fuccaro, 2005; Onley, 2005). The absence of a political centre coupled with its spontaneous development along the coast explain Manama's foundation and development as an accretion of labourers' houses and a market place.[7]

In terms of religion, the co-existence of the two main branches of Islam, Shia and Sunni, may blur the real social mosaic that makes up the city. The Shia are represented by several distinct groups: the Baharna, the local people speaking Arabic; the Ajam; the Persians; the Hasawis; and the Qatifs (Belgrave, 1960, p. 102). The Sunni are also made up of several groups, mainly the Arab Bedouin tribes who arrived with the ruling family in the eighteenth century, and the Hawala, the Arabic speaking Persians who are mostly merchants and who still keep in touch with their origins in Persia. Each of these groups comprised large families that had specific features distinguishing them from the others (Khuri, 1980, pp. 4–5). These two branches of Islam also co-existed in Manama with other non-Muslim entities such as Oriental Christians, Indians of various sects, and Jews (Lorimer, 1908, p. 1160; Qubain, 1955). Such a mosaic was further enhanced by the arrival of other communities, initially as a consequence of economic prosperity, later due to the geopolitical context which characterized the colonial period (Fuccaro, 2005).

The physical impact of this structure was evident in the morphology of the city which was subdivided into many quarters, locally called *fareeq* (pl. *furgan*). In 1919, the city comprised fourteen quarters: Bada', Barr, Dawarbah, Dawawdah, Al-Fadhel, Hammam, Hatab (Suq-Al), Haiyak, Hawalah, Jana'at, Mukharqah, Mishbar, Shuyukh and Abu-Surra (Lorimer, 1915, p. 1161). This structure seems to have continued and further developed prior to administrative reforms and the discovery of oil in the 1930s (Fuccaro, 2000, p. 67).

The names of the city's quarters had various origins. Some, such as Al-Fadhel, Shuyukh and Hawalah, were named after their residents' ethnicity, others, such as Mukharqa and Haiyak and Hatab, took the name of the crafts or commercial activities which were carried out there. Often the boundaries of these quarters overlapped with the main streets, a fact that motivated some academic studies for their reconstruction (Fuccaro, 2000, p. 67; Mandeel, 1992, p. 159). However, the mosaic character of Manama's social structure and its development as a city of workers have blurred the boundaries and reduced the degree of separation of these quarters.

As is the case with most other Muslim cities, residential quarters enjoyed an autonomous internal life that was reflected in the decentralized socio-political system.[8] Such a structure, used as a support for the British 'divide-and-rule' policy, has also been adopted in the modern municipal organization. During the elections of 1945, the city was subdivided into wards of nearly equal population, for the selection of representative members of the Municipal council (BAR, Vol. VII, 1956, p. 80).

At the individual level, freedom to build seems to have shaped the architecture and planning of each quarter. Houses, through their diversity, reflected individuals' actions and an incremental process of development which was determined by local customs and the know-how of masons, craftsmen and laymen (Hakim, 1994). Disputes among neighbours and partners were often solved amicably in the gathering places, in the presence of other community members.[9] At the second stage, they were brought to the Sheikhs and judges for decision according to Islamic law and local customs. Two supreme judges, one Sunni and one Shia, were nominated for this purpose, while there were many others of a lower rank in villages and other localities. When describing the shift from the traditional jurisdiction system to a centralized pro-Western one in Manama, Charles Belgrave noted that '… disputes [were] no longer settled by private arbitration, and the courts [were] resorted to on the least provocation' (RB, Vol. 5, 1932–1942, p. 633). There was a significant increase in the number of court cases involving boundary disputes, disagreements over water rights, and houses overlooking one another (BAR, Vol. I, 1924–1937, p. 364; Belgrave, 1972, p. 76; Khalifa, 2000, p. 92).

Bureaucratic Urbanism

The original autonomous urbanism was gradually but firmly replaced by a bureaucratic system along with the increasing involvement of the British Imperial administration in the internal affairs of the city (Ben-Hamouche, 2004). Before the Protectorate Treaty, which was officially established in 1892, British interests in Bahrain were mainly commercial and were little concerned with local affairs (Rumaihi, 1976, pp. 9–14; Khuri, 1980, p. 86; Lawson 1989, pp. 27–46). The strategic location of Bahrain in the Gulf, coupled with the continuous threats from other colonial superpowers, motivated the British to make the small city a regional capital for Arabia, and a model for the local societies, a fact which significantly influenced its future urban development (RB, Vol. 4, 1923–1932, p. 573). Manama was then considered as a regional port city and a residence of the Political Agent from which trade and political affairs in the Gulf were conducted together.

The urban impact of this geopolitical role became evident from 1919 onwards in the gradual and comprehensive administrative reforms which covered customs, justice, police, and local management. By this date, the city had come under a municipal authority and 3 years later its land tenure was subjected to a registration system which covered the territory of Bahrain following the national land survey launched in 1934 (BAR, 1934–1935, p. 539; Lawson, 1989, p. 42; Fuccaro, 2000, p. 57).

The bureaucratic system then expanded in all aspects during the British presence. Many departments reflecting this expansion, such as Public Works, Agriculture, Electricity, Water Supply and later on Housing and Physical Planning, were installed (Belgrave, 1960, pp. 42–45).[10]

Fifty years later, this sophisticated bureaucratic system passed to the Bahraini government when the country gained independence in 1971. Like many developing countries on independence, the inherited administrative structure was maintained. In the case of Bahrain the oil-based economy continued to flourish, thanks to the expanding international oil market, and development, reflecting the marriage of bureaucracy and oil-based economy, continued in the same pattern. Politically, Khuri (1980) suggests that Bahrain witnessed a shift from a tribal system to a modern State through a process of adaptation, while Lawson (1989) considers the event as a mere modernization of autocracy. Whatever the case, the bureaucratic urban pattern seems to have kept its essence during these major political and economic changes.

Manama under the British Authority

The urban impact of the British colonial authorities on Manama could be summed up as the ever-increasing involvement of the public authorities in shaping the city and the simultaneous shrinking of the previous autonomous system.

The discovery of oil in 1931 was a turning point in the intensity of bureaucracy as a result of the increase in financial resources on one hand and the collapse of the private economic sector, based as it had been on agriculture and the pearl trade, on the other. In the early stages, 1931–1936, oil contributed only moderately to the total income of Bahrain, representing around 30 per cent of the government income. After 1937, however, it increased to 65 per cent, and so helped to reinforce the hegemonic policies of the British authority.

In contrast to other forms of colonialism, the French in Africa and Spanish in South America for instance, a magic formula was invented by the British authorities in Bahrain and other parts of the Empire. As a compromise between full domination, which ensures Imperial interests, and indirect control, which masks the presence of the colonial power, Bahrain was placed under an advisory political system which was then extended to other Gulf countries (Haworth, 1929, p. 502; Rumaihi, 1976, p. 227). Political agents were continuously concerned with keeping the British presence low profile. On expressing this concern, F. Johnson, the Political Resident in the Persian Gulf, noticed a growing British interference in the Bahrain administration that was incongruent with the 'policy of avoiding undue westernization of Bahrain'. Such a tendency was confirmed by the Deputy Secretary to the Government of India, J.C. Acheson who stated that '… the introduction of reforms in Bahrain was originally intended only to remove the worst features of Arab misrule'. However, 'the process [today] has overrun its limited objectives. There are in Bahrain today a British Financial Advisor, a British Police Officer and a British Customs Officer, that is actually more British administration than in an ordinary Indian State…' (RB, Vol. 4, 1929, p. 538).

Regulations and Municipality: New Tools for Ruling

The autonomous system, mainly based on Islamic law, community structure and freedom of action of the individual, was gradually but radically overwhelmed by Western bureaucracy through a comprehensive reform that took place from 1919 onwards (BAR, 1931–1932, p. 364; Khalifa, 2000, p. 92).[11] Reforms covered major parts of public life such as justice, the pearl trade and customs. Describing the impact of the reform of the courts on the local society, Belgrave mentioned that during the last 30 years of the British presence, there had been significant changes in Bahrain, and life had become very complex. Private arbitration in daily disputes was replaced by legal action in court and regulations regarding building permits, tax collection and setback standards for road width gradually developed along with the direct involvement of the municipality in the daily affairs of the city (RB, Vol. 5, 1938, p. 633).

The divide-and-rule policy fed by the community divisions was camouflaged by the pretext of justice and equity (Fuccaro, 2005, p. 40). Minorities were gradually empowered at the expense of the ruling family and their allied tribesmen. A council of eight to ten members, half of whom were appointed by the British Political Agent, was formed (Khuri, 1980). In 1951, it was further extended to twenty-four members representing the spectrum of sects and nationalities such as Sunni Arabs, Shia Arabs, Sunni Persians, Shia Persians, Hindus, Jews, Muslim Indians and Saudi Arabs living in the city. The territory of the city was divided into seven wards each of which was represented by one or two elected members according to the number of inhabitants in the ward (RB, Vol. 6, 1942–1950, pp. 76–77). Elections and representatives were continually a matter of dispute and there were clashes between different sects in which the British became the master arbiter. While the power of merchants and local population was eroded due to the new world trade context, the collapse of the pearl trade and of agriculture (Khuri, 1980, p. 254; Al-Tajir, 1987, pp. 52–960), the enormous financial resources generated by the oil trade further reinforced the growing bureaucratic machinery.

A flow of information in relation to the regulations and administrative measures taken by the municipality are documented in the Records of Bahrain. The boundaries of the municipality for tax collection and council action as well as bye-laws were defined as early as 1921 (RB, Vol. 3, 1892–1923, p. 648; Khalifa, 2000, p. 473). However, in 1957 the boundary of the municipality was pushed back to include all the villages on the western side of Juffair Road, up to the souq – al-Khamis and the area north of Awali Road up to Sanabis, including Budayye Road (BAR, 1957, p. 53). The boundaries were defined by the coastline on the north and east, and a series of stone pillars constructed by the municipality in both Manama and Muharraq (BAR, Vol. I, 1934–1935, p. 548).

The municipality was in charge of cleaning, maintaining and controlling the internal roads and streets as well as providing fire services and inspection of food, shops and markets. The fees for these services were covered through a system of taxes fixed on each house and shop. Gradually, municipal duties were expanded to include inspection of building construction and road surfacing. According to the municipal bye-laws, no building work was to begin without the prior sanction of the chief of the municipality. New incomes were also generated through taxes fixed on new houses and shops (RB, Vol. 6, 1942–1950, pp. 650–657). In 1956, sources of the municipality revenues were as follows: 40 per cent from shop taxes; 40 per cent from house taxes; 10 per cent from government subsidies; and 3 per cent from rent of municipal properties (BAR, Vol. V, 1956, p. 28).

In the early 1960s many other works were undertaken by the municipality for aesthetic and entertainment purposes. Gardens, avenues of trees along major roads, and cemetery walls to prevent dogs from digging up graves, improved the image of the city facing the desert in the south.

Land Registration

Land tenure, despite its political sensitivity in the local context, was a major concern of the British authorities and was debated as early as 1923. Registration of land and verification of ownership began in 1925–1926. It was immediately followed by the creation of a Land Department (Rumaihi, 1976, p. 52). A thorough survey which lasted 6 years covered all properties and legal issues. The collection of aerial photographs and maps, going from 1934–1935 to 1970, made by Jarman (1996) showed the increasing concern of the authorities for the control of land and hence, the territory and the society. Each plot was identified through a government title deed containing details of tenancy, boundaries, measurements and special conditions such as water. On the reverse of the sheet, a plan of the property was drawn. Despite some fluctuation, registration continued until the last days of the colonial administration. Records of Bahrain show that from 1926 to 1946 there were 12,111 title deeds issued, while from 1946 to 1956, the number dropped to 9,246 titles (RB, Vol. 4, 1923, p. 187; BAR, Vol. VII, 1956, pp. 74–77).

One direct consequence of this procedure was that all unclaimed land passed to the government, a condition which deprived some individuals of the land they acquired by inheritance and extended the sphere of influence of the administrative machinery. Mechanisms of *Ihiya*, the right of individuals in Islam to develop un-owned land, which had existed in all Muslim cities, were implicitly abolished (Akbar, 1988, p. 48).

Registration procedures also showed a shift in land ownership which was to have an undesired socio-political impact. Due to the collapse of the date trade, much agricultural land was sold at low prices, giving the wealthy group of the new

Persian migrants an opportunity to acquire assets. Consequently, a corrective rule promulgated in 1939 forced Persians living in Bahrain either to obtain Bahraini nationality or sell their properties, other than their houses and places of business (BAR, Vol. VII, 1956, pp. 74–77; Fuccaro, 2005, pp. 45–49; Rumaihi, 1976, p. 52).

However, this regulation did not end the trend. Many parcels were sold by members of the ruling family to the new elite of wealthy merchants, a fact that increased the proportion of private property in the city (Rumaihi, 1976, p. 52; Fuccaro, 2005, pp. 42–44). The shift continued as a result of the development of the monetary economy which began just before the oil era. The decline in the date market, as dates ceased to be a main constituent in the Bahraini diet, allowed many people to purchase large date groves and transform them into private gardens. Over time these groves were developed into private housing and investment sites. For instance, between 1952 and 1959 the number of vegetable gardens increased from 150 to 576 (Rumaihi, 1976, p. 52). A map of Manama in 1946 (M. 675.32) shows such a shift in real estate on the outskirts of the city. Many large private gardens known as *Dūlab*,[12] such as the *Dulab*(s) of Madan, Mansoor al-Aryad, Muhammad Khunji, Al-Fadhel bin-Muhanna, and Gasaibi gardens, and Hutat Ali Abul, surrounded the governor's palace. This shift in land ownership was to have an impact on the development of Manama and seems to have prevented the public authorities from undertaking major urban extensions and developments on the new fringes of the city.

Reclamation Work

The increase in amount of land in private ownership coupled with the absence of major topographic constraints led to land reclamation to enable new development. As most of Bahrain is flat, water was the major obstacle for the urban development of Manama. In 1965, a planning study showed that in addition to the 676 km² of existing land, a further 274 km² could be gained through reclamation (BAR, 1965, p. 95). Within the main island, swamps covered considerable areas due to the abundant springs and tidal flows. For instance, Umm al-Hasam, an area now part of Manama, was described in 1818 as a large island totally detached from the main island (Tailor, 1818, p. 113). Some lagoons were turned into public gardens such as Andalus Garden and Water Garden.

In addition to the need for land for development, reclamation work was also undertaken for health reasons. The combination of high humidity and heat exacerbated the spread of many diseases and epidemics in Bahrain, such as malaria and cholera. Tailor (1818, p. 120) described Manama as a place where cholera epidemics had decimated the population. And nearly a century later, in 1904, it was reported that 3,000 people fell ill and 2,000 died (Mahdi, 1994, p. 37).

Early reclamation work took place around the pier to increase its area and improve landing and shipping of cargos. Large ships had difficulty in approaching the city because of shallow water except at high water seasons (Tailor, 1818, p. 113).

A scheme was approved by the British government in India in 1903 for reclamation (RB, Vol. 3, 1903, p. 561). By 1923 a hump-like line between the sea and the city had been created that became a sea road, now called Shari' al-Hukuma. Successive projects were carried out on both sides of the port where most of the new public buildings and offices were built. By 1967, an area of 8,400 m² along the sea road, east of the Customs House had been reclaimed. Consequently, the sea which originally reached the foot of the main gate, Bab-al-Bahrain, was pushed back 200 m, providing more space for public facilities (figure 8.5). At the back of the present Municipality building, stagnant pools which were an eye sore and danger to the public health (BAR, 1934–1935, p. 548) were filled-in in 1967 to establish a new bus park which is still in use (BAR, 1967, p. 116).

The present suburban areas in Manama, such as Hura, Mahuz and Qudhaibiyya, owe their existence to the successive reclamation works. For technical and health reasons, early reclamation works were carried out by the hygiene service of the municipality. Thousands of cubic metres of town rubbish once collected were discharged into marshes and then were covered with earth and sand (BAR, 1956,

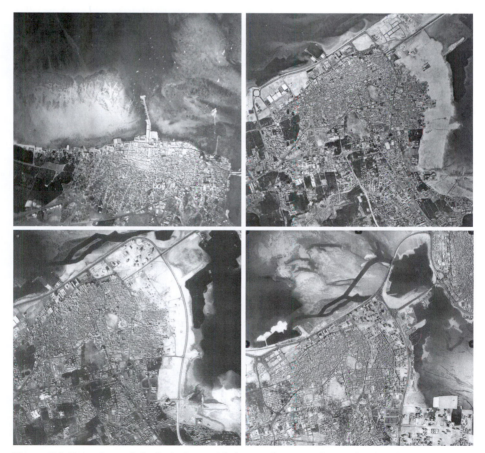

Figure 8.5. From the top left, clockwise: aerial photos of Manama during the years 1951, 1977, 1980 and 2002 showing the reclamation works and stages of growth.

p. 81). A sea wall was first constructed around the area in order to prevent the encroachment by the sea. In 1957, around 1.5 million m³ of refuse were removed and used to reclaim land from the sea at Hoora, (BAR, 1957, p. 53). Work at the same location continued until 1967 (BAR, 1967, p. 26). Similarly, Umm-Ghuraifa sea shore witnessed continuous work from 1963 to 1968 (BAR, 1963, p. 60; 1967, p. 26; 1968, p. 77).

Reclaimed land was considered as government property and most was used for public projects. However, when compared with the old urban fabric, the new areas are often developed at a low-density with free-standing public buildings surrounded by greenery, and thus denoting uneconomic use.

Planning and Design of the Road Network

One of the challenges which faced the urban fabric of old Manama was the advent of the motor car. Its use by British officers, members of the ruling family and a few wealthy tradesmen gave the roads a priority over other aspects of urban development and planning. Widening roads in the old city and the development of the national network linking the city with the other settlements took place as early as the arrival of the first car in 1914. At the city level, a shift in road pattern from the irregular form to straight arteries and a grid layout was an evident sign of this influence, a model that spread to other Gulf cities such as Riyadh, Jeddah, Kuwait, and Dubai later.

The continuous increase in the number of cars from 395 in 1944, to 3,379 in 1954, and then to 18,372 in 1970 focused urban development on the extension of the road network, widening of carriageways and the establishment of more parking places. Motorization has thus been the driving force which dominated the planning of extensions, new settlements as well as the old core. Many tracks which can be seen in the pre-oil period maps (M675.18: 1904–1905) have gradually been surfaced, widened and turned into arteries. Within the city, the market area, the *souq*, was the place to start. Its main artery was subjected to successive 'surgical' operations to widen its main road by demolishing encroaching houses. Its small shops gradually turned into wide ones with glazed façades (BAR, Vol. I, 1930, p. 165).

On the outskirts, successive extensions of the city can be easily traced back owing to the road system as shown in figure 8.6. Two types of roads can be identified from the map: ring roads and roads in finger-like patterns. Ring roads on the east side – namely Isa-al-Kebir Avenue (built in the 1930s), Palace Avenue (1950s), Exhibition Avenue (1960s), and finally Al-Fatih Highway (1980s) – have been constructed by successively pushing back the coastline and extending the city area in belt-like forms. To the north, the foreshore, which was defined by Government Avenue in the 1920s, by the early 1930s had been shifted to a new sea road, now known as King Faisal Road which has become the coastal edge of the city. Ring roads, following the oval form of the core, were built in response to the

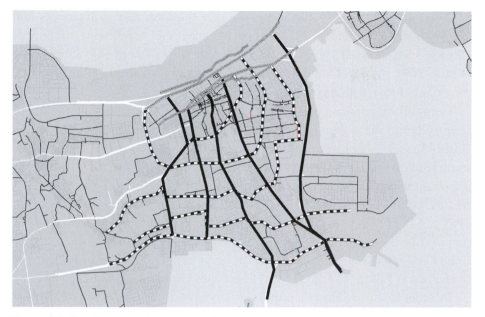

Figure 8.6. Development of Manama road system 1903–2006.

traffic congestion that arose in the city centre where most public services, banks and commercial activities were located.

The finger-like pattern of roads converging on the old core ensured the link between Manama and other areas of the island. They gradually restructured the sprawl and generated a linear urban development which conditioned the land use of future extensions. While plots located along these arteries were subject to intensive use, empty pockets in interstitial spaces, some of which still maintained their agricultural character, remained undeveloped. To the east, Manama had been linked to Muharraq, the former capital, via a traditional causeway since 1929 (Buhajji, 1998, p. 70; Jarman, 1996, p. 14). A new causeway was built in 1941 to replace the old wooden bridge. The intensity of traffic between the two cities then grew continuously, especially after the development of the airport on Muharraq island which came into service in 1932, the date of the first flight. Urban sprawl from both sides of the bay continued to shrink the distance between the two cities.

To the south, the large groves, lagoons and marshes in Hoora, Adlyia (formerly known as Zulm-Abad), Qodaibiya and Juffair areas, were pierced to link the remote villages to the city. Villages and hamlets, such as Mahooz, Umm-Shuum, Suqaya, Ghuraifa, and Halat-bin-Anas, were the end points of the new arteries.

Other recent attraction poles such as the Old and New palaces in Qodaibiya, the British military base (RAF) in Juffair, and later on, the new Salmaniyye port at the extreme south opposite to the old one, have been linked to old Manama by Shaikh Isa, Al-Mutanabbi, Al-Adliyya and Juffair north–south Avenues. To the west, a new road pierced the green belt towards Budaiyye village, the extreme point of the island.

From as early as 1919 the increasing concentration of social services and employment opportunities in Manama attracted the populations of remote villages, such as Budaiyye, Aali and Riffa, and turned them into dormitories (Khuri, 1980, p. 254). Under the pressure of commuting, tracks were gradually turned into roads, then highways.

Compulsory purchase procedures were introduced to enable the building of new roads and the widening of existing ones. In 1930, four houses south of the British Agency garden were purchased and demolished in order to start a north–south road passing by the Agency entrance (BAR, Vol. I, 1930, p. 291). In 1963, an important widening operation and compensation took place on Tijjar, Sheikh Al-Khalifa, Jasim Al-Mehza, and Sheikh Abdullah roads in Manama (BAR, Vol. VII, 1963, p. 61). However, in the absence of major topographical constraints, the high cost of compensation in such operations seems to have determined the routes of some roads and explains the segmentation, irregularity and curving of some major roads such as Palace, Al-Adliyya, Bani Utbah and Umm-Al-Hasam Avenues.

In order to ensure smooth traffic flow and avoid hotspots at intersections, a system of roundabouts was adopted in the early 1960s. The first were in Ras-Rumman, opposite the British Agency and in Salmaniyye, opposite the present Ministry of Health (Buhajji, 1989, p. 64); by the end of the 1970s there were forty in the country.

Managing the Extensions of the City

Unlike most old Muslim cities, including neighbouring ones such as Riyadh and Kuwait, and to some extent Muharraq,[13] which were surrounded by city walls well into the twentieth century, Manama seems to have been without walls for far longer (Abu Hakima, 1965). The statement of Belgrave (RB, Vol. 3, 1923, p. 76), confirming the existence of a city wall in 1819, is thus doubtful as there is no archaeological or historical evidence to support it.[14] However, earlier maps such as (M675.05) drawn in 1825 show that the city had clear edges that contrast it to its rural surroundings. The coastline defined the city's border to the north and east, while burial mounds and palm groves defined its western and southern boundaries. With the exception of the Qala't al-Bahrain fort, built during the Portuguese period (Belgrave, 1952, pp. 61–63), there seems to be no other building outside this boundary. Maps show the existence of the American Mission house built in 1892 and the British Agency built in 1900 partly on reclaimed land outside the urban edge (Jarman, 1996, p. 9). Early extensions to Manama seem thus to be the spontaneous, engulfing adjacent villages, Ras-Rumman and Naeem, on both sides, (M675.16: 1933).

The first planning action appears to have been in 1923 when a new village was created in open desert between the British Agency and the American Mission. A Persian community was moved, probably for health reasons, from a hut village named Zulmabad (Land of Injustice) to the new area (RB, Vol. 4, 1923, pp.

195–198) which was then called Adl-abad and later Adliyya. This first suburban area was described as being covered with fine houses belonging to well-to-do Arabs and Persian merchants, and as having good roads (RB, Vol. 4, 1923, p. 196). Such an extension appears to have pushed back the perimeter of the city towards the two other coastal villages, Halat Bin-Iswar and Halat Bin-Anas, mentioned in Lorimer's map drawn in 1904 (M675.18).

Despite the heavy involvement of the British Agency in the local affairs of Bahrain, the development of Manama does not reflect a clear structural plan. Its growth was a combination of major public actions and small, incremental private actions. The terms 'town planning' and 'building regulations' first appeared in the Annual Report documents in 1965 and 1966, while the Physical Planning Unit was established in 1968 (BAR, Vol. VII, 1965, p. 95; 1966, p. 107; 1968, p. 4). Despite the ordered rings that show the successive extensions, construction took place in a sprawling form that often preceded the planning of roads. Many scattered hamlets grew prior to the planning process and gave rise to fragmented development of the city. Conversely, some new areas such as Qodhaibiyya (1937–1938), Ghufool (1960s) and Khodhor (1963), which are characterized by their grid pattern, witnessed an intensive planning process (BAR, 1956; Jarman, 1996, p. 28). For instance, in 1946, land in Qodhaibiya district was planned with wide straight roads and sold to the public for development (BAR, 1956; 1963, pp. 60–61).

Extensions to the south-east corner of the island started from the former villages of Juffair and Ghuraifa, where the cap-like site called 'Essex Point' was selected for the establishment of the British military headquarters in 1927 and its development in 1935 (Jarman, 1996, pp. 14, 27; Fuccaro, 2005, p. 50). Due to its strategic location, the Juffair area was selected by the Royal Navy for a Rest House and a pier as early as 1933 (Jarman, 1996, p. 15). Similarly, a few hundred metres to the south, another pier on the map (M675.16: 1933) had increasingly witnessed marine activities. In 1962, it was turned officially into a new harbour, now called Salman Port, with docking facilities for up to six large ocean-going ships and extensive warehousing. It thus replaced the old port in Manama which was judged unsuitable as a deep-water anchorage (Rumaihi, 1976, p. 62). The two developments became major attractors for urbanization to the south. They were then linked to the Old Manama and formed the southern suburbs.

To the west, another road linked Manama to Riffa, the former headquarters of the ruling family, beyond which the desert dominated the territory. In this direction, Manama witnessed continuous sprawl along the fertile coastal green belt. The main track connecting the villages of Sanabis, Jidd Hafs, Diraz and Budaiyye became a spine for commuting to and from Manama. The attraction of the city coupled with the collapse of agriculture and the flourishing oil industry and monetary economy gradually led to the interconnection of these settlements and their attachment to the city. Table 8.1 shows the population growth in Manama, while table 8.2 shows that of expatriates both as a percentage of the population.

Table 8.1

Year	1941	1950	1959	1965	1971	1981
Population of Manama	27835	39648	61726	79098	88785	121986
Total population of Bahrain	89970	109650	143135	182203	216303	350457
Manama population as a percentage of total population	31	36	43	43	41	35

Sources: Rumaihi, 1976, p. 24, Lawson, 1989, p. 12; BAR, Vol. III, 1959, p. 733.

Table 8.2.

Year	1941	1950	1959	1965	1971	1981
Bahrainis	74040	91179	118734	143814	178393	
Non-Bahrainis	15930	18471	24401	38389	37910	
Total Population	89970	109650	143135	182203	216303	350457
Bahrainis as a percentage of total population	17.70	16.85	17.05	21.07	17.53	

Sources: Rumaihi, 1976, p. 24; Lawson, 1989, p.12; BAR, Vol. VII, 1959, p. 73.

Housing Policy

Housing delivery was initially based on the land market and private action rather than the direct involvement of the government. Stone houses gradually replaced the large area of huts surrounding the city. Fires that often happened during the dry windy months of May and June pushed the authorities to plan for their replacement. Until the mid-1960s Manama comprised 2,464 *barasti* houses (BAR, Vol. VII, 1965, p. 120). However, in 1961 for instance, 440 *barasti* houses were destroyed and many others were deliberately pulled down for fear of fire (BAR, Vol. VI, 1961, p. 62).

Early housing policy consisted of the sale of plots of land acquired through reclamation, from ruler's properties or from un-owned parcels. However, despite the powerful administrative system, private building development and land speculation were so rapid that the municipality lost control of new developments. Buildings were often erected prior to any urban infrastructure. A map from 1938–1939 shows, for instance, the water supply system for Manama which was adapted to the existing urban fabric (M675.32).

Public housing also increased in accordance with the growth in the expatriate workforce, most of whom were employed by the government in areas such as health, the army, police, the oil industry and teaching. For instance, the growth of the police force required the expansion of the headquarters located close to the Old Fort and bungalows for European police officers were constructed in 1955 (BAR, Vol. V, 1956, p. 30).

During the 1960s, public housing became part of the urban policy which introduced apartment buildings. In 1963, Manama comprised 8,341 ordinary stone houses and 959 flats in addition to 1,456 shops and mixed premises (BAR, Vol. VII, 1963, p. 63). For instance, in 1960 fifty new houses were built as labourers' accommodation, adding to the existing 196 (BAR, Vol. VI, 1960, p. 49).

From 1963 onwards the State became the major provider of social facilities and housing and a welfare policy aimed at achieving social justice and increasing living standards was adopted. Many programmes were launched throughout Bahrain to meet the housing needs of both expatriates and locals. As a means of relieving congestion in Manama, many local families were granted housing units in the new settlements, for instance in Isa New Town. However, the old core, which maintained its attraction as a business and service centre, gradually became an area of low-income rental housing.

In architecture, the new Western styles such as the flats for labourers, the Awali bungalows for European expatriates, and Isa New town designed by British planners and architects served as a reference for the local population (Faroughy, 1951, p. 20). From this period onwards modern architecture dominated both new housing schemes and private house design.

Services, Utilities and Social Facilities

The growth of bureaucracy can be traced through the expansion of public buildings in Manama. The nucleus of the administration was initially based in two main buildings, the Municipality and the British Agency. Gradually it was reinforced by other offices such as the Police, Customs, Courts, and Postal Service most of which were located on reclaimed land near the main gate of the city. As an image of the administrative reforms, a grandiose political district, known as Bab-al-Bahrain, was then created. Major government offices were designed around a formal plaza on which converge in a 'T' form the main road from the bazaar, the pier and the two parts of the new Government Road. A monumental arch was erected bridging the two sides of the main road towards the *souq* along which luxurious shops were opened (BAR, Vol. VIII, 1942–1947, p. 79) (figure 8.7*a* and *b*). Despite the traditional elements which characterize the building and made of it a landmark and logo of Bahrain, it contrasts starkly with the existing morphology and local architecture. Its formal architecture opposes the traditional, organic form and it stands as a screen covering the old town when approached from the sea. Sited in the face of the prevailing wind, it deprives the streets from the breezes, and caused climatic discomfort in the old core during the long hot humid season.

The government's efforts to provide utilities such as electricity, water supply and drainage, coupled with the health measures to combat epidemics and health hazards, greatly improved living standards in Manama. However, the recourse to large-scale technology had deeply marked the landscape of the city. Power stations such as Stations A, B and C and water towers, such as Mahooz tank which is

Figure 8.7a. Aerial view of Bab al-Bahrain gate showing the early political and administrative district in Manama.

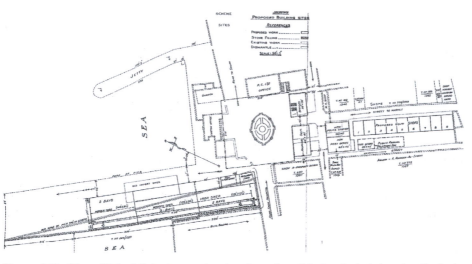

Figure 8.7b. Plan of Bab al-Bahrain gate showing the early political and administrative district in Manama.

23 m high with a capacity of 750,000 gallons, occupied large plots in the suburbs of Manama and dominate the skyline (BAR, Vol. VIII, 1968, p. 138).

Social facilities also reflect to a large extent the direct involvement of the government in Manama's urban development and the domination of the urbanism of bureaucracy. Education moved from small Islamic schools of fifteen to twenty pupils, which were scattered all over the city, to a few large, modern institutions. Early schools were established as private initiatives, mostly reflecting ethnic and religious structures. The first Western schools which opened in Manama were founded by the American Mission in 1892 for girls and in 1905 for boys. This was followed by the Persian minority school which opened in 1910. A Sunni and an Arab Shia school opened consecutively in 1921and 1927 (Rumaihi, 1976, pp. 115–121). In order to overcome social disputes, promote female education and control social movements, a committee was formed to unify education and make it a sector of government. At the physical level, the growing number of schools, mostly concentrated in Manama, had deeply affected land use in terms of space and the generation of traffic (BAR, Vol. V, 1956, pp. 84–91) (figure 8.8).

Figure 8.8. Zahra, Manama and Iranian Schools in the heart of the old urban fabric showing the contrast in typology and size.

Since the early days of British administration, health care facilities were provided to local populations suffering from epidemics and acute diseases. They were linked to missionary works; early hospitals – the American Mission (1892) and Victoria Hospitals (1900) – were attached to churches and educational facilities. They were, however, located on the outskirts of the old city where space was available. Other health centres such as the women's hospital, isolation hospital, government hospitals and clinics, were developed in Manama's suburbs and thus further expanded the city (Al-Khalifa, 1986).

Financial institutions represent another side of Manama's urban development. Since the pre-oil era, the city developed as a financial centre which flourished under the pearl trade. The prosperity of the oil economy, which jumped from 32.6 per cent of the total revenues in 1935–1936 to 64.3 per cent in 1936–1937, coupled with the massive presence of expatriates, most of whom transferred their money outside Bahrain, generated many offshore banks in Manama (Rumaihi, 1976, p. 75; Lawson, 1989, p. 49). Eastern Bank, established in 1920 (Bassam, 2000, p. 32) and the British Bank of the Middle East were the early ones which were gradually followed by other financial institutions which dramatically marked the landscape of the city.

Manama after Independence

In 1971, the country witnessed a smooth transition from the colonial era to independence. The administrative structures and regulations which were entirely inherited from the colonial authorities continued to play their role in shaping and guiding the urban development of Bahrain. Politically, this role was justified and endorsed by the welfare policy which aimed at achieving social justice through the equitable distribution of oil resources. Being the major employer, the government witnessed an increase in the size and number of its institutions as most of the previous departments, such as education, agriculture, municipalities, commerce, housing and public works, were turned into ministries. Bureaucratic proliferation took place at all levels of the administrative machinery. At the top, there was a pressing need for the provision of high positions for members of ruling families, the massive recruitment of educated locals, and the recruitment of highly qualified expatriate consultants. At the bottom, there was a need for masses of expatriates to perform low-paid jobs such as street cleaning and building maintenance (Khuri, 1980, p. 117, quoting Hunter, 1969, p. 194).

Massive buildings accommodating various departments and ministries were constructed in the new areas of Manama. The need for a central location was, however, challenged by the scarcity of land, a factor which led to further land reclamation on Manama's three land sides.

A diplomatic area comprising most of the ministries, courts and embassies gradually emerged on reclaimed land on the north-east side of Bab-al-Bahrain. As a sign of progress, most new buildings were high-rise and of Western style in sharp contrast to the 'backward' traditional city.

Tourism and finance were the two growing sectors supposed to substitute oil and lead the Bahraini economy into the post-oil era. As early as the 1970s, a new generation of banks and first-class hotels such as the Diplomat, Sheraton and Crown Plaza were established around old Manama within the diplomatic area. By 1986 hotels provided a total of 5,700 beds while the number of financial companies and banks was estimated to be 173, among which is the 26-storey glass and steel tower of the National Bank of Bahrain.

In a desperate move to tackle the increasing traffic, a new peripheral road with a series of roundabouts was developed along the edge of the peninsula, parallel to the three coastlines. Within the new belt of roads many pockets of land are unused as a result of the dispersed development. Mixed scenes make up the landscape of present day Manama; along the new highway, the driver passes empty plots, dying palm groves, a few remaining historic buildings, and modern glazed towers, with views of the sea never far away.

The primacy of Manama was further strengthened by the new network of highways and causeways which converge on the city. To the east, a second bridge joining Manama to Muharraq and the airport was inaugurated in 1997. To the south, a third causeway was created to link Manama to Sitra island and Riffa where most industrial complexes, the oil refinery and Bahrain Aluminum Company are located. At a regional level, the 24 km King Fahd Causeway, linking Bahrain to Saudi Arabia and other Gulf States was opened in 1986. By 2007 the causeway was carrying some 20,000 vehicles per day.

To further alleviate the pressure on the old city, the public authorities continued to provide housing in new settlements, namely in Isa New Town (last stages 1963–1983) and Hamad Town (1982–1986). A total of 15,000 dwellings were constructed between 1976 and 1990 outside Manama (MOH, 1993, p. 125). However, as these new settlements were very close to the city and consisted solely of housing and social facilities, most turned into dormitories whose residents commute daily to Manama and other places of work.

During the 1990s, the city witnessed a series of beautification and entertainment projects, mostly located on the recently reclaimed land along the northern and eastern coastlines. Walkways, corniches and public parks have been established. These leisure areas are interspersed with prestigious buildings such as the National Museum, Marina Club, the Al-Fateh Mosque, and children's play areas.

The Degradation of the Historical Core

With the diminution of urban development in Manama, as most projects were focused in other areas, the old core witnessed continuous degradation due to the absence of a serious preservation policy. With the exception of the urban fabric that preserves its organic character manifested in the irregular narrow streets and interlocked buildings, many architectural features of the city have disappeared and been replaced by modern buildings.

The old core, which now represents only about 10 per cent of the total area of Manama, suffers from various problems which reflect the timid efforts by the government in its preservation and revitalization.

In a 1987 study of the old city, it was found that only 41.9 per cent of the population were Bahraini, while the expatriate presence was growing at 6.1 per cent per annum. The outward migration of the original population and its partial replacement by expatriates changed the tenure of the housing from owner-occupier to tenant. This shift contributed enormously to the degradation of old buildings.

Old districts also witnessed significant over-crowding, as the density reached a peak of 952 persons per hectare, which is three times the average density of the rest of Manama. Old houses were mostly rented to male expatriates who generally work in restaurants, hotels, retail shops and other low-income activities in central Manama. Low rents together with neglect and the lack of maintenance by landlords contributed to the continuing dilapidation of houses and thus the creation of slums in some of the old residential quarters namely, Hammam, Makharga, Kanu, and Fadhel (MOH, 1987, p, 29).

Another cause of physical degradation is the dominance of male only enclaves and the disintegration of social networks. However the presence of *ma'atams* (Shia religious buildings), which are the focal point during *Muharram*, *Ashura* and other Shia religious festivals, are regularly maintained and upgraded with the help of endowments from the Jaffari Waqf (Fuccaro, 2005, pp. 48–49; 2000, pp. 75–76; 1999, pp. 1–4).

Urban spaces, including dead-end streets and small open areas within housing compounds, known as *baraha*, were considered as a continuation of the domestic space and thus were under the care of the residents. Under municipal law, they became the sole responsibility of the government in terms of ownership, hygiene and maintenance. Residents have consequently lost any interaction with their environment and limited their concern to their homes.

Regulations and building permits do not apply to construction in the old city. With the exception of some restrictions regarding the outlook of the houses, they are mostly concerned with the enforcement of modern planning requirements, such as zoning, set-backs, number of floors and plot ratios of built-up area, open spaces, etc. Old customs and practices mostly based on social agreements and Islamic law, such as inheritance (*mirath*), pre-emption (*shufa'a*), endowment (*waqf*), usufruct rights (*'ihiya*), custom's law (*urf*), and right of precedence (*sabq*), although still considered by local people in their daily life are unknown to municipal administrators (Hakim, 1994; Hakim and Zubair, 2005; Ben-Hamouche, 2004; Leeuwen, 1999; Khuri, 1980, pp. 28–29).

An exception is the pious foundation or *waqf*; two such institutions, Awaqf al-Sunna and Awaqf al-Shia, have fortunately not been abolished and continue to manage their assets in the city and throughout Bahrain (BAR, Vol. I, 1924, p. 162).[15] Part of their revenues are being spent on the repair and maintenance of endowed properties, a fact that has extended the life span of many old religious buildings.

One consequence of this legal co-existence between the traditional system and modern regulations is the dispute among partners and inheritors which usually leads to degradation due to the neglect of pre-emption and inheritance laws and their enforcing bodies. The continuous increase in the number of inheritors and partners, sometimes as many as 250 persons, makes agreements on the use and usufruct very difficult and can lead to building abandonment.

These factors explain the unsatisfactory state of the built environment as reflected in the 1987 report. While 32 per cent of the buildings were in a good state of repair, 38.8 per cent were poor, and 5.9 per cent were threatening collapse. Houses which had already collapsed, 2.5 per cent of the total area, were left as empty pockets and are often rented as private parking places or are simply used as garbage collection areas.

Global Urbanism

Bahrain might be taken as a good example of the influence of globalization on small countries of limited resources. The depletion of oil since the early 1990s, which now represents only 17 per cent of the economy, and reliance on market economy has had a profound effect on Manama and the whole territorial structure.[16]

Over the last 4 or 5 years action has been taken in two strategic sectors: tourism and finance. The first seems to be based on long experience in the off-shore banking system, which was developed by the British authorities in response to accumulation of oil revenues and the need for the means to transfer funds by both foreign companies and expatriate labour. The second is based on the physical potential of the Bahraini islands and the reputation of Arabian life which draws Western tourists.

The two sectors sometimes overlap through the investment projects which target foreigners as well as regional investors. This policy is realized in physical terms through a series of mega-projects involving tourist resorts, shopping centres, banks and office towers, and luxurious residences.

The increasing monetary fluidity in the region, resulting from the oil boom and the presence of multi-national finance companies, reflects to a large extent the slogan 'Form follows Finance' (Willis, 1995). Deregulation of the economy and administrative inducements led to the emergence of investors as the new actors on the urban stage. Recent changes in Manama serve as an example for what would be the dramatic effects of 'marketing a city image'.

Manama and the Mega-project Trend

The ready availability of information on current projects enables us to enumerate them and assess some of their common features and urban impacts. Four of these are situated around the old city of Manama of which three are along King Faisal Road, the vital artery that connects Manama with Muharraq and the international airport.

One of the most ambitious projects is the Bahrain Financial Harbour. Seeking a place on the globalization map and 'entering' the third millennium, this over-ambitious project is located opposite the old gate of Manama.[17] Metaphorically as well as economically it is intended to be a gate to Bahrain and an international financial hub. Within the Gulf region, the project is intended to compete with similar projects in other cities in order that Manama might become again the financial capital of the Middle East, as it was before. The project is a $1.5 billion integrated master-plan developed by a local consultant in joint venture with regional and international companies. It takes the form of twin 53-storey towers, whose design is inspired by a sailing boat, located on a reclaimed land located in line with the old pier and the bazaar (figure 8.9). The development, whose

Figure 8.9. Bahrain Financial Harbour.

first phase was inaugurated in May 2007, spreads over 380,000 m² of reclaimed land with office, residential, retail, dining and leisure space. The first occupants were announced as thirty-five key financial sector and retail companies including MENA TELECOM, DHL and ARAMEX, Kheliji Commercial Bank (KHCB).[18]

Next to Bahrain Financial Harbour (figure 8.9), on the other side of the same road, is Bahrain World Trade Center. Its twin towers have coincidently the same pyramidal form and height, as those of Bahrain Financial Harbour. They create dramatic landmarks visible throughout the city and they look out onto spectacular views of the city and the coast. The towers are linked by three bridges each of which supports a giant wind turbine said to improve the energy performance of the buildings. At the ground level, the centre comprises many facilities such as a shopping centre and a five-star hotel. The project was designed by W. Atkins, and is being developed by a consortium of international contractors. Started in June 2004 and scheduled for completion in 2009, the scheme will provide a space of 35,000 m² at a cost of approximately US$1 billion.

To the south, the old core of Manama is marked by Al-Zamel Tower, an office complex in two parts on either side of Sheikh Khalifa Avenue which forms a new gate to the city from the roundabout nearby. The taller of the two towers facing the busy Government Road has a height of 95.5 m with twenty-two storeys. The second tower, has only ten storeys and overlooks Sheikh Khalifa Avenue. In order to smooth the sharp contrast between its high-tech envelope and the old urban fabric, a hybrid treatment has been adopted for its architecture. The lower floors, including the gate has an 'Islamic', mostly Egyptian style, while the upper floors are of glass and steel.

To the west, close to the main roundabout, a high-rise, luxurious residential complex is being constructed. Abraj al-Lulu towers, due for completion in May 2008, are being developed by Pearl Development and Real Estate. Its cost is said to be BD95million or US$252 million for a floor area totalling 18,600 m². It comprises three multi-storey residential towers with 860 state-of-art apartments and is equipped with all the amenities for a luxury lifestyle, including a four-storey car park with 1000 spaces. The apartments are to be sold to upper-class locals and foreigners.[19]

The fourth project, which is to cost US$1.25 billion, is an artificial island of some 560,000 m² created at the northern corniche of old Manama. The Lulu Island development, due for completion in 2009, is a real estate development of thirty-nine residential buildings, an iconic residential tower, a 300-room five-star hotel, sixty-five villas and forty-nine chalets, with shopping and leisure amenities.[20] The luxury residences, far beyond the reach of the local population, are intended to attract Gulf and foreign investors and to put the capital city of Bahrain on the world's tourism map.

Away from the old core, 5 km inland, a new business district, Al-Seef area, is becoming a platform of several towers and luxurious buildings. Located along the major highway leading to Saudi Arabia, it accommodates many office towers, three shopping malls and several new five-star hotels.

Similar resort and leisure projects such as Amawaj, Riffa Views and the Bahrain International Circuit were also undertaken elsewhere in the hinterland of Bahrain. Durrat Al-Bahrain, which is being developed in the same way as Dubai's three Palm Islands and Qatar's Pearls, is a residential resort city on 20 km² of reclaimed land on the southern coast of Bahrain.

Because of Manama's proximity to the airport most of these new developments generate traffic which directly affects the old core. To mitigate this in the absence of an efficient public transport system, many flyovers and bridges are being constructed at junction points around Manama, while roads and highways are widened to accommodate more lanes.

Effects of Globalization

The scale of these transformations as well as their urban form have deeply affected the morphology of Manama. The new projects surrounding the old city mask its oriental identity and envelop the historic core, so projecting a 'globalized' image of the city. Their vertical character and exhibitionist architecture contrast sharply with the low-profile skyline and local style of the old town. The coastline which once defined the old Manama has been shifted seawards so depriving the old town of its original character which was for centuries shaped by water. Further projects are being developed in the bay and along the two bridges linking Manama and Muharraq thus gradually closing the views onto the sea and interlocking the two cities.

At the social level, the nature of the projects, mostly prestigious and targeting foreign investment, bypass the local reality and thus fuel social reactions. Such effects would threaten the fragile social stability that is already affected by the fluctuating political context of the region. While the Ministry of Public Works and Housing has estimated the shortage in low-income and social housing to be 30,000 units, these iconic projects will provide 10,000 high standard residential units, destined for foreign investors and the local wealthy class. On the regional scene, the ethnic conflict between Shia and Sunni in Iraq, coupled with the tension between Iran and the United States, Hezbolla in Lebanon and 'Israel', have direct reverberation within Bahrain.

Environmental sustainability is the least consideration in these developments. Besides their undesirable microclimatic effects on the old core (which are yet to be investigated), most of these projects are designed in fashionable glass envelopes which disregard energy saving and climatic performance.

While their architectural and construction details and finishes are scrutinized, none of these projects seems to have been based on studies of either the existing context or the possible impacts on the urban structure. Being decided at a higher political level, their approval bypassed the traditional planning process and so disregarded consideration of respect for heritage, land-use and other building standards. Similarly, the selection of their sites has been made on the basis of profit and pressure from investors.

An interesting project, Manama Souq, which covers the area of the old market starting from Bab-al-Bahrain, is finally being undertaken to regenerate the market area and give an impulse to its eroding micro-economy (Ministry of Commerce, 2004, pp. 6–25). However, in the absence of studies of socio-economic structure, land tenancy, and the physical state of the area, the project turned into a simplistic approach that is interested in the visual effects of design. Traditional architecture which recalls some symbols of the oriental city would certainly be of interest to tourists and visitors, but would not revive the dying heart of the city.

Perspectives for Future Development

There is clear evidence that, in the light of the present financial boom in the Gulf, Manama will continue to attract other development projects. Given the space shortage and high population growth, the extension of other remote villages and towns with regard to the short distances separating them will generate a multi-conurbation phenomenon that will make of Bahrain a single metropolis.

Encroachments on the coastline will also continue through reclamation work until it reaches the physical limits defined by the depth of the sea. The Bahrain bay would in this perspective shrink and become a narrow channel on which the three present causeways will be simple bridges. Similarly, the north coastline will move back further to make room for other prestigious projects in the interstitial spaces that still exist between the present scattered areas of reclamation.

Many pockets of undeveloped private land in the southern Manama suburbs will inevitably be subjected to speculation and unplanned development. An infill policy which consists of monitoring the development of these interstitial spaces within the modern urban fabric would therefore be of interest to the municipality in response to the pressure of land market and planning.

The old core faces two scenarios which depend on the official attitude of the public authorities. The first consists of the continuation of the present *laissez-faire* attitude with respect to the urban heritage, which will be subject to market forces, including pressure from wealthy merchants, investors, members of the ruling family seeking the bright lights of modernization. In this scenario the old core will witness a gradual but irreversible replacement. A similar process happened in other Gulf cities such as Kuwait, Dubai[21] and to a lesser degree Muscat, during the 1970s and 1980s, where the old fabric was entirely replaced by modern building which retained some nostalgic detailing. Permanent elements of the urban fabric, such as the street network, land subdivisions and property lines will, however, persist and mark the new morphology.

The second scenario, which is based on an 'interventionist' role of the State, would require a firm political attitude to consider the historic site as national patrimony to be preserved and protected for future generations. Examples of preserved cities such as Tarragona, Dénia, Córdoba and Seville in Spain, Durham, York, Oxford, and Bath in England, and Bari, Trani and Venice in Italy, abound.[22]

Inventive solutions for issues such as car parking, garbage collection, drainage, networks and cabling, could support this policy. A preservation policy will, however, require a multi-faceted approach which goes beyond the present pro-design approach to include legal, financial, social and informational considerations. For instance, a special legal framework which combines local customs, social customs and Islamic law would help to accommodate community participation and motivate individuals in its implementation. Financial incentives, such as grants to preserve old houses, and taxes on their demolition would encourage preservation. Empowerment of non-government agencies to safeguard old Manama would work to counter-balance pressure from developers. A thorough study to list the buildings and properties in the historic core, which has never been carried out, would be a starting point.

Conclusion

Manama has passed through many stages of development which have had direct impacts on its urban fabric. Initially, it was a port city which grew in symbiosis with its physical environment, cosmopolitan social structure and the local know-how of its citizens. The federal-like system of tribal governance and the freedom of individual actions which its residents enjoyed were reflected in the autonomous urbanism that marked its urban morphology.

British colonialism established a bureaucratic system through a long process of gradual substitution of local institutions, customs and practices, and the reduction of individual freedom. While health conditions improved and social facilities were provided, so raising the living standard of the local population, freedom of people and their autonomy shrank significantly in the face of the increasing role of government and its administrative machinery.

The growing role of the municipality and the 'divide-and-rule' policy rendered all decisions regarding the city the sole responsibility of the public authorities. The discovery of oil coupled with the erosion of private and community sectors, due to the degradation of the pearl trade, agriculture and local industry, further reinforced administrative reform. A new form of urbanism, reflecting the bureaucratic machine, dominated urban development in the outskirts, where the government became a major urban actor.

After independence, the inherited bureaucratic system flourished due to the increase of oil resources and the welfare policy adopted by the government. In contrast to the common academic belief that the Gulf cities of today developed as a consequence of oil, Manama presents evidence that oil has not been a determining factor but rather an accelerator in the bureaucratic/autocratic political system.

With the depletion of oil, and the partial withdrawal of government, globalization forces are now taking the front seat in the making of the city. Iconic projects are mushrooming all over the territory, with the aim of marketing the city and pinpointing it in the financial global market. Manama's old city is thus open to two possible scenarios depending on the role of authorities and civil agencies. Either, it will enter a further stage of disintegration and remodelling – the outcome if its future is left to market forces – or it will be preserved as national patrimony for future generations –and this requires a determinist public policy to be established by the government.

Notes

1.   The number of 300 villages and 30 cities and towns, that existed prior to the arrival of Al-Khalifa as noted in some historical references, has been discounted by Khuri (1980, pp. 28–29) as there is no evidence on the ground to support this. See also Al-Araiyadh (2006), p. 18.

2.   The code number of the map and its date are taken from Jarman (1996). From here onwards only the code of the map (M) and the date will appear in the text.

3.   *Ain* is the Arabic word for spring or source.

4.   The map of Manama and its outskirts 1969–1970 shows that until 1970 canals and streams flowing towards the sea shaped land parcels in Karrana, Toubli and other places in Bahrain.

5.   *Hareem* can be translated literally as 'the forbidden area', and is the buffer zone around a palm tree, a well or along a river on which no construction or other uses are permitted.

6.   However this technique, and Persian architecture in general, dominated Manama's landscape only after the influx of Persian migrants between 1860 and the 1920s, among whom there were builders and craftsmen (Fuccaro, 2005). There are no signs of Manama being under the influence of Persian civilization before this.

7.   According to some local sources, the name Manama comes from the Arabic word *nawm*, 'a place for sleeping'. It used to be a rest area for the ruler and was thus a secondary residence to

Muharraq, which was the ruler's headquarters and that of the allied Arab tribes (Ben-Hamouche, 2004, pp. 522–524).

8.   Residential quarters in old Muslim cities are mostly compact blocks, often accessed through gates, and much of the street network is made up of dead-ends (Raymond, 1985), features that are not present in Manama.

9.   This system was described by Belgrave (1972) as primitive. He called it a 'justice of the palm-tree' where the Sheikh used to listen to petitioners while sitting under the palm, his back on its trunk (Khalifa, 2000, p. 92).

10.   Charles Belgrave, the father of the author, had been working, as an 'advisor' to the Bahraini ruler for 30 years. In 1957, he left Bahrain, 'confident that he had been able to guarantee for the State the means to achieve steady and organized progress in the future' (Belgrave, 1960, p. 42).

11.   In his memoirs, Charles Belgrave considers that the replacement of Sunni and Shia judges by secular institutions was among his successes in Bahrain (Khalifa, 2000).

12.   Land irrigated by wheels once turned by oxen (Khuri, 1980, p.63).

13.   Tailor (1818) stated that '… at present there is only one fortified town on the island Awal and not more than 40 or 50 villages on the neighbouring islands'.

14.   Opposite to the city wall of Muharraq, which can be seen on the map M675.04-1828 (Jarman, 1996), Manama at this time was made up of scattered houses located on open land.

15.   The report on Sunni *waqf* states that: 'it was in an extremely unsatisfactory condition: valuable gardens, houses and shops in Manama and fish traps were lacking supervision. The revenues were not properly collected, and there were no check on the way in which they were spent'. For the abolition of *waqf* the same report added that: 'an attempt was made by Major Daly, the Political Resident in Bahrain during the 1930s but failed to face the huge opposition from local population' (BR, Vol. IV, 1928–1932, p. 460).

16.   Measures to cope with the post-oil era have been envisaged since the late 1960s. Heavy industrial complexes were developed in three locations outside Manama, in consortium with other Gulf states. The major industrial complexes in Bahrain are: ALBA (Aluminum of Bahrain) established in 1968, ASRY (the Arab Shipbuilding and Repair Yard) founded in 1977, GPIC (Gulf Petrochemicals Industries Company) developed in the early 1980s, and BAPCO (Bahrain Petroleum Company) which was established in 1929 (Al-Yousef, 1985, pp. 124–129).

17.   In fact many similar projects are being developed in Saudi Arabia, Kuwait and the Emirates, and will all be inaugurated soon. While the three countries' economies are still based on oil, Bahrain ironically relies on foreign and regional investors that mostly come from these countries. In Bahrain, some office towers which have been put up for rent, such as Bahrain National Bank tower and Al-Muayyed tower, have to date many unoccupied floors.

18.   http://www.ameinfo.com/103260.html. Accessed 28 March 2007.

19.   http://www.ameinfo.com/68693.html. Accessed 28 March 2007.

20.   http://realestate.theemiratesnetwork.com/developments/bahrain/lulu_island.php. Accessed 28 March 2007.

21.   For the impact of globalization on Dubai for instance see Marchal (2005)

22.   The stated cities were subjected to a personal visit by the author.

References

Abu Hakima, M. (1965) *History of Eastern Arabia 1750–1800: The Rise and Development of Bahrain and Kuwait*. Beirut: Khayats.
Abuzid, M.A. (1998) Fareej al-Shuyukh (part 2). *Akhbar Al-Khaleej*, 13 March.
Akbar, J. (1988) *Crisis in the Built Environment*. Singapore: Media Press.
Al-Araiyadh, A. (2006) Amkina Bahriniyya (part 2). *Al Watan*, 31 March.

Al-Khalifa, A. (1986) The inception and development of health services in Bahrain. *Al-Watheekah*, No. 8, pp. 219–241.

Al-Khalifa, M.A. (1994) *Ziraat al-Nakheel fi al-Bahrain*. Manama: Al-Matbaa al Hukumiyya.

Al-Tajir, M.A. (1987) *Bahrain 1920–1945*. London: Croom Helm.

Al-Yousef, A. (1985) An evaluation of Bahrain's major industries and their future prospects, in Nugent, J. and Thomas, T.H. (eds.) *Bahrain and the Gulf: Past Perspectives and Alternative Futures*. London: Croom Helm, pp. 107–123.

Bahrain Society of Engineers (2003) Editorial. *Al-Mohandis Magazine*, No. 38, p. 1.

BAR (Bahrain Government Annual Reports) (1924–1970) *Annual Reports*, 8 Volumes. Reprinted by Archive Editions, 1993.

Bassam, A. (2000) Establishment of the Eastern Bank in Bahrain 1920 in Delmun. *Journal of the Bahrain Historical & Archaeological Society*, **19**, pp. 22–33.

Belgrave, C.D. (1972) *The Pirate Coast*. Beirut: Librairie du Liban.

Belgrave, J.H.D. (1952) A brief survey of the history of the Bahrain Islands. *Journal of the Royal Central Asian Society*, **39**(1), pp. 57–68.

Belgrave, J.H.D. (1960) *Welcome to Bahrain*, 4th ed. Stourbridge and Manama: Mark & Moody.

Ben-Hamouche, M. (2003) Decision-making system and urban geometry in traditional Muslim cities: the case of Algiers 1516–1830. *Journal of Architectural and Planning Research*, **20**(4), pp. 307–322.

Ben-Hamouche M. (2004) The changing morphology of the Gulf cities in the age of globalization: the case of Bahrain. *Habitat International*, **28**, pp. 521–540.

BGWO (British Government War Office) (1916) *Handbook of Arabia*, Vol. 1, Part 1, pp. 320–321.

Broeze, F. (1997) Kuwait before Oil: the dynamics and morphology of an Arab port city, in Broese, F. (ed.) *Gateways of Asia: Port Cities of Asia in the 13th–20th Centuries* London: Kegan Paul, pp. 149–190.

Buhajji, A.M. (1989) *Lamahat min tarikh al-murur fil Bahrain 1914–1969*. Manama: Al-Muassassa Al-Arabiya.

Datta, S. and Nugent, J. (1985) Bahrain's pearling industry: how it was, why it was that way and its implications, in Nugent, J. and Thomas, T.H. (eds.) *Bahrain and the Gulf: Past Perspectives and Alternative Futures*. London: Croom Helm, pp. 25–40.

Durand, E.L. Ct. Description of the Bahrain Islands (Topography and archaeology: Durand Reports, 1878–1879) in Records of Bahrain Vol II, pp. 535–559.

Faroughy, A. (1951) *The Bahrein Islands, 750–1951*. New York: Verry, Fisher.

Fuccaro, N. (1999) Islam and urban space: Ma'tams in Bahrain before oil. *Newsletter of the Institute for the Study of Islam in the Modern World (ISIM)*, 3 July, p. 12.

Fuccaro, N. (2000) Understanding the urban history of Bahrain. *Critique*, No. 17, pp 49–81.

Fuccaro, N. (2005) Mapping the transnational community: Persians and the space of the city in Bahrain 1869–1937, in Al-Rasheed, M. (ed) *Transnational Connections and the Arab Gulf*. London: Routledge, pp. 39–57.

Hakim, B. (1994) The 'Urf' and its role in diversifying the architecture of traditional Islamic cities. *Journal of Architectural and Planning Research*, **11**(2), pp 108–127.

Hakim, B. (2001) Reviving the Rule System, an approach to revitalizing traditional towns in Maghrib. *Cities*, **18**(2), pp. 87–92.

Hakim, B. and Zubair, A. (2005) Rules for the built environment in the 19th century. northern Nigeria. *Journal of Architectural and Planning Research*, **23**(1), pp 1–24.

Haworth, L. (1929) Persia and the Persian Gulf. *Journal of the Central Asian Society*, **16**, pp. 495–509.

Jarman, R.L. (ed.) (1996) *Historic Maps of Bahrain 1817–1970*. Slough: Archive Editions.

Kemball, Lieutenant A.B. (1845) Tribes inhabiting the Arabian shores of the Persian gulf. Memoranda submitted to Government on 6th January 1845, in Records of Bahrain, Vol.1, pp. 95–107.

Khalifa, M. (2000) *Charles Belgrave; al-seera wa al mudhakkirat 1926–1957*. Beirut: Al Mu'assassa al Arabiya.

Khuri, F. (1980) *Tribe and State in Bahrain*. Chicago, IL: University of Chicago Press.

Larsen, C. (1983) *Life and Land Use on the Bahrain Islands: The Geography of an Ancient Society*. Chicago, IL: Chicago University Press.

Lawson, F. (1989) *Bahrain: the Modernization of Autocracy*. Boulder, CO: Westview Press.

Leeuwen, R.V. (1999) *Waqf and Urban Structures*. Leiden: Brill.

Lorimer, J.G. (1908 and 1915) *Gazetteer of the Persian Gulf, Oman and Central Arabia*. Official Records of the Government of India. Reprinted in 6 volumes, 1986. Archive Editions.

Mahdi, A. (1994) *Taste of the Past Bahrain*. Manama.

Mandeel, F. (1992) Planning Regulations for the Tradional Arab-Islamic Built Environment in Bahrain. MPhil thesis, University of Newcastle.

Marchal, R. (2005) Dubai global city and transnational hub, in Al-Rasheed, M. (ed.) *Transnational Connections and the Arab Gulf*. London: Routledge, pp. 93–110.

Ministry of Commerce (2004) Souq al Manama. *Commerce Magazine*, no. 3, pp. 6–25.

Ministry of Housing (1987) *Manama Urban Renewal Project*. Manama: Government Press Bahrain.

MOH (Ministry of Housing-Bahrain) (1993) *Masirat al-Injaz wa al Aata' Al Muassassa al arabiyya*. Manama.

Onley, J. (2005) Transnational merchants in the nineteenth century Gulf: the case of the Safar family, in Al-Rasheed, M (ed.) *Transnational Connections and the Arab Gulf*. London: Routledge, pp. 59–89.

Qubain, F. (1955) Social classes and tensions in Bahrain. *Middle East Journal*, **9**(3).

Raymond A. (1985) *Grandes villes arabes à l'époque ottomane*, Paris: Sindbad.

RB (Records of Bahrain) (1820–1970) *Primary Documents 1820–1970*, 8 volumes. Reprinted by Archive Editions, 1993.

Rumaihi, M.G. (1976) *Bahrain: Social and Political Change since the First World War*. New York: Bowker.

Tailor R. Ct. (1818–1856) Extracts from brief notes: The Persian Gulf Records of Bahrain, Vol. 1 pp. 85–93.

Walls, A.G. (1987) *Arad Fort*. Manama: Bahrain Government Printing Press.

Willis, C. (1995) *Form Follows Finance*. New York: Princeton Architectural Press.

Acknowledgments

This chapter is part of a research project entitled 'Land use in Bahrain; Past, Present and Future' which is funded by the Research Deanship, University of Bahrain, Project no 23/2005. I would like to thank Ranjieth Daraytnee and Ahmed Al-Jawder for reviewing the early draft of the chapter, and Nelida Fuccaro for providing me with her precious papers on the urban history of Bahrain.

Chapter 9

Rediscovering the Island: Doha's Urbanity from Pearls to Spectacle

Khaled Adham

When a man rides a long time through wild regions he feels the desire for a city.
                                        Italo Calvino, *Invisible Cities*

The bedouin who had at first refused to go near the sea or take part in unloading cargoes from the small boats were soon won over. It seemed to them curious, arousing and somewhat risky, and before long they went closer to the sea. They did so hesitantly, in stages, with a sense of experimentation and secrecy.
            Abdelrahman Munif, *Cities of Salt*

The island of my title alludes to the threefold components which I weave together to describe and analyse the current urban condition of Doha city. First, it refers to the semi-island, peninsula of Qatar, a barren land inhabited by people who, throughout history, have always been able to support and rediscover themselves by finding a product from the sea to sell: pearls, oil, natural gas, and today real estate. Second, it refers to 'The Pearl Island', the two and a half billion dollar real estate, commercial island being reclaimed off the coast of the Qatari capital, Doha; a mega-project I use as a prime representative of the current development efforts to re-dress the city for global audiences. Finally, it alludes to new forms of urban-archipelagoes prevalent in Doha, and elsewhere in the region. This emerging urbanity is a confluence of the strategies of consumerism, entertainment, and global tourism.

To locate the recent developments and the urban condition of today's Doha in their historical context as well as to inquire into the interrelationship between international capitalism and urban developments in Doha, I shall attempt to capture three paradigmatic scenes from the history of the city. The first scene depicts the city during the decline of the pearl industry in the 1930s and its impact on urbanization and development. The second scene is highlighted by the discovery of oil, which transformed the country between the mid-1950s and the mid-1980s from a poor British Protectorate into an independent modern state. Much of the urban development in this period was state-funded projects geared towards modernizing the infrastructure, public services, and housing. Not unlike many other cities in the world, Doha's development has always been tied to global geopolitics and prevailing economic conditions. Thus we find the city periodically experiencing times of relative austerity and slowdown in construction activities due to sharp declines in oil prices, such as the period between the mid 1980s and early 1990s. In the late 1990s, however, an economic upsurge marked a watershed in the country's modern urban history. Instigated by some geopolitical imperatives, the government, once again, searched in the surrounding sea for sources of capital, which it found in and extracted from the North Field, the world's largest natural gas field.

In the third exemplary scene, the sea was not only a source for natural energy supply to the world's industrialist countries, but also a commodity-space to be conquered by an ever growing global real-estate market. Like recent offshore projects in Dubai, Doha's largest real-estate adventure, The Pearl-Qatar, is land reclaimed from the Gulf, promising to be a controlled, sanitized, urban experience, or an Arabian Riviera, to use the words of its managing director. Although its new spaces are promising to be isolated physically and perhaps culturally from the city, these spaces will be (hyper-) linked, I shall suggest, to other spaces and urban experiences that are dotting the cityscapes in various parts of the world.

Scene I. Colonialism and the Urbanity of the Pearl Industry

We are all from the highest to the lowest slaves of one master, Pearl.

Sheikh Mohammed bin Thani

Rosemarie Zahlan (1979) tells us that the first mention of Qatar in the Western media appeared in a couple of newspaper articles around the beginning of 1935. With the popularity of the tales of the Orient in nineteenth-century Romantic literature in the West, both articles provided complete Arabian Nights accounts of Sheikh Abdullah bin Jasim al-Thani, the ruler of Qatar at that time, lolling idly on silken cushions, surrounded by eighty members of his beautiful harem, thousands of slaves, and piles of pearls. They went on to describe his sensational court and romantic country. Zahlan suggests that the intelligence units of US oil companies deliberately leaked the newspaper articles to solicit public attention to the lands of the Gulf in order to break the British policy of maintaining monopoly, which they had sustained through the suppression of all information on the region. The muffling of discourse was part of the contention between the two empires: the waning British and the waxing American. This geopolitical rivalry in the Middle East began over the acquisition of oil concessions in Qatar and the Gulf region. While these articles do not seem to have created interest outside the official circles of the British government, they marked a significant moment in Qatar's modern history. It was the start of the dislodging of Qatar from the British ambit, which was finally concluded with independence in 1971. It was also the moment when the country began to reinvent its economic system, from an economy based on pearling and, therefore, linked with limited global networks in Asia and Europe to an economy interwoven with the global political and economic circuits through the selling of vital world energy products, oil and gas.

But before Doha's arrival at this historical juncture, the daily realities of the city's life would prove further removed from the romantic, orientalists' depictions found in the two articles. On the contrary, travel accounts during the nineteenth and early twentieth centuries, and there are very few of them, usually described the miserable and desolate conditions of Doha, and the whole province for that matter. For example, in his narratives of his one year travel in Arabia during 1862, Wilfred Gifford Palgrave (1826–1888) reflected the prevalent sentiments towards the peninsula when he described for his readers the barren, monotonous land of 'Katar'.[1] Reinforced by the harshness and severe weather conditions, particularly during the summer, as well as the scant supply of fresh water and vegetation, this insipid picture of the peninsula explains the paucity of human presence throughout most of its early modern history. The scarcity of human and natural resources mirror the dearth of available historical literature. Jenny Walker (2004) rightly, and poetically, remarks that the early history of Qatar is the history of the Bedouins, who traverse a land 'taking only memories, and leaving only footprints', which are dusted away with every erupting sandstorm. It was towards the end of the nineteenth century when the recorded events began to leave more lasting impressions on the memory of the place. The chain of events in Qatar between the end of the nineteenth century and discovery and export of oil in the middle of the twentieth century seems to have been shaped by four interrelated domains or forces: pearling, territorial disputes, the Al-Thani family, and the British geopolitics to curb other colonialist interests in the region, particularly the Turkish, German, and later American.

Most historians refer to 1868 as the most significant date for Qatar, because it signified the beginning of a transition leading to the establishment of a Qatari identity (Al-Mansour, 1980). A year before this date, a war had erupted between Qatar and Bahrain, which was finally settled when the British Political Resident in the Gulf, Colonel Lewis Pelly, signed an agreement, but not a protection treaty, in September 1868 with Sheikh Mohammad bin Thani, who acted as a representative for the people of Qatar. It is important to mention that before this agreement, events in Qatar and Bahrain were closely entwined, and the Al-Khalifa ruling family in Manama was practically the accepted ruler of Qatar. In this treaty, Sheikh Mohammad conceded to desist from maritime warfare and regulate the tribute to be paid for Bahrain. The significance of this agreement is twofold. It was the first implicit recognition of Qatar as a sovereign sheikhdom with Sheikh Mohammad bin Thani as its ruler. Secondly, it strengthened the position of the al-Thani family against other tribes through the recognition granted to it by the highest British official in the Gulf region. The Al-Thani family is a branch of the Ma'adhid tribe, who originally settled in the 'Gibrin' oasis in southern Najd and claim descent from the Bani Tamim tribe of central Arabia (Mehanna, 2001, p. 83). Following similar tribal migration patterns from central Arabia during the early eighteenth century, the Ma'adhid found the living conditions in coastal areas more lucrative than the interior, mainly because the Gulf waters were the site of rich oyster beds for harvesting pearls and there was easy access to India, the major market. The tribe initially settled in the coastal areas around Zubara in the north of the peninsula, where they fished and dived for pearls. In 1847, under the leadership of Sheikh Mohammad bin Thani, they moved to Al-Bidaa, later renamed Doha (Mehanna, 2001, p. 83). The name is derived from the Arabic *Dawh* or *Tadweeh*, which meant circle-ness, or to encircle, referring to the shoreline of the city, which extended inland in a shape similar to a circle. We learn from John Lorimer's *Gazetteer of the Persian Gulf*, that in 1908 the Ma'adhid tribe was the sixth largest in the peninsula and was mainly settled in the eastern villages of al-Bidaa, Wakrah, and Lusail (Lorimer, 1970).

Just three years after the agreement with the British Political Resident, the son of Sheikh Mohamed bin Thani, Sheikh Jasim, who became the *de facto* ruler of Qatar after his father's retirement, agreed to raise the Turkish flag in Doha and establish Al-Bidaa Fort. For him, this was the most practical way to guarantee protection. The memories of the destruction of Doha during the earlier wars with Bahrain were still vivid. For the Ottomans, the opening of the Suez Canal in 1867 renewed their interest in the Gulf region and, under the leadership of the Baghdad *wali* (governor), their troops managed to extend their control over large parts of east and west Arabia. When in 1872, the one hundred Turkish troops landed in Al-Bidaa, they selected a site inland and south-east of the village and began building their fort, which became later known as Al-Koot Fort (figure 9.1). They also

Figure 9.1. Al-Koot Fort.

worked at deepening part of the port's shallow waters to accommodate the docking of their military vessels. The reason for selecting Al-Bidaa as the site of their fort is unclear, but probably it was because it was the largest of the existing villages on the east coast with a central geographical position on the peninsula. Moreover, it was easier to defend it against military attacks, particularly from the sea.

During the nineteenth century and the first few decades of the twentieth century, the urban conditions of Doha were very much influenced by two interrelated socio-economic forces: tribal affiliations and pearling.[2] While the social structure of the population remained, as elsewhere in the Gulf, tied to the tribal social system brought along with the migrant clan from central Arabia, it was during this period that a significant transformation in the economic structure began to take shape, which in turn led to what I shall call a 'fledgling capitalism'. Certainly, the process by which capitalism emerged and evolved in Qatar is a complex story that can only be sketchily dealt with here. I suggest that the process must be recognized as having roots in the transformation from a Bedouin economy based on tribes roaming, with their camels, sheep and goats, the unending sea of sand in search of grazing, to an economy based on criss-crossing the Gulf sea with boats in search of pearl banks lying offshore. There is no doubt that the pearling industry supplied some prerequisites for a capitalist system to emerge not only through the contacts, conditioned by the industry, with Indian and European traders, but also through the emergence of a primitive market and ownership systems with their peculiar relations and factors of production, particularly capital and labour. In short, the pearling industry was the principal axis around which the economic and social structures in the city revolved.

Kaltham al-Ghanim tells us that pearl trading had taught the Bedouins the value of money and the system of monetary exchange. According to her, this new system of transaction led to the emergence of new social strata that depended not only on the ownership of the tools of production, such as the camel or later the boat, but also monetary capital (Al-Ghanim, 1997, p. 53). Moreover, through the accumulation of capital, it was possible for the fledgling capitalists to expand the pearl trade by owning more ships or financing more diving expeditions, or both. Thus, the ship replaced the camel as the basic tool of production, and the number owned determined the social, political, and economic position of the owner (Al-Ghanim, 1997). From another perspective, the pearling industry ushered in a new division of labour and a new system of wage labourers selling their manpower in return for a share in the profit. According to Lorimer (1970) more than half of the male population in Doha was involved in the pearling industry with over 300 boats, constituting one of the largest fleets in the Gulf. But the emerging private ownership system did not totally replace the tribal communal one. It was the impact of the tribal social system that resisted a total transition. It is important to note that while the population of the peninsula at the beginning of the twentieth century was 27,000, that of Doha was not more than 12,000 inhabitants, including the 350 soldiers of the Turkish regiment stationed in Al-Bidaa Fort. Interestingly, the population estimates for Doha and Qatar remained unchanged throughout the first half of the twentieth century. We also learn from Lorimer's accounts that nearly one in five inhabitants of the peninsula was a slave brought from the eastern shores of Africa to work mainly as divers (*Ibid.*). The demographic mix in Doha included tribes from central Arabia and other coastal areas, slaves, and Persians. Before 1908, Persians had migrated to Qatar at different times, but from the 1939 population estimate we observe a large increase. This is so because of political and economic changes in Persia. Unlike all the other states in the Gulf region, strikingly absent from the country's demographic mix, particularly to those who are familiar with today's Doha, were people from the sub-continent. In fact, the issue of granting Indians, who were considered British subjects, residency permission in Doha was a constant dispute between the rulers of Qatar and the British Resident in the Gulf, even after the 1916 protection treaty.[3]

During this time, the total inhabited urban area was about one and a quarter square kilometres, which extended only a few hundred metres inland from the south side of Doha bay in an almost treeless environment. While in the first half of the nineteenth century, the settlements along the bay were limited to one specific area, Al-Bidaa, a century later they had metastasized into eight distinct *ferejan*, or districts: Al-Bin Ali (now renamed Al-Hitmi), Slata, Mirqab, Al-Dowayha (now renamed Al-Jasra), Al-Bidaa, and Al-Rumaila. Each *fereej* was occupied by a certain tribe or large family (figure 9.2). These *ferejan* stretched parallel to the irregular indentation of the salt marshes and tidal flats, which constituted large segments along the Arabian Gulf shoreline (Al-Kazim, 1993, p. 121). We learn from Nasser al-Othman (nd) that during the 1940s, and probably earlier, the main market place

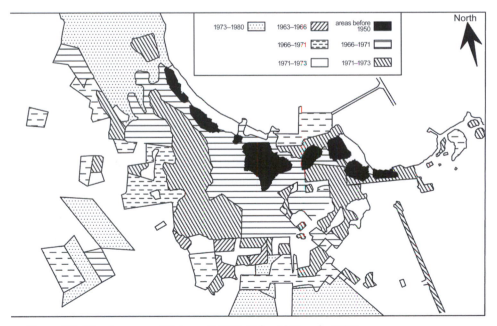

Figure 9.2. Development of Doha until 1980. (After Al-Kourdy, 1985)

in Doha stretched from the two-storey custom house at the harbour almost to Al-Asmakh Road, half a mile to the west. The market place – known at one point as Souk al-Zalam, the dark market – ran parallel to, and east, of the fort, separated from it only by a large vacant parcel of land. It is interesting to note that the fort was set apart from the densely populated areas of Al-Bidaa and Al-Jasra by a large tract on all sides. Part of this land was the main cemetery for the city. Another segment of this market stretched even further to the south and was chiefly a fish market. Between these two market places there was an open space reserved as a camel market. Mahmoud al-Kourdy (1985) observed that most alleyways which penetrated the *ferejan* of the urban area led to the harbour, which was the busiest part of the city, particularly during the preparation for the diving season between May and October. The harbour, therefore, was the hub where most of the activities were concentrated: shipyards, open markets, shops, and *majalis* (formal meeting rooms). It is important to note that social relations were determined more by blood and tribal affiliations than income and wealth. This is particularly apparent in the urbanization pattern, which put members of one tribe, regardless of their economic situation, in one area of the city.

The housing stock was composed of a few hundred simple one floor dwellings huddled closely together along narrow, winding alleys. Other structures that dotted the cityscape included the *barasti* and the Bedouin tents (Majed, 1987). Members of the tribe were given land by the sheikh upon their request, usually to accommodate a large increase in the family or for newlyweds to start a new one. A master mason was responsible for the design and execution of the house with the help of a few workers. Although we do not have accounts of the background of these workers, it is assumed that they were originally from Persia or other parts where masonry construction was the norm. This is attested by the fact that some house features, such as the *barajeel* (wind towers), were first developed in, and then imported, from Persia. In all houses, however, there was limited ornamentation in the façade, and the architectural style was similar to the architecture one would find elsewhere in the Gulf region. The most prominent house during these days was the old palace in Slata built by Shiekh Abdallah bin Jasim in the first decade of the twentieth century, which was used for both living and governance. The house was abandoned during the recession years of the 1930s until renovated as Doha's National Museum in the early 1970s (Al-Khalifi, 1990). It is interesting to note that today the prominent Parisian architect Jean Nouvel is expanding and renovating it once again.

While these urban scenes were almost unchanged during the first three decades of the twentieth century, the early 1930s came with some shattering developments that eventually caused the emergence of new urban patterns. First, the worldwide economic depression and the Japanese discovery of the cultured pearl proved a disaster for the Gulf's pearling industry. In Qatar, remembers Hussein al-Ferdan, the situation was very grim and extreme poverty forced people either to leave the peninsula or live in dismal conditions (Al-Ferdan quoted in Zearah, 2005). Some left their families in Doha and commuted to the eastern province of Saudi Arabia in search of jobs. It was in these days that the population of Qatar dropped for the first and last time during the century. The most optimistic population estimate shows a drop from 27,000 to 10,000 inhabitants (*Ibid.*). The outbreak of World War II aggravated the situation even further, but the final blow to the industry came with India's independence in 1947. One of the measures taken by India's new national government was to ban all imports of luxury items, including pearls.[4] With the decline of the pearl industry, a chapter of the city's urban history was sealed and another had begun.

Scene II: Modernization, and the Urbanity of Petrodollars

Oil is the greatest single post-war asset remaining with us. We should refuse to divide our last asset with the Americans.
        Lord Beaverbrook (1944)

Next to winning the war, the most important matter before the USA as a Nation was the world oil situation.
        Harold L. Ickes (1943)

Instigated by new geopolitical conditions, particularly the rise of American interest in the Gulf, the British Resident began negotiating with Sheikh Abdallah bin Jasim al-Thani the oil concession in Qatar which was finally signed in 1935.[5] According to Zahlan (1979) it was clear from all available evidence that 'Abdallah was at first totally unaware of the undreamed-of prosperity that lay ahead for Qatar with respect to oil'. Although oil was discovered in Qatar in 1939, the impact of World War II postponed its first oil exports for a decade. Both urban development and real oil wealth were slow in coming. While the population and construction boom began in the 1950s, urban development took off seriously only after Sheikh Khalifa bin Hamad al-Thani took power in 1972, one year after Qatar gained independence from Britain. The period of Doha's urban transformation between 1949 and the mid-1990s has a long, complex history that could be divided into four distinct periods, or sub-scenes. These urban scenes correspond to political and economic, international and local, changes: 1. urbanity of transition (1949–1955); 2. urbanity of necessity (1956–1971); 3. urbanity of modernization (1972–1984); and, 4. urbanity of stagnation (mid-1980s to early 1990s).

No doubt the oil wealth, which began to pour in during the 1950s, acted as a catalyst for the urban development that started to overtake the country. Many observers comment that the changes were slow in the beginning, mainly, as Helga Graham (1978) has pointed out, because the rulers at that time were conservative and it took time to exploit the country's resources fully. While this might be partially true, I want to suggest three other reasons for this sluggish start. First, the development pace seems to have grown in relation to the increase in oil revenue and amount of oil exploited. For example, while the revenue from oil was US$1 million in 1950, 5 years later it grew to US$35 million, and by the mid-1960s it was approaching US$70 million. Second, the transition period from a pearl- to an oil-based economy meant a transition in the relations of production, a new division of labour and, most importantly, the invention of new methods of wealth distribution. Finally, there was no apparatus in the system of governance to take responsibility for physical planning. The ruler remained directly involved, for example, in allocating lots for houses, with the size and location determined by a resident's social and political position in society. To put it differently, the political power and decision-making seem to have remained operating through a chain of personal orders rather than a generalized regime of government. What is interesting to note from this era is the direction of urban development in the city. While during the early years the city grew like an arc around and in relation to the harbour, the source of work, after the discovery and exploitation of oil – which was first inland before American oil giants were granted concessions in the waters of the Gulf – the city began to expand to the south and west, and in a matter of a few years the area of Doha had quadrupled. Mohamed al-Gabir (1977) says that during this period many residents began to move to the new added areas of the city, such as Meshirab and Remailah. The urban fabric and housing types of these new areas, however, remained the same.

It was around 1955 that a true sense of development began to be felt in the city. Asphalt roads were extended and lit; a new desalination plant was constructed with pipes connecting it to many houses nearby; an electric plant was built in Kahraba Street near Musheireb; new schools began admitting students; and a new hospital, Al-Remailah, opened its doors for the first time in the country, followed by maternity and children's hospitals. It is interesting to note that the design competition for the hospital was sponsored by the Royal Institute of British Architects and won by John Harris, the British architect who would later establish himself in Dubai and design some of its famous modern icons (Mitchell, 1976). According to Al-Kazim (1993), a visitor to the city in 1957 described Doha as if it were 'a city after an artillery bombardment', referring to the prevalent scenes of on-going construction.

The urban expansion of the built-up area of Doha during the two decades following the discovery of oil increased ten-fold, reaching around 12 square kilometres (Al-Kourdy, 1985). Simultaneous to this unprecedented urban expansion, which was likened by some observers to the days of the gold rush in California in nineteenth-century America, was an extraordinary demographic increase (Al-Khaiat, 1982). Of course, the construction activities as well as the expansion of governmental services necessitated the use of foreign skilled and un-skilled labour. No population survey was conducted in Qatar between 1939 and 1969, let alone of the percentage of foreign labourers or expatriates in the new demographic mix. But, we know from one governmental source that, in 1970, the population of Doha reached around 85,000, with foreigners constituting around 67 per cent. Thus the period between 1949 and 1969 witnessed a population increase of nearly 600 per cent and an increase in foreigners of more than 1,000 per cent. The increase in immigration patterns from abroad was echoed, with much smaller numbers, by the flight many Qataris took from the surrounding villages and small towns towards Doha (*Ibid.*). An interesting mix of locals and expatriates began to emerge in the city as a result of these immigration patterns. According to the 1970 census – which divided the city into four distinct areas – by and large, most Qataris preferred to live in the north, east and central districts of Doha, while expatriates chose to live more in the south, west and also central zones of the city. As we shall see, this distribution was to change during the 1970s and 1980s.

With the exception of the period between 1966 and 1971, when a foreign office began to introduce some planning consultations to the authorities, the urban expansion of this period can best be described as haphazard, without any preconceived plan. The housing and public buildings reflected specific needs to ease life for the increasing population of both locals and expatriates. True, the urban character of the city began to take shape around the end of the 1960s with developments along the Gulf shores, such as the construction of Al-Corniche Road, the opening of new routes through the city, such as Abdallah bin Thani Street, and the construction of two new hotels, the Gulf and the Oasis. These hotels were not built to accommodate tourists visiting Doha, but rather for the increasing number of businessmen and high ranking employees from Europe and US oil companies. Moreover, a new type of housing, the apartment building, began to appear, such as those in Abdallah bin Thani and Kahraba Streets. This new type reflected the increasing presence of an emerging social stratum of expatriate families within the city.

What is important to note from these days is that the haphazard urbanity in the 1950s and most of the 1960s mirrored the lack of modern urban governance. As Ahmed al-Shalaq (1999) explains, in the early 1950s the British annual report on Qatar discussed the slight improvements in the system of governance in the city, but it was not until 1970 that a full government in the modern sense was formed. During the last years of the 1960s, however, the city of Doha had a new apparatus in the fledgling government with a mandate to provide infrastructure and municipal services as well as to take charge of some of the city's built environment, namely, the Public Works Department. In coordination with the Ministry of Labour and Social Affairs and the Ministry of Finance, the new department's first task was to establish and implement a system of housing for the low-income Qataris.

Al-Shalaq notes that the period after 1972, when Qatar gained independence and Sheikh Khalifa Bin Hamad al-Thani became the ruler, witnessed an increase and/or restructuring of the governmental various bureaucracies. Thus we find new offices and governmental authorities sharing responsibilities for the built environment, such as the Ministry of Municipal Affairs and Agriculture and, later, the Ministries of Industry, Water and Power, and Telecommunications. Sharon Nagy (2000) rightly contends that the distribution of official responsibilities among various bodies within the government led to coordination problems. The relations among these various ministries were further complicated when the Emiri Diwan (the executive offices of the Emir) occasionally took 'control of particular projects, especially high-profile ones, overriding the jurisdiction of the ministries' (*Ibid.*).

No doubt, the years following Qatar's declaration of independence in 1972 were decisive to the modern urban history of the Middle East – perhaps, for decades to come. The use of the oil weapon during the 1973 October War sent shock waves to the Western hemisphere and caused an unprecedented leap in oil prices. As a clue to the scale of the increase, in 1972 Qatar's revenue from selling oil slightly passed the US$600 million dollars mark, 2 years later it tripled, and by 1980 it was more than US$5 billion. The incredible surge in oil prices swelled the government coffers and fuelled a construction boom which continued for the next decade. What made this period different from earlier booms was not only the magnitude of construction, or even the quality of buildings produced, but also the direct involvement of foreign, mainly Western, planners and designers in shaping the future development of the city. In most of what follows in this section, I shall concentrate on describing two planning projects from these days: the emptying out of the downtown and the reclamation of land from the sea. It is also important to mention that I was a resident of Doha during part of this period, specifically between 1978 and 1981.

To accommodate the population growth and the changing urban life, the government of Qatar in 1972 contracted the first foreign planning consultant, the British-based Llewelyn-Davies, to supply a master plan for Doha extending through to 1990. Llewelyn-Davies presented several proposals for different parts of the city and advised the Planning Department of the Ministry of Municipal Affairs on planning legislation. One of their recommendations for the central areas of the city was to acquire a number of older neighbourhoods from their residents and clear them for redesign and development (*Ibid.*). The intended goal for the city centre was to increase its commercial, governmental, and high-rise residential buildings. In short, the intention was to increase the population density by expanding vertically and using the extra land acquired either to expand the public ownership ratio or to add new land uses. Moreover, the plan intended to remove industrial warehouses and increase upscale shopping. This urban renewal policy proved to be a tedious and costly endeavour. Most of the central areas, around 90 per cent in one estimate, were composed of houses owned by Qataris, with a very complicated ownership system, laid along irregular *sikkas* (alleyways). Accordingly, the new Ministry of Municipal Affairs was given the task of acquiring these lands for development.[6]

The new action plan of land acquisition caused an immediate inflation in real-estate speculation, as many Qataris began to sell their homes for prices much higher than those of the market and to relocate in other, newer parts around the city peripheries. I agree with Fadila (1991) whom Nagy quotes suggesting that the government's policy to purchase the lands at inflated prices was a means to redistribute the oil wealth among Qataris. Among the obvious consequences of the urban renewal policy recommended by Llewelyn-Davies was the change in the demographic mix in the city centre. During the 1970s, the influx of expatriate Asian workers was at its zenith. While in earlier years, these newcomers were housed in peripheral parts of the city, such as the Tin District in Ne'aigah area, during the 1970s they began to move into the central district.[7] The houses that survived the bulldozing and clearance were usually divided internally and rented to low-income groups, particularly Asians, who lived in over-crowded conditions. A study conducted in Salata in 1980, for example, showed an average of thirteen people per dwelling (Al-Kazim, 1993). Another popular living area for Asian low-income workers was Um Ghowailenah. True, some Qataris remained in areas like Musheireb throughout the early 1980s, but they were the exceptions.[8] At the end of the 1970s and in the early 1980s, apartment buildings began to spread along the newly opened arteries, such as Abdallah bin Thani, Kahraba, and later Grand Hamad Streets. With all the demolition and clearance taking place, a survey conducted in 1980 showed that the residential population of the city centre had increased from that of 1970 by around 3,000 inhabitants. I recall that on Friday afternoons, thousands of low-income, Asian workers, who mainly lived around the downtown area, or commuted from other parts of the city, filled the streets of Doha's central area.

Other memories from these days in Doha centre are worth mentioning here. The apartment building where I lived with my family was located in Abdallah bin Thani Street (figure 9.3). It was a three-storey building, occupied by Egyptian, British, and Qatari families. All apartment buildings along the street, ours among them, formed a continuous urban wall, which ran from Al-Jeeda roundabout in the south until it almost reached the Emiri Diwan and the clock roundabout to the north. Looking to the east from the roof of our building, I recall how the dense urban fabric of Musheireb district, or Fereej Mohamed bin Jasim, dominated the scenery, with towering minarets occasionally changing the otherwise monotonous silhouette. The sharp contrast between the relatively high apartment buildings – most were three to five storeys – and the older low-rise dense area was striking. Like Potemkin villages, it looked from the street level as if the apartment buildings were fake drawings on canvas, erected to impress those who are traversing the street.[9] The most impressive building in this assemblage of relatively modern apartment buildings was Al-Jeedah office tower, which rose for over fifteen storeys (figure 9.4). Though it remained not in use, it was the highest building in Doha until very recently. Like other buildings of the 1970s and 1980s, such as Doha Sheraton, Qatar National Bank, Gulf Hotel, and Qatar University, Al-Jeedah tower appeared frequently on postcards and brochures of Doha (figure 9.5 and 9.6).[10] Such images were representative of the modernization that Qatar was undergoing. To put it differently, in addition to the use values of these buildings, they have acquired an image, which signalled the introduction of Qatar to the modern world.

Figure 9.3. The apartment building where I lived with my family between 1978 and 1981.

Figure 9.4. Until very recently, the Jeedah office tower was the highest structure in Doha.

What I also remember vividly from these days of modernizing Doha is the speed with which bulldozing and clearing were taking place in the central areas. I recall, for example, that in a few months, parts of the area around Souk Waqif were almost unrecognizable. Large swathes of the area were bulldozed to make way for a new route penetrating the old city, Grand Hamad Street, which ran through central Doha to the Corniche. Like Haussmann's boulevards in nineteenth-

Figure 9.5. Qatar Central Bank, one of Doha's architectural icons of the 1970s and 1980s.

Figure 9.6. Qatar University, an attempt to deal with the question of Qatar's architectural identity.

century Paris, the six-lane street was meant to be a ceremonial boulevard leading from the airport to the city. During the subsequent years, only a few banks, hotels, and small shopping centres were built along either side of the street. As we shall see, the attention of the government as well as private developers would shift to another part of the city. It is important to mention that a Lebanese firm, Dar al-Handasah, was also commissioned to prepare plans for the central areas of Doha in the early 1980s.[11] According to Corbett (2003), unlike Llewelyn-Davies, Dar al-Handasah's proposal placed greater emphasis on maintaining the traditional fabric of the central area, 'calling for a mix of new development together with renovation of older, historical buildings'. In fact, a third firm, the Hong Kong based Shankland Cox was hired before Dar al-Handasah, in 1979, to assess the earlier proposals and suggest new measures to be taken, particularly after it had become clear that the population projections made in the early 1970s were far less than reality (figure 9.7).

Among the other recommendations proposed by Llewelyn-Davies was to develop and reclaim a large area located north-west of the city centre along the shores of the Gulf. Henri Lefebvre (1991) said that any revolution which has not produced new spaces 'has not changed life itself but has merely changed ideological superstructures, institutions or political apparatuses'. As if answering to

Figure 9.7. Until today, large swathes of the cleared sites of old Doha are not built as they were intended in the 1970s.

Lefebvre's prophetic observation, this project was proposed immediately following independence and a new ruler, Sheikh Khalifa bin Hamad, assuming full power. The New District of Doha, as the area was formally designated, was Sheikh Khalifa's new revolutionary space for the city and the new era (figure 9.8). Nagy (2000) tells us that the project was meant not only to enhance Doha's new image of prosperity and development, but also allowed the State to possess 'large parcels of serviced residential and commercial land, which could be granted or leased to political allies'. According to Nagy, Llewelyn-Davies's original project proposal

Figure 9.8. Doha Corniche has become a defining image and a centre of activities for the city.

covered 2000 hectares, of which 750 hectares were reclaimed land. She also says the reclaimed land was to be used for up-scale housing and leisure facilities, but:

> The Emiri Diwan expanded the project to include housing for approximately 6000 residents (mostly Qatari), hotel and convention facilities, a diplomatic quarter, Qatar University, Doha Palace, a government center, and an elaborate waterfront promenade and park overlooking Doha bay. (*Ibid.*, p. 137).

An American office, William Periera Associates, was hired to develop the concept plan for the New District. One of the immediate effects of the reclamation project, which began in 1974, was the shaping of the Doha bay and the emergence of the long crescent-shaped Corniche (figure 9.9). Though the project required major earth moving and landfill, it proved a great instrument functionally and symbolically for the future of Doha. On the one hand, the Corniche opened new areas for development and was used by many residents during their leisure time; on the other, it became a symbol of the new city as most iconic and emblematic governmental and commercial buildings were lined up along its length. The Corniche indeed acquired a central character-defining position in the structural plan for Doha: the city was laid out in a semicircular pattern radiating outwards from the Corniche. A system of ring roads intercepted by radial ones, as presented by Llewelyn-Davies, formed the basic structure of the city. These ring roads were lettered progressively from the Corniche to the outer edges of the city. They encircled urban areas, separating and marking different zones in the city. For example, the old urban core of Doha became banded between the Corniche and the B ring road. Between B and C ring roads, there was a mix of old and new buildings. Llewelyn-Davies suggested that future extensions could be accommodated by creating new semicircular extensions defined by new ring roads. By 1980, few buildings existed beyond the C ring, or between C and D ring roads.

Figure 9.9. Doha's long crescent-shaped Corniche.

Figure 9.10. The Centre was the first Western-style department store and supermarket.

Along this six-lane road, a new Ramada hotel and two movie theatres marked the edge of the city to the south. Just a few hundred feet north of the hotel, and along one of the radial roads, Salwa, a modern shopping centre was constructed, known as The Centre, and this became popular for selling imported Western products and food during the late 1970s and 1980s (figure 9.10).

Much of the construction activities during the 1980s were taking place in the New District of Doha. Housing projects for Qataris, a new diplomatic quarter, the University, residential blocks for expatriates, compounds for Gulf Air employees, a football stadium, and the Sheraton Hotel were among the most prominent examples from this era (figure 9.11). Located on the new reclaimed land overlooking the Doha bay, the Sheraton hotel became the new icon of the city. Other governmental buildings began to appear along the Corniche, such as the Post Office and other ministerial buildings (figure 9.12). In the decade following independence, the area of the capital city doubled to over 20 square kilometres, with a population of around 200,000, of which nearly 70 per cent were expatriate workers. By the early 1980s, a drop in the oil price caused the government either to cancel or put on hold many of the infrastructure and building projects. For example, large areas designated in the original proposal by William Periera for commercial and leisure developments, particularly on the new reclaimed land, remained undeveloped. But the population growth continued to soar through the 1980s and early 1990s. By 1995, the metropolitan population of the city, which included Al-Wakrah to the south-east and Madinat Khalifah to the south-west, was close to 400,000 with Qataris constituting almost one of every four residents.

The development of Doha during the years following independence was

Figure 9.11. Sheraton Doha, the icon for Doha since it was built in the early 1980s.

Figure 9.12. The Emiri Palace is located on the Corniche.

interwoven with the recycling of the petrodollars earned by the government, which amounted to US$5 billion at the dawn of the fall in oil prices and recession period (Al-Ghanim, 1997, p. 112). At that time, the economy was not insulated against the inevitable swings in oil prices and the troublesome changes in government revenues which come with them. Functioning as a welfare state for its citizens, the government's policy was to supply every Qatari with a plot of land and an interest free loan for building a house, which was usually very large by Western standards. The expatriate workers also usually received free housing as part of their work contracts. As we have seen, the urban renewal policy of the 1970s re-channelled much of the resources to the citizens through land-acquiring policies. According to one estimate, the governments of the Middle East spent 80 per cent of their increased revenues during the 1970s boom either on modernization projects or purchasing goods from the United States and Europe. Only the remaining 20 per cent was saved in the form of equities or loans to developing countries, particularly in South America (Mouawad and Porter, 2006). I will argue that much of what was spent in construction activities, in the sphere of housing, infrastructure, or public amenities, was necessary to accommodate the increase in population and to modernize the capital city according to specific models. To put it differently, it was the era of an urbanity of necessity. It was during the second half of the 1990s that another type of urban development began to dominate the city as elsewhere in the Gulf region. It is to this emerging urbanity in Doha that I shall now turn and describe some of its prevalent scenes.

Scene III. Globalization and the Urbanity of the Spectacle

The [pearl] island will be an iconic development which will enhance the global image of Doha and Qatar as a premier residential, shopping and tourist destination.[12]
Nick Bashkiroff, Development Director for 'The Pearl-Qatar'

No doubt, the words 'globalization' and 'global' were the catch phrases of twentieth century *fin de siècle*. Journalists, academics, politicians, business executives, such as Nick Bashkiroff quoted above, and others use these words to signify that something profound is happening, that a new world economic, political, and cultural order is emerging, or to express their desire to join the club of global cities, global images, global corporations, or whatever. With hindsight, what has been taking place during the last two decades, in the aftermath of the collapse of the Soviet Union, can be described as part of a global restructuring process, a period that marked a critical turning point in the geo-economic history of capitalism. Moreover, the impact of these global changes on Qatar is aggrandized with a series of interconnected international, regional and local changes in the political and economic spheres: Iraq's invasion of Kuwait, the Second Gulf War, the bloodless coup and change of Emir in Qatar in 1995, the 9/11 terrorist attacks in New York and Washington DC, the occupation of Iraq, recent oil and gas price upsurge, and the emergence of Dubai as a centre for commerce and an entertainment hub in the Gulf region. Concurrent with these recent developments, particularly since the late 1990s, we observe a rapid urbanization and building frenzy in Doha that has been characterized by explosive expansion of the existing city in almost all spatial coordinates: building skyscrapers, constructing malls and gated residential communities, establishing iconic museums and libraries, erecting new stadia and sports facilities, importing water inland, and creating artificial lakes and islands. These recent developments represent the largest urban and real-estate explosion Doha has ever seen. It is customary to find almost every week one of

Qatar's growing numbers of real-estate developers either unveiling a new project or announcing the completion of a stage of an on-going one. Since the turn of the millennium an upward trend characterizes the total number of building and demolition permits issued across the city. While the building permits granted in 1999 slightly exceeded 1,500, in 2004 they reached over 1,000 in the first few months (OBG, 2005). Every previously-vacant lot appears to have been fenced for some construction activities; old houses and commercial blocks are being demolished to make space for higher-income earning towers, and the face of the city is changing from day to day. One needs only to observe the changing skyline of the West Bay area, which will host, when completed, more than 180 high-rise buildings (figures 9.13 and 9.14). A tell-tale sign of the magnitude of the construction activities in Qatar is to recall that the ambitious projects being built or in the pipeline for the next decade are worth some US$130 billion. Of course, this construction boom is backed by the fact that Qatar is blessed with the largest non-associated gas field in the world, with proven reserves that, according to one estimate, will be sufficient to support planned production of natural gas for the next two centuries (Gulf Construction, 2006*a*).

I believe that it is not a coincidence that these urban developments are concurrent with these political and economic transformations in the 1990s. I will argue that we cannot understand the emerging urban scenes with their accompanying phantasmagorical architectural forms and spaces in Doha, which strives to become a global city, without first mapping these emerging scenes in relation to other global trends, particularly in the economic regime of late capitalism. To describe how Doha is illustrative of the contemporary workings

Figure 9.13. West Bay from the Corniche.

Figure 9.14. The emerging Doha skyline in West Bay.

of global capital, therefore, I want to put forward five interrelated theoretical observations, or discourses, which I contend represent slightly different attempts to frame the dynamics of these global urban trends, particularly in relation to urban developments in Doha.

In the first discourse, many scholars have established that something different has been occurring in the nature of the capitalist system since the 1980s and early 1990s. The drive for capital accumulation in advanced, industrialist societies and their corollaries – the loosely connected, reproduced socio-economic and political nodes or clones in developing countries – is distending a second economic tier which accumulates capital through cultural rather than industrial production, a cultural capitalism tier (Rifkin, 2000). The main trade of this expanding economic tier is not the selling and buying of goods produced in factories but the performance and consumption of cultural experiences produced in specific spaces in the city. Interestingly, Jennifer Craik (1997) suggests that at about the same time a new phase of tourism, which highlights the cultural component of tourist experiences, has emerged. Thus we find a significant portion of these new hyper-spaces of capital has been claimed for the ever-expanding entertainment, cultural, and tourism industries. Some scholars are going so far as to claim that many contemporary cities are metamorphosing to accommodate these new spaces (Hannigan, 1998). But one must remember that tourism, which is a targeted sector for growth in Doha and most of the Gulf States, is one of the oldest cultural industries in the history of capitalism. Ever since it was launched as a formal business at the hands of Thomas Cook in the middle of the nineteenth century, the tourist industry has been involved in the business of packaging cultural experiences. Like a bud that has always been embedded in the bark of the capitalist tree, cultural capitalism has only recently accelerated its growth to the extent that very soon it might outgrow the tree. One striking observation in this current condition is the twinning of the cultural entertainment and tourist industries in producing spaces that cater for a new kind of 'cosmopolitan citizen' who, as Zygmunt Bauman (1993) has written, thinks of good life as equal to a 'continuous holiday'.[13]

From this perspective, the private and public sectors in Qatar seem to have responded to this new economic reality and put much emphasis on re-orienting the economy towards this expanding economic tier, which indeed explains much of the recent architectural development which uses culture as a backdrop to answer the lack of cultural and tourist venues in the city. To expand this fledgling economic tier, Qatar has recently announced an ambitious new tourism master plan with an investment of over US$15 billion into an array of prestigious projects to establish Doha as a high-quality destination for cultural tourism, beach and lifestyle resorts, business and sports events. Two years ago, at the National Tourism Conference held in Doha to celebrate World Tourism Day, Akbar al-Baker, Chairman of the Qatar Tourism Authority (QTA), outlined the government's vision to build its capital city as a leading quality destination for leisure, business and international sporting events. 'Our plan', said al-Baker, 'includes building hotels, lifestyle resorts, cultural products, sports facilities and building a stronger infrastructure to sustain the growth and appeal of our country'.[14] In 2004, over 500,000 tourists passed through Qatar, and the government is expecting that number to more than double, reaching 1.5 million visitors in 2010. Similarly, addressing leaders in business and finance, the Qatar Museums Authority (QMA) chairperson, Sheikha Mayassa bint Hamad al-Thani, revealed the government's cultural development strategy when she told her audience that 'it is in partnership with you that the vision of Qatar for the Mecca of Museums can become a vibrant reality' (*Gulf Times*, 2007). It is worth mentioning that these developments in the art scene in Doha are instigated, motivated, and inspired by Sheikh Saud al-Thani, cousin of the ruling Emir and one of the wealthiest art collectors in the world (Goswamy, 2004). Evidence of this aggressive plan promoted by Sheikh Saud abounds with several new developments and spectacular events, attesting to the growing interest in promoting culture as a way to attract tourists and enhance the image of the city for a global audience.[15]

Consider the new Museum of Islamic Arts, for example (figure 9.15). It was first conceived in an international competition coordinated by the Aga Khan Trust for Culture in 1997. From more than eighty contestants, the jury selected the Indian architect Charles Correa and the Jordanian architect Rasem Badran by a majority vote as finalists. Initially, although the client selected the project of Badran to be built, the final project was surprisingly passed to the Chinese-American superstar architect I.M. Pei, creator of the glass pyramid at the Louvre, who in his eighties was called out of retirement to design the building.[16] The museum building, which draws much influence from ancient Sumerian, Babylonian, and Assyrian architecture, is built on an off-shore artificial island in a prime location at the end

Figure 9.15. The Islamic Museum during construction.

of the Corniche and will house a large collection of Islamic arts. The museum is meant to join forces with four other national museums that will also be built or renovated in the Doha bay area, to form centrepieces in Doha's strategy to become a tourist destination.[17] It is worth mentioning that this strategy of enhancing the city's global brand-image through the construction of museums, which the government of Qatar has taken to distinguish itself from other development tracks in other Gulf emirates, is being echoed, or perhaps, challenged by the city of Abu Dhabi. A few months ago, the government of Abu Dhabi announced its future plans to construct four large museums designed by four superstar architects on Sadiyyat Island.

But the display strategy has not been limited to items framed within the boundaries of iconic museum buildings. For example, displaying the city's history is now expanding to incorporate framing certain sections of the old city (figure 9.16). Souk Waqif, the covered market which I mentioned earlier and which originally began as a Friday market place for Bedouins to trade their wool and meat in exchange for staple goods, has been recently transformed to become a showcase for Doha's past. The market was a bit modernized during the last few decades with neon lights, aluminium doors and windows, and new paints covering the otherwise characterless shop façades. Recently, Souk Waqif underwent a massive renovation and clearing effort so that it could be displayed to wandering tourists as an 'authentic' setting, replete with all signs of a refurbished, relived past (figure 9.17). Souk Waqif is re-dressing to signify an original that never existed in this sleek form (figure 9.18).[18]

The use of daily events in the market place as animated showcases for tourists is being replicated in a more organized and official manner. The tourism authorities in Doha have been using cultural events and festivals as animators of traditional

Figure 9.16. Souk Waqif is at the heart of the city and its historical memory.

Figure 9.17. Souk Waqif underwent a massive renovation and clearing before the Asian Games in 2006.

Figure 9.18. The clearings around Souk Waqif introduced new visual contrasts to the old city.

places and the past to encourage and levy tourist itineraries throughout the whole year. Consider the annual Doha Cultural Festival, which features a supposed blend of Eastern and Western cultures, ranging from Qatari Nabatean poetry recitals to Western musicals (*Gulf News*, 2007). Or take the newly launched heritage village, which is becoming a trademark for all cities in the Gulf. Not unlike its counterparts in the region, the Doha village hosts a variety of events which are meant to showcase traditional Qatari dances, music, and handicrafts (Bibbo, 2007).

In addition to developing art and local culture scenes, Doha authorities plan to attract sports fans with new facilities and major sporting events. I suggest that in Qatari society where staged cultural and sports performances are spreading, life is increasingly presenting itself as an immense accumulation of spectacles, to paraphrase what Guy Debord wrote 40 years ago about modern societies. The spectacular year-round spectator sports activities in Doha attest to this. According to a report on the overall view of the tourism activities in Doha, the number of high-level sports events organized in the city is dazzling: MotoGP, ATP tennis, gymnastics, volleyball, basketball, handball, football, Master's golf, Grand Prix fencing, Class One and Formula 3000 power boating, as well as non-stop round-the-world yachting, are but a few of the events which fill the calendar (OBG, 2005, p. 116). But the most important event which was the focal point used in boosting the cultural capitalism tier was the spectacular 2006 Doha Asian Games. Ever since Doha was awarded the hosting of the Games in 2001, nearly US$3 billon was spent on infrastructure developments directly related to the sports facilities (Qatar Business Report, 2005). These new venues include the renovation or construction of more than thirty-eight permanent and temporary sports venues to stage the forty sports which would draw nearly 11,000 Asian athletes (figure 9.19). The centrepiece of these facilities is Sports City. Located some 11 kilometres south-west of Doha's Corniche, the City covers an area of 130 hectares and includes Khalifa International Stadium, the Aspire Sports Dome, the Hamad Aquatic Center, the Orthopaedic Sports Medicine Hospital, the Energy Center, and a host of other facilities (figure 9.20). A bird's eye perspective of the overall development reveals that the design draws heavily on the elements of the desert, such as the car-parking which has been arranged in the shape of palm fronds.[19]

Figure 9.19. Ory, the mascot for the 2006 Asian Games in Doha, overlooks West Bay.

Figure 9.20. The Khalifa International Stadium.

The event itself was hailed as one of the most impressive, successful, and well organized of all Asian Games. To guarantee the success of the spectacular opening and closing ceremonies, the authorities hired the same Australian team who had organized the Sydney Summer Olympic Games to plan, to the minutest detail, the unfolding events of the two week spectacle. According to Barbara Bibbo (2006), the vast majority of the props, sets and scenery were shipped from Sydney, where a workshop was established to draw on 'the finest talent from the film and entertainment industry'. The organization of the sports event was a strategic focus which not only tied together a number of aspects of Qatar's ongoing development, but also used a flagship spectacle to promote the new brand-image of Qatar globally (OBG, 2005).

I want to conclude this discourse on the rise of cultural capitalism and its impact on Doha by shifting to the latest form of development which is taking place in many cities in the Gulf region, namely, the cities, as they are dubbed, of higher education. In 1995, the Emir of Qatar established the Qatar Foundation with a mandate to create an Education City, a fully functioning community, committed to imparting and creating knowledge, from early childhood education to postgraduate studies and applied research. Today, one of its key features is that it is co-located with the recently established Qatar Science and Technology Park, which is intended to spur development of Qatar's knowledge economy. The Science and Technology Park is based on free-trade zone incentives and aims to attract companies to develop their technology and help entrepreneurs launch new technology businesses. Christina Asquith (2006) says that inside the 2,500 acre, well-guarded compound on the outskirts of Doha, students from across the Arab world are enrolled in one of five premier US universities which have arrived in Qatar in recent years to deliver American-style education and degrees.[20] In the next few years, Education City will be joined by housing, shopping, sports and recreational facilities.

Arata Isozaki, the Japanese architect who designed the National Library, National Bank and other projects around Doha, including the Emir's private residence, is not only in charge of the master plan, but is designing the auditorium/convention and exhibition centre and the foundation headquarters, one of the emblematic buildings on the site, which appears on numerous postcards and periodicals about Doha. Ingeniously, the building, which was engineered by Arup, has a detached, outer screen shade controlling the amount of solar energy hitting its glassy external wall and ensuring that it never overheats. Another signature building by Isozaki planned for the Education City is a massive, state-of-the-art convention centre. The Mexican architects Legorreta & Legorreta are also leaving their mark on the vicinity with their designs for two academic buildings.

It is worth mentioning that Doha's enthusiasm to establish itself as an education hub for the Gulf region and South East Asia with an American-style education system is concurrent with the US government's desire, particularly since 9/11, to observe closely, and perhaps change, the education system in the Arab World, which has been surmised by the Western media and governments as one of the principal factors behind the ideological fanaticism of the New York and Washington suicide attacks. Moreover, the tense and acrimonious relationship between America and the Arab world in the aftermath of the attacks has been discouraging many Arab students, particularly from the Gulf region, to pursue higher education in the US. Thus, the opening of branches of several American universities in Doha might have become, particularly after 9/11, a shared goal of the different parties involved but for different reasons. It is also important to put in this context the fact that other Gulf States are also promoting American-style education by taking a similar course, for example, Knowledge Village in Dubai. In fact, this seeming competition among the various Gulf States constitutes the second discourse, to which I shall now turn and describe some of its prevalent features.

The main focus of the second discourse is on the ever expanding global capitalist corporations, whose aim today, just as in the past, is adding value to their products. It has been through branding, one of the primary instruments of capitalism, that the products assume the status of symbols and icons; in other words, products acquire sign values in addition to their use values. Thus, in the current development of hyper-inflated corporate power, we have entered the age of hyper-signification, in which the urban experience is increasingly cluttered with brand icons, 'sign wars', to use the words of Robert Goldman and Stephen Papson (1996). I want to suggest that in the Gulf region, beyond all the headlines and current media preoccupation with the situation in Iraq, an iconic war of hyper-signification is taking place in the realm of architecture. Today, architecture has become one of the primary instruments of brand communication, of lending tangible form to corporate brands. We may talk not only about making a brand into a place but also making a place or even a city into a brand. Of course, cities have always been stereotyped, or branded, because they always reflect a rational or an emotional attachment: Cairo is history; Paris is romance, and so on. As Simon Anholt (2005) has pointed out, what is different in today's globalized, networked world is that every city has to compete with every other city for the share of the world's tourists, consumers, businesses, capital, and so on. Of course, cities with powerful and positive brands find it easier to attract investment and tourists. Consider the negative image given to Qatar by the famous Lonely Planet guidebook of the 1980s which tells us that Doha has earned a reputation as the dullest place on earth. In fact, one cannot help but think that much of what is happening today has been instigated as a response to this negative image. In order to gain a share in the global economy, therefore, cities are consciously striving to construct, manage, and maintain a brand image. In this brand-setting of cities, architecture seems to have assumed the role of forging the backdrop for brand experiences with a high entertainment value, from flagship stores to themed residential gated communities, from innovative museum and mall concepts to spectacular, iconic office towers and hotels. Consider this brand-setting competition among cities in the Gulf.[21] Burj Dubai, for example, is set to top the list of the highest buildings in the world. However, three contenders from the Gulf region are lining up: Kuwait, Bahrain, and another structure in Dubai itself.

In addition to branding Doha using culture and art, as has been rehearsed in the previous discourse, the authorities are pioneering, in the Middle East, industry-based research and development to add the value of a knowledge economy to the brand. A similar project geared to differentiating Doha's developments from other cities in the Gulf is the Energy City. Located within the Lusail development and described by its developers as the only one of its kind in the region, the Energy City complex is anticipated to host a collection of regional headquarters for energy conglomerates and associated industries and suppliers.

But the centrepiece of these endeavours is the iconic 'The Pearl-Qatar' (figure 9.21). The US$2.5 billion Riviera-style, offshore island covers some 400 hectares

Figure 9.21. The Pearl-Qatar, the rediscovered island.

of reclaimed land and will triple, when completed in 2009, Doha's coastline. Built 350 metres offshore in the West Bay Lagoon area, the island is promising to house more than 35,000 inhabitants in an exclusive retreat, yet closely integrated with the mainland by an eight-lane, palm-tree lined super highway. It is worth mentioning that in keeping with the iconic rivalries and brand setting of cities in the Gulf States, The Pearl-Qatar is one of a series of emerging artificial or natural islands used to advance specific images: Bahrain has the Amwag Islands, Oman has the Wave, Dubai has three Palm islands and The World, and Kuwait is planning a major tourist investment on its existing island of Failaka.

The Seattle-based Callison Architecture Inc provided the master planning and conceptual design services for the whole reclaimed island. Clearly, Callison's main goal was to differentiate the island from the other islands in the Gulf and to create an iconic brand image for the country.[22]

In addition, both the island's name and location are of great complex significance. The Pearl-Qatar is supposedly being built on a reclaimed former pearl diving site. The name, therefore, alludes to the previous mainstay commodity of the economy, pearls. While the project clearly addresses global audiences, its progenitors waste no time in evoking a link between the cultural identity of the emerging spaces and the historical legacies of skills, stories, music, art, and poetry of the past times on the basis of their overlay with the old pearl-fishing site. Moreover, the shape of the island mirrors this illusion of pearls huddled together, extending into the Gulf waters. Now the old commodity of pearls is no longer a key economic factor. Its abstracted image and connotation, however, has become a circulating iconic fiction, while its actual spaces have been virtually non-existent until reclaimed from the sea, a reclaimed/recreated space-commodity to be conquered and sold in an ever growing global real-estate market. Apparently, for the developers of The Pearl, it is not sufficient for the new global cosmopolitan citizens to live in local historical times. Thus, we find the island encompassing ten variously themed residential and commercial districts, promising the 'ambience and lifestyle of the Mediterranean to the heart of Arabia'. I shall get back to this emphasis on lifestyles in a little while. As an incentive to attract people from across the globe, the property owners of The Pearl will automatically receive Qatari residency visas and will be granted unrestricted freehold titles to their property. According to official publications, The Pearl-Qatar is one of the designated areas that falls under the Prime Ministerial decree issued in June 2004 to allow non-Qataris to own residential units in Doha. Other designated areas in which foreigners can purchase land, buildings, and apartments include the Qutaifiya Lagoon and the Al-Khor projects – both these are projects developed by the state-owned Diar-Qatar.

The third discourse, though closely related to the second, focuses on the relationship between Dubai and Doha.[23] No doubt, a strong affinity between Dubai and Doha has grown over the years. Marriage between their ruling families and a unified currency until the early 1970s, the Qatar-Dubai riyal, are but two examples of these strong ties. Recently, a growing number of observers began to point out the impact Dubai has exerted on Doha as well as other cities in the region (Elsheshtawy, 2005; Sherwood, 2006). 'Is Doha the Next Dubai', 'The Dubai Effect', 'Dubaification', 'Dubaization', 'The Dubai Factor', 'Exporting Dubai', are but a few of the terms and titles used to reflect Dubai's growing influence and competition with Doha and other regional cities. 'Qatar and Dubai compete on many fronts', and 'Emirates and Qatar Airways slug it out for the title of the world's fastest growing airline' (Jones, 2006), and their airports, I shall add, will very soon follow suit. A quick look at a timeline of major developments in the past decade supports this argument. For example, The Pearl-Qatar was announced 2 years after the first Palm Jumeirah was being dredged; the Financial Center of Doha was established 2 years after Dubai International Financial Centre opened its doors; and the start of many of the large real-estate developments in Doha emerged in the shadows of their counterparts in Dubai. Moreover, Dubai investors have contributed to some key projects in Doha. For instance, Dubai International Properties, a member of Dubai Holding, has launched an 80-storey, 437 metre high development, Dubai Towers Doha, which will become Doha's tallest building; Dubai-based Tabreed has set up a joint venture, district cooling company with the United Development Company (UDC), which will be the first district cooling services provider in the State of Qatar; and DAMAC, the largest private developer in Dubai, made a foray into Doha with a US$300 million project, The Piazza, which will be part of Lusail City (Rahman, 2006).

From another perspective, Doha has followed the footsteps of Dubai in linking its new working and residential real-estate developments to urban ideas which, not unlike Dubai, also labels them cities. For instance, while in Dubai we find Media City, Internet City, Medical City, Studio City, International City and the ironic Residential City among many others, in Doha we observe developers increasingly using the same designations: Energy City, Entertainment City, Sports City, Education City, Bavaria City Suites, and so on. Increasingly relying on superlatives is another case in point: while Dubai has mastered this in the past few years with a series of world-breaking records such as the tallest building and the largest mall, Doha's developments are increasingly being defined in similar ways: Snow Xtreme is the only place in the Gulf where it snows all year round according to one flyer in the City Center Doha mall, another clone of Dubai's City Center in Deira. We have seen how the Aspire dome in Sports City was advertised as the largest sports dome in the world and Lusail City propagated as the largest real-estate development in the Gulf. Even the expansion of Dubai's private and state-owned business and real-estate companies in the Arab world is being replicated by Doha's emerging conglomerates. For example, following DAMAC, EMAAR, and Nakheel, the large real-estate developers in Dubai, Diar-Qatar, has recently announced two large real-estate projects: a US$170 million tourist development in Morocco near Tangier and an eco-tourist resort in Ras al-Haad, Oman. Other large projects in Egypt and elsewhere are in the pipeline.

Many observers will agree that Dubai has stirred the tourism and real-estate developments in the Gulf region. But it would be inaccurate to conclude that its influence is in a one-way direction. For example, Education City is a project conceived and launched in Qatar long before the Knowledge Village was established in Dubai and Al-Jazeera News state-owned channel has been operating since 1996, long before Al-Arabiya, the Dubai-based news channel, started broadcasting. Moreover, the emphasis on developing museums and cultural venues is unique to Doha, at least until the recent announcements in Abu Dhabi. State officials waste no time in distinguishing Doha from Dubai. For example, Jan De Boer, head of Qatar's tourism agency and a close associate of the Emir said that 'this [Dubai] gigantomania is precisely what we want to avoid. Of course, the speed of development here makes it seem like Dubai. But we have a different plan. We want to be more exclusive' (quoted in Follath, 2006). According to Follath, in Qatar, Dubai is seen as 'vulgar, boastful, nouveau riche and completely devoid of character'. On the other hand, 'Qatar wants to be a classy Portofino, not a tacky Benidorm. In fact, whether or not it wants to be like Dubai is no longer an issue' (*Ibid.*). I will argue that while it is true that Dubai may have instigated, or speeded up, Doha's recent developments and construction boom, these developments have lives and dynamics of their own. To put it differently, once the ball of development started rolling in Doha in the mid-1990s, it acquired its own dynamic energy, which is affected by both internal and external logics. It is, therefore, not a one directional predisposition, but rather a complex web of influences and interactions. Again, many of these developments in Doha started after the current Emir took power in 1995. Of course, this regime change is not related to Dubai, but to internal politics in the Al-Thani family.

In the fourth discourse, many social critics call attention to the fact that today the selection of brands has become an important factor in defining people's identities and lifestyles. For example, the American writer Naomi Klein (2002) reckons that lifestyles are becoming increasingly intrinsic markers of who one is and as a means to connect to others. Akin to an individual's possession of commodities, adoption of a certain brand or lifestyle marks and conveys to his or her peer group meaning, status, and prestige; it displays in the individual's society some sort of cultural capital. To put it differently, while for the individual the display function of commodity-signs remains a significant source for prestige and identity actualization, the accumulation of cultural experiences – travel accounts, souvenirs, and exotic photo images – represents an increasingly dominant source for identity formation and status. Illustrative of this reliance on exotic experience as a symbolic, cultural capital is the eagerness of many tourists to take photographs in certain sites so that they can tell their peers back home that they were in a particular place, the 'I have been there' feeling to paraphrase what Jean Baudrillard calls the 'I did it' feeling (Mestrovic, 1997).

It was Max Weber, according to Mark Gottdiener (2000), who first taught us that the cultural or symbolic aspects of society define people's behaviour as much as economic needs. Weber's insight has profoundly influenced numerous subsequent scholars, who emphasized the importance of symbolic or sign values in the realization of self and the exercise of identity through lifestyles, particularly in those societies that are increasingly characterized by consumption. I have in mind the long haul that runs from Thorstein Veblen (1899) to Daniel Boorstein (1961) to Guy Debord (1970) to Jean Baudrillard (1983). This semiotic approach to culture led many contemporary social observers to conclude that today's culture is about image and that consumption consists of appropriating signs (Kellner, 1995; Gottdiener, 2000). Although proponents of this approach are criticized often for being one-dimensional and one-sided, their analyses are very useful in shedding light on the importance of sign values in everyday culture (Gottdiener, 2000). There is little doubt, I want to emphasize, that signs and images play an increasingly important role in identity formation, including the identity of buildings and cities. In addition, because cultural productions in general are increasingly standardized, it became imperative that they 'attach themselves to signs that carry an additional element of value' (Goldman and Papson, 1996). Thus we find in contemporary Doha, which is trying to attract tourists, a plethora of cultural entertainment venues devising and using some overarching symbolic themes in their proliferating spaces. One may say that these tourist spaces have become like staged commercial entertainment settings replete with signs which, in addition to their function in differentiating tourist products, communicate meanings embedded in their signs that promote specific lifestyles and patterns of consumption. It is to gain cultural capital that a large segment of tourists is increasingly motivated to experience differences and the exotic; and to supply this exotic experience the urban developers and tourist industries in Doha are manufacturing the exotic brands and lifestyle spaces.

Consider, for example, how the progenitors of The Pearl-Qatar describe the main intention of the project. Catering to a particular lifestyle, the project intends to create a hybrid place of fantasy with a permanent atmosphere of festivity. In a secure and exclusive environment, the up-scale residential community, announces an editorial on the island, will bring 'the ambience and lifestyle of the Mediterranean to the heart of Arabia' (*Acari* Editorial, 2005, p. 31). Nick Bashkiroff, the Development Director of The Pearl-Qatar, tells us that 'the Porto Arabia lifestyle will be akin to that in Cannes or Nice but within the clean waters of the Arabian Gulf' (*Ibid.*). Or take the names given to the various residential areas or buildings within The Pearl island: Monaco, Tuscan, Provencal, Florentine, Catalan, Andalusian, Riviera, La Croisette, among many others. 'Select a destination. Then, select a home', says one advertisement for The Pearl-Qatar. It has been 'conceived to facilitate the most exclusive lifestyles within an environment that will constantly surprise', says another company publication. Obviously, these designations suggest the illusion of vitality, enjoyment, and fun through their semantic associations with Mediterranean destinations known for their ambience of dissociated festivity and up-scale lifestyle.

Another emerging project, which also emphasizes the lifestyle component of the development, is the US$5.5 billion Lusail City. Launched by the state-owned company Qatari-Diar and headed by the newly appointed premier Sheikh Hamad bin Jabor bin Jassim al-Thani, the new city, which will be located a few kilometres north of the West Bay area, will cover over 35 square kilometres with 8 kilometres beach-front and will accommodate up to 200,000 people. A key component for the development is the Energy City, the multibillion dollar hub for the energy industry in Qatar and supposedly the region. While the Energy City is a business hub, its advertisements evoke a lifestyle of surrounding posh houses, golf courses, themed malls, sleek restaurants, which as Sharon Zukin (1995) has observed, is a precondition for global corporations to settle in a city. In addition, the Lusail development will include, when completed, comprehensive leisure and entertainment facilities including an Entertainment City, an estimated US$500 million project developed by the Abu Dhabi Investment House. Entertainment City is a mixed-use theme park: themed hotels, themed restaurants, shopping, cinemas, and theatres. Part of Lusail and spanning over 1.6 million square metres is Fox Hills. Not unlike its neighbour, The Pearl-Qatar, it is presumably inspired by Qatari heritage and draws much influence from Mediterranean architectural themed environments and lifestyles.

Why these developments in their urban and physical environments are happening at this magnitude at this historical juncture is a question asked in the fifth discourse with the usual answer given by the authorities: to diversify the economy. Since the beginning of this real-estate boom a few years ago, the idea of diversifying the economy provided a mode of seeing, a way of diagnosing, and a remedy for improving and reaching a sustainable urban and economic growth. Of course, other possible, interrelated answers to this question have been addressed in the four discourses discussed above: the changing leadership in Doha; the rise of cultural capitalism as a paradigm for capital accumulation; the rivalry with other cities in the Gulf; the increasing influence of American and European lifestyles and business models; the growing importance of brands and lifestyles to the identity formation of citizens and cities; and the growing importance of the brand-setting of cities to attract businesses and tourists. I want to add here one further possible answer to this question: the repatriation of Arab wealth following the events of 11 September 2001 and the recycling of petrodollars.

Akin to the 1970s, the development of Doha during the past few years is interwoven with the recycling of the petrodollars earned by the government. Mohsen Khan, the Director of the Middle East and Central Asia Department at the International Monetary Fund, suggested that the export revenues collected by the oil-producing countries of the Middle East, particularly the Gulf region, would be shown to have exceeded US$500 billion in 2006 (Khan, 2005). By subtracting the import expenditures from the revenue accumulated from selling oil, Khan says that over US$200 billion would be available for saving or spending. If one's first reaction was amazement at the scale of wealth accumulated in such a short time, one soon begins to wonder about how this money is invested. Khan states that although it is difficult to trace the money, 'we can say that a large share has been likely invested in US dollar financial assets' (*Ibid.*). There is no mention in the IMF of the frenzied explosion of cities and the financing of many mega real-estate projects around the Gulf as a possible explanation for the missing petrodollars.

In a similar vein, Jad Mouawad and Eduardo Porter of the *New York Times* contend that after the 1973 oil shock, governments in the Middle East spent 80 per cent of their increase in revenue; by contrast, between 2003 and 2005, they spent less than 40 per cent of their new revenue (Mouawad and Porter, 2006). Other reports contradict these possible answers. For example, an online project tracker report published in the *Gulf News* estimates that the value of the projects planned or under development in the Gulf exceeds one trillion US dollars (Gulf News Staff Report, 2006). 'The value of more than 1400 projects', states the report, 'rose by more than 250 billion US dollars in the first quarter of 2006 and exceeded one trillion in the first week of April' (*Ibid.*, p. 37). While it is true that, historically, oil revenue has been converted into dollars or dollar-denominated assets, this time around, it is possible that a large portion of the petrodollars is invested in stock markets around the Gulf, financing large real-estate developments. Ironically, as Mike Davis (2005) has observed, terrorism deserves some of the credit for this real-estate boom. According to him, 'since 9/11, many Middle Eastern investors, fearing possible lawsuits or sanctions, have pulled up stakes in the West' (*Ibid.*). Estimates suggest, Davis contends, that 'the Saudis alone have repatriated one-third of their trillion-dollar overseas portfolio' (*Ibid.*). It is also possible to assume that much of the petrodollar surpluses are pumped back into the global economy, to the oil exporting countries. A glimpse at the number of Western companies operating in the construction as well as other industries in the Gulf attests to this observation.

Concluding Remarks

Ultimately, though, the current urban scene is mostly being driven by a projected image of Doha as a global city, an emerging command and control centre for the global economy which will be hyper-linked to other cities and other spaces. From an academic point of view, Jennifer Robinson (2002) tells us that the 'global city' emerges as a new concept for the post-colonial, one super power era, and I shall add, neo-liberal political-economic paradigm. It categorizes selected cities in the world as global or not-global on the basis of the presence and/or absence of specific concentrated transnational activities within them as well as entertainment and lifestyle venues. My first thought is precisely that what has been emerging out of the social and material production of Doha's new spaces is a specific urbanity, which functions as the city's membership card for joining the club of global cities. In a sense, the concept of 'a global city' is akin to a brand image bestowed upon some world cities, which have managed to create new spaces for work and leisure that cater for global audiences. Several of the examples discussed above suggest that the strategies of urban development in the past decade reflect a conscious approach to enhancing the city's global image through the construction of cultural, tourist, and commercial projects. Moreover, the creation of Doha's global image through the creation of spectacular, iconic built environments seems to have helped the city to conjure up an image to be marketed to tourists and visitors. This is how cities are competing under today's global capitalist system. In this iconic global-brand war, the success of architectural forms and spaces is contingent on their entertainment and fantasy qualities. Could it be that this aspiration to become a global city categorizes cities by establishing certain ones, or specific spaces and images, as the standard towards which all cities should aspire? One may wonder then which city constitutes the image-model for Doha. Is it Dubai? Is it Paris? Or is it an assortment of hybrid spaces which have neither specific geographic locale nor time frame? Or could it be that in the neo-liberal paradigm, the brand 'global city' is late-capitalism's way of expanding its grip over new territories by 'making others desire what we want them to desire', to paraphrase Joseph Nye (2004)? But one must not forget that changes in urban and architectural spaces are generated by agents and forces both local and global.

Certainly, the interaction of Qatari and international capitalism is not new. What is new, however, is that in this phase of interaction, desires and new urban values and images have been enticed to stoke the construction boom. Following Baudrillard's tripartite value system, one may suggest that if in the first urban scene, urban spaces developed on the basis of a natural use of the world, in the second urban scene, urban spaces began to develop in reference to the logic of the commodity – recall the emptying out of central Doha during the 1970s (Baudrillard, 1990). Moreover, in this scene, and perhaps due to the increasing presence of foreign planning offices, urban spaces were developed by reference to a set of modern planning models imported and localized. In the third contemporary urban scene, urban spaces have no specific reference; they are developing with references radiating from all directions: local and global signs and codes, other places, other times, interminable theming, various lifestyles. From another perspective, parallel to this tripartite account of value embedded in urban spaces is a tripartite account of the development of the relationship between Qataris and the Gulf sea. While the Gulf sea in the first scene was the source of life for Qataris through fishing and pearling and in the second scene, through extracting oil and natural gas, in the third scene it is as if suddenly the people of Qatar have discovered yet another value: real estate. In the urban dynamics of contemporary capitalism, for Doha to become a global city it must reinvent and rediscover itself, but in this round through real estate and spectacular, iconic mega-projects.

Notes

1. After travelling for a year from Syria, through Najd, and on to Bahrain and Oman, William Palgrave returned to Europe, where he wrote a narrative of his travels in Arabia. When travelling

in Qatar, he told his readers, 'to have an idea about Katar, my readers must figure to themselves miles on miles of low barren hills, bleak and sun-scorched, with hardly a single tree to vary their dry monotonous outline: below these a muddy beach extends for a quarter of a mile seaward in slimy quicksands, bordered by a rim of sludge and seaweeds. If we look landwards beyond the hills, we see what at extreme courtesy may be called pasture land, dreary downs with twenty pebbles for every blade of grass'. This quotation of Palgrave is from Arnold Wilson's article on the Gulf (Wilson, 1927).

2.   Absent in the period between the landing of the Turkish troops and the beginning of the twentieth century is any descriptive account of the physical environment, demographic distributions, and other urban characteristics. This period is, however, rich in historical documents describing the political affairs of the peninsula, such as the collected historical documents 'Précis of Qatar Affairs from 1873 to 1904' written by J.A. Saldanha. Most of these documents and letters were between the chief British officer in the region, the political resident in Bushire, on the coast of Iran, and his political agents, who were stationed in various Sheikhdoms in the Gulf, but specifically in Bahrain as there was no agent in Qatar.

3.   This was perhaps in fear of the competition with them over the pearl industry.

4. Ironically, today, there is a growing interest in Gulf pearls. But whereas in the old days pearls were shipped to Bombay and sold there, today, pearls are making the journey back to the Gulf, through the acquisition by rich sheikhs from the Gulf region.

5.   Helmut Mejcher (1976) tells us that experts in the US State Department's committees who dealt with post-war foreign economic policy and long-range oil strategies became fully aware that the British government might monopolize the post-war oil-thirsty European market and expand its sterling oil empire in the Gulf in order to help its tattered economy.

6.   Sharon Nagy says that 'while most of the land targeted for acquisition was eventually purchased, the acquisition of lands took much longer and was much more expensive than had been anticipated. The funds allotted for the acquisition and redevelopment of these areas were depleted in acquisition, preventing the implementation of the redevelopment phase. Additionally, by the time all the land was acquired, official planning priorities and preferences had shifted to other projects' (Nagy, 1997, p. 111).

7.   It was named the Tin District because of the type of cheap temporary dwellings made out of tin that occupied much of it.

8.   In fact, two of my Qatari schoolmates lived in Salata during the time I was a resident of Doha.

9.   The myth has it that Potemkin villages were fake, hollow façades painted on canvas and erected at the direction of the Russian minister Potemkin to impress Empress Catherine II with the value of the new conquered lands during her visit.

10.   Qatar University was founded in 1977 with four colleges: Education; Humanities & Social Sciences; Shariaa, Law, & Islamic Studies; and Science. The university campus was designed by the Egyptian architect Kamal Kafrawi.

11.   I could find no information about this project in their main headquarters in Cairo. I was told that before the digital age, many of the files and folders were lost between their Cairo and Beirut offices.

12.   http://www.asiatraveltips.com/news05/131-Qatar.shtml.

13.   See Bauman (1993). The concept of an emerging cosmopolitan citizenship is borrowed from Chris Rojek (2000).

14.   See an online MICE edition: http://www.miceonline.net/qatar/infrastructure.htm. Accessed 19 August 2007.

15.   In March 2005, Sheikh Saud al-Thani, who has spent hundreds of millions of dollars during the last decade buying some of the most important works, has been placed under house arrest after being abruptly removed as head of his country's National Council for Culture.

16.   The client of the competition, the State of Qatar, selected Rasem Badran's project to be built.

I found no information available about the reason for eventually giving this commission to I.M. Pei. It is possible that the selection of the designer of the pyramid of the Louvre was seen as a way to raise the profile of the building.

17. The other museums include the iconic photography museum that the famous Spanish architect, Santiago Calatrava, is designing to showcase mainly Sheikh Saud's photography collection which, when completed, 'will probably itself become a favorite target for flashbulbs' (Sherwood, 2006). The building is an ultra-light structure consisting of two immense curved wings, which will open and close with the light. Equally astounding is the iconic Qatar National Library and National History Museum designed by the Japanese architect, Arata Isozaki. The library is a futuristic-looking mega-structure, which will be hovering on top of three large pillars. While these pillars will support an inverted pyramid and house the library, the National History Museum will be located at ground level. Standing back from the Corniche, the existing Koot Fort will soon be refitted as a Museum of Traditional Clothes and Textiles by the Scottish architect Catherine Findlay (Goswamy, 2004). The last major museum in this array of impressive buildings is the renovated and extended former Emir's palace, mentioned earlier, which houses the Qatar National Museum. The project is designed by the French architect Jean Nouvel and planned to incorporate the most up-to-date concepts of musicology in presenting Qatar's past.

18. It is interesting to note the existing mix of modern and old shops in Souk Waqif. While the souk contains numerous traditional shops selling food and clothes as well as shoemakers, etc., it also contains exhibition halls for modern art and photography and other amenities geared to the taste of up-scale tourists.

19. The focal feature of the complex is the upgraded Khalifa Stadium. Arup, the world-class structural engineering firm, initially worked with Cox/PTW Architects to develop the scheme for the stadium expansion. It is worth mentioning that the Australian-based office PTW is currently designing the National Swimming Center for the 2008 Summer Olympic Games in Beijing, China. A key criterion in designing the Khalifa stadium was that it had to be highly distinctive. Built in 1976, this 20,000 seat stadium with no roof was converted into a 50,000 seat stadium with a tensile fabric roof over the western stand and a signature, distinctive lighting arch over the eastern stand (Gulf Construction, 2006b). Equally impressive is the Aspire Academy, which has been designed by a joint venture of the local Cico and the world famous sports facilities architect, Roger Taillibert, who also designed the Parc des Princes stadium in Paris and the Montreal Olympic stadium in Canada. Taking a cue from Dubai's infatuation with superlatives and world breaking records, Sports City is the home of the Aspire Dome, which claims to be the world's largest sports dome. The 250 metre free-span, multipurpose sports dome consists of two hemispheres covering numerous fitness halls and other sports facilities. But one of the most visible and iconic structures in the sports complex is the 300 metre high Aspire Tower. Designed by the Turkish architect, Hadi Seenan, the tower was intended to support the Olympic flame at the top, and to become after the games a high standard hotel, with revolving restaurant and sports museum.

20. The institutions include Carnegie Mellon University, the Georgetown School of Foreign Service, Texas A&M University, Virginia Commonwealth University School for the Arts and Weill Cornell Medical Center.

21. According to Peter Stanford (2004) of The Independent, neighbouring Bahrain has taken up this challenge by making itself into a centre for offshore banking. Dubai is now aiming to be a global tourist destination, with hotels and luxury holiday homes built on palm tree-shaped artificial sand spits in the Persian Gulf. Qatar shares the urge to modernize. Since the current Emir deposed his father in a bloodless coup in 1995, there has been a concerted effort to join the twenty-first century. Its chosen path to achieving this is by becoming a latter-day Florence.

22. Nick Bashkiroff, the Development Director tells us that 'Callison demonstrated immense creativity and style and produced designs which clearly differentiated the project and were aligned with the vision of the island's developers and promoters to produce an iconic asset for Qatar capable of attracting international investment' (Bashkiroff, 2004).

23. Exemplary of the comments and observations concerning this complex relationship is the

following waggery, which circulated on the internet in 2006 and describes and contrasts systems of governance in Dubai and Doha among other Arab Cities:

'DUBAI SYSTEM: You have two cows. You create a website for them and advertise them in all magazines. You create a Cow City or Milk Town for them. You sell off their milk before the cows have even been milked to both legit and shady investors who hope to resale the non-existent milk for a 100% profit in two years time. You bring Tiger Woods to milk the cow first to attract attention.

QATAR SYSTEM: You have two cows. They've been sitting there for decades and no one realizes that cows can produce milk. You see what Dubai is doing; you go crazy and start milking the heck out of the cows' boobs in the shortest time possible. Then you realize no one wanted the milk in the first place.'

The 'story of two cows': http://culturefusion.blogspot.com/2006/01/story-of-two-cows.html. Accessed 20 August 2007.

References

Acari Editorial (2005) The Pearl-Qatar. *Acari*, **2**(19), pp. 30–35.

Al-Gabir, Mohammed (1977) Al-Goghrafiya al-Bashariyya be-Qatar. Master Thesis, Cairo University.

Al-Ghanim, Kaltham (1997) *Al-Mogtama' al-Qatari men al-Ghawss ila al-Tahadour*. Doha: Dar al-Sharq.

Al-Kazim, Amina Ali (1993) *Al-Taghayour al-Igtima'I wa al-Thaqafi fi al-Mogtama' al-Qatari*. Giza: Hagr Publishers.

Al-Khaiat, Hassan (1982) *Al-Rasseed al-Sokani Le-Dewal al-Khaleeg*. Doha: University of Qatar.

Al-Khalifi, Mohammed J. (1990) *Al-'emarah al-Taqlediya fi Qatar*. Doha: Wizarat al-I'lam wa al-Thaqafa fi Qatar.

Al-Kourdy, Mahmoud (1985) *Al-Doha: al-Madina al-Dawla*. Doha: Markaz al-Wathaiq wa al-Derassat al-Insaniya bi Gami'at Qatar.

Al-Mansour, Abd al-Aziz (1980) *Al-Tatawor al-Siyassi li-Qatar fi al-Fatra ma bin 1868–1916*. Doha: Dar Dhat al-Salassel.

Al-Othman, Nasser (nd) *Al-Sawa'id al-Somer*. Doha: Manshorat Dana lil 'ilaqat al-'amah.

Al-Shalaq, Ahmed (1999) *Fossoul min Tareekh Qatar al-Siyassi*. Doha: Matabi' al-Doha al-Hadeethah.

Anholt, Simon (2005) How the world sees the world cities. *Place Branding*, **2**(1), pp. 18–31.

Asquith, Christina (2006) Accepted in Education City. *Diverse*, 1 June. online edition: http://www.diverseeducation.com/artman/publish/article_5931.shtml.

Bashkiroff, Nick (2004) The Pearl Qatar Appoints Callison for Main Marina Design and Construction Architecture. Online Press release 29 September: http://www.thepearlqatar.com/SubTemplate1.aspx?ID=167&MID=86. Accessed 27 September 2007.

Baudrillard, Jean (1983) *Simulations*. New York, NY: Semiotext(e).

Baudrillard, Jean (1990) *The Transparency of Evil*. New York, NY: Verso.

Bauman, Zygmunt (1993) *Postmodern Ethics*. Oxford: Blackwell.

Beaverbrook, Lord (1944) Oil, the United States, and the Middle East. Memorandum by the Lord Privy Seal, 11.2.1944. F.O. 371/42, 687 W2486.

Bibbo, Barbara (2006) Doha all dressed up to welcome the athletes. *Gulf News*, 7 October, p. 12.

Bibbo, Barbara (2007) Sixth Doha cultural festival reaches out to all. *Gulf News*, 22 March, p. 14.

Boorstein, Daniel (1961) *The Image*. New York, NY: Vintage.

Calvino, Italo (1974) *Invisible Cities* (translated by William Weaver). Orlando, FL: Harcourt Brace Jovanovich.

Corbett, Christopher (2003) Planning for explosive growth on the shores of the Arabian Gulf. American Planning Association (APA). Online edition: http://www.planning.org/hottopics/internationalplanning/qatar.htm. Accessed 19 August 2007.

Craik, Jennifer (1997) The culture of tourism, in Rojek, C. and Urry, J. (eds.) *Touring Cultures*. London: Routledge.

Davis, Mike (2005) Sinister paradise: does the road to the future end at Dubai? Online article: http://www.tomdispatch.com/index.mhtml?pid=5807. Accessed 20 August 2007.

Debord, Guy (1970) *The Society of the Spectacle*. Detroit, MI: Black and Red.

Elsheshtawy, Yasser (2005) Reversing Influences: The Dubaization of Cairo. Paper presented at the XXII UIA World Congress of Architecture – 'Cities: Grand Bazaar of Architecture', Istanbul.

Fadila, A. (1991) Urban Development and Planning in Qatar. PhD thesis, University of New Mexico, Albuquerque.

Follath, Erich (2006) Natural gas is catapulting Qatar into modernity. *Der Spiegel*, online edition: http://www.spiegel.de/international/spiegel/0,1518,428963,00.html. Accessed 13 November 2007.

Goldman, Robert and Papson, Stephen (1996) *Sign Wars*. New York: Guilford.

Goswamy, B.N. (2004) Art hub in the desert. *The Indian Tribune*, 2 May. On line edition: http://tribuneindia.com/2004/20040502/spectrum/art.htm. Accessed 20 August 2007.

Gottdiener, Mark (2000) Approaches to consumption, in Gottdiener, M. (ed.) *New Forms of Consumption*. New York, NY: Roman & Littlefield.

Graham, Helga (1978) *Arabian Time Machine: Self-Portrait of an Oil State*. London: Heinemann.

Gulf Construction Report (2006*a*) Focused on the future. *Gulf Construction*, **27**(3), pp. 42–47.

Gulf Construction Report (2006*b*) Going for gold. *Gulf Construction*, **27**(3), pp. 53–61.

Gulf News Report (2006) Gulf projects exceed $1tr in value. *Gulf News*, 23 April, p. 37.

Gulf Times Business Reporter (2007) Islamic museum to be platform for peace: Mayassa. *Gulf News*, 15 March. Online edition: http://www.gulf-times.com/site/topics/article.asp?cu_no=2&item_no=138293&version=1&template_id=36&parent_id=16.

Hannigan, John (1998) *Fantasy City*. London: Routledge.

Ickes, Harold L. (1943) Ickes to Roosevelt, 18.8.1943, Franklin Roosevelt library, P.S.F. Diplomatic Box 68.

Jones, Rhys (2006) Tussle for the top between Gulf centers: Dubai and Qatar vie for the crown. *Gulf News*, 14 October, p. 43.

Kellner, Douglas (1995) *Media Culture*. London: Routledge.

Khan, Mohsen (2005) How are the petrodollars invested in the Middle East. Online article: http://www.sagia.gov.sa/InvestInSaudi/Newsroom_7117.htm. Accessed 30 March 2007.

Klein, Naomi (2002) *No Logo*. New York, NY: Picador.

Lefebvre, Henri (1991) *The Production of Space*. Oxford: Blackwell.

Lorimer, J.G. (1970) *Gazeteer of the Persian Gulf: Oman and Central Arabia*. Vol. II. Westmead: Gregg International.

Majed, Ebrahim Issa (1987) *The Traditional Construction of Early Twentieth Century Houses in Bahrain*. Doha: Arab Gulf States Folklore Center.

Mehanna, Mohamad N. (2001) *Qatar: al-Tareekh, al-Syassah, al-Tahdeeth*. Alexandira: al-Maktab al-Game'i al-Hadeeth.

Mejcher, Helmut (1976) American oil interests and politics of penetration in Saudi Arabia and the Gulf in World War II, in *Papers presented to the Historical Studies Conference on Eastern Arabia*. Doha: Dar al-'Uloom.

Mestrovic, Stjepan (1997) *Postemotional Society*. London: Sage.

Mitchell, Christopher (1976) Development in the Middle East: the practice of architecture. *Bulletin of the British Society for Middle Eastern Studies*, **3**(2), pp. 89–91.

Mouawad, Jad and Porter, Eduardo (2006) New money, new ideas; this time, OPEC nations temper their extravagance. *New York Times*, 1 February, Section C, p. 1.

Munif, Abdelrahman (1989) *Cities of Salt* (Translated by P. Theroux). New York, NY: Vintage.

Nagy, Sharon (1997) Social and Spatial Process: An Ethnographic Study of Housing in Qatar. PhD Dissertation, University of Pennsylvania.

Nagy, Sharon (2000) Dressing up downtown: urban development and government public image in Qatar. *City & Society*, **12**(1), pp. 125–147.

Nye, Joseph (2004) *Soft Power*. New York, NY: Public Affairs.

OBG Report (2005) Stay a while longer, in *Emerging Qatar 2005*. London: Oxford Business Group.

Qatar Business Report (2005) The sporting spirit. Supplement to *Gulf Business*, **9**(11), pp. 32–36.

Rahman, Saifur (2006) Damac makes foray into Qatar with Dh1b project. *Gulf News*, 6 June, p. 43.

Rifkin, Jeremy (2000) *The Age of Access*. New York, NY: Jeremy P. Tarcher/Putnam.

Robinson, Jennifer (2002) Global and world cities: a view from off the map. *International Journal of Urban and Regional Research*, **26**(3), pp. 531–554.

Rojek, Chris (2000) Mass tourism or the re-enchantment of the world? Issues and contradictions in the study of travel, in Gottdiener, M. (ed.) *New Forms of Consumption*. New York, NY: Roman & Littlefield.

Saldanha, J.A. (1989) *Précis of Qatar Affairs from 1873 to 1904* (translated by Ahmed al-'anany). Doha: Qism al-Wathaiq wa al-Abhath bi Maktab al-Amir.

Sherwood, Seth (2006) Is Qatar the next Dubai? *New York Times*, Travel Section, 4 June.

Stanford, Peter (2004) The Guggenheim of the Persian Gulf. *The Independent*, 7 July. http://www.findarticles.com/p/articles/mi_qn4158/is_20040707/ai_n12803300.

Veblen, Thorstein (1899, 1953) *The Theory of the Leisure Class*. New York, NY: New American Library.

Walker, Jenny (2004) *Arabian Peninsula*. London: Lonely Planet.

Wilson, Arnold (1927) A periplus of the Persian Gulf. *Geographical Journal*, **69**(3), p 250.

Zahlan, Rosemarie Said (1979) *The Creation of Qatar*. London: Croom Helm.

Zearah, Khaled Abdallah (2005) *Loaa Loaa al-Khaleeg*. Doha: Al-Majlis al-Watany lel-Fenoon wa al-Thaqafa wa al-Torath.

Zukin, Sharon (1995) *The Cultures of Cities*. Oxford: Blackwell.

Chapter 10

Cities of Sand and Fog: Abu Dhabi's Global Ambitions

Yasser Elsheshtawy

'Your majesty, my lord, you know better than any other man there has been oil under this land for thousands of years, untouched in its place, until your late father after seeking counsel far and near, asking questions and making inquiries, told them, "Now carry out the will of God!"' He paused and drew a difficult breath, then added, 'The oil might have stayed in the bowels of the earth, Your Majesty, for hundreds of thousands of years, but divine care, approval and the good fortune that comes only from Almighty God, said, "Be!" and it was. Now, more than at any other time, and here, above any other place, Your Majesty, you can transform Mooran into a paradise on earth and rule over the far and the near!'

Abdulrahman Munif, *The Trench* (Cities of Salt), p. 24

Prologue

Abdulrahman Munif, well known Saudi writer, in *The Trench*, the second volume of his epic pentology 'Cities of Salt', describes the transformations which have occurred in the fictional city of Mooran – initially a desert settlement from where an entire city is created from scratch. In the process he evoked the fears and desires of its residents, giving a voice to those bearing the brunt of modernization. At the same time he articulates in clear terms the extent to which such desert cities are shaped by their rulers, and how their whims, opinions and personalities direct their development. The above quote suggests an almost messianic vision, a destiny that is bestowed upon the rulers to *create* a city – to turn it into *paradise* (figure 10.1). But they are also cities without history, or memory. Where do we find such cities? What do they look like? And do these visionary proclamations have a place in a globalizing world? This chapter is an attempt to answer these questions.

Introduction

Cities such as Abu Dhabi are invariably known as sudden cities, instant cities, and rapidly urbanizing cities. Such connotations evoke a sudden transformation

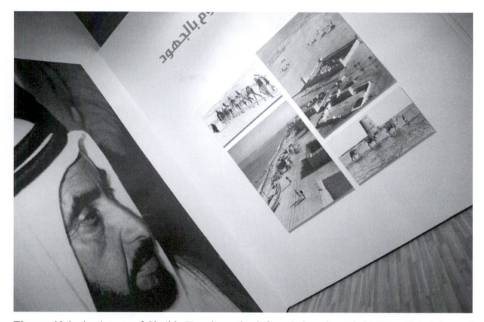

Figure 10.1. An image of Sheikh Zayed on the left and the Abu Dhabi Fort, Corniche and watchtower as they appeared in the 1960s.

from nomadic origins, characterized by constant movement, to an urban entity. These depictions underlie a certain dismissal; they are not 'real', but rather artificial creations fuelled by wealth generated from oil. They lack layers of history which shape and characterize traditional settlements. This chapter's title evokes and responds to this by using two metaphors: the shifting nature of sand and the ambiguous perception associated with fog – cities that constantly change and transform; there is no permanence, no fixity – everything is subjected to change. Or, so it seems on the surface.

The necessary city ingredients are there – streets, high-rise buildings, landmarks – but there is a certain detachment between these urban symbols and the city's citizens as well as its surrounding barren, desert landscape, imparting a strong sense of artificiality. Nowhere is this more evident than in Abu Dhabi, the capital of the United Arab Emirates, a city which owes its very existence to oil. It is currently entering a fifth phase in its urban development, continuing a process that began in 1962 with the first commercial extraction of oil and which continued until 2004 (figure 10.2). This was the year that Sheikh Zayed, its ruler, died. He is credited with transforming Abu Dhabi from a provincial backwater to a modern city. Yet his reluctance to fully open Abu Dhabi to international investment prevented it from becoming global – unlike its 'noisy' neighbour Dubai. This is set to change, however, as the current phase of its urban development is set to unleash a financial windfall generated from oil, as well as extensive overseas investment. Among the visible manifestations of this are high-rise buildings, a newly refurbished Corniche and of course 'mega-projects'.

This chapter traces the history of Abu Dhabi's urban development – its

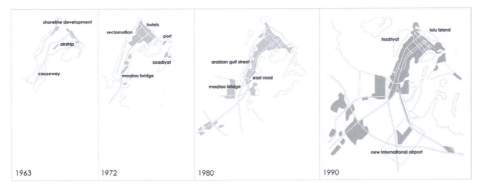

Figure 10.2. Abu Dhabi's growth from 1963 to the late 1990s.

transformation and metamorphosis. There are obvious difficulties in constructing such a narrative. For the most part, studies in this region focus on its history (e.g. Halliday, 2002; Heard-Bey, 1982; Maitra and Al-Hajji, 2001). Other writings are travellers' accounts (Thesiger, 1991; O'Brien, 1977; Raban, 1979) or depictions by political residents (Trench, 1994). There are a few studies dealing with its urban environment such as Unwin (1982) who examined the formation of town plans in the UAE; others looked at the general development of urban planning in the region (e.g. Melamid (1980)). Written mostly from a geographical perspective such studies tend to focus on what Fuccaro (2001) called a 'macro-level' of urbanism. They do not constitute a substantive urban discourse by being tied to a larger theoretical framework. Furthermore, most are quite dated – recent developments, the extent to which Abu Dhabi is attempting to globalize, have not been researched at all. It is here that examining 'artificial' cities such as Abu Dhabi may prove particularly useful. Recent global city theory has moved towards establishing uniqueness and differences rather than similarities, among cities. Some have described this as globalization from below, a transnational paradigm – in short establishing a connection between global processes and local lives.[1] The very recent urbanization process in the region has allowed for the emergence and intersection of various localities with global orientation, thus Abu Dhabi may offer some useful lessons for the current debate on global and/or transnational cities.

With that in mind, this chapter will attempt to develop a more substantive discourse by relying on these historical narratives and complementing them with first hand accounts provided by locals (e.g. Al-Fahim, 1995) as well as media accounts (both local and international). Thus the first section will deal with the city's history from 1761 to 1962. The second section will investigate its contemporary developments – from 1962 to the present – relying on official reports from planning authorities (e.g. Abu Dhabi Municipality Report, 2003) as well as research centres (e.g. the Oxford Business Group, 2006). In addition to these sources, aerial photographs will be used to study the city's morphology and its growth with the objective of understanding its current urban form. This part, by its very nature and given the dearth of urban studies in the region, is general and aims at providing an overview. Furthermore, it paves the way for the chapter's third section, titled 'Spaces of Exclusion', which will provide an in-depth examination of two case studies – the Central Market project and the Saadiyat Island – seen as being representative of the city's current effort to globalize. An argument will be made that these constitute spaces responding to what David Harvey (2006) calls 'geographies of exclusion' – essentially catering to a wider capitalist context. A conclusion will situate these developments within the current debate on global cities.

It is perhaps necessary before discussing Abu Dhabi, to establish the extent in which it differs from its neighbour Dubai – even though this may in and of itself constitute a separate area of study. Abu Dhabi, a relatively obscure and for many Westerners exotic place,[2] is now trying to emerge from the shadow of its sister city Dubai. It is quite telling that until recently highway signs leading from Al-Ain and Dubai, in addition to indicating remaining distance to Abu Dhabi had to ascertain that it also is the 'Capital of the UAE' – a reminder of the city's position within the federation which is somehow lost under the constant media attention devoted to Dubai. Differences between the two cities are quite striking: Dubai has an established historic centre, is cosmopolitan, liberal, and forms a trading hub between East and West. Abu Dhabi, on the other hand, lacks any significant historic centre (or structure), is conservative and lacks the liberal entertainment facilities of its rival. Furthermore, Dubai aims at a global audience and Abu Dhabi seemed – until recently – to be looking primarily to be a regional centre. One of the main differences is that unlike Dubai, there is no merchant tradition. Based on a nomadic way of life Abu Dhabians had limited exposure to the outside. Furthermore, while Dubai's development was guided by its merchant families (see Al-Sayegh, 1986), in Abu Dhabi there is a strong history of state intervention (see Davidson, 2007). Sheikh Shakhbut (ruler from 1928 to 1966) was an extreme manifestation of this trend as will be discussed below. And while his successor, Sheikh Zayed (ruler from 1966 to 2004) began a process of modernization this was held back by what one might describe as the city's conservative roots. In fact contemporary developments could be understood within this context – a conflict between a desire to modernize while still harking back to the old ways of the Bedouin (something perfectly illustrated in Munif's second book *The Trench*).

Looking at population numbers will also show some striking differences. Dubai's population according to the latest census (Tedad, 2005) is 1.2 million, while Abu Dhabi's is 600,000. Locals' representation in Dubai ranges from 5 to 12 per cent, while in Abu Dhabi the percentage tends to be higher – it is officially 21 per cent. Estimates of growth in Dubai suggest that the population will increase to 3 million by 2015; in Abu Dhabi the number is not expected to rise beyond 800,000. Visitors to the former are expected to be 15 million per year, whereas the latter is planning for 3 million.[3] The total built up area in Dubai is expected to reach 1000 km^2 by 2015 (Elsheshtawy, 2006b) against 400 km^2 for Abu Dhabi (Abu Dhabi Municipality Report, 2003). Thus, the growth of Abu Dhabi while still quite phenomenal is not – according to these figures – anything like the scale of Dubai, perhaps precluding the common perception of a competition.

Thus, while these comparisons are always made they do belie a few misconceptions and the fact that both cities are engaged in what one might call a symbiotic relationship. Dubai's boom, for example, would not be possible without the wealth of its neighbour, and Abu Dhabi is using some of Dubai's real-estate strategies for its own developments (Davidson, 2005). Yet Abu Dhabi is also engaged in a series of constructions (and demolitions) through which it is trying to (re)claim its title as the region's centre. However, its historical background – essentially a temporary shelter for nomadic residents and subsequently a fishing and pearling village – as well as its multiple players and decision-makers has not, until recently, led to a coherent urban strategy or direction. An examination of the city's urban character suggests a certain reluctance to become fully global and to engage the region (it never claimed to become another Singapore). Rather it aims at being the country's administrative and political centre without sacrificing its traditional (and conservative) roots. At the same time it is trying to become modern – and in turn global – as well. This paradox has resulted in a series of projects currently underway (and some completed) illustrating this struggle and ambivalence which this chapter aims at unearthing.

Origins and History: 1761–1962

*This was Mooran as it had been since the beginning of earthly time, but when the doctor arrived there for the first time he saw only a cluster of continuous mud houses. Except for the Rawdh Palace and the emirate building, no building could be distinguished from any other… Mooran's neighborhoods were tortuous and overlapping, their narrow streets crowded with dust, children and flies… Mooran was inhabited by Bedouin, and though some had settled, they kept their Bedouin way of life. Camels roamed the small squares and were tied by the doorways, tents were set up by the mud room… Even after the oil had begun to flow, and ships started arriving daily at Harran to offload tons of cargo every hour, Mooran was barely affected; **she still waited for rain that never came, for caravans that had lost their way**.*
Abdulrahman Munif, *The Trench* (Cities of Salt) (my emphasis), p. 21

The city of Abu Dhabi, shaped like an elongated triangle, is situated on Abu Dhabi Island on the Arab Gulf coastline extending to the mainland and neighbouring islands (figure 10.3). Residential clusters date back to 1761, when Bedouins, the Beni Yas, who were settled in an inland oasis, moved to the coastline looking for better living conditions. The Beni Yas were one of the principal tribes of the Arabian Gulf and resided in Al Dhafrah, in the interior, tending their flocks and herds. But some individuals, reduced to poverty through the loss of their cattle, migrated to the Gulf Coast between Dubai and the island of Abu Dhabi. The area was uninhabited as it was presumed to have no water (Maitra and Al-Hajji, 2001). Their living conditions were described by British traveller William Thesiger

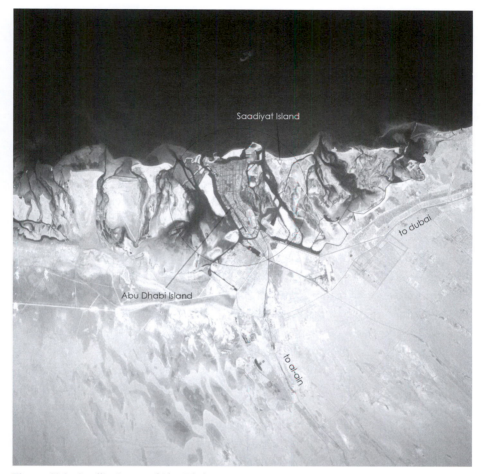

Figure 10.3. Satellite image of Abu Dhabi.

(1991), who notes that homes were rectangular cabins made from palm fronds – also known as *barasti*. These cabins were enclosed by a high fence and inhabited by one family.

Towards the close of the eighteenth century the threat of the Wahhabi forces on Saudi Arabia forced the tribe to consider moving their headquarters. Thus, in 1761, the tribe's leader, Sheikh Dhiyab bin Isa led his people to Abu Dhabi, which at that time had 20 *barasti* huts. The presence of water in the settlement became a significant factor in attracting more people and within 2 years there were more than 400 houses.[4] The village grew rapidly and became a permanent settlement devoted to fishing and pearling. The only visible landmark was the ruler's fort built of stone which contrasted sharply with the surrounding huts. The reason behind the sub-standard conditions imposed on these houses is that the ruler wanted to exercise effective control over his subjects; building in stone would make them too independent.

An Abu Dhabi Municipality report on the city's planning in these early stages of its existence notes that in 1793, Sheikh Shakhbout bin Dhiyab, moved his headquarters from Maria Oasis to Abu Dhabi Island – effectively making it the capital. This was followed by the construction of the Hosn Palace – the only remaining historic structure in Abu Dhabi today. The report makes a clear effort at situating these early origins within an Islamic context, noting that the conventional Islamic elements are all there: the palace; the *souq*; the mosque; and the narrow winding roads. Such official views establish the city's Islamic credentials as it were – similar to Cairo, Baghdad, Damascus etc. However, accounts of early travellers seemingly dispute this official version – essentially describing scenes of extreme primitiveness, thus conveying a very different image.

Early accounts of life in the settlement were based on travellers' notes and visits by missionaries, which taken together comprise a fascinating view of a primitive town which lasted until the early 1960s. Thesiger (1991) on a visit in the 1950s notes that a '… small castle dominated the small dilapidated town which stretched along the shore. There were a few palms, and near them was a well where we watered our camels'. Furthermore, 'the ground around us was dirty, covered with the refuse of sedentary humanity' (*Ibid.*, p. 263). He describes a visit to a 'dilapidated' house near a market where he and his companions stayed for twenty days. The market itself was a place where they 'sat cross-legged in the small shops, gossiping and drinking more coffee' after which they 'wandered along the beach and watched the dhows being caulked and treated with shark-oil to prepare them for the pearling season, the children bathing in the surf, and the fishermen landing their catch' (*Ibid.*, pp. 265–266). Mohamed Al-Fahim in his 1995 biography *From Rags to Riches* writes that the houses were clustered together for security reasons, in addition to providing warmth during the winter months. Furthermore, the houses were built away from the sea, presumably for protection from rising tides. The population at that time was estimated to be around 1,500 – a significant decline from its early origin, attributed to a decline in the pearling trade.

The turning point of Abu Dhabi's history came in 1953 when Abu Dhabi Marine Areas Ltd (ADMA) obtained offshore oil concessions resulting in royalty payments.[5] Expectations were aroused that Abu Dhabi would be eventually transformed from a Bedouin Sheikhdom to a modern state.[6] The ruler at that time was Sheikh Shakhbout, popularly known as a 'stubborn conservative' who 'refused to part with any of his money' (Halliday, 2002). Other observers, such as Donald Hawley, noted that one reason for this conservatism is his nostalgia for the traditional Arab way of life (Hawley, 1970).

A few developmental steps were taken towards improving living conditions such as the construction of a new school which was opened in 1958. However the ruler expressed a clear desire not to engage foreign teachers. Furthermore, when the British political officer at the time, Edward Henderson, prepared a map of the town, he wanted all names to be written in Arabic. In addition he envisioned Abu Dhabi as having an architectural style that would be suitable to its tradition, unlike American buildings which he had seen during a tour of the country (Maitra and Al-Hajji, 2001). However the city remained in a remarkable state of underdevelopment. Bernard Burrows, the Gulf political resident described the 'muddy' conditions of the road from the political agency to the ruler's palace, to the extent that his Land Rover got stuck in the sand (Burrows, 1990). Aside from the political agent only a few people had cars. Water was still being hauled using goat skin bags. According to Al-Fahim, in 1961 the ruler took an extended leave, leaving Sheikh Zayed (the future president) in charge, who promptly built Abu Dhabi's first mud road – extending from what is now known as the Maqtaa bridge to the palace. Aside from these sporadic efforts, conditions did not improve. He offers a remarkable depiction:

> We lived in the eighteenth century while the rest of the world, even the rest of our neighbors, had advanced into the twentieth. We had nothing to offer visitors, we had nothing to export, we had no importance to the outside world whatsoever. Poverty, illiteracy, poor health, a high rate of mortality all plagued us well into the 1960s. (Al-Fahim, 1995, p. 88)

The discovery of oil and the signing of concession agreements initiated a process that would transform what was in essence a provincial backwater, a collection of mud huts, into a recognizable urban entity. This process, however, was not immediate and took some time as will be discussed in the next section.

Urban Developments: 1962–2004

Once, Harran had been a city of fishermen and travelers coming home, but now it belonged to no one; its people were featureless, of all varieties and yet strangely unvaried. They were all of humanity and yet no one at all, an assemblage of languages, accents, colors and religions. The riches in the city, and underneath it, were unique in the world, yet no one in Harran was rich or had any hope of becoming so. All of them were in a race, but none knew where to or for how long. It was like a beehive, like a graveyard. They even greeted one another differently from people in any other place – a man greeted others and then looked searchingly in their faces, as if afraid that something might happen between his greeting and their reply.
Abdulrahman Munif, The Trench (Cities of Salt), p.162

Munif's depiction of the fictional city of Harran is quite typical of the alienation and the sense of loss accompanying massive urban transformation within cities in the Arabian Peninsula. To understand this fully it is necessary to provide a general overview of the main phases of urban development which occurred in Abu Dhabi. A superficial view would divide these phases into pre-oil and oil, however the process was quite complex and tied to a variety of factors, one of them of course oil. But other factors range from the personal (a ruler's whims and personal preferences) to the global (being part of a capitalist scheme). The Abu Dhabi Municipality report states that there are four main phases: 1962–1965; 1966–1968; 1969–1988; and 1988–2004. A fifth phase, 2004 to the present will be added to reflect the dramatic shift in the city's development following the death of its ruler,

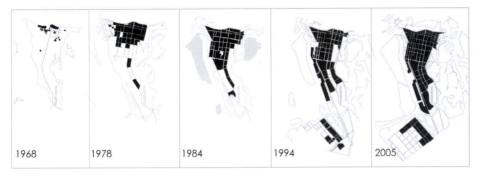

1968   1978   1984   1994   2005

Figure 10.4. Abu Dhabi's changing urban morphology from 1968 to 2005.

Sheikh Zayed (figure 10.4). The following is a brief outline of each phase, based on the previously mentioned report, but also relying on archival material from *The New York Times* which provides a first hand account of changes taking place in the 1960s and early 1970s; in addition literary narratives will be used to add a human dimension, showing how the city was perceived by ordinary people – Westerners and locals. To that end Mohamed Al-Fahim's excellent biography *From Rags to Riches* will be used, in addition to Edna O'Brien's poetic accounts of Abu Dhabi in its early urban stages in *Arabian Days*, and Jonathan Raban's inquisitive observations in *Arabia through the Looking Glass.*

Phase 1: 1962–1965: Emerging from a Provincial Backwater

Following the first exports of oil in 1962, Abu Dhabi started a much awaited urban development process beginning with the establishment of the municipality which was primarily concerned with the improvement of living conditions – mainly provision of adequate drinking water supplies and public health. Sheikh Shakhbout was reluctant to engage in any large-scale projects. While consultants were hired for the development of a masterplan he is said to have remarked that '... this is Paris! We don't want a Paris in Abu Dhabi!' (Trench, 1994, p. 260). Commissioned from Halcrow & Co., the plan had a series of features which included: north facing buildings; a road network which was not based on straight lines; and raising the ground level through dredging and reclamation. In addition, the report also recommended the removal of all buildings except for the Hosn Palace (Abu Dhabi Municiaplity, 2003). Projects initiated at that time included two water distillation plants, a few schools, a power station and a basic road system. The only hospital available in the emirate of Abu Dhabi was in the nearby town of Al-Ain. The population at that time was about 4,000. Accordingly Abu Dhabi was '... still a tribal society existing at subsistence level' (Trench, 1994, p. 248).[7]

At that time a Lebanese family built the Abu Dhabi Beach Hotel on the beach next to the present Sheraton Hotel. Its relatively distant location from the city at that time, as well as its high prices prevented locals from going there. It was used primarily by oil company representatives. Within this early phase of Abu

Dhabi's urbanization, the ruler was still adamant about preserving a traditional life style. For example, he refused to generate electricity, with the exception of the palace which was lit using portable electrical generators, making it look like 'Disneyland' (Al-Fahim, 1995, p. 116). As a further hindrance to development, in 1961 he imposed a ban on any new construction; business ventures had to get permission which was not always forthcoming; he also disliked non Abu Dhabian Arab merchants (Davidson, 2007). As a result the town remained in a persistent state of underdevelopment – with many residents leaving for nearby Dubai which was flourishing. Recognizing the difficulties posed by Shakhbout, Sheikh Zayed in 1966, with British help, removed his brother and was installed as Abu Dhabi's ruler – ushering in a new phase of the city's urban development.

Phase 2: 1966–1968: Creating a City: Contrasting Developments

Following the succession of Sheikh Zayed as ruler of Abu Dhabi the process of urban development continued. Modifications were made to the 1962 Halcrow plan, which was a task assigned to Arabicon Consultants, under the supervision of an Egyptian planner, Abd al-Rahman Makhlouf in 1968.[8] Accordingly, main roads in the northern part of the island were designed in straight lines. Also, a series of public works projects were constructed such as governmental buildings, airport, desalination and electricity plants, and the Maqtaa bridge. The municipality report points out that these improvements aimed at: 'Promoting interest of higher authorities to maintain the Arab Islamic architectural style of public and main buildings of the city' (Abu Dhabi Municipality, 2003, p. 47). This period also featured extensive greening; dredging a canal around the island; allocation of certain areas for development such as the Mussafah area; sports city; the international airport, Raha beach, residential townships, and the wave breaker. Al-Fahim (1995, p. 136) describes a scene of bustling activity, noting that a 'whole city was being created from scratch'. *Barasti* houses, where many people had lived, were being torn down, and people were re-housed in newly constructed homes. To further development, the ruler gave each Abu Dhabian three (and in some instances four) pieces of land, to be used for residential, commercial and industrial purposes.[9] Following the abject poverty of the Shakhbout era, the sudden release of oil funds resulted in an urban scene that was quite captivating – filled with contrasting images of Bedouin primitiveness and a modern lifestyle, which captured the attention of the international press.

A number of reporters were dispatched to describe the changes that were taking place. A typical account by *The New York Times*' Gloria Emerson mentions that '… The big, thick, glooming banks make a mockery out of the squat, peeling buildings next door'. The airport terminal '… consists of two bare rooms where passengers cannot sit or find a glass of water'.[10] It is also noted that the ruler, Sheikh Zayed, strongly influenced by the British, began to display an attitude of tolerance towards foreigners – officially opening a church, for example.[11] In another article she writes that '… the town of Abu Dhabi itself is not more than a village built on sand, where men squat to urinate in the streets and where the roads are full of lumps and holes'. She also notes that there are only two hotels in the city, there is no cinema and restaurants are only in the two hotels. Thus, 'Europeans must learn to waste time'.[12]

Phase 3: 1969–1988: Settling the Nomad

The time frame from the late 1960s and early 1970s to the 1980s saw a surge in construction activity and the final emergence of Abu Dhabi from a small fishing village to an actual city, recognizable internationally, which is also symptomatic of an 'instant' city whose existence is derived from its oil wealth. This is also associated with the emergence of the United Arab Emirates as a political entity in 1971 after seven emirates decided on a confederation. Furthermore, a decision was made to build a permanent capital between Abu Dhabi and Dubai, however the former was designated as a temporary capital further enhancing its status (Melamid, 1980).[13]

Symptomatic of the fascination with Arabia, journalists and writers flocked to the city, in an attempt to discover this new land, continuing a process that began in the 1940s with the travels of Wilfred Thesiger and others. One of them was Edna O'Brien, well known Irish writer, whose travel accounts were published in a pictorial book called *Arabian Days* in 1977. Filled with poetic depictions, encounters with locals – among them Sheikh Zayed – as well as a series of local women. Her experiences evoke a sense of wonderment, and at times bewilderment, at how those residents of the desert are coping with modernity. Pervading the text is a sense of nostalgia for an authentic Arabia that is simply not there anymore. For example she notes that 'Abu Dhabi had taken a plunge into the twentieth century' and she could not have imagined that she would see '… towers of concrete as far as the eye could see, cranes, tanks, a sense of unfinishedness as if the place had just been dropped higgledy-piggledy from the sky' (p. 30). She criticizes the fast pace of development, and the danger of being 'oblivious of the past', thus '… the illiterate have to be made literate, a breakwater built for the harbour, flats built, mobile homes hauled in, sodium streetlights installed, a traffic system and a traffic sense developed, kerbstones put down, paving slabs, polythene greenhouses, feed drips for the trees' (p. 147).

Continuing along similar themes, journalist Edward Lee writes that Abu Dhabi is in '… the midst of a construction boom that makes the capital look like an American beachfront development'.[14] Another writer Edward Sheehan argues that it is 'a paradigm of instant development' – noting that it consists of 'boulevards of Parisian scope and a corniche that rivals Alexandria's crisscross sand as white as moonlight; cranes and scaffolds are more numerous than trees. Here is a salt flat, there a city dump; blink and see a bank, a school, a hospital, a Hilton hotel'. Anticipating current migratory problems he observes that 'the streets murmur with Omanis and Iranians, with Indians and Baluchis; they are the labor force and many of them live in hovels'.[15] Others observe with a hint of sarcasm (and racism) that this '… is a culture starting from scratch, from scratching in mere sand'.[16] Jonathan Raban, journalist/writer, in his 1979 *Arabia through the Looking Glass* describes the city in a chapter titled 'Temporary People' as 'conscienceless' and that it 'had the appearance of something obtained ready-made in bulk' (p. 120). This sense of newness, seen in 'shimmering towers' represents for the Abu Dhabian, according to Raban, innocence and the wide possibility of urban life. He further delves into the nature of its residents, their 'bedu' character, and says that this constitutes the main fabric, the infrastructure, of the city regulating life in all its aspects – albeit hidden. Thus he poignantly illustrates the temporality of Abu Dhabi's urbanity.

As these accounts illustrate, one of the main problems facing planners was the settling of nomads/bedu who were used to a lifestyle that was quite different from what was being offered – a Western-style way of living, and most importantly a way of life that is based on permanent settlement.[17] This was difficult since the bedu life 'had been evolved as a means of regulating a society composed of wanderers and migrants' (*Ibid.*, p. 146). Sheikh Zayed's aim was to lure these 'nomadic tribes that used to roam this barren Arab sheikdom' to governmental jobs, trade, farming and of course a booming oil industry.[18]

A key figure at that time was the Director General of Town Planning, Abdel Rahman Makhlouf, an Egyptian who arrived in 1968, after starting town planning in Saudi Arabia in the city of Jeddah. Among his achievements was the design of a 'national house', which aims to help the Bedouin adapt to urban life. It consists of a large one-storey structure of concrete blocks with open and closed spaces 'suited to Bedouin traditions'. Each has two bedrooms, a kitchen, bathroom, garden, courtyard and other open spaces. A wall hides the women's quarters. In early depictions of these developments a Bedouin boy notes that 'We love our new house because it's big and we can play outside like we did in the desert'.[19] Another Makhlouf project was the modern *souq* or market (to be discussed in more detail later in the chapter). Sheikh Zayed had a strong influence on these early phases of development with the primary aim of settling the Bedouin who were used to a traditional migratory existence.[20]

Some of the main elements of the city, recognizable today, originated at that time. In 1969 the central area project was introduced which specified that the height of buildings should be between eight and ten storeys; the construction of four markets (*souqs*) – also known as the central market; and the development of a cultural centre around the Hosn Palace designed by The Architects Collaborative (TAC)[21] who won an open competition for the project in 1973 (completed in 1981). The prominent site shares the block with the historic old palace and is across from the Grand Mosque. Its architecture is a response to the conservative climate present at that time – an attempt to re-interpret traditional 'Islamic' architecture – in many ways reflecting similar trends in the region. Building façades are plain with small window openings; where large areas of glass are used, deep arcades provide shelter from the sun.

The 1973 Egyptian-led war against Israel resulted in an increase in oil price as is well known, further spurring growth within the region. As a result, according to Al-Fahim (1995), the price of land rocketed, and the building code for maximum height was changed to thirteen storeys. The city also saw an expansion of its luxury hotels which included a Hilton and Ramada, in addition to plans for an Intercontinental.[22] The last was to be, according to the wishes of the ruler, a 'tall, prestigious and eminent building' (Frampton and Khan, 2000). The design was completed and the hotel opened in 1981. Mostly modernist in appearance, it consists of a twenty floor tower, 'local' elements are added such as 'screens, coloured tile work, and calligraphic ornamentation'. However, constructing such a large number of buildings within a short time span led to fears of overdevelopment. Thus, a slowdown began in 1977 when many high-rise buildings were completed, causing an excess supply in the housing sector, which had around 15,000 empty apartments – 'to let' signs were visible everywhere. To counter this Sheikh Zayed declared a freeze on new residential and office buildings. Furthermore, recognizing the problems associated with giving land to locals, the Khalifa Committee was established in 1976 – whose role will be examined in more detail below – with the purpose of administering and granting land to nationals (Al-Fahim, 1995). There was also a concern about the oversupply of port facilities in the Gulf area, and in turn plans for port expansion at Abu Dhabi were reduced. However, the economy recovered, and extensive work of land reclamation and waterfront development, which started in the 1970s, continued unabated increasing the original size of the island to 6,000 hectares – or 60 km^2 (in 1994 the total area became 9,400 hectares, or 94 km^2). The 1980s witnessed continuous extensive development, land reclamation and development of townships as well as major public works projects.

Phase 4: 1988–2004: The Abu Dhabi Masterplan

Given the piecemeal development which characterized the previous phase, there was a need for the development of a comprehensive masterplan (Abusham, 2005). Thus, in 1988 the Abu Dhabi Executive Council decided to implement the plan which was prepared by Abu Dhabi Town Planning department with the assistance of the UNDP and Atkins.[23] The plan comprised five main phases up to 2010. It was also called the Master Directive Plan for Abu Dhabi and its Environs – 1990–2010 (figure 10.5). Anticipating rapid growth, and given the limited area of the island, the plan recommended several areas of 'extensions'. These included the development of the islands surrounding the city which number 200 – particularly Saadiyat and Hadriyat. Further growth towards the mainland was suggested along two axes: highways leading to Dubai and Al-Ain. However, significant modifications were made to the plan. Particularly, the development of Saadiyat has been put on hold, although the report notes that it '… is a natural extension of urbanization in Abu Dhabi island'. The same applies to Hadriyat, which represents

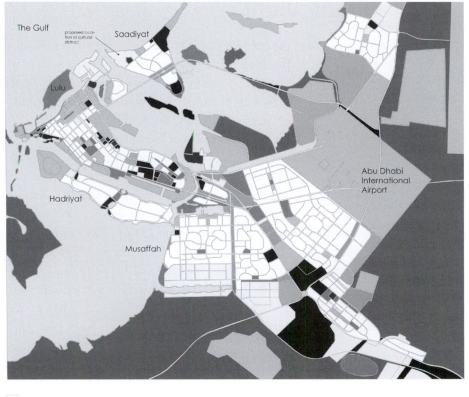

The Gulf

proposed location of cultural district

Saadiyat

Lulu

Hadriyat

Musaffah

Abu Dhabi
International
Airport

Residential

Special Residential/Palace

Mixed Commercial/Residential

Institutional/Community Uses

Industry/Warehousing

Master Directive Plan
1990–2010

Figure 10.5. Abu Dhabi's Master Plan 1990–2010 (now modified to Abu Dhabi Master Plan 2030).

the natural expansion of urbanization from the western side.[24] The masterplan also recommended the conversion of Mussaffah area from an industrial to a residential zone. Furthermore, the direction of growth would be limited to the Dubai and Al-Ain axes (Abu Dhabi Municipality & Town Planning Department, 2003, p. 94). While the plan had significant impact on the overall growth of the city in the 1980s and 1990s, other factors contributed to the urban character of Abu Dhabi shaping its general appearance.

One of these was the Khalifa Committee, named after Sheikh Zayed's son and the current ruler of Abu Dhabi and the UAE, an institution set up to distribute state owned land to Emirati citizens, and subsequently developing the land on behalf of those citizens (households with a male head). The committee was responsible for building a large part of the city of Abu Dhabi. Thus, according to the Oxford Business Group (2006) over 200 apartment blocks were constructed every year in the 1980s and 1990s. While these 'were often not very inspired in their architecture', they did adequately address housing needs for the emirate's developing population.

The current urban form of the city was strongly influenced by this policy since plots handed out were small, resulting in the construction of towers which are particularly evident in the city's centre. Some 95 per cent of plots in Abu Dhabi range between approximately 25 m x 15 m and 30 m x 30 m, occupied by multistorey buildings with an average height of twenty floors. The overall effect is a stereotyped repetition of buildings with no sense of urbanism (Antoniou, 1998). Mixed-use developments such as malls, schools, entertainment and recreational facilities were therefore rare. This centralized process – the committee was responsible for the design, contracting builders, as well as receiving a share of the income – resulted in the uniform and repetitive appearance of buildings characterizing the city today (Oxford Business Group, 2006). The report further notes that this system ensured that Abu Dhabi nationals received housing, land and a major income stream, as well as keeping the emirate's property firmly out of the hands of foreign residents – a policy that on the one hand Emiratized a segment previously dominated by Lebanese, Syrian and Egyptian businesses, while on the other hand 'ensured that the armies of expatriate workers ... were prevented from putting down any serious roots' (*Ibid.*, pp. 157–158). However, one negative outcome for such a policy was a high turnover of tenants, as there is little incentive to sell a house or apartment, and an overall 'shabby' appearance of buildings due to poor maintenance. As a result of these rapid modernization efforts one of the characteristic sights in the city centre is the contrast between crumbling 1970s and 1980s style building and recently constructed ultramodern towers (figure 10.6).

Figure 10.6. Central area of Abu Dhabi contrasting developments from the 1960s with recent additions.

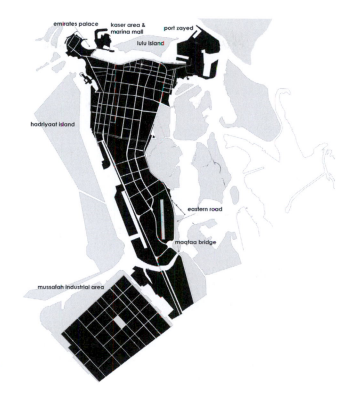

Figure 10.7. Abu Dhabi's current built-up area.

The city's urban character is characterized by wide grid-pattern roads, and high-density tower blocks (figure 10.7). On the northerly end of the island, where the population density is highest, the main streets are lined with 20-storey towers. Inside this rectangle of towers is a normal grid pattern of roads with lower density buildings (2-storey villas or 6-storey low-rise buildings). Away from the high-density areas, land is primarily used for government buildings and private villas. Principal thoroughfares are The Corniche, Airport Road, Sheikh Zayed, Hamdan and Khalifa. Many streets are known for specialized businesses that tend to cluster on them. Hamdan is the main shopping street, Khalifa is lined with banks, Al Najdha is known for hardware stores, Defense is filled with mobile telephone shops and Sheikh Zayed (also known as Electra) is the computer street.

This phase also saw the construction of 'quirky' projects characterized by an exaggerated scale and a peculiar choice of architectural style. Chief among these is the Emirates Palace Hotel, heralded as the most expensive hotel ever built (figure 10.8).[25] Located on the city's Corniche, its detailing is in a neo-orientalist style, which is dominated by an assortment of domes and lavish 'Islamic' decorative patterns. Along these same lines is the Grand Mosque, a project initiated by Sheikh Zayed. Plagued by construction problems and a halt in construction, it is currently being completed. Massive in scale, it is using a Mughal (Indian) style and is located at the entrance of Abu Dhabi, next to the Maqtaa bridge. These projects underlie a certain ambivalence – a desire to set the city apart from Dubai by constructing monuments that reflect some sort of Islamic renaissance. These remained singular

Figure 10.8. The Emirates Palace Hotel.

projects however – and while they are significant landmarks within the city, the following phase is set to change this.

Phase 5: 2004 to the Present – Going Global: The Age of the Mega-projects and Star Architects

According to Mohamed Abusham, chief urban planner at Abu Dhabi Municiaplity, after the preparation of the Abu Dhabi Comprehensive Development Plan in 1988 the actual rate of growth of urban development was so immense that it surpassed all its expectations and proposals. The UAE in general and Abu Dhabi Emirate in particular witnessed a significant urban development that leapt outside the framework predicted for 2010. This factor coupled with a change in leadership led to a complete reworking of the original plan (Abusham, 2005).

The year 2004 witnessed the death of Sheikh Zayed and the transfer of power to his son Khalifa. In addition a number of cabinet changes saw the introduction of young, Western educated ministers – most belonging to the ruling family. Intent on transforming Abu Dhabi into a global player a number of changes were introduced which would significantly impact the cities growth and urban form. Chief among these is a change in the property ownership law, allowing the sale of government granted land by nationals, as well as introducing a form of ownership by foreigners[26] – moves previously prevented by Sheikh Zayed to counter real estate speculation.[27] The generous welfare state is thus being 'corporatized and privatized'. These developments are 'expected by many industry insiders to lead to around a 25% per annum increase in construction activities over the next three years' (Oxford Business Group, 2006, p. 157).

Abu Dhabi had kept a low profile up until 2004 – investing its vast oil income through its main overseas financial arm – the Abu Dhabi Investment Authority (ADIA) (figure 10.9). According to *The Economist* (2006) it has steadily accrued wealth for the last 30 years; estimates of its size range from $200 billion to 'way north of $500 billion'. Furthermore, Abu Dhabi is witnessing an increase in capital which is due to two factors: increasing oil prices and a changing political climate which is responsible for a move home of Arab money – a 'repatriation of capital' – due to post 9/11 security measures in the West. Thus, 'phenomenal amounts of liquidity produced by the current conditions have found a welcome home in real estate' (Oxford Business Group, 2006, p. 157). Real estate accounts for about a third of the $100 billion which the emirate expects to spend on itself in the next 5 years. Projects range from entire new residential and tourist complexes to vast malls and town-sized commercial and industrial developments – as well as developing the vast number of islands surrounding the city. More recent estimates suggest that the total value of projects has reached $270 billion.[28]

Figure 10.9. Abu Dhabi Corniche with the ADIA building on the left and the Hilton Baynouna on the right.

As a way to enhance the city's appeal to foreign investors, foreign ownership will be allowed – under certain restrictions and limitations – within specially designated investment zones. These would specifically include the various islands surrounding Abu Dhabi. Other areas within the city, such as the Central Market project, are considered as well. A major difference from Dubai, however, is that ownership would only be allowed for a certain amount of time (99 years) as opposed to the freehold concept. Further enticing investors as well as tourists, a new airline has been introduced – Etihad, dubbed 'The National Airline' – with a new airport planned to open in 2010 accommodating more than 40 million passengers.[29]

Another significant development pertains to consolidation plans among these recently formed real estate companies. Four of Abu Dhabi's major property developers have teamed up to create a new company. Named as *Al Maabar*, meaning 'The Gateway', it is a joint venture between Al Qudra Real Estate, Sorouh Real Estate, Aldar Properties and Reem Investments, the four main operators in the emirate's property market. While it is nothing new for the Gulf's leading property developers to spread their wings and target major investment projects overseas, the forming of such a joint venture with the specific objective of going global is according to a research study 'a major step forward' (Oxford Business Group, 2007). Such a venture is similar to the Dubai based Dubai Holding – which includes some of the big names in the industry.

In light of these massive developments the government of Abu Dhabi announced a modified masterplan – 'Plan Abu Dhabi 2030: Urban Structure Framework Plan'.[30] Under the plan, the city is projected to grow to over three million people by 2030. A series of principles are outlined, emphasizing the city's focus on identity and sustainability (implicitly contrasting with Dubai). Thus the plan states that Abu Dhabi will be a 'contemporary expression of an Arab city' and will continue its practice of measured growth, reflecting a sustainable economy. Furthermore it 'pledges' to respect the natural environment of coastal and desert ecologies, and to manifest the role of Abu Dhabi as a capital city. Curiously – drawing lines of separation – the plan provides for large areas of new Emirati housing inspired by traditional family structures, and a diverse mix of affordable housing options for low-income (expatriate) residents. The plan specifies land uses, building heights and transport plans for the city – this will include an expansion of the business district and the creation of new business and governmental centres.

Thus, the notion of a paradigmatic shift in planning is no exaggeration. However, such efforts raise a series of issues – among them whether there is sufficient population to sustain these developments. Unlike Dubai which is planning for a 3 million population and 15 million visitors by 2015, estimates in Abu Dhabi according to the Urban Structure Framework Plan suggest that the population in 2013 will reach 1.3 million, with 3.3 million visitors. Meanwhile development plans are underway and continue unabated. For example, as of 2006, the Abu Dhabi government is demolishing eighty-five old buildings with plans to replace them with modern skyscrapers. Thus within a span of 40 years the city has been transformed quite dramatically. However, this has also led to a series of problems typical of cities in the Gulf. Among them are an acute housing shortage, an increased cost of living as well as a simmering labour problem due to lack of appropriate housing conditions. [31] While the previous sections provided a general overview of these developments, the following section will take a closer look at two projects symptomatic of Abu Dhabi's attempt to join the rank of globalizing cities: The Central Market and the cultural district in Saadiyat Island.

Case Studies: Spaces of Exclusion

*They drove the whole length of Mooran which appeared to him a harsh, repulsive city. This had been his first impression upon his arrival, though the city had changed drastically over the years and become filled with villas, with Japanese-style and English-style buildings and still others that were a mélange of styles: in hidden places, behind the wide streets and the tall new buildings, lay the low mud-houses. Broad boulevards and sweeping traffic circles had blanketed the city in the last few years; people's circumstances had changed, and so had their looks: they were fatter … he did not like this city and still was not used to it. Now as he traversed the city the brilliance of the sun showed him only dark clods of hard, unruly earth that throbbed with hostility. **He wished that he had never come to this city. He wished he had never heard of it**.*

Abdulrahman Munif, *The Trench* (Cities of Salt), (my emphasis), pp. 430–431

Munif's narrative of a city being transformed, and in the process alienating its citizens, offers a rare look into the mindset of Arabia's citizens (even though they are fictional). Modernity created a city that no longer resonated with its occupants. Unfortunately such depictions are for the most part restricted to the realm of literature. Urban planning studies in the Gulf tend to emphasize a 'voyeuristic view from above' – to quote Michel de Certeau (1984) – where the daily, everyday life of people is simply ignored. Fuccaro (2001) argued for a shift in urban studies in the region that would place more emphasis on what she termed 'micro studies' – examining local processes that shape the form and structure of cities, which in turn would provide a more significant insight. The previous section provided an overall view. The following part aims at addressing this by situating and contextualizing these developments through two case studies – seen as representative of the changes taking place in Abu Dhabi – and taking us closer to the city as lived space.

The Case of the Central Souq: From Makhlouf to Norman Foster

One of the memorable sights for anyone visiting Abu Dhabi in the 1990s was the central market nestled between high-rise buildings in its central business district. Entering it was like encountering a different world – a *Foucaultian Heterotopia*

Figure 10.10. The central market prior to demolition. View from the pedestrian bridge.

– composed of small, informal shops, populated by low-income migrant workers – a sense of chaos contrasting sharply with the ordered appearance of its immediate context. It projected an air of provinciality and informality (figure 10.10). Ironically, in Abu Dhabi this was the only place that conveyed some sense of history and tradition even though the market was built in the early 1970s.

One could argue that this project's story captures the transformation currently underway in Abu Dhabi – in all its contradictions. It was part of a general scheme to modernize, devised by the city's town planner, the Egyptian Abd al Rahman Makhlouf. This was in 1972. Early references to the project describe it as a 'modern souq or market, built along old Arab principles of lanes, spaces, and partly covered passages'. Addressing the city's primarily nomadic population, and in an attempt to settle them within an urban entity '… each tribe was given a quota for shop space, with Sheik Zayed checking the list'.[32] Even though references were made to Arab-Islamic principles, the market is laid out along strictly geometric lines, following the general grid pattern of the city. This seeming contradiction caught the eyes of some Western observers.

Jonathan Raban (1979) in his account of Abu Dhabi in the 1970s uses the *souq* as a narrative device anchoring his experience in the city – characterized by restlessness, anomie, etc. The symptoms of decay, even squalor become signs that there are elements of life in an 'artificial' city such as Abu Dhabi. His first depiction of the market notes its generic qualities and that it could be home in 'Levittown'. Its straight geometry and grid-like arrangement are lifeless. However, its inhabitants with their shops and stalls have taken over the space and ignored 'all the architects design on them' (p. 125). In one particular insightful observation he writes:

… and under one umbrella an old man with a mouthful of gold teeth was crouched over the Koran. The book, which looked older than he was, was coming apart in his hands. Its pages were brittle and grey; the oldest, grimiest, most battered object in the whole of Abu Dhabi. (*Ibid.*)

The space is thus subjected to a certain level of informality – enhancing its appeal for 'Western' sensibilities. While the familiarity – or banality – of the architecture is evident, the arched backs of the praying inhabitants, and the old man gave the architecture 'a fierce ironical twist' and thus the *souk*'s 'remoteness was accentuated rather than diminished by the banality of its appearance' (*Ibid.*, p. 128).

The project remained a major landmark not just for foreign tourists and travel writers but also for residents of Abu Dhabi. Popular accounts describe it as being as 'old as Abu Dhabi, an intrinsic part of the city'.[33] For many tourists coming to the area the place was reminiscent of a *souq*, conveying an Arabic atmosphere. Some of the shops which sold everything from utensils to spices, etc. were considered among the oldest in the area. The Abu Dhabi bazaar – as it was sometimes called – cuts across the capital's two main streets, of Hamdan and Khalifa. It housed more than 700 shops selling a variety of consumer items, in an area covering roughly 50,000 square metres (figure 10.11). Most of the shop owners are from Pakistan, India and Iran, giving the marketplace '… more an Asian identity than a local aura' according to one observer. The architectural character of the *souq* is described as 'shabby two-storey buildings and tiny shops' – in essence suggesting that it is time for the *souq* to be demolished. While it did serve its purpose in the early days of the city – when it looked 'like a giant modern market place monopolizing shopping in

Figure 10.11. A storefront in the central market.

Figure 10.12. General view of the central market surrounded by the high-rises of Abu Dhabi's central district.

the city' – it is now a 'dwarf amidst surrounding skyscrapers and modern shopping complexes' (figure 10.12).[34]

Thus, the image of the *souq* is incompatible with the new, modern Abu Dhabi. But, architectural criticism aside, such places have qualities that go beyond the physical, evoking memories, and suggesting a sense of rootedness. Longtime residents would associate their very arrival in Abu Dhabi with the market – a place for buying cheap merchandise as well as a hang-out.[35] However, the sense of a curiosity prevailed – the very fact that such a market with its chaotic appearance would not fit with the neat and orderly image that officials would like to project. Plans for renewal and removal were under consideration for some time but it was not until 2002 that authorities finally decided to build a new market in 'traditional Arab and Islamic design'.[36]

This initial announcement, and subsequently the proposed replacement, did not seek a radical departure from the existing layout. Officials were suggesting that '… the new market will retain its traditional atmosphere', or that it will be 'almost a facial copy of the old one'.[37] Furthermore, the new market will retain the same number of shops, even trying to keep them all in the same spot. Needless to say that such assurances did not help in alleviating the sense of loss that was felt among shop owners as well as shoppers with some going so far as to argue that '… the country will lose something if it is demolished'.[38] A watch dealer insightfully notes that '… this market is deeply associated with the memories of who first came to Abu Dhabi. It is history and culture and I don't think it will be easily forgotten'.[39]

Urban renewal projects are of course a hallmark of modernist planning principles occurring all over the world in different forms and disguises, always eliciting similar responses of loss (one can go as far back as Jane Jacobs's criticism of urban renewal in New York in the 1960s or Herbert Gans's depiction of the North Enders in Boston). What is striking about this particular project, however, is how it has developed from a simple re-incarnation of an old, architecturally un-inspiring structure, to a world-class shopping destination.

Initially, Abu Dhabi Municipality awarded the project for the new market to the Arab Engineering Bureau (AEB), a major multi-disciplinary consulting firm based in the Gulf. Its Abu Dhabi branch, Al Arabi Engineering Bureau, was supposed to be carrying out the design and supervision work. Architects at the firm were quick to affirm the historical character of the *souq* ('The old *souq* is Abu Dhabi history') and that every attempt will be made to 'rebuild or reconstruct history'. As a further bonus, the new project will be 'similar to those ancient bazaars in Damascus and Cairo as it has Islamic and Arabian structural designs that contain arcades, old lanterns, alleys and traditional shop lines'.[40] The rather contradictory nature of these statements is never questioned – the original *souq* a repetitive, modernist arrangement of shops is equivalent to old Arab-Islamic bazaars!

Aside from these historical musings, the project was in these initial stages still viewed mostly in humanistic terms. The small, intimate scale will be retained; it is contrasted with the high-rise towers and so on. A municipality official emphasizes the human nature of the project and that it will be an 'attempt to restore life to the heart of Abu Dhabi and resurrect old memories that are being obliterated by rapid changes and modernity'.[41] As such the new *souq* will be built to preserve these goals – perhaps also alluding to rapid changes taking place, reflecting some sort of anxiety among local residents.

From the initial announcement of a new market in 2002 until the old *souq*'s demolition in 2005 a series of newspaper articles periodically documented shopkeepers' and shoppers' moods, eliciting reactions and more or less playing into this notion of loss, and that Abu Dhabi is losing an 'historical landmark'. Plans or images for the project were never made public. However, initial plans by the Arabi Engineering Bureau were scrapped and a competition was held for a larger scheme. The winning design by award winning architect, Jordanian Rasem Badran, shows a three-storey inward oriented structure, in addition to a five-storey building. The project displays a cultural sensibility by incorporating elements of what is considered Gulf-Arab architecture: a requisite non-functioning wind-tower; window patterns modelled after reconstructed houses and a colour scheme that evokes mud-brick buildings.[42] Since Abu Dhabi had no significant urban tradition to begin with these elements resemble historic buildings in Dubai in their architectural detailing. Overall, however, the project did not show the breadth, scope or ambition that characterizes similar ventures in Dubai. Rather, it still was relatively conservative, fitting in with the overall image of the city – slow development and avoidance of commercialization.

However, the project was put on hold and no significant effort at demolition took place. In 2004 after the death of Sheikh Zayed, Abu Dhabi embarked on a significant construction effort entering a new phase of urbanization as outlined above. This stage witnessed the destruction of many well known landmarks in the city such as the GCC roundabout, the Volcano fountain and clock tower – the only reminder that was left was the *souq*. This was set to change however. Among the many development players entering the scene was government owned AL DAR – modelled after similar ventures in Dubai such as Emaar or Nakheel. They replaced the municipality as the principal developer for the site. Things moved quickly once the replacement was made, resulting in an announcement about the cancellation of the previous scheme and a complete reworking of the design, and the issuance of eviction notices for shopkeepers – made more urgent by a fire which partially destroyed the *souq*. Parallel to this, newspaper articles promptly began to suggest that the new project will be a 'gleaming showpiece for the UAE's constant push toward modernization', and that it is 'part of a broader modernization scheme', although it is quickly noted that '… a lot of people are quite happy with the old, burnt, dusty, permanently dying souq this city currently has'.[43]

Figure 10.13. An area of the central market which was destroyed by fire and a store-front.

Figure 10.14. The outer edge of the central market was a popular gathering place for many low-income expatriates.

A site visit by the author prior to demolition shows the *souq* still in operation with significant commercial activity (figure 10.13). Some shops were openly displaying their wares to the public which included a cross-section of Abu Dhabi residents: the usual assortment of Arabs and Asians, in addition to locals. The place still showed its attraction as a gathering point for low-income residents who were sitting along the *souq's* sidewalks in large groups (figure 10.14). However, a sense of loss and sadness pervaded the market – no doubt enhanced by the prominence of eviction notices plastered throughout the crumbling complex (figure 10.15*a* and *b*). The project was finally demolished on 2 March 2005.

Following the demolition a new scheme was introduced by star architect Norman Foster, replacing the Arab architect Rasem Badran. This new Dh1.3 billion ($360 million) project hopes to create 'a prestigious and fully integrated mixed-use scheme at the heart of Abu Dhabi'. This will include a hotel, luxury shops, flats, restaurants, offices and a traditional market (figure 10.16).[44] The company intends the Central Market to 'redefine the city centre of Abu Dhabi'. Addressing cultural concerns, '… the traditional Arabian Souq will aim to recapture the heritage of the site by offering authentic Middle Eastern goods including textiles, jewellery, gold, spices, perfume, tailoring, carpets and gifts'. An ominous note is cast about the potential clientele, noting that the centre will have '… high-end lifestyle stores and boutiques in the retail podium' and 'floors will

Figure 10.15*a*. Demolition notices plastered throughout the crumbling complex.

Figure 10.15*b*. Close-up of the demolition notice.

be occupied by the world's leading retail brands covering all possible categories, from specialist food stores to designer fashion, with at least one level becoming the "Bond Street" of Abu Dhabi'.[45] Norman Foster's website includes an interesting description of the project essentially confirming its historical origin, but then noting that the market will be a 'reinterpretation of the traditional market place

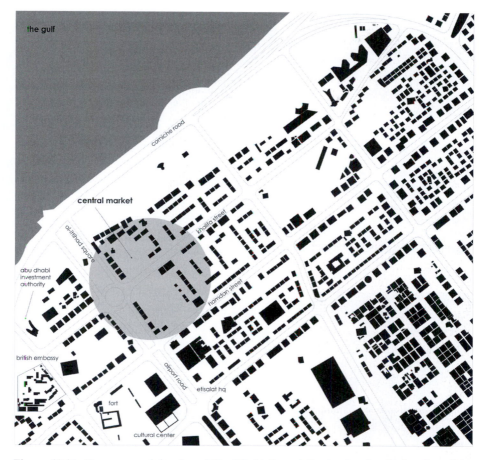

Figure 10.16. Figure ground drawing of Abu Dhabi Central district showing the location of the old central market and the site of the new project.

and a new civic heart for Abu Dhabi'. A cluster of towers will create a 'striking new urban landmark' (Foster & Partners, 2007).

In 2006 a media blitz was launched which began by displaying a darkened Abu Dhabi skyline, with faint images of a skyscraper, and the words 'Future under construction'. Anticipation thus heightened, the next stage included a brightened skyline with three gleaming towers rising from the back and the ominous words: 'Abu Dhabi will never be the same again'. The project received further exposure in the 2006 Cityscape real estate extravaganza in Dubai where a large model and an extensive exhibition stand displayed it to the (cash rich) public (figure 10.17*a*, *b* and *c*). A pamphlet, actually a fancy book, repeats the same ideas arguing in all seriousness that this scheme will 'restore Central Market to its former glory' and 'just as it was in the 60s, Central Market will be the focal point of business and social life'. The entire book is sprinkled with images of local Arabs as well as foreigners enjoying the finer things in life. Advertisements for the project are placed in a variety of locations such as the Abu Dhabi airport where one is greeted with posters displayed throughout the arrival terminal.

Figure 10.17a: ALDAR stand in Cityscape 2006, Dubai showing the model for the new Abu Dhabi Central Market project.

Figure 10.17b. View from above of the model showing the new mall section and the rising towers at the back.

Figure 10.17c. Advertisements for the new Central Market project in Cityscape 2006, Dubai.

The physical facts illustrate the sheer enormity of the project – standing in stark contrast to the original plan of creating a humane, small-scale environment, which would foster a sense of community and intimacy. This is exemplified by the three towers, which include a 52-storey five star luxury hotel; a 58-storey office tower; and the *pièce de résistance*, an 88-storey residential tower. The tower is clad in a shimmering, gleaming curtain wall which is meant to dominate the Abu Dhabi skyline. The lower podium is clad in a lattice-like screen, meant to evoke some sort of *mashrabiy'ya*. What is in essence a modern, luxurious shopping mall is covered with such a device to address this dubious notion of an Arabian *souq*.

Now, these are of course common pronouncements in any mixed-use, high-end development scheme that can be found anywhere in the world. For the Gulf, this has almost become the *lingua franca* of architecture. It is as if a project in Dubai is being described. Most significantly, however, is the transformation which has occurred – from a small dilapidated row of shops, which nevertheless catered to a very significant part of the population, to an ultra-luxurious shopping mall. What underlies all this, it seems, is a desire to exclude these elements which were in some way 'spoiling' the modern metropolitan image that officials are trying to portray. There simply is no room for loitering Pakistani shoppers looking for a cheap bargain, or a gathering of Sri Lankan housemaids exchanging news (figure 10.18). As such this development by its very nature responds to the capital schemes

Figure 10.18. The old central market – a popular meeting place.

depicted by Harvey (2006) when he argues that capitalism favours a geography that caters to the rich and is based primarily on social exclusion – seen here in unmistakably clear terms. However, this project pales next to what is in store: the Saadiyat Island development which will be discussed in the next section.

Saadiyat Island: Integrating with a Global Cultural Network

Development plans for Saadiyat Island – located approximately 500 m from the main shoreline of Abu Dhabi, and encompassing an area of 25 km^2 – go as far back as 1992 when it was conceived initially as a major financial centre (Allison, 2000).[46] Described by *The Economist* in 1999 as an 'an elongated triangle of desiccated scrub and scorched sand criss-crossed by camel tracks' but where 'skyscrapers will sprout, bankers and stockbrokers will congregate – and a financial centre on the scale of New York, London or Tokyo will blossom'. In 1996, authorities created the Abu Dhabi Free Zone Authority to regulate the development. It, in turn, hired legal and financial consultants to develop the island's financial infrastructure. It seems the project was well under way – in spite of concerns that it would compete with Bahrain, the traditional financial centre of the area. More significantly, however, were developments taking place in Dubai which has been more attractive to foreigners for a variety of reasons, representing a counterpoint to what Abu Dhabi was trying to achieve.[47] Completion of the project was expected by 2002, with an entire city planned to house 25,000 people; it was also described as a 'digital city' (Allison, 2000). The entire project faltered, however, and developments were put on hold. Soon thereafter the Dubai Financial Market was founded in 2000, and in 2002 the Dubai International Financial Centre (DIFC) was announced, opening officially in 2004 in a state-of-the art building meant to be a contemporary interpretation of the Arc de Triomphe (*The Economist*, 2002, 2005). It seems, however, that Saadiyat Island was destined for bigger, and more ambitious, plans.

Harking back to its conservative and traditional role, Abu Dhabi always saw itself as the centre of culture in the UAE. In the 1970s, as already mentioned, it hired a well known architectural firm to design a cultural centre and a national library. This would become a main venue for staging classical concerts, art exhibits, as well as a major book fair. It seemed only natural that its sights would eventually turn towards creating a more substantive cultural venue. Changes following the death of Sheikh Zayed – which were noted above – involved the redevelopment of the islands surrounding Abu Dhabi resulting in a series of projects announced on an almost daily basis. Most significantly, in 2004, the Abu Dhabi Tourism Authority (ADTA) embarked on a project to develop Saadiyat Island into a 'world-class', 'environmentally sensitive' tourist destination that included as its centrepiece the creation of a new cultural district for Abu Dhabi and the UAE. This was translated into a masterplan through the appointment of the USA's Gensler Associates and under UAE Law No: 12, the establishment of yet another organization, the Tourism Development Investment Company (TDIC). Included within the

Figure 10.19. Saadiyat Island development. View from above of a model at an exhibition at the Emirates Palace Hotel. A bridge connects the island to Abu Dhabi city.

massive project was an array of features and amenities, such as commercial and residential properties, resort hotels, recreational facilities, nature preserves, and perhaps most significantly, the creation of a cluster of 'world class' cultural facilities and institutions that would be operated in partnership with established museums and performing arts institutions from around the world. Thus, 'Abu Dhabi had embarked on one of the most ambitious urban and cultural development projects ever conceived' (figure 10.19).[48]

Through this project it was hoped that the city would finally emerge from the shadow of its neighbour, Dubai, and place itself squarely on the map of 'globally significant' cities. In July 2006 an agreement was signed between TDIC and the New York based Guggenheim Museum to establish a 'world-class' museum devoted to modern and contemporary art to be built as part of the cultural district. The museum – designed by world renowned architect Frank Gehry – would be called the Guggenheim Abu Dhabi (GAD) covering an area of 30,000 m² – the largest of that franchise of museums (figure 10.20). Accompanied by numerous press releases, Sheikh Mohamed, Abu Dhabi's crown prince, noted that this project 'will become an international cultural hub for the Middle East on par with the best in the world'.[49] Statements as to the significance of this project were characteristically hyperbolic, emphasizing its global dimensions, with Thomas Krens, director of the Guggenheim Foundation arguing that 'when this comprehensive and inclusive vision is realized, it will set a standard for global culture that will resonate for decades to come'.[50] Gehry, after admitting that he knew little about the place, stated that his initial reluctance was overcome by

Figure 10.20. Frank Gehry's proposed Guggenheim Museum.

three hours of 'quality time' with Sheikh Sultan, chairman of TDIC, in his office in California, which convinced him otherwise.[51] Asked about his vision for the project, he said that its main 'draws' 'were the "magic" of the Arabian desert – with its undulating peach-colored dunes and the turquoise Persian Gulf' – a curious statement given the fact that there is no immediate desert surrounding the island, which is for the most part a barren landscape.

The announcement was met with widespread acclaim in the local media, with pictures of Gehry standing in the opulent Emirates Hotel lobby appearing in a variety of newspapers. Criticism came from abroad with some noting that the project by its very nature could 'arouse conservative sensibilities' – for example, the depiction of nude paintings or religiously sensitive subjects.[52] Or, that it has 'brought striking cultural juxtapositions' since the museum is named for a major Jewish-American family and designed by a Jewish-American architect' and that it 'would rise in the capital of an Arab country'.[53] Furthermore, many critics argued that Abu Dhabi (and others) are simply buying art and culture without a substantive cultural scene – such views are sometimes cloaked in a downright racist language.[54] Adding another twist to the project is the New York based Human Rights watch who have called on the Guggenheim Museum board to 'publicly pledge that it will enforce labour rights during construction and maintenance' (no response was received).[55] While such projects are announced all over the world, it is rare that they elicit similar reactions. As the historical review in this chapter showed, these expressions of 'bewilderment' go back as early as the late 1960s when Abu Dhabi began its urban development process. However, they do underscore significant issues related to identity, and Abu Dhabi's globalizing efforts both at a regional and global level. In addition, it also makes an interesting contribution to the current debate about the role of museums and art.

The project in its final form was unveiled in 2007. In addition to Gehry's Guggenheim Museum, the development included a classical museum by Jean Nouvel (affiliated with the French Louvre), a maritime museum by Tadao Ando, and performing arts centre by Zaha Hadid (figure 10.21), while nineteen art pavilions, designed by an assortment of international architects (only one UAE local architect was included – Khalid Al-Najjar), were proposed along a meandering water canal within the cultural district (alluding to the Venice Biennale). The original masterplan was revised by US based firm Skidmore, Owings and Merrill, described as a disappointment since it 'represents nothing so much as an outmoded 19th-century planning formula – an axial Beaux-Arts scheme with hotels, marinas and cultural monuments sprinkled along the edges'.[56] Some

Figure 10.21. Zaha Hadid's concert hall and another view of Gehry's Guggenheim showing its location within the island.

observers noted that 'it probably would be hard to build them all in one district anywhere else' and that taken together 'it could be the world's largest single arts-and-culture development project in recent memory'.[57]

The architectural designs are signature pieces characteristic of the architects chosen; each is a unique tribute to his/her style and taken together are a fascinating display of state-of-the-art architectural design in the twenty-first century. Yet they, as *New York Times* Middle East correspondent Hassan Fattah poignantly observes, represent 'a striking departure from Abu Dhabi's crumbling 1970s-style concrete buildings and more modern glass-and-steel high-rises'.[58] The notion of the *tabula rasa* designing within an unconstrained setting figures prominently in the design discourse of some architects.[59] Yet as architectural critic Charles Jencks recently observed, in effect there is no such thing as a *tabula rasa* – there are always contextual constraints of some sort, which seems to be the case in the conceptual ideas proposed (Jencks, 2007; personal communication).[60] Architects are creating their own context. Frank Gehry in a recent internet blog, titled 'My Abu Dhabi Adventure', agues that his design alludes to the traditional alleyways of Arab towns, as well as paying homage to traditional ways of cooling and controlling climate.[61] None of these images have existed in any way in Abu Dhabi – they are more an evocation of towns in Syria and Egypt, or amazingly Dubai. Similar contextual references are made by Nouvel (an 'Arabian' town covered with a gigantic dome – a homage perhaps to Buckminster Fuller's 1950s proposal for a dome covering the city of New York), Ando (evoking the shapes of the *dhow*, the traditional Gulf boat) (figure 10.22). Zaha Hadid, on the other hand, utilizes some organic growth

Figure 10.22. Jean Nouvel's Louvre Abu Dhabi – a view under the dome.

metaphor – which could be applicable anywhere.[62] Whether the references are regional or universal, the significant aspect of these pronouncements is twofold: first, by evoking linkages to traditional towns the project positions itself as the region's centre and second the universalizing aspect of these designs establishes its global credentials. Taken together these two factors supposedly show that the project represents a perfect fusion between East and West, a model of happy co-existence – a politically correct hybrid.

The notion of Abu Dhabi becoming a 'new' cultural centre in the Middle East has in fact occupied a central position in announcing the project and in providing a justification for such a massive undertaking. Officials note that 'culture crosses all boundaries and therefore Saadiyat will belong to the people of the UAE, the greater Middle East and the world at large' thus effectively establishing the project's main credentials.[63] Taking this a step further the chairman of the TDIC proclaims that 'What is happening is unfortunate in places like Beirut … we want it to come back to its old days'.[64] Nicholas Ouroussoff, the *New York Times* architecture critic, in a major article on this development titled 'A vision in the desert' offers a similar view, arguing that the traditional centres of the Middle East could effectively be replaced by Abu Dhabi which offers '… the hope of a major realignment, a chance to plant the seeds for a fertile new cultural model in the Middle East'.[65] Viewed in these terms such projects could be interpreted in relation to the larger notion of a new Middle East, imposed on the region by a hegemonic power such as the US. Richard Haass, a US policy advisor, in fact notes that if the US would like to change the Middle East it needs to 'intervene' in its affairs 'with nonmilitary tools' (Haass, 2006). Echoing similar sentiments, Thomas Krens – Guggenheim director – suggests that these museums could become a 'tool of diplomacy'.[66] Viewed from another angle they could also be tools of cultural imperialism!

The project raises another interesting issue, namely the role of the museum within a global world. The Guggenheim has in fact become symptomatic of what has been described as the 'McDonaldization' of culture. It has in effect been turned into a brand that can be placed anywhere. Abu Dhabi by acquiring this brand is thus plugging itself into this global cultural network – becoming another stop on the world circuit of art aficionados. However, Krens argues that this is not about 'exporting a commodity' or 'setting up a franchise'. Instead, it becomes a tool for communication – the museum would bring modern works of art to the local settings; in addition these institutions would help in fostering and nurturing local talent.[67] There are many who disagree, however. An art critic sarcastically observes that '… it's people here who would like to think that if they send this stuff to the other side of the world, it's going to have some impact… I think the other side of the world isn't the slightest bit interested'.[68] Others dispute the notion of cultural exchange, pointing out that 'there are very few exhibitions at the Guggenheim Bilbao which relate specifically to Spanish artists and many of the exhibitions are the same ones that rotate to other Guggenheim sites' (Hynes, 2006).[69] At the end it is all about attempting to 'juice up, globalize, and glamorize the museum, to market it, turn it into a world wide entertainment network ... and pad the pockets of this institution'.[70]

In this context the French reaction was quite interesting. Jean Nouvel's classical museum, proposed for the Island, was envisioned as carrying the Louvre name. Naturally, a French resistance emerged which tried to derail these attempts on the grounds that France is 'selling its culture'. A website was created to rally support for their cause, enlisting more than 4,700 petitioners – the website was in turn promptly blocked by UAE authorities. However, French government support was strong and, for a reported price tag of $0.5 billion, the then French President, Jacques Chirac, agreed to the deal, thus allowing for the creation of a Louvre franchise in the UAE.[71] While dismissed by some as typical French snobbery, it shows an intersection of local resistance, global capital and neo-colonial ambitions. In the end, culture and art become pawns within a global market – Abu Dhabi is simply catering to this emerging trend. There have even been talks with the British Museum to open another franchise![72]

Abu Dhabi is of course not the first city in the world to embark on such an ambitious venture. Bilbao's Guggenheim museum is perhaps one of the first attempts at using both a signature architect and an art institution to establish global significance for a city. More recent efforts are at a much larger scale such as the Galician City of Culture by Peter Eisenman. A more poignant example – and perhaps aligned with the scale attempted by Abu Dhabi – is the West Kowloon Cultural District designed by Norman Foster in Hong Kong. The project was conceived as an attempt for Hong Kong to become a world city and to further enhance its status as a major global financial centre. Thus private corporations were invited to build a series of world class museums, among them the Guggenheim. Interestingly a similar strategy of 'spectacular' architecture (for example, the world's largest outdoor roof) was adapted to enhance the projects appeal. However, as Cecilia Chu (2006) pointed out the project was met with widespread opposition questioning its scale and its relevance within the context of Hong Kong, which in her view led to the opening 'of new spaces to imagine alternative modernities based not on the official "world city" rhetoric but on *social responsibility and ongoing cultural work*' (p. 19; emphasis added). Such debates – for a number of reasons – could not be conceived in Abu Dhabi. However, such discourses need to be adapted in order to critique the Saadiyat Island project with the general objective of making it ultimately useful for everyone. If these buildings were to emerge from being a mere spectacle, or a pawn within some global cultural scheme, a local art scene would need to be nurtured which would in effect sustain such a development. Schools of art and architecture, openness towards an exploration of ideas are all necessary ingredients for a vital art scene. Furthermore, a more effective and substantive engagement with Arab talent – which has not been part of the official rhetoric – will add significance and perhaps address concerns that Abu Dhabi is simply using its 'oil money' to buy art. It should be noted that when the project was unveiled in February 2007, a large exhibition dedicated to the development, displaying the architects' models and renderings, was held at the opulent Emirates Palace hotel. The exhibition lasted until April 2007 and has in fact stirred a debate among residents and intellectuals. Perhaps unprecedented in the history of the UAE – projects in Dubai, for example, are simply unveiled without any public participation – such events need to be substantiated by being accompanied by debates about their merits and relevance. Hong Kong may offer some lessons in this regard.

Conclusion

*A city that had no pity on itself or its citizens: a mound of debris that rose higher every day. People looked around them, **bewildered or gratified**, but with a single wish: to get this all over with.*

Abdulrahman Munif, *The Trench* (Cities of Salt) (my emphasis), p. 222

Leftist writer Mike Davis in a 2006 article on Dubai entitled 'Fear and Money in Dubai' – an allusion to Hunter S. Thompson's novel *Fear and Loathing in Las Vegas* – argued, while using the writings of Marxist writer Baruch Knei-Paz, [73] that 'backward societies' (and he is using both Dubai and China as examples) adapt products in their final stages of development without going through a necessary evolutionary process. In his words 'the arduous intermediate stages of commercial evolution have been telescoped or short-circuited to embrace the "perfected" synthesis of shopping, entertainment and architectural spectacle, on the most pharaonic scale'. Looking at Abu Dhabi a similar analysis would be applicable. One must ask here: What is the validity of such claims? They do belie the sense of dismissal and derision hurled at cities in the Gulf which is – at its worst – racism and at its most benign a form of neo-colonialism. Based on brief visits – usually a few days – they impart to the writer a sense of superiority and significance. Unfortunately this is the general view of many writers on cities in the Gulf – though sometimes cloaked in more palatable language. Being unfamiliar with the intricacies of this region, its daily life, the aspirations and struggles of its citizens – both local and expatriate – they cannot grasp that these are real cities as significant to their inhabitants as are New York, Boston, Los Angeles or London to theirs. However, how these cities are built, the nature and appropriateness of the projects that are being proposed should not be taken at face value. They do underscore significant issues that are of direct impact and relevance for Arab cities but also for cities elsewhere.

Tracing a trajectory of Abu Dhabi's urban development in the twentieth century, as this chapter has tried to do, has shown that the city has changed quite significantly from the construction of its 'Disneyesque' fort in the 1920s to the proposed Gehry museum in Saadiyat. During the course of such rapid change one of the main problems seems to be that no alternative discourse or new planning paradigm is proposed. Instead Western models are adapted as is, resulting in the current repetitive grid like patterns of its centre, or a lack of any significant urban realm due to the reliance on cars. Yet by looking at cities elsewhere and perhaps adapting a mode of thinking that is more sustainable – both in its environmental as well as socio-cultural aspects – the city could truly make a contribution to urbanism in the twenty-first century. One only needs to look at places like Shanghai's Eco City project or the grassroots resistance against Hong Kong's Kowloon cultural district, to realize that alternative ways of thinking are possible.

The Urban Structural Framework Plan announced at the time of writing this chapter with its focus on sustainable development, as well as a series of new projects such as the Norman Foster designed Masdar walled city (a business park and research centre) which promises to be zero carbon and zero waste,[74] suggest that a new way of thinking is shaping the city's growth – yet it remains to be seen if this truly represents a departure from conventional practices.

Abu Dhabi has, however, adapted a global city rhetoric, a natural development given that it is strongly integrated within the global financial network. Its aspirations to become global are – as this chapter has shown – not meant as a competition with its neighbour, Dubai, but to complement its emergence as a financial and service centre, by becoming a cultural centre within the region. Its conservative roots, as well as the welfare system created by its late ruler, are being replaced by policies that cater to the rich resulting in spaces that are exclusionary – the Central Market project discussed in this chapter is symptomatic of this transformation. Of particular significance is the Saadiyat Island cultural district – which aims at replacing the Middle East's traditional centres of knowledge, art and learning – essentially completing a process which began in the 1980s and 1990s when a rich Arab Gulf clientele was busy acquiring Orientalist paintings in London as Christa Salamandra (2002) has shown in her excellent study on the construction of Arabia in London. Through these – and other – efforts, a New Middle East, is being forged in this region (figure 10.23). The institutions of global capital – multi-national companies and increasingly museums as well – are being used to transform cities in the Gulf which are offered as a model for the rest of the dysfunctional Middle East. This has become part of the official rhetoric adapted by local officials and scholars. Abd al-Khaleq Abdullah, a UAE University Professor of political science talks about 'the Dubai moment' and that the significance of cities such as Cairo, Beirut or Baghdad has effectively diminished (Abdullah, 2006). Abu Dhabi is increasingly following a similar path.

Yet such proclamations need to be looked at with caution. Accepting the validity of the claim that developments in Abu Dhabi may in fact constitute a model of some sort, its applicability within a context such as Cairo for example, is quite questionable. This has been discussed at great length elsewhere using the case of Dubai (Elsheshtawy, 2004, 2006a, 2008). But a more significant question is whether Abu Dhabi is in fact on its way to becoming a global city? Samir Amin, well known economist, in an article questioning the applicability of the global city concept to Dubai, argues that such cities while more or less formally becoming

Figure 10.23. Entrance gate to the Emirates Palace Hotel with the city skyline in the background.

centres for finance, culture etc. are not what Saskia Sassen (2001) calls command posts within a global economy. They are not sites of production or technological innovation. More significantly their financial status is not linked to a decision-making process that allows for the control and flow of capital – which are typically associated with the financial centres of the USA, Europe and Japan (Amin, 2006). Increasingly the 'global city discourse' is moving away from the Western, economic bias and is becoming more inclusive, accepting the distinctiveness of cities – using terms such as world city, transnational city, or globalizing city.[75]

Thus, cities such as Abu Dhabi may adopt the forms of a global city – exclusive mixed-use developments, international museums and centres of learning, world-class airports etc. – but in the end one could argue that they are merely recycling ideas, or serving global capital – without adding a substantive, alternative discourse to urban development. The question then becomes: Going beyond the glitter of *Gheryesque* museums or high-tech *Fosterian* towers – what does Abu Dhabi offer to the world? Are these developments at the end geared to its citizens, enhancing their daily lives or are they – like Munif's fictional people in the quote above – left as bewildered as everyone else?

Epilogue

Abu Dhabi was like a hotel. Everyone was in transit. Some people, like myself and the traveling salesmen, were here for a few days, living out of suitcases and calling up sandwiches on room-service. Others ... were out on two year contracts; the Palestinians were here until that mythical day when Haifa and Tel Aviv would be liberated; the Baluchi's, in their encampment on the sand, were passing through; even the bedu had been turned into guests of the state, en route *from a nomadic past to a sketchy future.*

'Temporary people. Migrants. Passengers' (Raban, 1979, p. 145)

Notes

1.   See, for example, Benton-Short, Price and Friedman (2005) and Robinson (2002); also Peter-Smith (2002) and of particular importance is Ley (2004).

2.   As an interesting indication of the exotic allure of Abu Dhabi in the 1980s, the cartoon cat Garfield would often put the kitten Nermal in a box and ship him to Abu Dhabi. The phrase 'Abu Dhabi is where all the cute kittens go' is sometimes used in the comic. In one episode of Garfield and Friends, Garfield himself is sent to Abu Dhabi and he finds it inhabited by dozens of cute kittens which people keep sending there. This is the song that accompanied these adventures (http://en.wikiquote.org/wiki/Garfield_and_Friends. Accessed 30 September 2007):

> Abu Dhabi, it's far away. Abu Dhabi, that's where you'll stay.
> Abu Dhabi, the place to be. For any kitten who's annoying me, yeah!
> Abu Dhabi, it's off the track. Abu Dhabi, now don't come back.
> Abu Dhabi, it's quite a thrill. For any kitten who can make me ill!
> Now some take a train, and some take a plane.
> But I am sending you, not on a boat, or even by goat. But in a box marked 'Postage Due'.
> Abu Dhabi, you're what they lack. Abu Dhabi, now you're all packed.
> Abu Dhabi, a far commute. For any kitten who is too darn cute!

3.   The official website for the UAE 2005 census: http://www.tedad.ae/english/index.html. Accessed 15 April 2007.

4.   The settlement at that time used to be known as Mleih *(*salty) due to its salty water. It changed to Abu Dhabi which in Arabic means Father of the Gazelle, which was an animal that roamed the desert and which was reportedly found drinking water from a well; hence the name (Al-Fahim, 1995).

5.   First reference to Abu Dhabi in *The New York Times* was in a 1951 article titled 'No quick decision likely in oil suit; two companies seeking right to drill of sheikhdom of Abu Dhabi in Persian Gulf'.

6.   The 1951 *New York Times* article notes that: 'Sheik Shakhbut Bin Sultan Bin Za'id left his homeland for the first time to appear at the arbitration hearings, expected to end Tuesday. The Sheik maintains he can legally give the American company an underwater concession. Trucial Coast has a concession dating back to 1939'.

7.   At that time rivalry with neighbouring Dubai did exist. Sheikh Shakbut on a visit to Dubai was impressed by a 2,400 foot bridge over Dubai's creek. Even though Abu Dhabi did not have a creek he was determined that it should have a bridge, the principal characteristic of which must be that it be larger and longer than Dubai's. And so it was built over a dry wadi. [Adams Schmidt, D. (1969) Tiny Arab Sheikdom strives to outdo its neighbor. *The New York Times*, March 22.]

8.   For an interesting profile of Makhlouf see Hassan, F. (2001) Abdel-Rahman Makhlouf: A passion for order. *Al-Ahram Weekly Online,* Issue 565, 20–26 December. http://weekly.ahram.org.eg/2001/565/profile.htm. Accessed 31 March 2007. And a recent *Khaleej Times* profile described him as the masterplanner of Abu Dhabi and Al-Ain and mostly influenced by modernist Western planning principles developed after World War II as a result of witnessing the reconstruction of destroyed German cities where he studied planning (Aziz, A. (2007) The 'master' planner of Abu Dhabi, Al Ain. *Khaleej Times Online*, 10 March. http://www.khaleejtimes.com. Accessed 31 March 2007).

9.   The population of Abu Dhabi in 1966 was 17,000. The number increased to 70,000 in 1972 following unification. A remarkable increase mostly attributed to immigrants (Halliday, 2002).

10.   Emerson, G. (1968*a*) Abu Dhabi gushes instant wealth. *The New York Times*, 28 February.

11. Emerson, G. (1968b) Abu Dhabi: the unsociable baby boom town. *The New York Times*, 10 March.

12. Describing scenes of extreme primitiveness contrasted with emerging signs of modernity she observes: 'The camels, the goats and the mongrel dogs of Abu Dhabi still meander through the market place, a honeycomb of stalls and huts and stands, speckled with pocket-sized supermarkets and pharmacies too. The screech of tires and the horns of big foreign cars, driven too fast by men who learned to steer in Mercedes and Cadillac, do not startle the animals any more' (Emerson, G. (1968c) A mixture of goats and cadillacs: Abu Dhabi is rolling in oil wealth. *The New York Times*, 24 February).

13. Also see New York Times (1969) 9 Sheiks launch Gulf Federation; Abu Dhabi designated as provisional capital. *The New York Times*, 23 October.

14. Lee, J. (1970) Unity eludes nine Persian Gulf Sheikhdoms. *The New York Times*, 29 November.

15. Sheehan, E. (1974). Unradical sheiks who shake the world. *The New York Times*, 24 March.

16. Broyard, A. (1978) Books of the Times: Arabian days. *The New York Times*, 27 June.

17. Jonathan Raban (1979, p. 179) writes: 'The bedu had been resettled. All over the emirate, the nomads who had been the companions of Thesiger, Philby and Bertram Thomas now lived on new breezeblock estates in the desert'.

18. Howe, M. (1979) Emirates seek development controls. *The New York Times*, 4 August.

19. Howe, M. (1972) Abu Dhabi adapting to modern world. *The New York Times*, 14 January.

20. Howe (1972) writes: '"Town planning is Sheik Zayed's hobby", Mr. Makhluf said. "Although he's had no formal schooling he has a very good sense of orientation, space and correlation. He used to walk about the oases and dream of modern cities and now it's happening"' (see note 19).

21. An architectural firm established by Walter Gropius, one of the pioneers of modernism and founder of the Bauhaus School in Germany

22. Howe (1979) (see note 18).

23. The municipality report does not state that Atkins was involved in the project. However, the company's website indicates that they were involved in preparing the masterplan. (www.atkinsglobal.com/skills/planning/urbanplanning/regionalandstrategicplanning/abudhabimasterplan/. Accessed 6 October 2007.

24. No clear reason is given for this change at that time – although a planner with the Abu Dhabi Planning Department suggested that the concept of 'investment' was not applicable (Abusham, 2005).

25. The price tag is billed at $3 billion. For more information see Otto Pohl's (2005) article in *The New York Times* titled 'Abu Dhabi Journal; What $3 Billion, More or Less, Buys: A Hotel Fit for Kings'; or Katherine Zoepf's (2006) 'The Land with the Golden Hotel'.

26. According to Article 3 in the new law, GCC citizens and legal personalities wholly owned by them may own properties, provided that the property should be located within the precinct of investment areas. However, they shall have the right to dispose and arrange any original or collateral right over any of those properties… According to Article (4) – Non-UAE nationals, natural or legal persons, shall have the right to own surface property in investment areas. Surface property refers to that property built on land. Thus, the non-nationals can own the property, but not the land on which it is built… This shall be done through a long-term contract of 99 years or by virtue of long-term surface leasing contracts of 50 years renewable by mutual consent' (Gulf News (2007) Foreigners get rights to own surface property. *Gulf News*, 12 February, p. 37).

27. A government report notes: 'Sheikh Zayed nipped in the bud an onslaught from US property speculators to buy into Abu Dhabi in the 1970s; they were intent on buying up properties in the largest emirate at what constituted high prices for UAE nationals, but which were very low by international standards. Sheikh Zayed agreed with the speculators that property prices would soar as oil-wealth flowed into the economy; the then poor majority of UAE nationals would be squeezed

out of the market and have to compete with international all-comers to buy back into the property market at a later date at inflated prices' (Gulf States Newsletter (2003) Abu Dhabi and Dubai's paths diverge over real estate development. *Gulf States Newsletter*, 1 December).

28.   Gulf News (2007) Abu Dhabi projects worth close to Dh1tr. *Gulf News*, 13 February, p. 37.

29.   Gale, I. (2007) New Abu Dhabi airport terminal to be ready in 2010. *Gulf News*, 20 March, p. 36.

30.   Roberts, L. (2007) Abu Dhabi plans future of capital. *Arabian Business*, 20 September. http://www.arabianbusiness.com/500636-abu-dhabi-plans-future-of-capital. Accessed 21 September 2007.

31.   Salama, S. (2007*a*) Hundreds vie for affordable flats: Abu Dhabi's shortage affects many residents. *Gulf News*, 25 February, p. 8.; Salama, S. (2007*b*) Landlords find new ways to get around rent cap rule: soaring rates force many expats to leave jobs and return home. *Gulf News*, 31 March, p. 3; Salama, S. (2007*c*) Hundreds of workers forced to live in cramped attics. *Gulf News*, 19 February, p. 3.

32.   Howe (1972) (see note 19).

33.   Daniel, K. (2002) Bazaar buzz: The old world charm of Hamdan Souk in Abu Dhabi makes shopping a pleasure. *Gulf News*, 17 June, Tabloid, p. 16.

34.   Kowch, N. (2003*a*) Abu Dhabi souq prepares to fade into history: Demolition of three-decade old bazaar to start in November, shopkeepers express sadness. *Gulf News*, 31 August, p. 5.

35.   'J.P. an Indian chartered accountant, who came to the UAE in 1967, "When I first came out here we only had the Souk to shop and meet people. It was not in the same shape as you find it now. They were ordinary shops with tarpaulins for roofs and sand as flooring. But, it was the only place to buy cheap stuff and spend time in the cafeterias"' (Daniel, 2002) (see note 33).

36.   Gulf News (2002) Designs underway to build new market in Abu Dhabi: Central Souq to be replaced with a new facility in traditional Arab and Islamic design. *Gulf News*, 29 December, p. 4.

37.   Gulf News (2002) and Kowch (2003*a*) (see notes 36 and 33).

38.   A local newspaper includes the following accounts (*Gulf News*, 2002):

'Tariq Mubbarak of Mubbarak Jewellers said: "This is a shocking news. I have been here for 27 years doing good business. I even get customers from the GCC countries and Europe. This is very painful for me, if I go somewhere else I will lose customers… If the municipality repairs the souq, turns it into a more antique style like the Gold Souq in Dubai it will be better".'

A studio attendant: 'There are around 3,000 to 4,000 people from different countries who work here and if the market is knocked down, their source of income will be cut off and they may go home.'

A Syrian shopper: 'The way the souq is now it invites more customers. An old market has its own special atmosphere which attracts tourists. It is similar to a heritage site. There are enough modern stores around. I think the country will lose something if it is demolished (see note 36).

39.   The full account: 'There are too many things to remember in this market. It has a unique character, the mixture of nationalities and cultures, the family atmosphere and closeness among the shop owners, and the smell of perfume and incense. Above all, this market is deeply associated with the memories of who first came to Abu Dhabi. It is history and culture and I don't think it will be easily forgotten' (Kowch, 2003*a*) (see note 34).

40.   *Ibid*.

41.   'It will give a human and cultural touch to the city. We are trying to create a balance in this aggressive modernity and construction drive that engulfs the capital. At least this will preserve part of its culture and prompt the residents to interact with it. Modernity and development do not mean that we have to line up all these high-rise towers along our roads. Development should take into consideration our history and culture, otherwise no memories will be left to the people. The human needs this kind of rhythmic and diverse scene and the new souq will be built to serve this goal. In other words this project is an attempt to restore life to the heart of Abu Dhabi and resurrect old memories that are being obliterated by rapid changes and modernity' (Kowch, 2003*b*).

42.   Al-Khaleej (2006) Al-Dar postpones Central Market bidding; in order to conduct changes to the project design. *Al-Khaleej*, 14 April, p. 14. 'Designed by international prize-winning architect RTKL following an international design competition in which five of the world's leading urban designers took part, RTKL has been commissioned by ALDAR to progress the project through to construction. To supplement and enhance this landmark development, ALDAR has also appointed award-winning architects Jafar Tukan and Rasem Badran to design this project's new Mosque and Souk; whose achievements are evident throughout the Middle East and worldwide – both of them have won many major architectural awards, including the coveted Aga Khan Award for Architecture'.

43.   Sands, C. (2005) End of an era: at midnight, Abu Dhabi's old souq will be history. *Gulf News, Tabloid*, 1 March, p. 2.

44.   *Ibid.*

45.   ALDAR CEO Christopher Sims commented: 'This will not be a "Mall" in the traditional sense, but will be a destination offering the visitor or resident myriad leisure, entertainment and retail experiences… It will be a unique experience – the first of its kind in the UAE. We are already in negotiation with some of the most exciting and original names in the retail world.' (http://www.ameinfo.com/74169.html. Accessed 1 March 2007).

46.   It is interesting to observe that this project was conceived immediately following the BCCI banking scandal in which Abu Dhabi was implicated and which received considerable coverage in the international press at that time (see, for example,. Ibrahim, Y. (1991) Behind B.C.C.I., a Sheik with power and wealth. *The New York Times*, 10 July. http://select.nytimes.com. Accessed 1 March 2007).

47.   According to The Economist (1999): '… until Saadiyat takes off, foreigners will prefer to live in Dubai. It has the region's busiest port and airport, not to mention hotels, bars, restaurants, shops and brothels. Its free zone has already achieved a critical mass of importers and light manufacturers. The tight anti-laundering rules drawn up by Saadiyat's consultants will make it hard to attract some of the more suspect sorts of deposits. And Abu Dhabi's rulers lack Dubai's flair for publicity'.

48.   Trade Arabia (2007). Andrew visits Saadiyat. http://www.tradearabia.com/news/newsdetails.asp?Sn=INT&artid=120234. Accessed 26 March 2007.

49.   Ameen, A. (2006) Frank Gehry to design Guggenheim museum. *Gulf News*, 9 July, p.3.

50.   Property World Middle East (2006). Abu Dhabi to build Gehry-designed Guggenheim Museum. http://www.propertyworldme.com/content/html/1461.asp. Accessed 6 February 2007.

51.   Krane, Jim (2006) Frank Gehry wonders whether he can top Bilbao. *The China Post*, 10 July. www.chinapost.com.tw/art/detail.asp?ID=85658&GRP=h. Accessed 12 July 2006.

52.   Goldenberg, S. (2006) Guggenheim to build museum in Abu Dhabi. *The Guardian*, 10 July. http://arts.guardian.co.uk/news/story/0,,1816806,00.html. Accessed 6 February 2007.

53.   Israel Insider (2006) Jewish architect builds Guggenheim's largest museum in booming Abu Dhabi. *Israeli Insider Online Edition*, 9 July. http://web.israelinsider.com/Articles/Briefs/8833.htm. Accessed 6 February 2007.

54.   Conrad, P. (2007) When oil and paint mix… *Guardian Unlimited*. 11 March. http://arts.guardian.co.uk/art/visualart/story/0,,2031070,00.html. Accessed 1 April 2007.

55.   Arabian Business (2007) Guggenheim called on to protect rights. *Arabian Business*, 28 July. http://www.arabianbusiness.com/index.php?option=com_content&view=article&id=496634. Accessed 6 August 2007.

56.   Ouroussoff, N. (2007) A vision in the desert. *The New York Times*, 4 February. Section 2, pp. 1, 30

57.   Fattah, H. (2007) Celebrity architects reveal a daring cultural xanadu for the Arab World. *The New York Times*, 1 February, Section E, pp. 1, 5.

58. *Ibid.*

59.   Gehry on context: 'It's like a clean slate in a country full of resources… It's an opportunity

for the world of art and culture that is not available anywhere else because you're building a desert enclave without the contextual constraints of a city (*Ibid.*).

60.   A conversation with Charles Jencks, speaker at a symposium organized by Ajman University of Science & Technology. 'Architectural & Urban Development in the UAE'. 19 March 2007. Fairmont Hotel, Dubai.

61.   The complete statement is quite fascinating: 'Abu Dhabi's going to be very different – a take on a traditional, spread out, organic Arab village or town. Not literally, but it'll have the equivalent of streets and alleys, souk-like spaces and plazas, some shaded and others covered. It'll be the biggest Guggenheim yet. There'll be fresh air and sunlight, and we'll be bringing in cooling air through a modern take on traditional Middle Eastern wind towers. Of course, the core of the building, or complex, will need to be air-conditioned, but this won't be a hermetic building; it'll be an adventure, a kind of walk through a town with art along the way' (Gehry, F. (2007) My Abu Dhabi adventure. *The Guardian Unlimited, Art Blog*. 5 March. http://blogs.guardian.co.uk/art/2007/03/my_abu_dhabi_adventure.html. Accessed 25 March 2007.)

62.   Both the Gehry and Nouvel projects are described as being a perfect representation of a successful fusion of East and West: 'Mr. Nouvel and Mr. Gehry have ingeniously harnessed local architectural traditions without stooping to superficial interpretations of historical styles. Intrinsically their designs acknowledge that the flow of culture between East and West has not always been one-sided. If they convey nostalgia, it is for a belief in the future... Yet overall it is heartening to see Western architects engaged in seeking a balance between the brute force of global culture – its ruthless effacement of differences, its Darwinian indifference to the have-nots – and the fragility of local traditions' (Ouroussoff, 2007) (see note 56). Zaha Hadid's design on the other hand 'springs from the complex nature of the site rather than an exploration of cultural memory'.

63.   Haider, H. (2007) Saadiyat projects' designs on show. *Khaleej Times*, 1 February, p. 3.

64.   As quoted in Ouroussoff (2007) (see note 56).

65.   'Now the city is on the verge of another audacious leap. Over the next decade or so it aims to become one of the great cultural centers of the Middle East: the heir, in its way, to cosmopolitan cities of old like Beirut, Cairo and Baghdad... With once-proud cities like Beirut and Baghdad ripped apart by political conflict bordering on civil war, Abu Dhabi offers the hope of major realignment, a chance to plant the seeds for a fertile new cultural model in the Middle East... the buildings promise to be more than aesthetic experiments, outlining a vision of cross-cultural pollination' (*Ibid.*).

66.   Taylor, K. (2007). Abu Dhabi lures Western museums. *The New York Sun*. http://www.nysun.com/article/47795. Accessed 10 February 2007.

67.   He further notes: '... this interest in using culture as a tool for communication as a vital part of the urban fabric is taking place all over the world. In the last three years, we have been approached by more than 120 cities from around the world that wanted to do this sort of thing'. (Krens, T. (2006) Interview on the Charlie Rose Show. Aired 3 January 2006 on PBS).

68.   Taylor (2007) (see note 66).

69.   Hynes, F. (2006) The goog effect – American imperialism or visionary museum practice. http://blogs.usyd.edu.au/bizart/2006/08/the_goog_effect_american_imper_1.html. Accessed 10 February 2007.

70.   Saltz, J. (2007) Downward spiral. The Guggenheim Museum touches bottom. *Village Voice*. www.villagevoice.com/issues/0207/saltz.php. Accessed 29 March 2007.

71.   The announcement made front page news in the local media. See, for example, Habib, Rania and Ezz Al Deen, Mohammad (2007) Louvre comes to Abu Dhabi as UAE and France seal pact. *Gulf News*, 7 March. http://archive.gulfnews.com/articles/07/03/07/10109389.html. Accessed 8 October 2007; also the international press was quite keen on reporting the deal, for example: Riding, Alan (2007) The Louvre's Art: Priceless. The Louvre's Name: Expensive. *New York Times*, 6 March. http://www.nytimes.com/2007/03/07/arts/design/07louv.html. Accessed 8 October 2007.

72.   Flanagan, B. (2007) Abu Dhabi in talks with British Museum. *Arabian Business*. 7 February. http://www.arabianbusiness.com. Accessed 9 February 2007.

73.   The reference in question is: Knei-Paz, Baruch (1978) *The Social and Political Thought of Leon Trotsky*, Oxford: Clarendon Press, p. 91.

74.   The scheme was recently announced and represents a 6 km² completely self-sufficient city located in Abu Dhabi. See, for example, Miller, V. (2007) Foster unveils green utopia in the desert. *Building*, 8 May. http://www.building.co.uk/story.asp?storycode=3086562. Accessed May 9, 2007.

75.   For more on this see Robinson (2002); Peter-Smith (2002); and of course Marcuse and Van Kempen (2000).

References

Abdullah, A. (2006) Dubai: an Arab city's journey from localism to globalism. *Al-Mustaqbal Al-Arabi (The Arab Future)*, No. 323, January, pp. 57–84.

Abu Dhabi Municipality & Town Planning Department (2003) *Abu Dhabi: Planning and Urban Development*. Abu Dhabi: Studies and Research Section.

Abusham, M. (2005) Abu Dhabi Comprehensive Development Plan. Abu Dhabi City Planning Conference: Planning & Design for Sustainable Development, 10–12 April.

Al-Fahim, M. (1995) *From Rags to Riches*. London: The London Centre of Arab Studies.

Al-Sayegh, F. (1986) Merchants' role in a changing society: the case of Dubai, 1900–90. *Middle Eastern Studies*, **34**, pp. 87–102.

Allison, T. (2000) Abu Dhabi's US$3.3bn desert isalnd dream. *Asia Times*, 20 October. http://atimes.com/reports/BJ20Ai01.html. Accessed 9 March 2008.

Amin, S. (2006) Discussion of Abdul Khaleq Abdallah's article – Dubai: an Arab city's journey from localism to globalism. *Al-Mustaqbal Al-Arabi (The Arab Future)*, No. 328, June, pp. 157–160.

Antoniou, J. (1998) The architectural review in the Gulf – conference on sustainable architecture and construction in the Middle East, March 30–31, 1998. *The Architectural Review*, May 1998.

Benton-Short, L., Price, M. and Friedman, S. (2005) Globalization from below: the ranking of global immigrant cities. *International Journal of Urban and Regional Research*, **29**(4), pp. 945–959.

Burrows, B. (1990) *Footnotes in the Sand: The Gulf in Transition 1953–1958*. Salisbury: Michael Russell Publishing.

Certeau, Michel de (1984) *The Practice of Everyday Life*. Berkeley, CA: University of California Press.

Chu, C. (2006) Visioning a cultural hub for 'Asia's World City': The controversy of the development of Hong Kong's West Kowloon cultural district. Unpublished abstracts for the International Symposium on Environment, Behaviour and Society 'People in Place in People', Sydney, Australia 9–11 February.

Davidson, C. (2005) After Shaikh Zayed: the politics of succession in Abu Dhabi and the UAE. *Middle East Policy*, **18**(1), pp. 42–59.

Davidson, C. (2007) The emirates of Abu Dhabi and Dubai: contrasting roles in the international system. *Asian Affairs*, **38**(1), pp. 33–48.

Davis, M. (2006) Fear and money in Dubai. *New Left Review*, **41**, September/October. http://newleftreview.org/?page=article&view=2635. Accessed 8 April 2007.

The Economist (1999) Sandcastles in the air. *The Economist*, **22** July, p. 67.

The Economist (2002) In the shadow of Saddam: Bahrain's troubles could boost Dubai's ambitions. *The Economist*, 28 November. http://www.economist.com/finance/displaystory.cfm?story_id=E1_TQGRSQT. Accessed 22 March 2007.

The Economist (2005) Do buy, do sell: a new stock exchange for the Middle East opens for business. *The Economist*, 29 September. http://www.economist.com/finance/displaystory.cfm?story_id=E1_QQGNRJR. Accessed 26 March 2007.

The Economist (2006) Sitting pretty: haven of prosperity in a turbulent sea. *The Economist*, 20 June 10. http://www.economist.com/displayStory.cfm?story_id=7041338. Accessed 22 September 2007.

Elsheshtawy, Y. (2004) Redrawing boundaries: Dubai, the emergence of a global city, in Elsheshtawy, Y. (ed.) *Planning the Middle Eastern Cities: An Urban Kaleidoscope in a Globalizing World*. London: Routledge.

Elsheshtawy, Y. (2006a) From Dubai to Cairo: competing global cities, models, and shifting centers of influence? in Ammar, P. and Singermann, D. (eds) *Cairo Cosmopolitan: Politics, Culture, and Space in the New Middle East*. Cairo: American University in Cairo Press

Elsheshtawy, Y. (2006*b*) Transitory sites: mapping Dubai's 'forgotten' urban public spaces, in *Tradition and the Hyper-Modern, IASTE Working Paper Series*, Vol. 188. Berkeley, CA: Center for Environmental Design Research, University of California Berkeley.

Elsheshtawy, Y. (2008) The global and the everyday: situating the Dubai spectacle, in Kanna, A. (ed.) The Superlative City: *Dubai: and the Urban Condition in the Early Twenty-first Century*. Cambridge, MA: Harvard University Press.

Foster & Partners (2007). *Official Office Website*, http://www.fosterandpartners.com/Projects/1431/ Default.aspx. Accessed 8 April 2007.

Frampton, K. and Khan, H. (eds.) (2000) *World Architecture 1900–2000: A Critical Mosaic*. Volume 5. New York: Springer.

Fuccaro, N. (2001) Visions of the city: Urban studies on the Gulf. *Bulletin of the Middle East Studies Association of North America*, **35**(2), pp. 175–188.

Haass, R. (2006) The New Middle East. *Foreign Affairs*. November/December. http://www.foreign affairs.org/20061101faessay85601/richard-n-haass/the-new-middle-east.html. Accessed 26 November 2007.

Halliday, F. (2002; first published in 1974) *Arabia without Sultans*. London: Saqi Books.

Harvey, D. (2006) *Spaces of Global Capitalism: Towards a Theory of Uneven Geographical Development*. London: Verso.

Hawley, D. (1970) *The Trucial States*. London: Allen & Unwin.

Heard-Bey, F. (1982) *From Trucial States to United Arab Emirates*. Harlow: Longman.

Ley, D. (2004) Transnational spaces and everyday lives. *Transnational Institute of British Geography*, **29**, pp. 151–164.

Maitra, J. and Al-Hajji, A. (2001) *Qasr Al Hosn: The History of the Rulers of Abu Dhabi, 1793–1966*. Abu Dhabi: Centre for Documentation and Research.

Marcuse, Peter and Van Kempen, Ronald (eds.) (2000) *Globalizing Cities: A New Spatial Order*. Oxford: Blackwell.

Melamid, A. (1980) Urban planning in Eastern Arabia. *Geographical Review*, **70**(4), pp. 473–477.

O'Brien, E. (1977) *Arabian Days*. London: Quartet Books.

Oxford Business Group (2006) Real Estate Overview: Big developments ahead. *Emerging Abu Dhabi Intelligence Report*. London: Oxford Business Group, pp. 157–162.

Oxford Business Group (2007) Opening the Gateway. http://www.oxfordbusinessgroup.com/ weekly01.asp?id=2762. Accessed 7 April 2007.

Peter-Smith, M. (2002) Power in place: retheorizing the local and the global, in Eade, J. and Mele, C. (eds.) *Understanding the City: Contemporary and Future Perspectives*. Oxford: Blackwell, pp. 109–130.

Raban, J. (1979) *Arabia through the Looking Glass*. London: Collins.

Robinson, J. (2002) Global and world cities: a view from off the map. *International Journal of Urban and Regional Research*, **26**(3), pp. 531–554.

Salamandra, C. (2002) Globalization and cultural mediation: the construction of Arabia in London. *Global Networks*, **2**(4), pp. 285–299.

Sassen, S. (2001) *The Global City*. Princeton, NJ: Princeton University Press.

Tedad (2005) http://www.tedad.ae/english/index.html. Accessed 26 November 2007.

Thesiger, W. (1991, reprint; originally published in 1959) *Arabian Sands*. London: Penguin Books.

Trench, R. (1994) *Arab Gulf Cities*. Slough: Archive Editions.

Unwin, P. (1982) The contemporary city in the United Arab Emirates, in Seragledin, I. and El-Sadek, S. (eds.) *The Arab City: Its Character and Islamic Cultural Heritage*. Riyadh: Arab Urban Development Institute, pp. 120–241.

Index